CW00498089

The
Bible Reader's
Joke Book

*A collection of over 2,000
jokes, humorous stories, puns,
and funny sayings
connected to
Bible passages*

from Genesis to Revelation

Stephen J. Bramer, Ph.D.

Jokes by their very nature are passed around (orally and electronically), changed, reinvented, adapted and told in various ways and so it is usually impossible to determine the original author of the vast majority of them. The copyright of this book refers to the collection and manner of presentation of this material, not to the original creation of each joke.

The purpose of this book is to provide a resource for Bible study leaders, youth pastors and preachers and so I fully expect you to use this material in your ministry without reference to this book (though if you did I'd sure appreciate the promo!). However, no significant portion of this book (e.g. the collection of jokes for an entire biblical book) may be reproduced or transmitted in any form or by any means mechanically or electronically, including scanning, photocopying, recording, posting on a blog or website, or by any information storage and retrieval system, without the expressed written permission of the author.

Violators of the above restrictions will be subject to something lingering, involving tar and feathers (or boiling oil) I suppose or an appeal to our legal system.

Please read the section "Read This First, Before You Use This Tool!" on page ix. However, even after reading this section, the author desires you to know that if you "bomb" or otherwise mess up the telling of a joke with dire consequences, you are on your own and are expected to accept full responsibilities for your own actions and communications. Please don't come crying to me. I have enough problems of my own due to my speaking and have neither the time nor the money to help you with yours. I know you'll understand.

First Edition, 2014

DEDICATION

To my 90 year old father
Douglas Clifford Bramer
who instilled in me a love for the Bible
and who always, always had a joke ready to share.

For his entire life he has lived Proverbs 17:22
"A merry heart doeth good like a medicine."

TABLE OF CONTENTS

ACKNOWLEDGMENTS

For over 39 years my wife Sharon has loved me, supported me in my
ministry, sacrificed in the Lord's work and encouraged me in many,
many more ways. I love her with all my heart. She, along with my
wonderful children Sarah Grace Hau (husband John Hau), Charity
Ruth Hartweck (husband Justin Hartweck) and Joshua Stephen
Douglas Bramer (wife Haleigh), have loved me and then smiled (and
sometimes even laughed) in support of my humor in my public
ministry. Thanks, especially when you had heard them before! Thanks
too for giving me my wonderful grandkids Soren, Marlow, Madelin,
Holden, Norah, Juliet and Harper (and others still to come!) on whom
I can lavish my love and practice my new jokes! Thanks.

My students at Dallas Theological Seminary, Jordan Evangelical Theological
Seminary, Word of Life: Hungary, Montana Wilderness School of the
Bible and Briercrest Bible College have listened with a grin or a grimace
and then often shared with me their favorite jokes about the Bible.
Thanks.

Members of my Adult Bible classes at RBC Phase 1 and Stonebriar's Impact,
and listeners of my sermons at Waterbrook Bible Fellowship, as well as
others at various family camps, churches and conferences, have all
encouraged me. Thanks.

My friends are a special gift from the Lord, especially Charles Savelle and
Greg Hatteberg, who have supported me and encouraged me in
unbelievable ways. Thanks guys.

Read this First, before you Use this Tool!

All manuals for tools come with a warning page. I want to give you full value and be like everyone else who produces a potentially dangerous tool (that was a joke, oh no, I'm sweating, someone didn't realize that was a joke ... just keep reading and we'll pretend that I didn't write that last, lame sentence)!

Please:

1. Make certain that the jokes you select are suitable and relevant to your presentation. The user takes full responsibility for the use of any of the jokes in this book.
2. Be aware, some people don't think the Bible and humor belong together. Guess they never heard the one Jesus told about the camel with the hump attempting to go through the sewing needle! Still, be sensitive to your audience and try not to offend.
3. Avoid saying, "and that reminds me ..." because we all know you don't have that good of a memory! Just tell the joke already.
4. Make the assumption, even when telling a familiar joke, that this is the first time the audience has heard it otherwise your overwhelming excitement might hurt someone!
5. Tell it in your own style even if your friends have been telling you that you have no style!
6. If you are going to use someone in the audience as a "target" for a joke, select that person carefully. Unless you know the person well and the joke is appropriate without causing too much embarrassment, avoid using a specific person because, as you probably have read in the news, people can carry (guns) in many places (like Texas)!
7. Jokes concerning biblical content, like all jokes, should be told with the proper spirit and never with intent to hurt (although a little guilt sometimes doesn't maim and may be good for the soul).
8. Be aware of the ethnicity and culture of your audience (never be offensive) because there are over 4 billion people who aren't like you.
9. If you tell a joke and it goes over "like a lead balloon" keep going. Do not try and explain it, do not retell it, do not sweat, just keep going. And then don't be surprised if five minutes later someone breaks out laughing (they finally got it!). Are you laughing yet about my first line of introduction above?

GENESIS

Genesis 1

Children's Church teacher: "Who is the first man in the Bible?"
Student (peeking at the first page of Genesis): "I guess it's Chap Number One."

[man]

Genesis 1:1

Baseball is talked about a great deal in the Bible, in fact right from the first verse: In the big inning ... then Eve stole first, Adam stole second, later, Cain struck out Abel, the Giants and the Angels were rained out, Gideon rattled the pitchers, Goliath was put out by David, and finally, the Prodigal Son made a home run!

[sports]

Genesis 1:1

In the beginning, God created the heavens and the earth.
Quickly, God was faced with a class action suit for failure to file a temporary permit for the project, but was stymied with the cease and desist order for the earthly part.
Then God said, "Let there be light!"
Immediately, the officials demanded to know how the light would be made. Would there be strip mining? What about thermal pollution? God explained that the light would come from a large ball of fire. God was granted provisional permission to make light, assuming that no smoke would result from the ball of fire, and that he would obtain a building permit and to conserve energy, He would have the light out half the time. God agreed and offered to call the light "Day" and the darkness "Night." The officials replied that they were not interested in semantics.
God said, "Let the earth put forth vegetation, plant yielding seed, and fruit trees bearing fruit."
The EPA agreed, so long as only native seed was used.
Then God said, "Let the waters bring forth swarms of living creatures, and let birds fly above the earth."
The officials pointed out that this would require approval from the Department of Game coordinated with the Heavenly Wildlife Federation and the Audubon Society. Everything was okay until God said the project would be completed in six days.

The officials said it would take at least two hundred days to review the applications and the impact statement. After that there would be a public hearing. Then there would be ten to twelve months before...
At this point God created Hell.

[creation, environment, hell]

Genesis 1:2

Surgeon: "I think the medical profession is the first profession mentioned in the Bible. God made Eve by surgically removing a rib from Adam."
Engineer: "No, engineering was first. Just think of the engineering job it was to create things out of chaos."
Politician: "That's nothing ... who do you think created the chaos?"

[medicine, politics, science]

Genesis 1:2

Did you know God was a helicopter pilot?
"... and the Spirit of God was hovering over the waters." (NIV)

[God, Holy Spirit]

Genesis 1:3

Dear God,
We read in school that Thomas Edison made light. But in Children's Church they said that you did it. So I bet he stole your idea.
Sincerely,
Madelin

[creation, light]

Genesis 1:3

In the beginning there was nothing, then God said " Let there be light" And there was light. There was still nothing, but you could see it a lot better.

[creation, light]

Genesis 1:4

Recently the first draft of the Book of Genesis was discovered. It begins: "In the beginning the world was without form, and void. And God said, 'Let there be light.' And God separated the light from the dark. And did two loads of laundry."

[laundry, light]

Genesis 1:5

God is talking to one of his angels.
He says, "Boy, I just created a 24-hour period of alternating light and darkness on Earth."
The angel says, "What are you going to do now?"

2

God says, "Call it a day."

[creation, rest, work]

Genesis 1:11

The Christian school teacher was teaching a lesson on creation to a class of children.

Now, children," she said, "who can tell me what makes the flower spring from the seed?"

"God does it," answered one little boy, "but my dad says fertilizer helps."

[farming, fertility]

Genesis 1:16

"Who put the stars in the sky?" asked the Christian school teacher, reviewing the previous week's lesson on creation.

"I know," said Paul. "It was America."

"Why do you say it was America?" asked the surprised teacher.

"A lady sang about it in church," Paul explained. "You know the song that goes, 'It took America [a miracle] to put the stars in place.'"

[creation, music]

Genesis 1:18

A newly discovered chapter in the Book of Genesis has provided the answer to the question, "Where do pets come from?"

Adam said, "Lord, when I was in the garden, you walked with me everyday. Now I don't see you anymore. I'm lonesome here and it's difficult for me to remember how much you love me."

And God said, "No problem! I will create companion for you that will be with you forever and who will be a reflection of my love for you, so that you will love me even when you cannot see me. Regardless of how selfish or childish or unlovable you may be, this new companion will accept you as you are and will love you as I do, in spite of yourself."

And God created a new animal to be a companion for Adam. And it was a good animal. And God was pleased. And the new animal was pleased to be with Adam and he wagged his tail. And Adam said, "Lord, I have already named all the animals in the Kingdom and I cannot think of a name for this new animal." And God said, "No problem, because I have created this new animal to be a reflection of my love for you. His name will be a reflection of my own name, and you will call him 'Dog.'"

And Dog lived with Adam and was a companion to him and loved him. And Adam was comforted. And God was pleased. And Dog was content and wagged his tail.

After a while, it came to pass that Adam's guardian angel came to the Lord and said, "Lord, Adam has become filled with pride. He struts and preens like a peacock and he believes he is worthy of adoration.
Dog has indeed taught him that he is loved, but perhaps too well."
And the Lord said, "No problem! I will create for him a companion who will be with him forever and who will see him as he is. The companion will remind him of his limitations, so he will know that he is not always worthy of adoration."
And God created CAT to be a companion to Adam. And Cat would not obey Adam.
And when Adam gazed into Cat's eyes, he was reminded that he was not the supreme being. And Adam learned humility.
And God was pleased. And Adam was pleased. And the Dog was pleased. And ... the Cat didn't care one way or the other.

[animals, pride]

Genesis 1:24

Two caterpillars were crawling across the lawn in the Garden of Eden when a butterfly flew over them. As they looked up at the beautiful fluttering creature, one nudged the other, "You couldn't get me up in one of those things for a million dollars."

[ignorance, insects, transportation]

Genesis 1:24 (KJV)

I have been told that freeways were first mentioned in Genesis:
"The Lord made every creeping thing... ."

[speed, transportation]

Genesis 1:24

QUESTION: What do you get when you cross a praying mantis with a termite?
ANSWER: A bug that says grace before it eats your house.

[prayer, insects]

Genesis 1:24

A cat's view of creation
On the first day of creation, God created the cat.
On the second day, God created man to serve the cat.
On the third, God created all the animals of the earth to serve as potential food for the cat.
On the fourth day, God created honest toil so that man could labor for the good of the cat.
On the fifth day, God created the sparkle ball so that the cat might or might not play with it.

On the sixth day, God created veterinary science to keep the cat healthy and the man broke.
On the seventh day, God tried to rest, but he had to scoop the litter box.

[animals, pride]

Genesis 1:25

Dear GOD,
Did you mean for the giraffe to look like that or was it an accident?
Sincerely,
Norah

[animals, creation]

Genesis 1:25

QUESTION: Which came first, the chicken or the egg?
ANSWER: The chicken, of course, God couldn't "lay an egg."

[animals]

Genesis 1:26

We finally figured out what distinguishes humans from all the other beasts – financial worry!

[humans, image of God, worry]

Genesis 1:26

After her first lesson in zoology, the high school girl came home and asked her mother, "Is it true, mother, that I'm descended from an ape?"
"I'm not sure," her mother said. "I don't know your father's family very well."

[evolution, heredity]

Genesis 1:26

Some people can't understand the idea of a Trinity. But this concept is fundamental to the creation story. Did God tell Adam to add? No, he told Adam to go forth and MULTIPLY! And $1 \times 1 \times 1 = 1$.

[numbers, procreation, trinity]

Genesis 1:27

And here are Adam and Eve living together in paradise. You can tell it's paradise because Eve never asks Adam to take out the garbage.

[paradise, roles]

Genesis 1:28

Wife: "This article on overpopulation of the world says that somewhere in the world there is a woman having a baby every four seconds!"
Husband: "I think they ought to find that woman and stop her!"

[birth control, fertility]

Genesis 1:28

Adam and Eve had many advantages, but the principal one that many mothers with small babies think of was that they escaped teething.

[babies]

Genesis 1:28

A wealthy old farmer was having a family reunion with his large family and as they all sat down to the table for a Sunday dinner, the old man looked around at his six sons. All had been married for a few years and so the old farmer said: "I don't see any grandchildren around this table of mine. I want you all to know that I will give $500,000 to the first one of you who presents me with a grandchild. We will now say grace."
When he raised his eyes again, he and his wife were the only ones at the table.

[fertility, money, sex]

Genesis 1:28

Two businessmen were having lunch and they started talking about world problems, high taxes, the cost of living, and their families. One of them said proudly, "I have six boys."
So the other guy said, "That's a nice family. I wish to heaven I had six children."
Then the proud father said with a touch of sympathy in his voice asked, "Don't you have any children?"
And the other guy said, "Yeah, ten!"

[birth control, size of family]

Genesis 1:28

A West Virginia man, considering getting a vasectomy, decided to discuss it with his priest.
The priest gave him various bits of advice, and suggested that he discuss it with his doctor.
The doctor likewise advised him on various aspects, but on discovering that he hadn't talked to his family about it yet, urged him to do so.
His family voted in favor, fourteen to four.

[birth control, size of family]

Genesis 1:28

William and Eleanor Bramer and their fifteen children visited the zoo. Upon arriving, they found the admission was one dollar per family. William guided his twelve kids through a gate and handed the ticket collector a dollar bill. "Are all these your kids?" he asked.
"Sure are," answered the proud father.

"Then here's your dollar back. It's worth more for the animals to see your family then for your family to see the animals."

[size of family]

Genesis 1:28

Mrs. Denton the Christian school math teacher was having children do problems on the blackboard. She was constantly trying to incorporate Christian themes in the classroom, but was having trouble making it work for math until she got some unexpected help from a student.

"Who would like to do the first problem, addition?"

No one raised their hand. She called on Tommy, and with some help he finally got it right.

"Who would like to do the second problem, subtraction?"

Students hid their faces. She called on Mark, who got the problem but there was some suspicion his girlfriend Lisa whispered it to him.

"Who would like to do the third problem, division?"

Now a low collective groan could be heard as everyone looked at nothing in particular. The teacher called on Suzy, who got it right

"Who would like to do the last problem, multiplication?"

Jeff's hand enthusiastically shot up. It surprised everyone in the room because he had previously been avoiding participation. The teacher finally gained her composure in the stunned silence.

"Why the enthusiasm, Jeff?"

He said, "The Bible says to go forth and multiply!"

[misunderstanding, sex]

Genesis 1:31

Adam and Eve in the Garden of Eden couldn't complain how much better things were in the good old days!

[nostalgia]

Genesis 1:31

QUESTION: Why did Eve have no fear of the measles?
ANSWER: Because she'd Adam [had 'em].

[sickness]

Genesis 2:2

Some smart students don't believe that God created the world in seven days. They think, from their own experience, that He probably rested for six and then pulled an all-nighter.

[rest, students]

Genesis 2:2

In the middle of the children's sermon, the pastor was telling the preschoolers that God makes trees and water and apples and cherries. In fact, he said, "God makes everything."
Immediately one little boy spoke up "God doesn't make my bed!"

[creation, impossibility]

Genesis 2:2

A workaholic was asked, "Why don't you take a day off? Even God took a day off to rest." He answered, "I am not as good a worker as God, I need that day to catch up."

[Sabbath]

Genesis 2:2

A little girl named Victoria explained the Sabbath: "In the first book of the Bible, Genesis, God got tired of creating the world, so he took the Sabbath off."

[Sabbath]

Genesis 2:3

In the beginning, God created earth and rested. Then God created man and rested. Then God created woman. Since then, some insist, neither God nor man has rested.

[creation, rest, woman]

Genesis 2:7

A Children's Church class had been carefully drilled for the visit of the senior pastor who was going to review what they had been learning. Donny was to answer "God" when the question "Who made you?" was asked. Jimmy was to pipe up "Out of the dust of the earth" in answer to the second question.
"Who made you?" asked the senior pastor when the great day of the review arrived. No one answered, Again the opening question. Still no answer.
"Please, pastor," spoke up a freckled-faces boy, "the boy God made is home with the measles."

[creation]

Genesis 2:7

QUESTION: Why was Adam a famous runner?
ANSWER: Because he was first in the human race.

[sports]

Genesis 2:7

QUESTION: At what time of day was Adam created?

ANSWER: A little before Eve.

[creation, timing]

Genesis 2:7

A minister in a southern church was preaching on the subject of creation and stated that the first created man was really a black man. The church was silent in shock. Then he went on to explain. "Yes," he said, "and then the Lord leaned him against a fence and when he dried out he had bleached out white."

One of his astonished congregation finally called out, "Who made the fence, pastor?"

"Brother Johnson," replied the minister, "them's just the questions that spoils religion."

[creation, races]

Genesis 2:7

One day a group of scientists got together and decided that man had come a long way and no longer needed God. So they picked one scientist to go and tell God that they were done with Him. The scientist walked up to God and said, "God, we've decided that we no longer need you. We're to the point that we can clone people and do many miraculous things, so why don't you just go on and get lost."

God listened very patiently and kindly to the man and after the scientist was done talking, God said, "Very well, how about this, let's say we have a man-making contest." The scientist replied, "OK, great, you're on!" But God added, "Now, we're going to do this just like I did back in the old days with Adam."

The scientist said, "Sure, no problem" and bent down and grabbed himself a handful of dirt.

God just looked at him and said, "No, no, no. You go get your own dirt!"

[creation, science]

Genesis 2:10

Adam and Eve were walking along the bank of the river in Eden arm in arm. Adam looked poetically out to the river and eloquently cried out: "Roll on, thou deep blue river, roll on!"

Eve gazed at the water for a moment, then in hushed tones gasped, "Oh, Adam, you wonderful man! It's doing it!"

[manhood]

Genesis 2:15

A farmer purchases an old, run-down, abandoned farm with plans to turn it into a thriving enterprise. The fields are grown over with weeds, the farmhouse is falling apart, and the fences are collapsing all around.

During his first day of work, the town preacher stops by to bless the man's work, saying, "May you and God work together to make this the farm of your dreams!"

A few months later, the preacher stops by again to call on the farmer. Lo and behold, it's like a completely different place--the farmhouse is completely rebuilt and in excellent condition, there are plenty of cattle and other livestock happily munching on feed in well-fenced pens, and the fields are filled with crops planted in neat rows. "Amazing!" the preacher says. "Look what God and you have accomplished together!"

"Yes, reverend," says the farmer, "but remember what the farm was like when God was working it alone!"

[cooperation, farming, work]

Genesis 2:15

What a good thing Adam had going. When he said something, he knew nobody had said it before.

[speech]

Genesis 2:17

QUESTION: Why is a pair of skates like the forbidden fruit in the Garden of Eden?
ANSWER: Both come before the fall.

[failure, sports]

Genesis 2:18

An English professor wrote on the board the sentence, "Woman without her man is a savage." Then he asked the students to punctuate it correctly.
The males in the class wrote, "Woman, without her man, is a savage."
The females wrote, "Woman! Without her, man is a savage."

[men, women]

Genesis 2:18

QUESTION: Who was created first, Adam or Eve?
ANSWER: Eve. Everyone knows she was the first maid [made].

[creation, gender]

Genesis 2:18

Adam ... the one man in the world who couldn't say, "Pardon me, but haven't I seen you before?"

[creation]

Genesis 2:18

TOP TEN REASONS GOD CREATED EVE
10. God worried that Adam would always be lost in the garden because men hate to ask for directions.

9. God knew that Adam would one day need someone to hand him the TV remote. (Men don't want to see what's ON television, they want to see WHAT ELSE is on!)

8. God knew that Adam would never buy a new fig leaf when his seat wore out and would therefore need Eve to get one for him.

7. God knew that Adam would never make a doctor's appointment for himself.

6. God knew that Adam would never remember which night was garbage night.

5. God knew that if the world was to be populated, men would never be able to handle childbearing.

4. As "Keeper of the Garden," Adam would never remember where he put his tools.

3. The Scripture account of creation indicates Adam needed someone to blame his troubles on when God caught him hiding in the garden.

2. As the Bible says, "It is not good for man to be alone!"

1. When God finished the creation of Adam, He stepped back, scratched His head and said, "Let's give this creation-thing another try."

[gender, creation]

Genesis 2:19

Adam was naming the animals of the earth when along came a rhinoceros.
God: What are you going to call this one?
Adam: I think I'll call it a rhinoceros.
God: Why?
Adam: Well, it looks more like a rhinoceros than anything I've named yet.

[names]

Genesis 2:19

QUESTION: Why didn't God create Eve at the same time as Adam?
ANSWER: He didn't want them arguing about the names of the animals!

[names, argument]

Genesis 2:19

Son: "Father, why was Adam made first?"
Father: "I suppose to give him a chance to say a few words."

[speech, creation]

Genesis 2:19

QUESTION: What is the earliest history of the flea?
ANSWER: Adam had'em.

[insects]

Genesis 2:20

A Children's Church teacher asked Little Willie who the first man in the
Bible was.

"Hoss," said Willie.

"Wrong," said the teacher. "It was Adam."

"Ah, shucks!" Willie replied. "I knew it was one of those Cartwrights."

[names, television]

Genesis 2:21

The little boy was telling his parents what he had learned at Children's
Church about the creation of Adam and Eve and he got just a few facts
twisted.

"The teacher told us about how God made the first man and the first
woman," he said. "He made the man first and he got lonesome for
somebody to talk to. So God rocked him to sleep and then he took out the
man's brains and made a woman of them!"

[creation, gender]

Genesis 2:21

After hearing the story about how God took the rib out of Adam's side, a
little boy who had been running and had gotten a side ache, declared to his
mother, "I think I'm going to have a wife."

[creation, wife]

Genesis 2:21

God looks down and notices that Adam is all alone while all the animals
have companions so he decides to create a companion for man as well. He
comes to see Adam and says to him, "Adam, you are my greatest creation
and therefore, I am going to create for you the ultimate companion. She
will worship the very ground you walk on, she will long for you and no
other, she will wait on you hand and foot and obey your every command,
and all it will cost you is an arm and a leg." Thinking for a few moments,
Adam replies reluctantly, "I don't know God, an arm and a leg is an awful
lot, what could I get for, say, a rib?"

[man, woman, creation]

Genesis 2:21

For some men who don't understand either the Scriptures or reality,
woman has always been merely a side issue!

[woman]

Genesis 2:22

No man ever got so much out of a surgical operation as Adam did.

[creation]

Genesis 2:22

After Eve was created you might say Adam was "beside" himself!

[creation, man]

Genesis 2:22

Children's Church teacher, "Can anyone tell me the story of Adam and Eve very briefly?"
A little woman's libber, "Sure, first God created Adam. Then He looked at him and said, 'I think I could do better if I tried again.' So he created Eve."

[creation, woman]

Genesis 2:22

Mr. and Mrs. Howard were having a slight difference of opinion. "It's obvious that I am right," snapped Mrs. Howard. "After all, since God created women second, we must be an improvement on the original model."
Patiently Mr. Howard replied, "Actually, my dear, He created woman second because He didn't want any advice."

[creation, man]

Genesis 2:22

The first Adam-splitting [atom-splitting] gave us Eve, a force that ingenious men in all ages have never gotten under control.

[creation, woman]

Genesis 2:22

QUESTION: What is the first theatrical event the Bible mentions?
ANSWER: Eve's appearance for Adam's benefit.

[appearance]

Genesis 2:22

QUESTION: When was radio first referred to in the Bible?
ANSWER: When the Lord took a rib from Adam and made a loud speaker.

[noise]

Genesis 2:22

QUESTION: Why had Eve no fear of the measles?
ANSWER: Because she'd Adam.

[sickness]

Genesis 2:22

When Adam stayed out very late for a few nights, Eve became upset. "You're running around with other women," she charged.
"You're being unreasonable," Adam responded. "You're the only woman on earth." The quarrel continued until Adam fell asleep, only to be awakened

13

by someone poking him in the chest. It was Eve. "What do you think you're doing?" Adam demanded.

"Counting your ribs," said Eve.

[trust]

Genesis 2:22

Whilst Adam slept, Eve from his side arose:
Strange his first sleep should be his last repose.

[rest]

Genesis 2:22

Adam was the first man to know the meaning of rib roast.

[food]

Genesis 2:22

The best check-writing machine was made from Adam's rib.

[money]

Genesis 2:23

When Adam called the being God had created for him "Woman," he definitely was not using it as a short form for "Woe is man!"

[names, woman]

Genesis 2:23

QUESTION: Why is the female called woman?
ANSWER: When Adam saw her, all he could say was, "Whoa, man!"

[names woman]

Genesis 2:24

"Dad," said the small boy, "why isn't a man allowed to have more than one wife?"

"My son," replied the dad, "when you are older you will understand that the law protects those who are incapable of protecting themselves."

[marriage, polygamy]

Genesis 2:24

QUESTION: What did Adam never see or have, yet left two of them for each of his children?
ANSWER: Parents.

[parents]

Genesis 2:24

A Children's Church teacher was reviewing her pupils on a unit of lessons. She placed an apple on the table.

"This is my apple," she said. "If you see someone take it, what Bible verse does it bring to mind?"

"Thou shalt not steal," a wise pupil answered promptly.
"That's good. Now if you see two boys fighting, what verse comes to you?"
"Be ye kind one to another," a pupil answered.
Now the teacher wanted to remind the pupils about being kind to animals. "If two boys were fighting over a cat, "she said, "and one boy was pulling the cat's front legs and the other the cat's tail, what verse would that remind you of?"
All of the pupils thought a moment. Finally one raised his hand.
"What God hath joined together, let no man put asunder!" he answered.

[animals, marriage]

Genesis 2:24

"Oh, my darling, we are now a part of each other. You are part of me, and I, a part of you. Of course there'll be confusion when we get dressed in the morning."

[gender, marriage]

Genesis 2:24

Marriage is a union. A union of heart, a union of soul, a union of minds, but just wait till you have to pay those union dues!

[marriage]

Genesis 2:24

The way some nearly married men encourage their wives to dress, even in public, you'd think the important thing about marriage is cleavage!

[modesty]

Genesis 2:25

Conversation between Adam and Eve must have been difficult at times because they had nobody else to talk about.

[communication, gossip]

Genesis 2:25

QUESTION: What political persuasion were Adam and Eve?
ANSWER: Communist citizens, of course ...nothing to wear, no meat to eat, but living in Paradise!

[paradise]

Genesis 2:25

QUESTION: Can you spell "Adam's Express Company" with three letters?
ANSWER: E-V-E.

[business]

Genesis 2:25

Eve: "Adam, do you love me?"

Adam: "Who else?"

[love]

Genesis 2:25

"You remember Eve," said the husband to his wife, "the first and only
woman who could truly say, 'I haven't got a thing to wear' and mean it!"

[clothes]

Genesis 2:25

Adam and Eve lived thousands of years B.C. — before clothing.
[clothes, time]

Genesis 2:25

Sign over Adam's house: "We're Never Clothed."

[business, clothes]

Genesis 3:1-7

When Adam bit into the apple, you could tell it was from the Tree of
Knowledge. Adam looked at the apple, turned to Eve and said: "You call
this dinner? I'd say it's dessert."

[food, knowledge]

Genesis 3:6

QUESTION: At what season did Eve eat the fruit?
ANSWER: Just before the Fall.

[time]

Genesis 3:6

Since the dawn of recorded history, people have complained about the
terms of mortgages. Look at Adam and Eve. They had the world's easiest
deal, a life-long, no bite mortgage. Then they had to open their big mouth!

[business, house, sin]

Genesis 3:6

All the trouble started in the Garden of Eden when Eve bit into a piece of
fruit. I can empathize with her since you should have seen the trouble I had
in Mexico when I did the same thing.

[food, sickness, travel]

Genesis 3:6

QUESTION: Did Adam ever finish eating the fruit Eve gave to him?
ANSWER: No, the apple got stuck in Adam's throat [Adam's apple].

[body, food]

Genesis 3:6

When Eve suggested to Adam that they eat from the forbidden fruit, Adam should have said no and been <u>adam</u>ant!

[Adam, names}

Genesis 3:6

In the Garden of Eden one morning, Eve asked Adam, "What's wrong with eating this apple?"
"I'll bite," smiled Adam.

[temptation]

Genesis 3:6

QUESTION: What type of computer did Adam and Eve use?
ANSWER: Both of them used an Apple.

[computer]

Genesis 3:6

A teacher was winding up a discussion in her fourth grade class on the importance of curiosity.
Teacher: "Where would we be today if no one had ever been curious?"
Child: "Still in the Garden of Eden?"

[consequences, curiosity]

Genesis 3:6

Some men were discussing the Bible. They were wondering how many apples Adam and Eve ate in the Garden of Eden.
First man: I think there was only one apple in the Garden.
Second man: I think there were ten apples. Adam 8 and Eve ate 2.
Third man: I think there were sixteen apples. Eve 8 and Adam 8 also.
Fourth man: I think all three of you are wrong. If Eve 8 and Adam 82, that would be a total of 90 apples.
Fifth man: You guys don't know how to add at all. According to history, Eve 81 and Adam 82. That would be a total of 163 apples.
Sixth man: Wait a minute! If Eve 81 and Adam 812, that would make a total of 893 apples.
Seventh man: None of you guys understand the problem in the slightest. According to my figuring, if Eve 814 Adam and Adam 8124 Eve, that would be a total of 8,938 apples in the garden.
At that point all of the men gave up.

[curiosity, math]

Genesis 3:6

See Romans 5:14.

Genesis 3:7

Adam and Eve began to argue with each other almost immediately after the fall. In fact, for supper Adam came to Eve quite upset saying, "You've messed up again Eve, you've put my pants in the salad!"

[argument, clothes, food]

Genesis 3:7

A little boy opened the big and old family Bible with fascination, and looked at the old pages as he turned them. Suddenly, something fell out of the Bible, and he picked it up and looked at it closely. It was an old leaf from a tree that had been pressed in between the pages. "Momma, look what I found," the boy called out. "What have you got there, dear?" his mother asked.

With astonishment in the young boy's voice, he answered: "I think it's Adam's suit!"

[clothes]

Genesis 3:7

Adam and Eve were the first bookkeepers. They invented the loose-leaf system.

[business]

Genesis 3:7

One man to another as they sit on a bench in a mall waiting for their shopping wives, "I wonder how many fig leaves Eve tried on before she found one that she liked."

[clothes]

Genesis 3:7

I found this dry leaf in this old Bible. Do you suppose it belonged to Adam and Eve?"

[clothes]

Genesis 3:7

The expression 'turning over a new leaf' takes on a whole new meaning when it's used of Adam and Eve.

[new]

Genesis 3:7

Customer: "Why do you have an apple for a trademark? You're a tailor."
Tailor: "Well, if it hadn't been for the apple, where would the clothing business be?

[business, clothes]

Genesis 3:7

And now we take you to the Garden of Eden where a fig leaf is slowly wafting down from a tree. Eve looks up and says: "Look, Adam, look! The Invisible Man!"

[invisible]

Genesis 3:7

QUESTION: Where is the first mention of insurance in the Bible?
ANSWER:. When Adam and Eve needed more coverage.

[clothes, insurance]

Genesis 3:7

Here's to Adam
Father of us all,
He was Johnny on the spot,
When the leaves began to fall.

[clothes]

Genesis 3:10

In visiting members of his church one afternoon, a clergyman knocked at the door of a church member but received no response. He was annoyed because he could hear footsteps and knew the mother of the family must be there. The pastor left his calling card, writing on it: "Revelation 3:20. Behold, I stand at the door and knock: if any man hear my voice, and open the door, I will come in to him."
The next Sunday, as the congregation filed out of the church after the service, the woman who had refused to answer the door greeted the pastor and handed him her card, with "Genesis 3:10" written on it. Later, the pastor looked up the passage and read: "I heard thy voice in the garden, and I was afraid, because I was naked; and I hid myself."

[naked, visit]

Genesis 3:11-14

When God asked Adam why he had eaten from the forbidden fruit, man blamed it on the woman, the woman blamed it on the serpent, and the serpent was left without a leg to stand on!

[excuses]

Genesis 3:12

Most people would learn from their mistakes if they weren't so busy trying to place the blame on someone else.

[blame]

Genesis 3:12

Eve was nigh Adam; Adam was naïve (nigh Eve).

[gender]

Genesis 3:12

"Did he take his misfortunes like a man?"
"Absolutely. He laid the blame on his wife."

[manhood, blame]

Genesis 3:16

Judgment Day arrives. God reviews the billions of people assembled, and says, "Welcome to Heaven. Women, go with Saint Peter. Men, form two lines. One line shall be men who dominated their woman on Earth. The other line shall be men who were dominated by their woman." After much movement and shuffling, all the women are gone, and there remain two lines of men. The line of men that were dominated by their women is hundreds, perhaps thousands of miles long. The line of men that dominated women has but one man standing. God reviews the two lines, points to the long line, and in a voice that echoes angrily throughout Heaven says, "You men should be ashamed. I created you in MY image, and you all were dominated by your mates. Behold! Only one of my sons stood up and made me proud. You shall learn from him!" God turns to the one man standing, smiles, and says, "Tell them, my son, how did you manage to be the only one in that line?" And the man says, "I don't know, Lord. My wife told me to stand here."

[submission]

Genesis 3:17

Adam was rejected for Eden [eatin'] the apple.

[eating, rejection]

Genesis 3:19

A little boy came in to the kitchen and asked his mother, "Mom is it true that man was made from dust and that when he dies he goes back to dust like our Children's Church teacher said?"
The mother answered, "Son, that's true because it is what the Bible says."
The little boy looked up at his mother with all seriousness and announced, "Well, I just looked under my bed and I have someone either comin' or goin'!"

[creation, death]

Genesis 3:20

A little boy was asked to name the first man. He promptly answered, "Adam."

Then, he was asked to name the first woman. He pondered long and hard and finally suggested, "Madam."

[names]

Genesis 3:20

Children's Church teacher: "Class, what do you know about Adam's wife, Eve?"
Children's Church student: "I think her first name is really Christmas, you know, Christmas Eve."

[names, Christmas]

Genesis 3:20

The Children's Church teacher asked her class, "Does anyone know who lived in the Garden of Eden?"
I do, Madame," said little Jewel, "It was the Adams Family."

[names, television]

Genesis 3:23

QUESTION: How were Adam and Eve prevented from gambling?
ANSWER: Their pair-o-dice [paradise] was taken away from them!

[gambling, paradise]

Genesis 3:24

A little boy in Children's Church after hearing the story about the fall, drew a picture of a man and woman in the back seat of a chauffeur driven limousine. The chauffeur had a long white beard.
When asked what the picture was about, he replied, "That's God driving Adam and Eve out of the garden."

OR

A teacher asked her students to draw a picture of their favorite Old Testament story, and as she moved around the class, she saw there were many wonderful drawings being done. Then she came across Barry who had drawn a man driving an old car. In the back seat were two passengers, both scantily dressed.
"It's a lovely picture," said the teacher, "but which story does it tell?"
Barry seemed surprised at the question. "Well," he exclaimed, "doesn't it say in the BIBLE that God drove Adam and Eve out of the Garden of Eden?"

[rejection, transportation]

Genesis 3:24

QUESTION: What was the license number of the car that drove Eve out of the garden?
ANSWER: ADAM-812 [Adam ate one too].

[blame, transportation]

Genesis 3:24

QUESTION: How did Adam and Eve feel when expelled from the Garden of Eden?
ANSWER: They were really put out.

[feelings]

Genesis 3:24

After the fall in the Garden of Eden, Adam was walking with his sons Cain and Abel. They passed by the Garden of Eden. One of the boys asked, "Dad why did you ever leave such a beautiful place?"
Adam replied slowly, "Well, you might say your mother and I ate us out of house and home."

[blame, eating]

Genesis 3:24

QUESTION: What kind of motor vehicle does God drive?
ANSWER: God drove Adam and Eve out of the Garden in a 'Fury.'

[transportation]

Genesis 3:24

The first car in the Bible was owned by God — when he drove Adam and Eve out of the Garden of Eden.
For other motor vehicles mentioned in the Bible, see 1 Samuel 18:7 where David's Triumph was heard throughout the land, Acts 2:1 where the early Christians drove a Honda because the apostles were all in one Accord, and 2 Corinthians 4:8 which describes going out in service in a Volkswagen Beetle: "We are pressed in every way, but not cramped beyond movement."

[transportation]

Genesis 4:1

Children's Church teacher to noisy boy, "What do you mean there is biblical evidence that Adam and Eve were noisy?"
Little boy, "They raised Cain, didn't they?"

[noise]

Genesis 4:1

QUESTION: Who introduced the first walking stick?
ANSWER: Eve—when she presented Adam a little Cain [cane].

[names]

Genesis 4:2

Famous prophetic words: "Cain! Get off your brother! You're going to kill him some day!"

[brothers, murder]

Genesis 4:2

How do we know Cain was constipated? Unlike Moses who took two tablets, Cain just wasn't able [Abel].

[constipation]

Genesis 4:6-7

Cain just wasn't able [Abel] when it came to the sacrifice!

[names, sacrifice]

Genesis 4:8

QUESTION: How long a period of time did Cain hate his brother?
ANSWER: As long as he was Abel [able].

[hatred]

Genesis 4:8

Dear GOD,
Maybe Cain and Abel would not kill each other so much if they had their own rooms. It works with my brother.
Sincerely,
Rhys

[hatred, murder]

Genesis 4:8

QUESTION: Who sounded the first bell in the Bible?
ANSWER: Cain, when he hit Abel [a bell].

[names, music]

Genesis 4:9

Just recently an ape escaped from a city zoo. Several hours later the beast was finally found in the reading room of the main library. He was pouring over the first chapter of Genesis, and he also had a copy of Darwin's Origin of the Species.
When a policeman asked the ape what he was doing, the ape replied, "I am trying to figure out once and for all if I am my brother's keeper, or if I am my keeper's brother!"

[animals, brother, evolution]

Genesis 4:17

Heckler to a sincere but unlearned Preacher: "Who was Cain's wife?"

Preacher: "I respect any seeker of knowledge, but I warn you, young man, don't risk being lost to salvation by too much inquiring after other men's wives."

[mock, wife]

Genesis 4:17

QUESTION: How do you know when Enoch is at the door?
ANSWER: 'E knocks.

[names]

Genesis 4:19

Some feel that the extreme penalty of bigamy is having two mothers-in-law.

[polygamy]

Genesis 4:21-22

The human race has been able to improve on everything but people.

[improvement, race]

Genesis 5:5

You could say that Adam was so old that he could remember Eve when she was just a rib.

[age]

Genesis 5:27

To what do you attribute your long life?" the reporter asked Methuselah.
"I don't know yet," replied Methuselah, "I'm still dickering with a couple of vegetarian food companies."

[age]

Genesis 5:27

Methuselah ate what he found on his plate
And never as people do now,
Did he note the amount of calorie count,
He ate it because it was chow.
He never feared, as at dinner he sat,
Devouring a salad or pie,
To think it was lacking in granular fat,
Or a couple of vitamins shy.
He cheerfully ate each species of food,
Unmindful of troubles or fears,
Lest his health might be hurt
By some fancy dessert,
And he lived over nine hundred years.

[age]

Genesis 5:27

Methuselah, when celebrating his 900th birthday was asked, "What are you most proud of?"

Methuselah replied, "That I've lived 900 years and haven't an enemy in the world."

Noting that he had a feisty nature, he was then asked, "And how did you manage that?"

Came the retort, "I've outlived every last one of them!"

[age, enemies]

Genesis 5:27

Methuselah—The oldest man in history at 969 years old, which is 6,783 in dog years.

[age]

Genesis 5:27

I can believe it's true that Methuselah lived over nine hundred years. They had no cars back then.

[death]

Genesis 5:32

"What were the names of Noah's three sons, Tommy?" asked his Children's Church teacher.

"I can't remember them exactly," Tommy replied, "but I think one was called Bacon [i.e., Ham]."

[names]

Genesis 5:32

Skeptic: "How could Noah's wife have a son that age?"

Pastor: "She didn't. When she had him he was just a baby."

[age, birth]

Genesis 6

Two small children were talking when the first asked the second one, "What kind of lights did Noah's ark have?"

The second child answered, "I don't know. What kind did he have?"

"Floodlights!" screamed the delighted first child.

[light]

Genesis 6

Noah's Excuses For Not Completing His Ark On Time:

And the Lord said unto Noah: "Where is the ark which I have commanded thee to build?"

And Noah said unto the Lord, "Verily, I have had three carpenters off ill. The gopher wood supplier hath let me down—yea, even though the gopher wood hath been on order for nigh upon 12 months. What can I do O Lord?' And God said unto Noah: 'I want that ark finished even after seven days and seven nights."

And Noah said: "It will be so.' And it was not so."

And the Lord said unto Noah: "What seemeth to be the trouble this time?"

And Noah said unto the Lord: "Mine subcontractor hath gone bankrupt. The pitch which Thou commandest me to put on the outside of the ark hath not arrived. The plumber hath gone on strike. Shem, my son who helpeth me on the ark side of the business, hath formed a pop group with his brothers Ham and Japheth. Lord, I am undone."

And the Lord grew angry and said: "And what about the animals, the male and female of every sort that I ordered to come unto thee to keep their seed upon the face of the earth?"

And Noah said: "They have been delivered unto the wrong address but should arriveth on Friday."

And the Lord said: "How about the unicorns, and the fowls of the air by seven?"

And Noah wrung his hands and wept, saying: "Lord, unicorns are a discontinued line, thou canst not get them for love or money. And fowls of the air are sold only in half-dozens. Lord, Lord, Thou knowest how it is. And the Lord in his wisdom said: Noah, my son, I knowest, Why else dost thou think I have caused a flood to descend upon the earth?"

And the Lord grew angry.

[business, environment]

Genesis 6–9

And the Lord spoke to Noah and said: "In six months I'm going to make it rain until the whole earth is covered with water and all the evil people are destroyed. But I want to save a few good people, and two of every kind of living thing on the planet. I am ordering you to build Me an Ark.

And in a flash of lightning he delivered the specifications for an Ark.

"OK," said Noah, trembling in fear and fumbling with the blueprints. "Six months, and it starts to rain," thundered the Lord. "You'd better have my Ark completed, or learn how to swim for a very long time."

And six months passed. The skies began to cloud up and rain began to fall. The Lord saw that Noah was sitting in his front yard, weeping. And there was no Ark.

"Noah," shouted the Lord, "where is my Ark?" A lightning bolt crashed into the ground next to Noah. "Lord, please forgive me!" begged Noah. "I did my best. But there were big problems. First I had to get a building permit for the Ark construction project, and your plans didn't meet code. So I had to hire an engineer to redraw the plans. Then I got into a big fight over whether or not the Ark needed a fire sprinkler system. My neighbors objected, claiming I was violating zoning by building the Ark in my front yard, so I had to get a variance from the city planning commission. Then I had a big problem getting enough wood for the Ark because there was a ban on cutting trees to save the Spotted Owl. I had to convince U.S. Fish and Wildlife that I needed the wood to save the owls. But they wouldn't let me catch any owls. So! No owls. Then the carpenters formed a union and went out on strike. I had to negotiate a settlement with the National Labor Relations Board before anyone would pick up a saw or a hammer. Now we have 16 carpenters going on the boat, and still no owls. Then I started gathering up animals, and got sued by an animal rights group. They objected to me taking only two of each kind. Just when I got the suit dismissed, EPA notified me that I couldn't complete the Ark without filing an environmental impact statement on your proposed flood. They didn't take kindly to the idea that they had no jurisdiction over the conduct of a Supreme Being. Then the Army Corps of Engineers wanted a map of the proposed new flood plane. I sent them a globe. Right now I'm still trying to resolve a complaint from the Equal Employment Opportunity Commission over how many Croatians I'm supposed to hire. The IRS has seized all my assets claiming I'm trying to avoid paying taxes by leaving the country, and I just got a notice from the state about owing some kind of use tax. I really don't think I can finish your Ark for at least another five years," Noah wailed.

The sky began to clear. The sun began to shine. A rainbow arched across the sky. Noah looked up and smiled. "You mean you're not going to destroy the earth?" Noah asked, hopefully.

"No," said the Lord sadly, "Government already has."

[environment, government]

Genesis 6-9

A Pennsylvania citizen, arriving in heaven, was asked to be prepared to share at the next service some experience from his earthly days.

The new arrival jumped at the opportunity. "I survived the Johnstown flood of 1889. Over two thousand people perished in the destruction. I managed to save my family in an old boat we had bought years before. I've told the story to many on earth now I can tell it up here as well."

"That will be fine," said his heavenly guide, "But remember – Noah will be out there in the audience."

[boasting, flood]

Genesis 6-9

A traveling salesman found himself stranded in a very small town due to a heavy rainstorm that had washed out the road he normally took out of town. While having a cup of coffee in the hotel dining room, he looked out the window and remarked to the waitress, "Did you ever see such rain? It looks like the Flood."

"It looks like the what, mister?"

"The Flood. Surely you have read about the Flood and how Noah finally landed the Ark safely on Mount Ararat."

"Can't say as I have," replied the waitress. "But then I ain't seen a newspaper in days."

[flood, ignorance]

Genesis 6-9

All I Really Need to Know I Learned From Noah's Ark:

1. Don't miss the boat.
2. Don't forget that we're all in the same boat.
3. Plan ahead. It wasn't raining when Noah built the ark.
4. Stay fit. When you're 600 years old, someone might ask you to do something REALLY big.
5. Don't listen to critics, just get on with what has to be done.
6. Build your future on high ground.
7. For safety's sake, travel in pairs.
8. Two heads are better than one.
9. Speed isn't always an advantage; the snails were on board with the cheetahs.
10. When you're stressed, float awhile.
11. Remember that the ark was built by amateurs; the Titanic was built by professionals.
12. Remember that woodpeckers inside are a larger threat than the storm outside.
13. No matter the storm, when God is with you there's a rainbow waiting.

[experience]

Genesis 6:1

QUESTION: Why did early man have no need for a calculator?
ANSWER: Because men used to multiply on the face of the earth.

[math]

Genesis 6:1

As the last member of a family of 12, I have mixed emotions about this business of population control.

[population control]

Genesis 6:4

Baseball is talked about a great deal in the Holy Bible, in fact right from the
first verse: In the big inning ... , then Eve stole first, Adam stole second,
later, Cain struck out Abel, the Giants and the Angels were rained out,
Gideon rattled the pitchers, Goliath was put out by David, and finally, the
Prodigal Son made a home run!

[sports]

Genesis 6:13

Teacher: "Do you know who built the Ark?"
Confused Student: "Yes...NO...AH..."
Teacher: "Correct."

[confusion, names]

Genesis 6:14

QUESTION: Where did Noah hammer the first nail in the ark?
ANSWER: On the head.

[carpentry]

Genesis 6:14

QUESTION: What did God say when Noah told him he wanted to build
the ark out of steel?
ANSWER: "No, Noah—go for wood" [gopher wood].

[wood]

Genesis 6:16-20

Do you know how Noah spent his time in the ark? No, but we know he
couldn't play cards since there were animals sitting on all three of his decks.

[games]]

Genesis 6:17

Probably the last completely accurate weather forecast was when God told
Noah there was a 100 percent chance of precipitation.

[weather]

Genesis 6:17

Noah's wife to a neighbor: "I hardly know what to think. The general
consensus says always sunny, my arthritis says damp weather is coming,
and my husband says the Lord told him there'll be forty days of rain."

[weather]

Genesis 6:19

Boy: "Must have been lonely on Noah's ark."
Children's Church teacher: "Couldn't they have done a lot of fishing?"

Boy: "What — with only two worms?"

[boredom]

Genesis 7:7

One thing about Noah — he didn't miss the boat.

[procrastination]

Genesis 7:7

During a history class the teacher asked the question, "Who was Joan of Arc?"
After a long pause, one girl raised her hand and responded, "Wasn't she Noah's wife?"

OR

A little boy, just back from Children's Church, asked his non-church-going father if Noah had a wife.
"All the time, questions, questions, questions," replied the father. "Of course he did, Joan of Arc."

[names]

Genesis 7:8

QUESTION: Why did Noah have to punish and discipline the chickens on the Ark?
ANSWER: Because they were using "fowl" language.

[swearing]

Genesis 7:8

Don: "Was there any money on Noah's Ark?"
Jessie: "Yes. The duck took a bill, the frog took a greenback, and the skunk took a scent."

[money]

Genesis 7:8-9

You remember the story of the Ark. The ship that carried a male and female of every living creature on earth. I think it was the last cruise ship that was ever evenly matched!

[dating]

Genesis 7:8-9

As Noah remarked ungrammatically while the animals were boarding the Ark, "Now I herd [heard] everything."

[work]

Genesis 7:8-9

QUESTION: What animal took the most baggage into the ark?
ANSWER: The elephant. He took his trunk with him, while the fox and the rooster only took a brush and a comb.

[animals]

Genesis 7:8-9

QUESTION: Why did the people on the ark think the horses were pessimistic?
ANSWER: They kept saying neigh.

[pessimist]

Genesis 7:9

Noah was standing at the gangplank checking off the pairs of animals when he saw three camels trying to get on board.
"Wait a minute!" said Noah. "Two of each is the limit. One of you will have to stay behind."
"It won't be me," said the first camel. "I'm the camel whose back is broken by the last straw."
"I'm the one people swallow while straining at a gnat," said the second.
"I," said the third, "am the one that shall pass through the eye of a needle sooner than a rich man shall enter heaven."
"Come on in," said Noah, "the world is going to need all of you."

[animals]

Genesis 7:9

Scene: Two elephants entering Noah's ark.
One said to the other, "On the other hand, Clyde, who else has ever asked us to take a boat trip?"

[animals]

Genesis 7:9

Johnny volunteered to review the story of Noah and the Ark for the Children's Church class. "All the animals went into Noah's ark two by two," he said, "except the worms, they went in apples."

[pairs]

Genesis 7:9

I'd admire Noah for building the ark and preserving all the species by putting two of everything on board but I must admit, why did he have to include mosquitoes?

[questions]

Genesis 7:9

Where did Noah keep his bees? In the archives [ark hives].

[insects]

Genesis 7:9

Two zebras standing in the rain waiting to get into Noah's Ark. Says one: "It's enough to shake your faith. They would decide to take us alphabetically."

[names]

Genesis 7:9

QUESTION: What animal could Noah not trust?
ANSWER: The cheetah.

[trust, animals]

Genesis 7:9

"They just appeared two by two," whispered Noah arcanely.

[speech]

Genesis 7:9

Why didn't Noah swat those two flies when he had the chance?

[insects]

Genesis 7:11

QUESTION: Who was known to have bladder problems?
ANSWER: Wasn't it Noah, you know, with the water problem?

[sickness]

Genesis 7:12

A newcomer in one of the more arid plains of the Southwest continually complained about the lack of rain. One day he asked a native, "Tell me the truth, does it ever rain here?"
After reflecting for a moment, the native replied, "I wouldn't say it never rains here. Remember the story about Noah's ark when it rained forty days and nights?"
"Sure do," replied the newcomer.
"Well," said the native, "We got a quarter of an inch that time."

[weather]

Genesis 7:13

Noah had two pigs in the ark — plus a Ham!

[names]

Genesis 7:13

Japheth: "Do you think it is still raining outside?"

Shem: "Did you ever see it raining inside?"

[weather]

Genesis 7:13

QUESTION: Who introduced salted meat to the Navy?
ANSWER: Noah – he took Ham on the ark.

[food]

Genesis 7:17

Then it rained for forty days and forty nights. I've had vacations like that myself!

[vacation, weather]

Genesis 7:17

QUESTION: What was Noah's favorite country record?
ANSWER: "I Love a Rainy Night."

[music]

Genesis 7:17

Noah to wife: "Do me a favor. Quit saying, 'Into each life some rain must fall!'"

[talking]

Genesis 7:23

QUESTION: Who was the world's first, greatest, and wisest financier?
ANSWER: Noah, because he floated stock while the rest of the world was in liquidation.

[business]

Genesis 7:23

QUESTION: Who ran the first canning factory?
ANSWER: Noah — he had a boat-load of preserved pairs.

[business]

Genesis 7:23

QUESTION: In what place did the cock crow when all the world could hear him?
ANSWER: In Noah's ark.

[noise]

Genesis 8:1

QUESTION: How did Noah keep the milk from going sour on the ark?
ANSWER: He kept it in the cows.

[farming]

Genesis 8:1

Memo: From Noah to the creatures on the ark —

Alligators....stop nibbling on fellow passengers.

Flies....quit pestering the horses.

Elephants.....shovel up your own mess, it blocks the hallways.

Pigeons....the lions are not statues.

Mosquitoes and bats....quit biting the other passengers.

Myna birds....stop repeating everything you hear.

Cows....fly swatting is prohibited.

Lightening bugs....remember lights out at 9 pm.

Pigs.....clean up your room.

Raccoons....stop your midnight raids.

Hyenas....stop laughing at the other passengers.

Lions....quit stalking everyone.

Vultures....stop hovering.

Bugs....stay out of the pantry.

Snakes....pick up your own skins and throw them away.

Ants....bring your own picnic lunch next time.

Hoofed animals....please tiptoe after midnight.

Camels....no spitting at the other passengers.

Squirrels....quit hiding nuts in the bathtub drains.

Night Owls....keep your hooting down, it keeps the Morning Doves awake.

Turtles....your dinners are getting cold, start for the dining hall earlier.

All passengers.... be careful what you say around the parrots if you don't want it repeated.

Signed, Noah

[animals, behavior]

Genesis 8:4

QUESTION: What is the difference between Noah's ark and an Archbishop?

ANSWER: One was a high ark, but the other is a hierarch.

[difference]

Genesis 8:4

QUESTION: Why was Noah like a hungry cat?

ANSWER: He went almost a year without finding Ararat [a rat].

[names]

Genesis 8:6

In many ways, the Bible is a surprisingly modern story. Like Noah in the Ark? It took him over forty days to find a place to park!

[frustration]

Genesis 8:11

QUESTION: When was money first mentioned in the Bible?
ANSWER: When the dove brought the green back to the ark.

[money]

Genesis 8:12

QUESTION: Why didn't the last dove return to the ark?
ANSWER: Because she had sufficient grounds to stay away.

[lawyers]

Genesis 8:12

The last dove hasn't returned," said Noah <u>dryly</u>.

[weather]

Genesis 8:13

Do you know what state is mentioned in the Bible? Arkansas [Noah looked out of the "ark and saw".]

[geography]

Genesis 8:13

How to we know that Noah was constipated the entire time he was on the ark?
For an entire year all he passed was water.

[constipated]

Genesis 8:14

QUESTION: Was Noah the first one out of the Ark?
ANSWER: No, he came forth [fourth] out of the ark.

[speed]

Genesis 8:18

As Noah and his family were disembarking from the ark, they paused on a ridge of Mount Ararat to look back. "We should have done something, Noah," his wife said. "That old hulk of an ark will sit there and be an eyesore on the landscape for years to come."
"Everything's taken care of," Noah assured her. "I've left the two termites aboard."

[insects, beauty]

Genesis 8:24

Although it is not well known, during the great flood, Noah's Ark sprang a leak and Noah told his dog to put his nose against the hole. The water continued to rush in, so Noah asked his wife to stand over the spot. As the leak grew, Noah himself sat on the hole.

And to this day, a dog's nose is always cold; a woman's feet are always clammy—and men always stand with their backs to the fireplace.

[men, temperature, woman]

Genesis 9:1

QUESTION: What was one of the first example of math in the Bible?
ANSWER: God told Noah to go forth and multiply.

[math]

Genesis 9:3

The most enjoyable way to follow a vegetable diet is to let the cow eat it and take yours in roast beef.

[food]

Genesis 9:6

An unbeliever who has no understanding of the scriptural reasons for capital punishment, once said, "Anyone who believes in capital punishment ought to be hanged."

[capital punishment, hypocrisy]

Genesis 9:6

New York State is abandoning the electric chair. Henceforth criminals will have to cross Times Square against the light.

[capital punishment]

Genesis 9:7

The long journey was finally over. Noah set down the ramp and proceeded to usher the animals off, two by two. Each time a pair left the ark he would say the same thing: "God bless you. Now go forth and multiply." It was quite a job, but he finally got the ark emptied, or so he thought, until he came across a pair of snakes coiled up in a corner.
"Well, what are you two waiting for?" he asked. "God bless you. Now go forth and multiply."
"That's the problem," said one of the snakes. "We're Adders."

[math, procreation]

Genesis 9:7

A woman came to ask the doctor if a woman should have children after thirty-five. I say thirty-five children is enough for any woman.
--Gracie Allen

[population control]

Genesis 9:15

An elderly lady from the country visited her grandson who lived in a large city. He took her to see his apartment, which was on the thirty-third floor of the building. When he asked his grandmother what she thought of it, she replied as she looked out the window, "Well at least you'll never have to worry about floods."

[flood]

Genesis 9:19

A lady was trying to impress those at the party. "My family's ancestry is very old," she boasted. "It dates back to the days of King James." Then, turning to a lady sitting quietly in a corner, she asked condescendingly: "How old is your family, my dear?"

"Well," came back the woman with a quiet smile, "I can't really say. All our family records were lost in the Flood."

[ancestors. pride]

Genesis 10:5

Dear GOD,
Who draws the lines around the countries?
Sincerely,
Harper

[geography]

Genesis 11:8

Tower of Babel—The reason the Lord created different languages. He scattered the builders across the continents, only to have them reunite in New York as cabbies.

[languages]

Genesis 11:9

QUESTION: What was the Tower of Babel?
ANSWER: Wasn't that where Solomon kept his wives?

[noise, wife]

Genesis 11:9

The Tower of Babel was a din of iniquity.

[languages, noise]

Genesis 12:4

QUESTION: How do we know Abraham was smart?
ANSWER: He knew a Lot.

[knowledge]

Genesis 13:11

"Some people say the Baptist denomination started with John the Baptist, but it was much earlier than that," said a great Baptist leader as he spoke to a large gathering of Baptist ministers. "In fact, it started way back in the Old

Testament. In the 13th chapter of Genesis, it says Lot said to Abraham, 'You go your way and I'll go mine.' That's really the roots of the Baptists!"

[Baptist, denominations]

Genesis 14:3

The two boys were boasting.
First boy: You know the Panama Canal? Well, my father dug the hole for it.
Second boy: You know the Dead Sea? Well, my father killed it.

[boasting, geography]

Genesis 14:13

The term "Hebrew" is used here first, but not, as some assume, as the first beer [He—Brew] for men in the Bible.

OR

He'Brew — The Chosen Beer."

[alcohol, drinking]

Genesis 17:12

Two little kids are in a hospital, lying on stretchers next to each other, outside the operating room.
The first kid leans over and asks, "What are you in here for?" The second kid says, "I'm in here to get my tonsils out and I'm a little nervous."
The first kid says, "You've got nothing to worry about. I had that done when I was four. They put you to sleep, and when you wake up they give you lots of Jell-O and ice cream. It's a breeze!"
The second kid then asks, "What are you here for?" The first kid says, "A circumcision." And the second kid says, "Whoa! I had that done when I was eight days old. I didn't walk for a year after that!"

[circumcision, sickness]

Genesis 17:12

QUESTION: What is the technical term for an uncircumcised Jew who is older than 8-days old?
ANSWER: A girl.

[circumcision]

Genesis 17:17

The Young Couples' church class was studying the story of Abraham and Sarah, who in their nineties were blessed with a child. Among other things the teacher asked, "What lesson do we learn from this story?"
A young mother of three who was having financial difficulties blurted out: "They waited until they could afford it!"

[children, finances]

Genesis 17:17

Bert age 85, and Rebecca age 79 are all excited about their decision to get married. They go for a stroll to discuss the wedding, and on the way go past a drugstore. Jacob suggests that they go in. He addresses the man behind the counter:

"Are you the owner?"

The pharmacist answers, "Yes."

Jacob: "Do you sell heart medication?"

Pharmacist: "Of course we do."

Jacob: "How about medicine for circulation?"

Pharmacist: "All kinds."

Jacob: "Medicine for rheumatism?"

Pharmacist: "Definitely."

Jacob: "How about skin lotions?"

Pharmacist: "Of course."

Jacob: "Medicine for memory?"

Pharmacist: "Yes, a large variety."

Jacob: "What about vitamins and sleeping pills?"

Pharmacist: "Absolutely."

Jacob: "Perfect! We'd like to register here for our wedding gifts."

[gifts, wedding]

Genesis 18:20-21

You know what I like about the story of Sodom and Gomorrah? It comes right out and names names!

[geography, names]

Genesis 18:20-21

Sodom and Gomorrah — Where Old Testament pagan college students went on spring break.

[party, sin]

Genesis 19:26

Teacher: "Lot was warned to take his wife and <u>flee</u> out of the city. Sadly, she looked back and was turned into a pillar of salt."

Little girl: "What happened to the <u>flea</u>?"

[insect]

Genesis 19:26

A teacher was telling his Children's Church class that Lot's wife had looked back and had turned into a pillar of salt.

"That's nothing," exclaimed Little Holden, "Just last week when my mother was driving her car she looked back and turned into a telephone pole!"

[consequences, driving]

Genesis 19:26

When Lot's wife looked back," said the Children's Church teacher, "what happened to her?"

"She was transmuted into chloride of sodium," answered the boy with the glasses.

[knowledge, science]

Genesis 19:26

"Where are you scaredy-cats going?" asked Lot's wife <u>salti</u>ly.

[mockery]

Genesis 19:26

QUESTION: Why was the woman in the Bible turned into a pillar of salt?
ANSWER: Because she was dissatisfied with her "Lot."

[dissatisfaction]

Genesis 21:2

"I have something to tell you, Abraham," said Sarah <u>expect</u>antly.

[anticipation, birth, surprise]

Genesis 21:7

A woman went to doctor's office. She was seen by one of the new doctors, but after about 4 minutes in the examination room, she burst out, screaming as she ran down the hall. An older doctor stopped and asked her what the problem was, and she explained. He had her sit down and relax in another room.
The older doctor marched back to the first and demanded, "What's the matter with you? Mrs. Terry is 63 years old, she has four grown children and seven grandchildren, and you told her she was pregnant?"
The new doctor smiled smugly as he continued to write on his clipboard. "Cured her hiccups though, didn't it?"

[doctors, surprise]

Genesis 22:3

Isaac—The biblical figure who became anxious when his father, Abraham, wanted to spend some "quality time" with him.

[anxiety, fathers, parenting]

Genesis 22:7

But Father, where is the sacrifice?" asked Isaac <u>sheep</u>ishly.

[sacrifice]

Genesis 22:7

Bible scholars have long wondered how old Isaac was when his father Abraham took him up to the mountain top to offer him as a sacrifice. A careful study of the story, as related in the Old Testament, contains the following facts:
1) Isaac was old enough to understand the ritual of sacrifice,
2) Isaac was old enough to carry wood for the fire to the top of the mountain,
3) Isaac was old enough to notice that they were not bringing an animal for the sacrifice.
Therefore Isaac's age, at this time, was greater than 8 years old. Scholars also conclude that he was younger than 12 years old as supported by the following fact:
If Isaac had been older than twelve, he would have been a teenager and most parents believe this would not have been a worthy enough sacrifice.

[teenagers]

Genesis 22:8

Abraham wants to upgrade his PC to Windows 8. Isaac is incredulous. "Pop," he says, "you can't run Windows 8 on your old, slow 386. Everyone knows that you need at least a 2.40 GHz with a lot more memory in order to multitask effectively with Windows 8."
But Abraham, the man of faith, gazed calmly at his son and replied, "God will provide the RAM, my son."

OR

And Abraham said unto Isaac, "come with me, my son, and we will upgrade my computer."
And Isaac said unto Abraham, "O my father, whence shall we upgrade it?"
And Abraham said unto Isaac, "My son, we shall upgrade it unto Windows 8."
And Isaac said unto Abraham, "O my father, this is surely too great a task for us to embark upon, for your computer lacketh the resources for so lofty an upgrade. Its processor is barely capable; its hard disk is far smaller than optimum, and its memory is sorely lacking even the minimum required."
And Abraham said unto Isaac, "Yet even so my son we shall make the attempt."
Isaac said unto Abraham, "Yea, but we are here in the wilderness, far from any electronics stores. Where shall we find the hardware needed to meet minimum specifications?"

And Abraham said unto Isaac, "Fear not, my son: for God will provide the RAM."

[computer, provision]

Genesis 22:14

A young woman brings home her fiancé to meet her parents. After dinner, her mother tells her father to find out about the young man. The father invites the fiancé to his study for a drink.

"So what are your plans?" the father asks the young man. "I am a Torah scholar." He replies. "A Torah scholar. Hmmm," the father says. "Admirable, but what will you do to provide a nice house for my daughter to live in, as she's accustomed to?" "I will study," the young man replies, "and God will provide for us." "And how will you buy her a beautiful engagement ring, such as she deserves?" asks the father. "I will concentrate on my studies," the young man replies, "God will provide for us." "And children?" asks the father. "How will you support children?" "Don't worry, sir, God will provide," replies the fiancé. The conversation proceeds like this, and each time the father questions, the young idealist insists that God will provide. Later, the mother asks, "How did it go, Honey?" The father answers, "He has no job and no plans, but the good news is he thinks I'm God."

[daughter, marriage, provision]

Genesis 24:16

QUESTION: When was baseball mentioned in the Bible?
ANSWER: When Rebecca walked to the well with the pitcher.

[sports]

Genesis 24:45

How do we know Rebecca loved baseball? She walked to the well with a pitcher,

[sports]

Genesis 24:63-67

Boy: "Did you know, Dad, that Isaac didn't know his wife until he married her?"
Father: "Why single out Isaac?"

[marriage]

Genesis 24:64

Did you know that the first mention of a cigarette in the Bible was in Genesis? According to the KJV, as Rebekah saw Isaac approaching, she "lit off her camel."

[smoking]

Genesis 25:1

There were two elderly people living in Trailer Estates, a Florida mobile home park. He was a widower, and she a widow. They had known one another for a number of years.

One evening there was a community supper in the big activity center. The two were at the same table, across from one another. As the meal went on, he made a few admiring glances at her and finally gathered his courage to ask her, "Will you marry me?" After about six seconds of 'careful consideration,' she answered, "Yes. Yes, I will." The meal ended, and with a few more pleasant exchanges, they went to their respective places.

Next morning, he was troubled. "Did she say 'yes' or did she say 'no'?" He couldn't remember. Try as he would, he just could not recall. Not even a faint memory. With trepidation, he went to the telephone and called her. First, he explained that he didn't remember as well as he used to. Then he reviewed the lovely evening past. As he gained a little more courage, he inquired, "When I asked if you would marry me, did you say 'Yes' or did you say 'No?'"

He was delighted to hear her say, "Why, I said, 'Yes, yes, I will;' and I meant it with all my heart." Then she continued, "I am so glad that you called, because I couldn't remember who had asked me.

[age, marriage, memory]

Genesis 25:21-22

There is one thing for which a human is never fully prepared — TWINS.

[birth, children]

Genesis 25:24

Keturah: "I guess your husband was pleased when he found himself the father of twin boys."

Rebekah: "Was he! He went around grinning from heir to heir [ear to ear]."

[birth, pride]

Genesis 25:24

Among other things, a first-grade teacher told her students that nowadays more twins are born than in past years. One little boy asked, "Why is that?" Before the teacher could attempt an answer, another little boy spoke up: "Because these days little children are afraid to come into the world alone."

[fear]

Genesis 26:34-35

Manny was almost 29 years old. Most of his friends had already gotten married, and Manny just bounced from one relationship to the next.

Finally a friend asked him, "What's the matter, are you looking for the perfect woman? Are you THAT particular? Can't you find anyone who suits you?"

"No," Manny replied. "I meet a lot of nice girls, but as soon as I bring them home to meet my parents, my mother doesn't like them. So I keep on looking!"

"Listen," his friend suggested, "Why don't you find a girl who's just like your dear ole Mother?"

Many weeks past before Manny and his friend got together again.

"So Manny. Did you find the perfect girl yet. One that's just like your Mother?"

Manny shrugged his shoulders, "Yes I found one just like Mom. My mother loved her, they became great friends."

"Excellent!!! So ... Are you and this girl engaged, yet?"

"I'm afraid not. My Father can't stand her!"

[marriage]

Genesis 27:11

Dear GOD,

I want to be just like my Daddy when I get big but not with so much hair all over.

Sincerely,

Ben

[hair]

Genesis 27:40

The way to solve the Mid-east problem is to get the Arabs and the Israelis to live like Christians.

[fighting, race]

Genesis 27:41

After hearing much yelling and screaming, Isaac rushed into his son's room to find them in the middle of a fist fight.

"Who started this?" asked Isaac.

"It all started when Jacob hit me back," said Esau.

[fighting]

Genesis 28:12

A hypocritical clergyman had preached on the subject of Jacob's ladder, and his young son was very impressed. A few days later he told his father that he had dreamed about the sermon.

"And what did you see, my son?"

"I dreamed," replied the boy, "that I saw a ladder reaching up into the clouds. At the foot of the ladder were many pieces of chalk, and no one was allowed to climb up without taking a piece of chalk and marking on each rung for each sin committed."

"Very interesting, my boy, and what else?"

"Well, Father, I thought I would go up, but I hadn't gotten very far when I heard someone coming down."

"Yes," said the father, "and who was that?"

"You Father," replied the boy.

"Me? Whatever was I coming down for?"

"More chalk!" came the reply.

[dreams, sin]

Genesis 28:12

An atheist was teasing a Christian about his religious beliefs. "Come on now," he said, "Do you really believe that when you die you'll go up to heaven and fly around with wings? I understand it's not warm up there like where I'm going when I die. How in the world are you going to get your coat on over those wings?"

The Christian replied, "The same way you are going to get your trousers over your tail!"

[atheist, hell]

Genesis 28:12

The Children's Church class was reviewing the wonderful lesson of Jacob when he used a stone for a pillow and had the dream of the angels ascending and descending on the ladder above him. The young, recently graduated Bible college teacher asked if there were any questions.

"If the lovely angels had wings," asked a ten-year-old, "why did they have to climb up and down the old ladder for?"

"Ah-hem!" said the teacher, "Are there any more questions?"

[angels]

Genesis 28:12

In reviewing the story of Jacob's dream, a Children's Church teacher asked the class, "Why did the angels use the ladder when they had wings?"

One bright student quickly replied, "Because they were molting."

[angels]

Genesis 29:30

Old Ike Brown had been married twice and both wives had died and were buried in the family plot at the cemetery. Ike talked things over with the funeral director.

"I suppose one of these days you'll be burying me out there in the family plot, and I want to give you some instructions. My first wife was Millie. I loved her very much. My second wife was Tilly and I loved her as much as I

45

loved Millie. Between the graves of Millie and Tilly is the space for me when I die. Now I want you to measure the distances between the graves very carefully. I want to be buried exactly the same distance from Millie as I am from Tilly. But, if you happen to make a little mistake in the measuring, then tilt me a little toward Tilly.

[favoritism, marriage]

Genesis 29:31-35

Of Leah it could truly be said: "Four [For] crying out loud."

[children]

Genesis 30:21

"Well boys," said a proud Jacob, "how do you like your new sister?"
"Oh, all right," they replied, "but there were a lot of other things we needed instead."

[sister]

Genesis 30:21

When Leah finally gave birth to a daughter, young Levi ran over the fields to the neighbor's house and yelled, "Come on over and see our new baby. He's a girl!"

[gender]

Genesis 32:31

Addressing his students, the theology professor said, "Now notice how Jacob, because God has dislocated his thigh, is limping as he prepares to meet Esau, the brother who hates him. Students, what would you do in such circumstances?"
Replied one of the students, "I would limp, too."

[fear, retaliation]

Genesis 34:24

"I'll want $600 dollars for the job of circumcising the entire city," said the local doctor.
"Can't you do it for $300?" demanded Shechem.
"Sure. But I'll have to use dull knives."

[circumcision, doctors]

Genesis 34:25

There were two men at a doctor's office one day. The first man looked over at the second and says, "What are you here for, mister?"
The second man looks over at his new-found friend and replies, "Well, I'm here to be circumcised."

The first man turns his head to make an awful face as he thought of the extreme pain, then returns to face the second man. "Well, buddy. I was about six or seven days old when I had that done to me..."

"Really?" inquired the second man, growing nervous as he continued.

"Yeah," he replied. "I couldn't walk for a year after I had that done."

[circumcision, doctors]

Genesis 37:3 (KJV)

"Joseph was the boy who never had a cold neck," the boy told his mother when she quizzed him about the Children's Church lesson.

"How do you know that?" asked the mother.

"Because," replied the lad, "Joseph had a coat of many collars [colors]."

[clothes]

Genesis 37:5

Why is it when we talk to God, we're said to be praying, but when God talks to us, they say we are schizophrenic?

[praying, psychology]

Genesis 37:5-7

"I had a profoundly disturbing dream about the wheat harvest," said Joseph, shocked.

[dreams]

Genesis 41:40-41

QUESTION: Who was the straightest man in the Bible?

ANSWER: Joseph, because Pharaoh made a ruler out of him.

[leaders]

Genesis 41:46

QUESTION: Where is tennis mentioned in the Bible?

ANSWER: When Joseph served in Pharaoh's court.

[sports]

Genesis 42:21

Fear is the tax that conscience pays to guilt.

[conscience, fear]

Genesis 43:23

He didn't know the meaning of "fear." (He was too afraid to ask.)

[fear]

Genesis 50:2, 3

Two little girls were visiting the museum of natural history. They had been standing for an hour in front of the mummy exhibit of the Egyptian room.

Finally, one of them asked the attendant, "Do you catch them and stuff them yourself?"

[curiosity]

Genesis 50:2-3

Two young children stood in front of a mummy case in the museum. On the bottom of the mummy case they noticed "1286 B.C."
"What does that number mean?" asked the first one.
The second one thought a moment and said, "That must be the license number of the car that hit him."

[date, transportation]

Genesis 50:26

An archeologist to a new student: "To be a mummy you had to be rich or of royal blood."
New student: "I thought you had to be dead."

[death]

EXODUS

Exodus

A bashful pastor found the young ladies in the congregation too helpful. At last it became so embarrassing that he left.

Not long afterwards he met the young pastor who had succeeded him.

"Well," he asked, "how do you get on with the ladies?"

"Oh, very well indeed," said the other. "There is safety in <u>numbers</u>, you know."

"Ah!" was the instant reply. "I only found it in <u>Exodus</u>."

[dating]

Exodus 1:7 (KJV)

After his first few weeks in Children's Church a boy said, "Daddy, I want to ask you a question. The teacher keeps telling us about the children of Israel as slaves in Egypt, the children of Israel crossing the Red Sea, the children of Israel in the wilderness, the children of Israel offering sacrifices. Didn't the grown-ups do anything?"

OR

At Children's Church , Kevin, the new teacher, finished the day's lesson. It was now time for the usual question period.

"Mr. Kevin," announced little Joey, "there's something I can't figure out."

"What's that Joey?" asked Kevin.

"Well according to the Bible, the Children of Israel crossed the Red Sea, right?"

"Right."

"And the Children of Israel beat up the Philistines, right?"

"Er – right."

"And the Children of Israel built the Temple, right?"

"Again, you're right."

"And the Children of Israel fought the Egyptians, and the Children of Israel fought the Romans, and the Children of Israel were always doing something important, right?"

"All that is right, too," agreed Kevin. "So what's your question?"

"What I wanna know is this," demanded Joey. "What was all the grown-ups doing all that time?"

OR

A Children's Church teacher told her class, "The children of Israel crossed the Red sea and Pharaoh's army drowned. Then the Children of Israel walked around Jericho 7 times and the walls fell down, then the Children of Israel killed all the Philistines."
A little girl raised her hand, and said, "I want to know something. Just WHERE WERE their parents all this time?"

[Israel, parents]

Exodus 1:15

Definition of a midwife: The second wife of a man who marries three times.

[polygamy]

Exodus 1:22

Greg: A man just sold me the Nile River.
David: Egypt you [He gypped you].

[cheating]

Exodus 2:2

A Children's Church teacher who had presented each student with special study Bibles asked: "When does your Bible say Moses lived?"
After the silence had become painful she suggested: "Open your Old Testaments to the Introduction to Exodus. What does it say there?"
A boy answered: "Moses, 4,000."
"Now," said the teacher, "why didn't you know when Moses lived?"
"Well," replied the boy, "I thought it was his telephone number."

[phone]

Exodus 2:3

What do you call all the little rivers feeding the great Nile River?
The Juveniles.

[children, puns]

Exodus 2:3

Don't give up. Moses was once a basket case.

[psychology]

Exodus 2:5

Did you know that pharaoh's sister was an excellent financier?
She took a little prophet [profit] from the bulrushes.

[finance, prophet]

Exodus 2:6

QUESTION: When is high finance first mentioned in the Bible?
ANSWER: When Pharaoh's daughter took a little prophet [profit] from the
bulrushes.

[finance]

Exodus 2:10

Description of person with name altered by one letter:
MOOSES — Hebrew prophet who parted the Maine woods.

[names]

Exodus 3:4

George W. Bush, in an airport lobby, noticed a man in a long flowing white
robe with a long flowing white beard and flowing white hair. The man had
a staff in one hand and some stone tablets under the other arm.
George W. approached the man and inquired, "Aren't you Moses."
The man ignored George W. and stared at the ceiling.
George W. positioned himself more directly in the man's view and asked
again, "Aren't you Moses."
The man continued to peruse the ceiling.
George W. tugged at the man's sleeve and asked once again, "Aren't you
Moses."
The man finally responded in an irritated voice, "Yes I am."
George W. asked him why he was so uppity and the man replied, "The last
time I spoke to a Bush I had to spend forty years in the desert."

OR

George Bush died and went to heaven and St. Peter met him at the gates.
George ask St. Peter if the people in heaven were as friendly as the people in
Texas. St. Peter said, "Sure they are." Well George goes for a walk and
passes by Moses and decides to speak to him. Moses just looks the other
way and keeps on walking. Slightly upset by this, George goes back to St.
Peter and tells him what happened with Moses. St. Peter seemed confused
so he seeks Moses and ask him why he ignored President Bush. Moses
looked St. Peter in the eye and said, "Well, Peter, if you will remember, the
last time I spoke to a bush I spent 40 years in the wilderness."

[consequences, politics]

Exodus 3:5

QUESTION: Where is coffee first mentioned in the Bible?

ANSWER: In Exodus 3:5 where the place Moses is standing is "holy grounds."

[coffee, holy]

Exodus 3:8

Pessimist: Someone who can look at the land of milk and honey and see only calories and cholesterol.

OR

Israelite mother: "What do you think the land flowing with milk and honey will be like?"
Israelite boy: "Probably very sticky!"

[Israel, land of Israel]

Exodus 3:11

You might say that Moses begins to "beat around the bush."

[procrastination]

Exodus 4:10

A man told his boss he was called to be a preacher and resigned his job.
But he was back on the job in two weeks.
"I thought you were called by God to preach," he was asked.
"Yes," he replied, "but that was before He heard me preach!"

[commitment, preaching]

Exodus 4:14

Children's Church teacher: "Charlie, what can you tell me about Aaron?"
Charlie: "His name was the first in the telephone book."

[names]

Exodus 4:14

QUESTION: How do we know Moses wore a wig?
ANSWER: Sometimes he had Aaron [hair on] and sometimes he didn't!

[names]

Exodus 5:19-21

Moses is sitting in the Egyptian ghetto, things are going terrible: the Pharaoh won't even talk to him, the rest of the Hebrews are mad at him for making the overseers even more irritable than usual, etc. He's about ready to give up.
Suddenly a booming, sonorous voice speaks from above: "YOU, MOSES, HEED ME. I HAVE GOOD NEWS, AND BAD NEWS."
Moses is staggered. The voice continues:

"YOU, MOSES, WILL LEAD THE PEOPLE OF ISRAEL FROM BONDAGE. IF THE PHARAOH REFUSES TO RELEASE YOUR BONDS I WILL SMITE EGYPT WITH A RAIN OF FROGS.

"YOU, MOSES, WILL LEAD THE PEOPLE OF ISRAEL TO THE PROMISED LAND. IF THE PHARAOH BLOCKS YOUR WAY I WILL SMITE EGYPT WITH A PLAGUE OF LOCUSTS.

"YOU, MOSES, WILL LEAD THE PEOPLE TO FREEDOM AND SAFETY. IF THE PHARAOH'S ARMY PURSUES YOU, I WILL PART THE WATERS OF THE RED SEA TO OPEN YOUR PATH TO THE PROMISED LAND."

Moses is stunned. He stammers, "That's, that's fantastic, I can't believe it! — but what's the bad news?"

"YOU, MOSES, MUST WRITE THE ENVIRONMENTAL IMPACT STATEMENT!"

[environment]

Exodus 7:10

QUESTION: When did Aaron's automobile break down in Egypt?
ANSWER: The time Aaron threw a rod trying to impress pharaoh's court.

[transportation]

Exodus 7:14ff

Teacher: "Today I am going tell you a Bible Story about Moses and the plagues sent on the people of Egypt. First of all, does anyone know what a plague is?"
Student: "Not exactly, but my mother says my brother is one."

[judgment]

Exodus 9:8-12

QUESTION: What might have been the most appropriate response Pharaoh could have given Moses before the sixth plague?
ANSWER: "So it all boils down to this, Moses."

[consequences]

Exodus 12:18

A young girl was part of a larger group that spent a week attending the church's Vacation Bible School. The week's theme focused on Moses and the Exodus.

When they returned home after the last day, the girl excitedly greeted her mother: "Guess what, Mommy. Today we made unleaded bread!"

[food]

Exodus 12:31

Passover is approaching. At the Seder table, every Jewish child will be told the story of Moses and the Pharaoh, and how God brought boils, locusts, hail and the other plagues onto the Egyptians. Yet in spite of this overwhelming evidence of God's intentions, Pharaoh refused to let the Jews go, until a tenth plague, the death of the first-born children was inflicted on every Egyptian home, passing over the Jewish homes. Only after this tragedy did the Pharaoh relent and let the Jews leave slavery and Egypt to begin their journey to the promised land.

This has been known for generations. What has not been known is why the Pharaoh, in the face of such overwhelming evidence would refuse to release the Jews after the first nine plagues. It took eight years of research by Elizabeth Kubler-Ross, the renowned psychologist, to find the definitive answer. Dr. Kubler-Ross spent those years studying the Dead Sea Scrolls before discovering the answer. And once found, it was obvious. The Pharaoh was still in de Nile [denial].

[psychology]

Exodus 12:35, 36

QUESTION: How were the Egyptians paid for goods taken by the Israelites when they fled from Egypt?

ANSWER: For this and the four hundred years of slavery of the Israelites, the Egyptians got a check on the Bank of the Red Sea.

[money]

Exodus 13:19

Can't you just hear all the little Israelite children asking Moses, "Why do you call that thing a mummy? I thought only ladies were mummies?"

[misunderstanding]

Exodus 14

A little boy home from children's church showed his parents a painting he had done, based on the lesson — the crossing of the Red Sea by the Israelites, chased by the Egyptians.

Surprised to see only a huge blotch of red, the parents asked for an explanation.

Pointing to the blotch of red, he said, "That's the Red Sea."

"Where are the Egyptians?" asked the parents.

"They were all drowned."

"And the Israelites?"

"They've already crossed over."

[children, logical]

Exodus 14

A non-religious teacher was trying to convince a sixth-grader that what he had learned in Children's Church about Moses crossing the Red Sea was nothing out of the ordinary. "Actually, " he explained, "Moses and the Israelites simply walked across Yam Suph or Sea of Reeds, probably a marsh no more than a few inches deep."

The bright sixth-grader responded, "Wow, it really was a miracle then — the entire Egyptian army drown in just a few inches of water!"

OR

A boy was sitting on a park bench with one hand resting on an open Bible. He was loudly exclaiming his praise to God. "Hallelujah! Hallelujah! God is great!" he yelled without worrying whether anyone heard him or not. Shortly after, along came a man who had recently completed some studies at a local university. Feeling himself very enlightened in the ways of truth and very eager to show this enlightenment, he asked the boy about the source of his joy.

"Hey" asked the boy in return with a bright laugh, "Don't you have any idea what God is able to do? I just read that God opened up the waves of the Red Sea and led the whole nation of Israel right through the middle."

The enlightened man laughed lightly, sat down next to the boy and began to try to open his eyes to the "realities" of the miracles of the Bible. "That can all be very easily explained. Modern scholarship has shown that the Red Sea in that area was only 10 inches deep at that time. It was no problem for the Israelites to wade across."

The boy was stumped. His eyes wandered from the man back to the Bible laying open in his lap. The man, content that he had enlightened a poor, naive young person to the finer points of scientific insight, turned to go. Scarcely had he taken two steps when the boy began to rejoice and praise louder than before. The man turned to ask the reason for this resumed jubilation.

"Wow!" exclaimed the boy happily, "God is greater than I thought! Not only did He lead the whole nation of Israel through the Red Sea, He topped it off by drowning the whole Egyptian army in 10 inches of water!"

OR

"Wow, man," Timmy said. "God parted the Red Sea and let all His people through on dry ground!"

"Sorry," said the 'biblical' scholar. "But that wasn't the Red Sea; it was the Reed Sea. And its water is only about 1 foot deep. No miracle was involved."

"Oh," said Timmy. Then, reading on a little more, he said,

"What a miracle! God drowned all those Egyptians in 1 foot of water!"

[miracle]

Exodus 14

A father who was concerned about his children's spiritual life asked his son what he had learned in Children's Church that morning.

"Oh dad," he sighed, "it was something about an Israelite general named Moses who found his army in a tight spot with a river in front of him and his enemy closing in fast from behind."

"So what did he do?" said the father quite intrigued.

"Well, he got his engineers to build a pontoon bridge across so his army could escape. After they had reached the other side, he noticed his enemy start to make their way across on the same bridge. Immediately he called for the engineers to blow up the bridge which they did. Many Egyptians were killed while the rest drowned."

Unable to take it any longer the father asked, "Did you really learn that in our Children's Church this morning?"

"Well, not really," said the boy. "But if I told you the story they told me, you'd never believe it!"

[miracle]

Exodus 14:6

"Prepare my chariot," commanded Pharaoh <u>hoarse</u>ly [horse–ly].

[speech]

Exodus 14:9

QUESTION: Why did Moses cross the Red Sea?
ANSWER: To avoid Egyptian traffic.

[transportation]

Exodus 14:10

Moses was leading the children of Israel as they fled from the Egyptians. When they came to the Red Sea, he begged God to rescue his people.

Suddenly he heard a voice from on high saying, "There is some good news and some bad news."

"I hear you, Lord," said Moses, "Tell your servant everything."

"The good news," said the voice from on high, "is that I will part the sea, so that you and your people can escape."

"And the bad news?" asked Moses.

"You'll have to file the environmental impact statement."

[environment]

Exodus 14:28

QUESTION: What became of the white clothes of the Egyptians army when the Red Sea came over them?
ANSWER: They became wet!

[clothes]

Exodus 14:30

See Exodus 12:35-36

Exodus 15:1

"Mark," asked the Children's Church teacher, "what did the Israelites do after they crossed the Red Sea?"
"I'm not sure, but I'm guessing they dried themselves off."

[children, logical]

Exodus 15:22

The Children's Church teacher was reviewing a lesson. She asked, "Who led the children of Israel out of Egypt?"
No answer. So she pointed to a small boy at the back of the room.
"Wasn't me, ma'am," he answered. "We just moved here from Tulsa."

[responsibility]

Exodus 15:24; 16:2

See Numbers 11:4.

Exodus 16:15

Manna—the trail of bread crumbs that God left for the Israelites so they could find their way out of the desert.

[directions, food]

Exodus 17:1

It was so dry that trees chased the dogs.

[weather]

Exodus 17:2

See Numbers 11:4.

Exodus 17:4

The trouble with being a leader today is that you can't be sure whether people are following you or chasing you.

[leader]

Exodus 17:6

The prime minister of Israel sits down with Arafat at the beginning of negotiations regarding the resolution of the conflict in their territories. Prime Minister Sharon requests that he be allowed to begin with a story. Arafat replies, "Of course."

The prime minister begins his story: "Years before the Israelites came to the Promised Land and settled here, Moses led them for 40 years through the desert. The Israelites began complaining that they were thirsty and, lo and behold, a miracle occurred and a stream appeared before them. They drank their fill and then decided to take advantage of the stream to do some bathing — including Moses. When Moses came out of the water, he found that all his clothing was missing.

"'Who took my clothes?' Moses asked those around him.

"'It was the Palestinians,' replied the Israelites.

"Wait a minute," objected Arafat immediately, "there were no Palestinians during the time of Moses!"

"All right," replied the prime minister. "Now that we've got that settled, let's begin our negotiations."

[land of Israel]

Exodus 17:14

After a particularly inspiring worship service, a church member greeted the pastor.

"Reverend, that was a wonderful sermon. You should have it published."

The pastor replied, "Actually, I'm planning to have all my sermons published posthumously." "Great!" enthused the church member. "The sooner the better!"

[ignorance]

Exodus 19:16

A mother noticed that it was about time for school to dismiss and since it looked like it would rain, she drove toward the school to pick up her eight year old daughter.

She turned down the street to see her daughter running towards her down the sidewalk. A lightning bolt flashed and the little girl looked up towards the sky, smiled and then began running towards her mother's van.

Another lightning bolt flashed and again the little girl looked towards the sky, smiled and resumed running. This happened several more times until the little girl finally arrived at where her mother was parked.

Her mom immediately inquired as to the strange behavior. "Why did you keep stopping and smiling at the sky," she asked her daughter.

"I had to, Mommy. God was taking my picture."

[weather]

Exodus 20:1

Moses was the greatest lawgiver; keeping the Ten Commandments short and to the point shows clearly he was no ordinary lawyer!

[lawyers]

Exodus 20:1f

A pastor was talking to the children before they were to be dismissed from the service and asked, "Where are the Ten Commandments found?"
There was a long pause before a young voice spoke out, "Have you tried a good search engine on your computer?"

[computer, lost]

Exodus 20:1f

One reason the Ten Commandments are so brief and concise, is that they didn't come through a committee.

[committee]

Exodus 20:1f

If God had believed in permissiveness, He would have called them the Ten Suggestions.

[commandments]

Exodus 20:1f

Different hermeneutical approaches to the Ten Commandments: some are looking for specific rules, some for a code of living, but most people are looking for loopholes."

[permissive]

Exodus 20:1f

This is a little known tale of how God came to give the Jews the Ten Commandments.
God first went to the Egyptians and asked them if they would like a commandment. "What's a commandment?" they asked.
"Well, it's like, thou shalt not commit adultery," replied God.
The Egyptians thought about it and then said, "no way, that would ruin our weekends."
So then God went to the Assyrians and asked them if they would like a commandment. They also asked, "What's a commandment?"
"Well," said God, "it's like, thou shalt not steal." The Assyrians immediately replied, "No way. That would ruin our economy."
So finally God went to the Jews and asked them if they wanted a commandment. They asked, "how much?"

God said, "they're free." The Jews said, "Great! We'll take ten."

[commandments]

Exodus 20:1-17

Ten Commandments—The most important Top Ten list not given by David Letterman.

[commandments]

Exodus 20:1-17

See Deuteronomy 5:6-21 for additional jokes on the Ten Commandments.

Exodus 20:4

A group of young children in a Children's Church were asked to discuss what God is like.

"What are his qualities?" asked the teacher.

Several responses were given. "He's loving; He's powerful; He's everywhere; He cares for you; He speaks to everyone in a still small voice; He created the world; He protects people." Then one child said, "He's jealous."

The class was aghast. God—great, good God—jealous?

The teacher said, "Well, let's see if we can find any evidence. Let's look in the Bible."

"But where shall we look?" asked several children.

"Try the Ten Commandments, the Book of Exodus, chapter 20," suggested the teacher.

The children opened their Bibles, and after a few minutes, one raised his hand and was called on. "Here it is! It says, 'Thou shalt not make for yourself an idol in the form of anything in heaven above or on the earth beneath or in the waters below. Thou shalt not bow down to them or worship them; for I, the Lord your God am a jealous God.'"

At that point a voice from the back of the room shouted, "Holy cow, He admits it!"

[attributes, God, jealousy]

Exodus 20:4

The pastor finished a powerful sermon on the Ten Commandments. One listener was momentarily depressed but soon perked up. "Anyway," he told himself, "I've never made a graven image."

[commandments, disobedience]

Exodus 20:5

Nancy was sometimes a very naughty seven year-old. On one of those occasions, her mother tried to have a "teachable moment" with her when she said, "Don't you know that if you keep being so naughty your children will be naughty too?"

Nancy started to giggle, louder and louder.

"And what is so funny, young lady?" the mother asked.

"So what did YOU do?!?"

[disobedience, mothers]

Exodus 20:8-11

QUESTION: What is the strongest day of the week?

ANSWER: Sunday. The rest are weekdays[weak days].

[Sunday]

Exodus 20:8-11

Legalistic Mother: "You shouldn't be flying that model airplane in the back yard on Sunday."

Johnathan: "Oh, it is all right to fly this one. It isn't a pleasure plane. It's a missionary plane going to the jungle to tell people about Jesus."

[Sunday]

Exodus 20:8-11

An itinerant musician was stranded in a town one Sunday morning, and as he was playing his cornet in the street, he was approached by the clergyman of the nearby church, who said, "Do you know the Fourth Commandment, my good man?"

"No," he replied, "but if you will just whistle it over, I'll do my best."

[music, Sunday]

Exodus 20:11

Steve Martin is reported to have said that union officials have only one basic thing against God — he worked a six-day week.

[Sunday, unions]

Exodus 20:12

A Children's Church teacher was discussing the Ten Commandments with her five and six-year-olds. After explaining the commandment "honor thy father and thy mother," she asked, "Is there a commandment that teaches us how to treat our brothers and sisters?"

Without missing a beat, one boy from a large family answered, "Thou shalt not kill."

[murder, siblings]

Exodus 20:12

The Fifth Commandment is *humor* thy mother and father.

[parents]

Exodus 20:12

A poor widow's son down in Texas struck it rich with oil and, as Mother's Day approached, made up his mind to show his appreciation by some unusual gift for all his mother had done for him. So he told the owner of a pet shop that he wanted the most unusual and expensive pet he had.

The merchant replied, "I have a myna bird worth $27,000. It is the only one in the world that can recite the Lord's Prayer, the 23rd Psalm and the 13th chapter of First Corinthians.

"I'll take it," said the Texan. "I don't care how much it costs. Mom is worth it and she will get so much comfort hearing it recite Scripture."

So he bought it and shipped it off to his mother.

On Monday following Mother's Day, he called her on his cell. "Did you get my bird?" he asked.

"Yes, Son."

"How did you like it?"

"It was delicious, Son."

[food, mothers]

Exodus 20:14

The Seventh Commandment is thou shalt not *admit* adultery.

[adultery]

Exodus 20:15

See Genesis 2:24.

[marriage]

Exodus 20:15

There was quite a bit of confusion in a church after the morning bulletin read: "Text for today, 'Thou Shalt Not Steal.' The choir will sing, 'Steal, Steal Away.'"

[music, stealing]

Exodus 20:17

A Children's Church class was studying the Ten Commandments. They were ready to discuss the last one. The teacher asked if anyone could tell her what it was. Marlene raised her hand, stood tall, and quoted, "Thou shall not take the covers off the neighbor's wife."

[covet]

Exodus 21:6

QUESTION: "Have you ever had your ears pierced?"
ANSWER: "No, but I have often had them bored."

[boredom, ears]

Exodus 22:29

The boy came skipping into the house with a big lollipop in his hands.
"Where did you get it?" his mother asked.
"I bought it with the quarter you gave me."
"The quarter I gave you was for Children's Church ."
"I know, Mom," said the boy, "but the minister met me at the door and got me in free."

[offering]

Exodus 23:19

When Moses went up to the Sinai to receive the oral explanation of God's laws, he was quite confused with the commandment "Do not boil a calf in it's mother's milk".
Moses (Perplexed): "I don't quite understand this line about boiling a calf in it's mothers milk. What does it mean?"
God: "It means, don't boil a calf in it's mother's milk."
Moses thinks for a while and replies: "Oh I get it, it means that we shouldn't eat meat products and dairy products on the same plate."
God: "No, it means don't boil a calf in it's mother's milk."
Moses: "Oh, I get it. We should have a separate set of dishes for dairy and meat products."
God: "No, it means don't boil a calf in it's mother's milk."
Moses: "Oh, I see. It means we should wait an appropriate amount of time after eating flesh before we can intake of milk or any dairy product. But fish is o.k. since it doesn't give milk."
God: "No, it means don't boil a calf in it's mother's milk."
Moses: "What about chicken? It doesn't give milk but it sort of tastes like the flesh of a milk producing beast?"
God: "MOSES! IT MEANS DON'T BOIL A CALF IN IT'S MOTHER'S MILK!"
Moses: "OK I think I got it all now. We should have a separate set of cooking and eating utensils for meat and dairy products. After partaking of meat we should wait an appropriate amount of time before we partake of any dairy products. Fish should not be considered as meat since it doesn't give milk. Chicken, on the other hand should be considered as meat even though it doesn't produce milk since it tastes a lot like it does."
God: "Have it your way."

[frustration]

Exodus 24:12

QUESTION: Where is medicine first mentioned in the Bible?
ANSWER: The place where the Lord gave Moses two tablets.

[medicine]

Exodus 24:12

Where is the first laxative mentioned? The Bible of course: Moses took the tablets and went into the wilderness, and it came to pass!

[constipation, medicine]

Exodus 25:10-22

Arc[ark] of the Covenant—The trajectory of the tablets when Moses threw them down the mountain.

[ark of the covenant]

Exodus 31:18

"Moses had indigestion like you have, mother," announced Faith at the Sunday dinner table.
"Why, what makes you think so?" questioned her astonished mother.
"Because our Children's Church teacher said, 'God gave Moses two tablets.'"

[medicine, sickness]

Exodus 32:19

QUESTION: Why might someone consider Moses an evil man?
ANSWER: He broke all the Ten Commandments at once.

[commandments, disobedience]

Exodus 32:2

My brother just got his ear pierced. Now he's got my father's looks and my mother's jewelry.

[ears, jewelry]

Exodus 32:34

Moses—The leader of the Israelites who should have gone up the mountain a third time for directions out of the desert.

[directions, leader]

Exodus 34:1

QUESTION: How do we know Moses was constipated?
ANSWER: He was told to go up a mountain and take two tablets.

[constipation]

Exodus 34:14

Dear GOD,
What does it mean You are a Jealous God? I thought You had everything.
-Madelin

[God, jealousy]

LEVITICUS

Leviticus 1:3

Mark: "My wife treats me like an idol."
Ray: "Why do you say that?"
Mark: "She feeds me burnt offerings."

OR

Two guys were at a bar talking about how highly their wives thought of them.
The first guy said, "My wife, she thinks so much of me that she won't let me do any work around the house. It's incredible."
The second guy says, "That's nothing. My wife thinks I'm God."
"She thinks you're God? What makes you say that?"
"Easy. Every night she places a burnt offering before me."

[marriage, sacrifice]

Leviticus 1:3-5

According to beef prices these days, all cows must be sacred.

[sacred]

Leviticus 1:1-9

At Children's Church the little children were told how sacrifices in the Old Testament were made. One child called from the back of the classroom, "My father does the same thing, but he calls it barbecuing."

[cooking, sacrifice]

Leviticus 10:8

The young man had just graduated from Seminary and was called to pastor a church close to his home town. The new Pastor was so nervous at his first service, he could hardly speak. Before his second appearance in the pulpit, he asked his former Pastor how he could relax. The older minister said, "Next Sunday, it may help if you put a little vodka in your water glass. After a few sips, as people assume you are just sipping water, everything should go smoothly as it relaxes you. I will be visiting your church next week to see how things go for you."

The next Sunday the young minister put the suggestion into practice and was able to talk up a storm. He felt great! However, after the service, his former Pastor pulled him aside and offered this advice for him.

1 .Next time sip rather than gulp.
2. There are 10 commandments, not 12
3. There are 12 disciples, not 10
4. We do not refer to the cross as the "Big T"
5. The recommended grace before meals is not "Rub-a-dub-dub, thanks for the grub. Yeah God!"
6. We do not refer to Our Savior, Jesus and His disciples as "J.C. and the Boys"
7. David killed Goliath; he did not, as you put it, "kick the you-know-what out of him."
8. Last, but not least, The Father, the Son, and the Holy Ghost are never referred to as "Big Daddy, Junior, and the Spook."

[alcohol, preaching, Trinity]

Leviticus 11:7

Priest: Rabbi, when are you going to break down and eat ham?
Rabbi: At your wedding, Father.

OR

Due to an oversight, the main dish at the interfaith banquet was a pork roast. The rabbi was taking it in good stride, although he wasn't eating, of course. His friend, the local priest, turned to him and said jokingly, "So, Rabbi, won't you ever try pork?" "Sure, Father, at your wedding."

[kosher, priest, rabbi]

Leviticus 11:7

Born losers = the business man who starts a hog farm in Israel.

[kosher]

Leviticus 13:2

QUESTION: What is a common Middle East skin disease?
ANSWER: Midrash [mid rash].

[sickness]

Leviticus 19:16

Gossip is information given by someone who can't use it to someone who won't!

[gossip]

Leviticus 19:18

See Luke 6:27.

[enemies, neighbors]

Leviticus 19:23

Forbidden fruits create many jams.

[consequences]

Leviticus 19:28

Dennis Miller's definition of body piercing: "A powerful, compelling visual statement that says, 'Gee, in today's competitive job market, what can I do to make myself less employable?'"

[body]

Leviticus 19:36

See Micah 6:11

Leviticus 20:27

Spiritualist: a trance-guesser [transgressor].

[sin, spirits]

Leviticus 23:2,3

Jewish mother: "What is it called when we break the laws of the Sabbath?"
Disinterested son: "Sabotage?"

[disobedience, Sabbath]

Leviticus 23:27

Monty goes to the rabbi and says, "I committed a sin and I want to know what I can do to repent."
"What was the sin?" the rabbi asked.
"It happened just once," Monty assures him. "I didn't wash my hands and recite the blessing before eating bread."
"Now, if it really only happened once," the rabbi said, "that's not so terrible. Nonetheless, why did you neglect to wash your hands and recite the blessing?"
"I felt awkward Rabbi," said Monty. "You see, I was in an un-kosher restaurant."
The rabbi's eyebrows arch. "And why were you eating in an un-kosher restaurant?"
"I had no choice," Monty said. "All the kosher restaurants were closed."
"And why were all the kosher restaurants closed?" the rabbi asked.
Monty replied, "It was Yom Kippur."

[compromise, Day of Atonement]

Leviticus 23:27-29

The rabbi of a synagogue was working on an exchange program with other churches of his town. Every few weeks he went to a church of some Christian denomination to speak. Last week he spoke at a Catholic church. The topic of his talk was religious holidays. He told the members about Yom Kippur, the Day of Atonement. They understood a great deal of what he was talking about as soon as he told them it was a sort of "Instant Lent."

OR

Next month the Jews have another great holy day–Yom Kippur, the Day of Atonement. Or, as a rabbi once defined it to a Christian audience, "Instant Lent."

[Day of Atonement, holidays, Lent]

Leviticus 24:17

"Did you hear the new joke about the murderer?" asked one teenager. "No," said another, "but I'll bet it's a killer."

[murder]

NUMBERS

Numbers

QUESTION: Who was the greatest mathematician in the Bible?
ANSWER: Moses — he wrote the Book of Numbers.

[Moses, numbers]

Numbers 6:3

The 98-year-old Mother Superior from Ireland was dying. The nuns gathered around her bed trying to make her last journey comfortable. They tried to give her some warm milk, but she refused.

Then one of the nuns took the glass back to the kitchen. Remembering a bottle of Irish whiskey received as a gift the previous Christmas, she opened it and poured a generous amount into the warm milk.

Back at Mother Superior's bed she held the glass to her lips. Mother drank a little, then a little more, and before they knew it, she had drunk the whole glass down to the last drop. "Mother," the nuns asked with earnest, "please give us some wisdom before you go to the Lord." She raised herself in bed and with a pious look on her face said, "Don't sell that cow."

[alcohol, nuns]

Numbers 11:4

"Who stole my porridge?" shouted Papa Bear as he came into the dining room and found no porridge where it should have been on the table. "Who stole my porridge?" cried Baby Bear who was right behind Papa Bear. "That's all I hear around here," screamed Mama Bear. "You're just like the Israelites, always complaining. Who stole my porridge? Who stole my porridge? Nobody stole your porridge. I haven't even cooked it yet."

[complain, food]

Numbers 11:4

"But I don't have any food to give you," Moses quailed.

[food, Moses]

Numbers 11:29

When you recruit people that are smarter than you are, you prove you are smarter than they are.

[wisdom]

Numbers 13:16

QUESTION: What man, besides Adam, had no parents?
ANSWER: Joshua, the son of Nun [none].

[Adam, Joshua, parents]

Numbers 13:32

God's work, like business, will put away encouraging profits when it puts away discouraging prophets [profits].

[business, prophets]

Numbers 14:34

A Bible Study teacher asked the question: "Why did Moses wander in the desert for 40 years?"
A new woman who had arrived late with her husband quickly answered: "Probably because, even then, men wouldn't stop and ask for directions."

[directions, men]

Numbers 22:21-35

In the course of a sermon, the preacher referred to the story of Balaam and his talking donkey. He explained that God made the donkey tell Balaam how to accomplish His business. "You might say," he added, "that the donkey was God's Better Business Burro [Bureau]."

[business, guidance]

Numbers 22:30

One man was arguing with another about the miracles in the Bible and about Balaam's donkey in particular.
"How could it be possible," the first one questioned, "for an ass to talk like a man?"
"Well," replied the other, "I can't see why it ain't just as easy for an ass to talk like a man as it is for a man to talk like an ass."

[miracle, speech]

Numbers 22:30

In biblical days it was considered a miracle for an ass to speak; now it would be a miracle if one kept quiet.

[miracle]

Numbers 22:30

In biblical days, it was considered a miracle when a donkey spoke. Listening to him, you can't help but realize how times haven't changed.

[miracle, speech]

Numbers 22:30

Children's Church teacher: What could possibly be smarter than a talking donkey?
Children's Church pupil: Maybe a spelling bee.

[miracle, speech]

Numbers 22:30

I'm thankful that the Lord has opened my mouth to preach without any larning," said an illiterate preacher who often misinterpreted the Word.
"A similar event took place in Balaam's time," replied a gentleman present.

[education, ignorance]

Numbers 22:38

I tell you, she did talk!" asserted Balaam.

[puns, speech]

Numbers 32:23

A certain woman, preparing to entertain guests, went to a small grocery store to buy food. She stopped at the meat counter and asked the attendant for a large chicken. He reached down into the cold storage compartment, grabbed the last chicken he had, and placed it on the scale. "This one weighs four pounds, ma'am," he said.
"I'm not sure that will be enough," the woman replied. "Don't you have a bigger one?"
The attendant put the chicken back into the compartment, pretended to search through the melting ice for another one, and then brought out the same bird, discreetly applying some finger pressure to the scale. "Ah," he said with a smile, "this one weighs six pounds."
"I'm just not sure," the woman frowned, "I'll tell you what—wrap them both up for me!"

[cheating, deception]

DEUTERONOMY

Deuteronomy 1:21

Husband: "Honey, you've got to stop your worrying. It doesn't do a bit of good."

Wife: "Oh, yes it does! Ninety percent of the things I worry about never happen."

[worry]

Deuteronomy 4:9

One of the world's greatest scientists was also recognized as the original absent-minded professor. One day, on board a train, he was unable to find his ticket. The conductor said, "Take it easy. You'll find it."

When the conductor returned, the professor still couldn't find the ticket. The conductor, recognizing the famous scientist, said, "I'm sure you bought a ticket. Forget about it."

"You're very kind," the professor said, "but I must find it, otherwise I won't know where to get off."

[forgetful, memory]

Deuteronomy 5:1

As Moses said to the multitude when he showed them the Ten Commandments, "You might say they're nonnegotiable demands."

[commandments]

Deuteronomy 5:1

A little lady was mailing her grandson a package for his birthday. One of the things it contained was a Bible.

The postal clerk inspected the package and asked, "Does it contain anything breakable?"

"Oh," replied the little old lady dryly, "only the Ten Commandments."

[commandments]

Deuteronomy 5:1

A conservative minister reprimanded a young girl for playing bits of snappy music on Sunday. "Young woman, he said, "don't you know the Ten Commandments?"

Answered the young girl, "I'm not sure. If you'll hum a few bars, I'll try to pick it up as we go."

[commandments, music]

Deuteronomy 5:6-21

The Ten Commandments in Ebonics
1. I be G-d. Don' be dissing me.
2. Don' be makin hood ornaments outa me or nothin in my crib.
3. Don' be callin me for no reason — homey don' play that.
4. Y'all betta be in church on Sundee.
5. Don' dis ya mama ... an if ya know who ya daddy is, don' dis him neither.
6. Don' ice ya bros.
7. Stick to ya own woman.
8. Don' be liftin no goods.
9. Don' be frontin like you all that an no snitchin on ya homies.
10. Don' be eyein' ya homie's crib, ride, or nothin.

[commandments]

Deuteronomy 5:6-21

See Exodus 20:1-17 for additional jokes on the Ten Commandments.

Deuteronomy 5:12-14

In a mental institution one patient suffered under a compulsion to tear off his clothes. The doctor offered him a payment of one dollar for each day he refrained from doing so.

The man kept his clothes on through Mondays, Tuesday, Wednesday, Thursday, Friday and Saturday, but on Sunday he tore them off again. The doctor chided him for his relapse.

"Well," retorted the astonished patient, "you didn't think I was going to work on Sunday, did you?"

[psychology, Sunday, work]

Deuteronomy 5:17,19

The Children's Church teacher was teaching about the Ten Commandments.

"Can anyone tell me which Commandments have only four words?" she asked. "Take a guess, there's more than one."

A little boy in the front row finally volunteered, "Keep off the grass."

[commandments]

Deuteronomy 5:22

A student was asked to list the 10 Commandments in any order. His answer? "3, 6, 1, 8, 4, 5, 9, 2, 10, 7."

[commandments, student]

Deuteronomy 6:4

A Jewish boy in grade school was listening to his Hebrew teacher quoting Scripture.

"The Lord our God is One," the teacher declared.
"When will He be two?" the youngster asked.

[attributes, God, unity]

Deuteronomy 6:4

Monotheism—When God speaks to you over the AM dial of your radio.

[attributes, God, music, unity]

Deuteronomy 6:7

A father and son went fishing one day. After a couple hours out in the boat, the boy suddenly became curious about the world around him. He asked his father, "How does this boat float?"
The father thought for a moment, then replied, "Don't rightly know, son."
The boy returned to his contemplation, then turned back to his father, "How do fish breath underwater?"
Once again the father replied, "Don't rightly know, son."
A little later the boy asked his father, "Why is the sky blue?"
Again, the father replied. "Don't rightly know, son."
Worried he was going to annoy his father, he says, "Dad, do you mind my asking you all of these questions?"
"Of course not son. If you don't ask questions, you'll never learn anything!"

[children, education, father]

Deuteronomy 7:6

"Tell me class, what do you know about Inuit, or as they are sometimes called, Eskimos?" asked the teacher.
Young Mike's hand shot up. "I know all about Eskimos," he bragged.
"They're in the Bible. They're God's frozen people."

[Israel]

Deuteronomy 8:6-9

During the first days of creation, God turned to the Angels and said: "I am now going to create a land called Israel. It will be a land of mountains and valleys, a wonderful fresh water lake, forests full of all kind of trees, cliffs overlooking sandy beaches with an abundance of sea life."
God continued, "I shall make the land rich so to make the inhabitants prosper, I shall call these inhabitants Israeli, and they shall be known to most people on earth."
"But Lord," asked the Angels, "don't you think you are being too generous to these Israelis?"
"Not really," God replied, "wait and see the neighbors I am going to give them."

[Israel, land, neighbors]

Deuteronomy 13:1-5

The ground hog is like most false prophets; it makes its prediction and then disappears.

[prophets]

Deuteronomy 14:8

At a banquet in New York City at which pork was the main dish, Daddy Hall, an Episcopalian rector and open-air preacher known for his homespun, down-to-earth phraseology, prayed this blessing, "Dear Lord, if thou canst bless under grace what you cursed under law, then bless this bunch while they munch this lunch."

[food, grace, prayer]

Deuteronomy 14:22

There were two men shipwrecked on this island. The minute they got on to the island one of them started screaming and yelling, "We're going to die! We're going to die! There's no food! No water! We're going to die!"
The second man was propped up against a palm tree and acting so calmly it drove the first man crazy.
"Don't you understand? We're going to die!!"
The second man replied, "You don't understand, I make $100,000 a week."
The first man looked at him quite dumbfounded and asked, "What difference does that make? We're on an island with no food and no water! We're going to DIE!!!"
The second man answered, "You just don't get it. I make $100,000 a week and I tithe ten percent on that $100,000 a week. My pastor will find me!"

[giving]

Deuteronomy 17:19

A child was being examined to test her reliability as a witness.
"Do you know anything that is in the Bible?"
"I know everything."
"What?" the judge exclaimed in astonishment. "Tell us some of the things that are in there."
"Well," she said, "there's a picture of sister's boyfriend, one of mother's recipes for tomato ketchup, a curl of mine and the lottery ticket of daddy's.

[Bible]

Deuteronomy 18:10

A new preacher preached a sermon in Kentucky against tobacco.
A deacon said, "Pastor, Kentucky is the heart of tobacco country."
The minister prepared a sermon on the evils of whiskey. Another deacon noted that Kentucky was famous for its whiskey.

Next, the pastor preached a sermon on the evils of horse racing. "Pastor, maybe you didn't know it, but horse racing is also very popular in Kentucky."

"Well, what can I preach on?" the pastor asked.

"Son," said the deacon, "Why don't you preach on witch doctors? There is not one in a thousand miles of here."

[hypocrisy, preaching]

Deuteronomy 18:10-11

Ungodly Israelite: "I can't decide whether to go to a palmist or a mind-reader."

Irritated Prophet: "Go to a palmist. It's obvious that you have a palm."

[ignorance, prophet]

Deuteronomy 18:11

A lawyer had a client who believed in reincarnation.

In his will he left everything to himself.

[reincarnation, wills]

Deuteronomy 20:7

Israelite military commander: "What are your objections to military duty?"

Israelite farmer: "My wife is not pregnant, sir, and I don't want to leave her in that condition."

[military, pregnant]

Deuteronomy 20:8

A young man shows up and claims a medical exemption for not serving in the army.

He explains: "Half my insides are missing!"

The military doctor proceeds to question him: "Explain a little more clearly the nature of your internal problem?"

Young man: "No guts!"

[coward, military]

Deuteronomy 22:5

The latest thing in men's clothing is women.

[clothes, unisex]

Deuteronomy 22:5

I went to a rock festival last summer and it was unbelievable. There were four hundred girls, five hundred boys and fifty uncommitted.

[unisex]

Deuteronomy 22:5

We're constantly amazed at these young things with their fancy hairdos and skintight pants. And the girls are even worse.

[hair, unisex]

Deuteronomy 22:5

Now that men and women are both wearing pants here's how to tell the difference: the one who is pretending to listen is the man!

[clothes, listening, unisex,]

Deuteronomy 24:1

A judge was interviewing a woman regarding her pending divorce, and asked, "What are the grounds for your divorce?"
She replied, "About four acres and a nice little home in the middle of the property with a stream running by."
"No," he said, "I mean what is the foundation of this case?"
"It is made of concrete, brick and mortar," she responded.
"I mean," he continued, "What are your relations like?"
"I have an aunt and uncle living here in town, and so do my husband's parents."
He said, "Do you have a real grudge?"
"No," she replied, "We have a two-car carport and have never really needed one."
"Please," he tried again, "is there any infidelity in your marriage?"
"Yes, both my son and daughter have stereo sets. We don't necessarily like the music, but the answer to your questions is yes."
"Ma'am, does your husband ever beat you up?"
"Yes," she responded, "about twice a week he gets up earlier than I do."
Finally, in frustration, the judge asked, "Lady, why do you want a divorce?"
"Oh, I don't want a divorce," she replied. "I've never wanted a divorce. My husband does. He said he can't communicate with me."

[communication, divorce, marriage]

Deuteronomy 24:3-4

A fellow bought a new Mercedes and was out on the interstate for a nice evening drive. The top was down, the breeze was blowing through what was left of his hair and he decided to open her up. As the needle jumped up to 80 mph he suddenly saw a flashing red and blue light behind him.
"There's no way they can catch a Mercedes," he thought to himself and opened her up further. His needle hit 90, 100, 110. Then the reality of the situation hit him. "What the heck am I doing?" he thought and pulled over. The cop came up to him, took his license without a word, and examined it and the car. Finally he came to the window looking steadily at the driver

and said, "I've had a tough shift and this is my last pull over. I don't feel like more paperwork so if you can give me an excuse for your driving that I haven't heard before, you can go!"

The driver blinked only once while his brain scrambled for a reply. "Last week my wife ran off with a cop," he said, "and I was afraid you were trying to give her back!"

"Off you go," said the officer.

[driving, marriage]

Deuteronomy 25:13

See Micah 6:11

Deuteronomy 28:38

The kid eats all day ... we practically inherited a famine.

[famine, food, hunger]

Deuteronomy 31:3

Teacher: "What countries are on the other side of the Jordan?"
Student: "That depends on what side of the Jordan you are on."

[directions, land of Israel]

Deuteronomy 32:7

First rule of history: History doesn't repeat itself—historians merely repeat each other.

[history, repetition]

Deuteronomy 32:50

QUESTION: When did Moses sleep with five people in one bed?
ANSWER: When he slept with his forefathers [four fathers].

[fathers, sleep]

Deuteronomy 34:5

A little four-year-old suddenly lost interest in Children's Church . She had enjoyed so much learning about Moses that her mother could not understand the change of attitude.

"Why don't you want to go, daughter?" she asked.

"Oh," was the astonishing reply, "I don't like to go to Children's Church since Moses died."

[death, Moses]

Deuteronomy 34:7

Bible school teacher: "Charlie, can you tell me what condition Moses was in at the end of his life even though he was one hundred and twenty-years-old?"

Student in the back row: "Sure, teacher — he was dead."

[age, death, Moses]

Deuteronomy 34:10-12

Teacher: "You can be sure that if Moses were alive today, he'd be considered a remarkable man."

Student: "He sure ought to be, he'd be almost 4,000 years old."

[age, Moses]

JOSHUA

Joshua 1:1,2

The Children's Church teacher addressed his class of small boys.
"Who led the children of Israel into Canaan?"
There was no reply volunteered.
"That little boy on the end seat," said the teacher, "You answer the question. Who led the children of Israel into Canaan?"
"It wasn't me, teacher, 'cause I just moved here last week."

{blame children, Israel}

Joshua 1:1

See Numbers 13:16.

[Adam, Joshua, parents]

Joshua 1:8

Unless you define success God's way, you'll soon discover that the formula for success is the same as for a nervous breakdown.

[success]

Joshua 1:8

A teacher of an adult Sunday School class who enjoyed dressing informally, remarked to his class during a lesson on Joshua and his successes, "I don't go along with this concept of dressing for success. Let's face it. Can anyone tell me what color of necktie Joshua was wearing when he conquered Jericho?"

[clothing, dress]

Joshua 2:14

Life is wonderful. Without it you're dead.

{death, life}

Joshua 3:15

QUESTION: Which area of Canaan was especially wealthy?
ANSWER: The area around the Jordan. The banks were always overflowing.

[Jordan, wealth]

Joshua 5:15

See Exodus 3:5.

[coffee, holy]

Joshua 6:15

Too many preachers have been influenced by the incident of Joshua's conquering of Jericho. When they preach they march around the subject seven times!

[Jericho, preaching]

Joshua 6:26

A tourist was visiting Israel. While gazing at the stones at Jericho, he turned to ask his guide some questions.

"How old are these ruins?" asked the tourist.

"Exactly eight thousand and seven years old," was the guide's reply.

"How can you be so definite?" inquired the tourist.

"Oh, an archeologist told me they were eight thousand years old when I took my guide exam," replied the guide, "and that was exactly seven years ago."

[age, archeology, Jericho}

Joshua 7:1

QUESTION: Why did <u>Achan</u> take that which was not allowed?

ANSWER: You might just say he was <u>aching</u> to take it.

[stealing]

Joshua 7:1

QUESTION: What deodorant did the people of Jericho use?

ANSWER: It must have been Ban because Joshua said "the city shall be under the ban!" (N.A.S.B.)

[smell]

Joshua 10:12

The greatest miracle in the Bible is when Joshua told his son [sun] to stand still and he obeyed him.

[miracle, obedience, son]

Joshua 10:12,13

A ten-year-old boy was heard to pray, "Dear God: My mother says I can stay out after school only until it gets dark. Please make the sun stand still. I figured if you did it once, you probably could do it again."

[dark, prayer, sun]

Joshua 10:13-14

QUESTION: When was there a longest day in the Bible than the day when the sun stood still for Joshua?

ANSWER: The day Adam was created because when he was created there was no Eve.

{Adam, long)

Joshua 24:15

Almost everyone knows the difference between right and wrong; some people just have to make decisions.

[decisions, morality]

JUDGES

Judges

QUESTION: What's the first Supreme Court case in the Bible?
ANSWER: Joshua Judges Ruth. (Joshua judges Ruth)

[court]

Judges 1:6

Five-year-old: Do you know what thumbs are for?
Seven-year-old: They're to hold up bottoms of sandwiches.

[body]

Judges 4:21

When Jael was asked what happened to Sisera after she had put a tent peg through his temple she wouldn't have been wrong to say, "He got a splitting headache!"

[head]

Judges 4:21

You might say that Sisera got the point!

[head]

Judges 4:21

On the day of Sisera's battle with Barak and Deborah, something new entered Sisera's mind that had never entered it before.

[head]

Judges 6:12

Gideon is the name of a special man who wrote a Bible used in motel rooms.

[Bible]

Judges 7:7

At one Army base, the annual trip to the rifle range had been canceled for the second year in a row, but the semi-annual physical fitness test was still on as planned.
One soldier mused, "Does it bother anyone else that the Army doesn't seem to care how well we can shoot, but they are extremely interested in how fast we can run?"

[military]

Judges 7:20

Baseball is talked about a great deal in the Holy Bible, in fact right from the first verse: In the big inning ... , then Eve stole first, Adam stole second, later Cain struck out Abel, the Giants and the Angels were rained out, Gideon rattled the pitchers, Goliath was put out by David, and finally, the Prodigal Son made a home run!

[sports]

Judges 8:20

"My daddy is eighty-six and has twenty children. Don't you think I should notify the papers?"

"Not yet. Why don't you wait for the final score?"

[birth control, conception, sports]

Judges 8:30

An old Jewish man was once on the subway and he sat down next to a younger man. He noticed that the young man had a strange kind of shirt collar. Having never seen a priest before, he asked the man, "Excuse me sir, but why do you have your shirt collar on backwards?"

The priest became a bit flustered but politely answered "I wear this collar because I am a Father."

The Jewish man thought a second and responded "Sir I am also a father but I wear my collar front-ways. Why do you wear your collar so differently?"

The priest thought for a minute and said "Sir, I am the father for many."

The Jewish man quickly answered "I too am the father of many. I have four sons, four daughters and too many grandchildren to count. But I wear my collar like everyone else does. Why do you wear it your way?"

The priest who was beginning to get exasperated thought and then blurted out "Sir, I am the father for hundreds and hundreds of people."

The Jewish man was taken aback and was silent for a long time. As he got up to leave the subway train, he leaned over to the priest and said "Mister, maybe you should wear your pants backwards."

[priest, population control]

Judges 11:30

Two men were shipwrecked. One of them started to pray. "Dear Lord, I've broken most of the Commandments. I've been an awful sinner all my days. Lord, if you'll spare me I'll vow ..."

The other one shouted, "Hold on, don't commit yourself just yet. I think I see a boat!"

[repentance, vows]

Judges 16:1

QUESTION: What is an ancient Philistine Belly Dance?
ANSWER: The Gaza Strip

[dance, geography]

Judges 16:6

A man is never so weak as when some woman is telling him how strong he is.

[flattery, men]

Judges 16:17

A Children's Church teacher asked her class to write a composition on the story of Samson. One teenage girl wrote, "Samson wasn't so unusual. All the boys I know brag about their strength and wear their hair long too."

[boasting, hair]

Judges 16:19

There's nothing worse than a homemade haircut—look what it did for Samson.

[hair]

Judges 16:20

How do you know that Samson was a Scottish golf addict?
For all his strength he couldn't break away from the links.

[golf, hair]

Judges 16:29,30

You know, Samson had the right idea when it came to advertising. He took two columns and brought the house down.

[business, communication]

Judges 16:30

QUESTION: What simple affliction brought about the death of Samson?
ANSWER: Fallen arches!

[death, sickness]

Judges 16:30

QUESTION: Who was the most popular comedian in the Bible?
ANSWER: Samson. He brought the house down.

OR

Did you know Samson and Delilah put on the first successful vaudeville show in history? Brought the whole house down!

[entertainment, humor]

Judges 19:30

QUESTION: Does he ever take any advice?
ANSWER: Occasionally, when nobody is looking.

[advice, pride]

Judges 20:1

Children's Church Teacher: "What was Dan and Beersheba?"
Student: "I think they were husband and wife almost like Sodom and Gomorrah."

[geography, land of Israel]

RUTH

Ruth 1:17

There was this crossword puzzle fanatic who died. They buried him six feet down and three feet across.

[burial, death]

Ruth 2:2

This morning," said the teacher of an early Children's Church class, "the subject of the lesson is Ruth the gleaner. Who can tell me anything about Ruth?" A small boy raised his hand.

"Well, Charlie, what do you know about Ruth?" said the teacher encouragingly.

Charlie piped out in a shrill little voice, "The Babe cleaned up sixty home runs in one season."

[sports]

Ruth 2:3

Student #1: "Did you know Ruth abused Boaz?"
Student #2: "Really! How?"
Student #1: "She pulled his ears and trod on his corn."

[abuse, dating]

Ruth 2:19

A black, female minister, while sharing the book of Ruth, said to the single women in her Bible study:" While waiting on your Boaz don't settle for any of his relatives. Brokeaz, Poaz, Lyingaz, Cheatingaz, Lockedupaz, Goodfornothingaz, Lazyaz, or his third cousin Beatyoaz. He also needs to respect yoaz.

[respect]

Ruth 2:20

QUESTION: What kind of man was Boaz before he got married?
ANSWER: Ruth-less.

[single, marriage]

Ruth 4:8

How did the closest relative to Ruth refuse to marry her? He did it <u>ruth</u>lessly!

[single, marriage]

1 SAMUEL

1 & 2 Samuel

Teacher: "Can you name a set of twins in the Bible?"
Student: "Sure, First and Second Samuel!"

[books of the Bible]

1 Samuel 1:28

When a crying infant was presented by its parents for dedication in the morning service, a little girl in church asked what was happening. Her father said, "His parents are giving the baby to God."
Seeing the minister return the baby to its parents, the girl questioned, "What's wrong? Didn't God want that one?"

[dedication]

1 Samuel 2:22-25

The children get together and decide to give their father for his 75th birthday a history of the family, drawn up by a professional. But they warn this man about the family's "black sheep," the skeleton in the closet, Great Uncle George. He went over to the States after the war and ended up being executed in the electric chair for murder. "It's all right," said the biographer. "I can handle that. I'll say that Great Uncle George occupied a chair of applied electronics at an important government institution in America. He was attached to his position by the strongest of ties and his death came as a terrible shock."

[shame]

1 Samuel 5:4

The Philistines stole the Ark of the Covenant and took it to Ashdod. There they placed it in the temple of Dagon at the foot of it's statue. The next day the Philistines were amazed when they saw the statue laying prostrate on the ground before the Ark. They restored the statue to it's feet, but low-and-behold, the next day the statue was not only laying prostrate, but it was shattered into a million pieces.
It was then, for the first time one of the southern Philistines was reported to exclaim, "Wa'ell be da'gone!"

[idols, names]

1 Samuel 8:18

The Israelites would have felt the same way as most Americans when a man stated, "It seems a little ridiculous now, but this country was originally founded as a protest against taxation."

[taxes]

1 Samuel 16:18

David was a Hebrew king skilled at playing the liar [lyre].

[lies, music]

1 Samuel 17:14,23

QUESTION: Do you know how you can tell that David was older than Goliath?
ANSWER: Because David rocked Goliath to sleep!

[age, sleep]

1 Samuel 17:14,23

QUESTION: Who is the greatest babysitter mentioned in the Bible?
ANSWER: David — he rocked Goliath to sleep.

[babysitter, names]

1 Samuel 17:40

The very first rock festival was staged by David and Goliath.

[music]

1 Samuel 17:49

On the day of David's battle with Goliath, something new entered Goliath's mind that had never entered it before.

OR

QUESTION: Why was Goliath so surprised when David hit him with a slingshot?
ANSWER: The thought had never entered his head before.

[head]

1 Samuel 17:49

After the short fight with David, Goliath had "something on his mind."

[fighting, head]

1 Samuel 17:49

"David swung. And God made his point. Anyone who underestimates what God can do with the ordinary has rocks in his head." (Max L. Lucado)

[ordinary]

1 Samuel 17:49

Goliath — a man "stoned" without the use of drugs!

[drugs]

1 Samuel 17:49

Baseball is talked about a great deal in the Holy Bible, in fact right from the first verse: In the big inning ... , then Eve stole first, Adam stole second, later, Cain struck out Abel, the Giants and the Angels were rained out, Rebekah: walked to the well with a pitcher, Gideon rattled the pitchers, Goliath was put out by David, and finally, the Prodigal Son made a home run!

[sports]

1 Samuel 17:49

QUESTION: If Goliath is resurrected, would you like to tell him the story about David and his sling?
ANSWER: No, he already fell for it once.

[resurrection]

1 Samuel 17:50

An archaeologist was digging in the Negev Desert in Israel and came upon a casket containing a mummy. After examining it, he called the curator of a prestigious natural history museum.
"I've just discovered a 3,000 year old mummy of a man who died of heart failure!" the excited scientist exclaimed.
To which the curator replied, "Bring him in. We'll check it out."
A week later, the amazed curator called the archaeologist. "You were right about the mummy's age and cause of death. How in the world did you know it was heart failure?"
"Easy. There was a piece of paper in his hand that said, '10,000 Shekels on Goliath'."

[archaeology, betting]

1 Samuel 17:50

"Triumphed" (NIV) See 1 Samuel 18:7.

1 Samuel 17:51

Talk about losing your head in competition!

[competition, head, sports]

1 Samuel 17:51

Do you know why David killed Goliath and then decapitated him?
He wanted to get a-head!

[ambition, head]

1 Samuel 17:54

David and Goliath: Prophet and loss.

[business, profit]

1 Samuel 18:7

QUESTION: When were motorcycles first spoken of in the Bible?
ANSWER: When David's triumph was heard throughout the land.

[transportation, victory]

1 Samuel 18:8,9

When small men cast big shadows, it means the sun is about to set.

[pride, size]

1 Samuel 18:11

"I hope I can still play the guitar," the youth minister <u>fretted</u>.

[music, puns]

1 Samuel 22:8

It's all right to sit on your pity potty every now and again. Just be sure to flush when you are done.

[selfish]

1 Samuel 25:3

The difficulty with marriage is that we fall in love with a personality, but must live with a character.

[character, marriage]

1 Samuel 25:25

Abigail: "You're lazy, you're worthless, you're bad-tempered, you're shiftless, you're a thorough liar."
Nabal: "Well, my dear, no man is perfect."

[character, perfection]

1 Samuel 28:7

Non-communicative Husband: "Do you think it is possible to communicate with the dead?"
Exasperated Wife: "Yes, I talk to you don't I?"

[after-death, communication, marriage]

1 Samuel 28:7

"I think it is just an allusion that anyone can predict the future with cards."
"I disagree. My mother can take one look at my report cards and tell me exactly what will happen when my dad gets home."

[prophecy]

1 Samuel 28:7

During a séance, a medium was bringing people back from the other world. A ten-year-old kid was among those who were present. "I want to talk to Grandpa," he insisted.

"Quiet!" hushed the medium, quite annoyed.

"I want to talk to Grandpa now," repeated the kid.

"Very well," said the medium, making a few hocus-pocus passes, "here he is."

"Grandpa," said the little boy, "what are you doing there? You ain't dead yet."

[after-death, spirits]

1 Samuel 28:7

See Leviticus 20:27.

[spirits]

1 Samuel 31:12

Little Tommy walks into his primary school classroom one morning to be confronted by his teacher.

Teacher "Ah, Good Morning Tommy, and where were you yesterday?"

Tommy "I'm sorry Miss, but my Granddad got burnt yesterday."

Teacher, "Was he burned very bad?"

Tommy "Yes Miss, they don't mess around at these crematoriums you know.

[cremation, death]

2 SAMUEL

2 Samuel 5:4

QUESTION: What is one of the worst cases of constipation mentioned in the Bible?
ANSWER: It's in Kings, where it says that David sat on "the throne" for forty years.

[constipation]

2 Samuel 6:20-22

Churchill got into a heated debate with a lady member of the Parliament. The lady became so irate with Churchill that she told him that if he were her husband, she would poison his tea. Churchill replied, "If you were my wife, I would drink it."

[anger, death, poison, rebuke]

2 Samuel 8:1

One Sunday a family was driving out in the country. The children were telling about the Bible story they had heard in Children's Church that morning — David and the giant. Suddenly little Sally interrupted the conversation and pointed to some Holstein cows. "There's some of the Philistines now!"

[communication]

2 Samuel 11:1f

Church Sign: David and Bathsheba ... you've seen the movie, now read the book.

[adultery, movie]

2 Samuel 12:23

The ninety-two year-old woman at a nursing home received a visit from one of her fellow church members. "How are you feeling?" the visitor asked.
"Oh," said the lady, "I'm just worried sick!"
"What are you worried about, dear?" her friend asked. "You look like you're in good health. They are taking care of you, aren't they?"
"Yes, they are taking good care of me."
"Are you in any pain?" she asked sympathetically.
"No, I have never had a pain in my life."
"Well, what are you worried about?" her friend queried.

She leaned back in her chair and slowly explained her major worry. "Every close friend I ever had has already died and gone to heaven. I'm afraid they're all wondering where I went."

[death, worry]

2 Samuel 13:11

Amnon: If you won't make love to me, I'll put a spear through my head and my brains will fall out!
Tamar: Really? That would be a great joke on Dad. He says you don't have any.

[stupidity]

2 Samuel 15:4

Absalom was being discussed by two Israelites, one of whom was quite impressed by him. "He's so tender," said the young men. "Perhaps," replied an older and wiser man, "that is because he has been in so much hot water!"

[disobedience, trouble]

2 Samuel 18:9

"My hair is caught!" <u>snarled</u> Absalom.

[hair, puns]

1 KINGS

1 Kings 1:1

As people grow older, they generally become more quiet. But of course, they have more to keep quiet about.

[age, silence]

1 Kings 1:2

The playful, older king sidled up to the young brunette. "Where have you been all my life? He asked.

She looked at him carefully and replied wisely: "Well, for most of it, I wasn't born!"

[age]

1 Kings 2:1

See 2 Samuel 5:4.

1 Kings 3:9

An angel appears at a faculty meeting and tells the dean that in return for his unselfish and exemplary behavior, the Lord will reward him with his choice of infinite wealth, wisdom, or beauty. Without hesitating, the dean selects infinite wisdom.

"Done!" says the angel, and disappears in a cloud of smoke and a bolt of lightning. Now, all heads of those in the meeting turn toward the dean, who sits surrounded by a faint halo of light. At length, one of his colleagues whispers, "Say something."

The dean looks at his faculty, sighs and says, "I should have taken the money."

[disappointment. wisdom]

1 Kings 3:16-27

Two women came before wise King Solomon, dragging between them a young man in a three-piece robe.

"This young lawyer agreed to marry my daughter," said one.

"No! He agreed to marry MY daughter," said the other.

And so they haggled before the King until he called for silence.

"Bring me my biggest sword," said Solomon, "and I shall hew the young attorney in half. Each of you shall receive a half."

"Sounds good to me," said the first lady.

But the other woman said, "Oh king, do not spill innocent blood. Let the other woman's daughter marry him."

The wise king did not hesitate a moment. "The attorney must marry the first lady's daughter," he proclaimed.

"But she was willing to hew him in two!" exclaimed the king's court.

"Indeed," said wise King Solomon. "That shows she is the TRUE mother-in-law."

[argument, mother-in-law, wisdom]

1 Kings 3:16-27

Two elderly woman on a commuter train got into an argument about the window: One insisted that it had to be open or she would suffocate; the other demanded that it be closed so she would not catch a cold. The conductor was asked to settle the noisy dispute.

A commuter nearby called to the conductor, "Open the window first, and let one of them catch a cold and die. Then close it and let the other one suffocate."

[argument, wisdom]

1 Kings 4:34

Four women got into a terrible argument. After much yelling, screaming, and pulling of hair, one of them called out, "I'm on my way to the cops to report you."

The other three wanted to get there first. What resulted was all four rushed into the office, each trying to be the first to relate her complaints. Charges and countercharges filled the air.

The cop called for order. When quiet had been restored, he showed some of Solomon's wisdom when he announced, "All right ladies, I'll hear one at a time. The oldest can speak first."

That closed the case.

[age, argument]

1 Kings 6:1

Teacher: "Where was Solomon's temple?"
Student: "On the side of his head."

[head, temple]

1 Kings 11:2

Solomon had the type of love that quickens all the senses—except common sense.

[common sense, love]

1 Kings 11:3

See Genesis 11:9.

1 Kings 11:3

Teacher: "Why was Solomon the wisest man in the world?"
Student: "Maybe because he had so many wives to advise him."

[advice, wife, wisdom]

1 Kings 11:3

How is it that King Solomon was considered a wise man when he has 1000 mother-in-laws!

[mother-in-law, wisdom]

1 Kings 11:3

"King Solomon," declared a little girl in Children's Church , "is my favorite character in the Bible — because he was so kind to ladies and animals." The startled teacher inquired, "Who told you that?"
"Nobody told me; I read it myself in the Bible," asserted the little girl. "It says Solomon kept seven hundred wives and three hundred porcupines [concubines]."

[animals, concubine]

1 Kings 11:3

In her book *Smile Please*, Mildred Spurrier Topp recalls the day she and her sister decided to send a valentine, supposedly from their widowed mother, to a prominent judge who had shown marked, if discreet, signs of interest. Mildred wanted to use a new word she had heard in Children's Church .
"I'm not sure what it means," she confessed to her sister, "But it's in the Bible so it must be OK. Besides, it was used about King Solomon, so it's bound to be romancy enough for a valentine."
That's how the judge came to receive a gaudy, lace-bedecked valentine that read:
If you will be my valentine, I will be your concubine ... .

[concubine]

1 Kings 11:3

See Proverbs 18:22.

1 Kings 17:1

A visitor to Israel during the drought-stricken area during the time of Elijah was engaged in conversation at the local gate about the "no-rain" situation.
"You think the drought is bad here," replied the old timer, "but down south the drought is so bad that the Levites are just sprinkling their hands, the woman going through purification rites are using a damp cloth, and the proselytes to Judaism aren't even being baptized anymore, just being issued rain checks!"

[drought, water]

1 Kings 17:1

A tourist traveling through the Texas Panhandle got into conversation with an old settler and his son at a service station.

"Looks as though we might have rain," said the tourist.

"Well, I hope so," replied the native, "not so much for myself as for my boy here. I've seen it rain."

[drought, weather]

1 Kings 17:6

Now where am I going to find food?" asked Elijah ravenously.

[food, hunger]

1 Kings 17:17

One night, as Al was watching TV, the doorbell rang. He went to the door and found a six-foot cockroach standing there. The bug grabbed him by the collar, threw him across the room, and then left. Al picked himself up and phoned his friend Tony to tell him the bizarre story.

"That's amazing," said Tony. "The same thing happened to me an hour ago! This huge cockroach rang my doorbell, and when I answered, the bug punched me in the gut and left!"

Al and Tony decided to visit their buddy Vince and get his advice. When they finished telling their tales, Vince said: "This is too weird, guys. When I got home from work this afternoon, a huge bug was waiting for me at the door. He beat me up real bad! I think we better go to the cops and get this settled."

So the three men went to the local police station and reported their experiences. The desk sergeant just shook his head. "Sorry, fellas, there's nothing we can do. There's just a nasty bug going around."

[insects, sickness]

1 Kings 18:19

QUESTION: How do you know that Elijah drove a standard automobile?
ANSWER: Elijah went up on high.

[driving, transportation]

1 Kings 18:33-35

The teacher of a Children's Church class explained the story of Elijah and the prophets of Baal — how Elijah built the altar, put wood upon it, and cut the bull in pieces and laid them on the altar.

"And then," she said, "he commanded the people to fill four barrels with water and pour it over the altar, and they did this four times. Now, can anyone tell me why this water was poured over the bullock on the altar?"

"To make the gravy?" came a prompt reply.

[sacrifice, water]

1 Kings 18:40

Now those false prophets and their gods will be put in their place," said Elijah <u>bale</u>fully.

[prophets]

1 Kings 18:40

The prophets bailed out when Baal didn't answer.

[prophets]

2 KINGS

2 Kings 2:23-25

Mark Twain was fond of telling the story of a small boy's account of Elisha in his less ingratiating mood.

"There was a prophet named Elisha. One day he was going up a mountainside. Some boys threw stones at him. He said, 'If you keep on throwing stones at me I'll set the bears on you and they'll eat you up.'" And they did, and he did, and the bears did."

[brevity, communication]

2 Kings 2:24

The minister was addressing a Children's Church class. He had taken for his theme the familiar one of the children who mocked Elisha on his journey to Bethel — how the youngsters taunted the poor old prophet and how they were punished when two she-bears came out of the wild and mauled forty-two of them. To heighten the drama, the pastor had the two she-bears eat the children as well.

"And now, children," said the pastor, wishing to discover whether his talk had produced any moral effect, "what does this story show?"

"Please, sir," came from a little girl well down in front, "it shows how many children two she-bears can hold."

[eating]

2 Kings 2:24

In light of the rising frequency of human/grizzly bear conflicts, the Montana Department of Fish and Game is advising hikers, hunters, and fishermen to take extra precautions and keep alert for bears while in the field.

We advise that outdoorsmen wear noisy little bells on their clothing so as not to startle bears that aren't expecting them. We also advise outdoorsmen to carry pepper spray with them in case of an encounter with a bear. It is also a good idea to watch out for fresh signs of bear activity. Outdoorsmen should recognize the difference between black bear and grizzly bear droppings. Black bear droppings are smaller and contain lots of berries and squirrel fur. Grizzly bear droppings have little bells in it and smells like pepper.

[animals]

2 Kings 4:40

Sharon prepared a pasta dish for a dinner party she was giving. In her haste, however, she forgot to refrigerate the spaghetti sauce, and it sat on the counter all day. She was worried about spoilage, but it was too late to cook up another batch. She called the local Poison Control Center and voiced her concern. They advised Sharon to boil the sauce again.

That night, the phone rang during dinner, and a guest volunteered to answer it. Sharon's face dropped as the guest called out, "It's the Poison Control Center. They want to know how the spaghetti sauce turned out."

[deceit, food]

2 Kings 4:41

A short history of medicine
"Doctor, I have an ear ache."
2000 BC — "Here, eat this root."
1000 BC — "That root is heathen, say this prayer."
1850 AD — "That prayer is superstition, drink this potion."
1940 AD — "That potion is snake oil, swallow this pill."
1985 AD — "That pill is ineffective, take this antibiotic."
2000 AD — "That antibiotic is artificial. Here, eat this root!"

[advancement, medicine]

2 Kings 8:1

QUESTION: Where is the first example of cannibalism in the bible?
ANSWER: Two Kings Ate One [2 Kings 8:1]!

[cannibalism]

2 Kings 9:20

For those who, like Jehu, enjoy driving fast — a few Hymns:
45mph.........God will take care of You
55mph Guide Me, O Thou Great Jehovah
65mph.....Nearer My God to Thee
75mph....Nearer Still Nearer
85mph.....This World is not my Home
95mph......Lord, I'm Coming Home
100mph.....Precious Memories

[driving, hymns, speed]

2 Kings 12:15

Jim had an awful day fishing, sitting on the lake all day without a single bite. On his way home, he stopped at the supermarket and ordered four catfish.

He told the fish salesman, "Pick out the four largest ones and throw them at me, will you?"

"Ok. But, why do you want me to throw them at you?"

"Because I want to tell my wife that I caught them."

[honesty]

2 Kings 17:7-23

A new flood is prophesied and nothing can be done to prevent it; in six days the waters will wipe out the world.

The leader of Buddhism appears on TV and pleads with everyone to become a Buddhist; that way, they will at least find harmony with nature.

The Pope goes on TV with a familiar message: "It is still not too late to join the church," he says.

The Chief Rabbi of Israel takes a slightly different approach and in keeping with his ancestors common response to God's judgment declares: "We have six days to learn how to live under water."

[judgment]

2 Kings 20:1

A man walks into a restaurant and says, "How do you prepare your chickens?"

The cook says, "Nothing special. We just tell 'em they're gonna die."

[death]

2 Kings 21:13

Wife: "Would you help me with the dishes?"

Husband: "That isn't a man's job."

Wife: "The Bible suggests that it is."

Husband: "Where does it say that?"

Wife: "In 2 Kings 21:13 (KJV) it says, '... and I will wipe Jerusalem as a man wipeth a dish, wiping it and turning it upside down.'"

[husbands, roles]

1 CHRONICLES

1 Chronicles 25:1

Definition of a Choir—A group of people whose singing allows the rest of the congregation to lip-sync.

[choir, worship]

2 CHRONICLES

EZRA

Ezra 6:8

A preacher was asking for contributions to the church's program to buy food for the needy. The town gambler, who also owned the saloon and several other shady operations, offered the preacher $500.

"You can't take that," a deacon told the preacher. "That's the devil's money."

"Well, brother," said the preacher, cheerfully accepting the gift, "in that case, the devil has had his hands on it long enough. Now let's see what the Lord can do with it."

[giving, money]

NEHEMIAH

Nehemiah 1:1

QUESTION: Who is the shortest man in the Bible?
ANSWER: It was Nehemiah [Knee-high-am-I-ah],
See also Matthew 26:40.

[height, size]

Nehemiah 1:6

A businessman who needed millions of dollars to clinch an important deal
went to church to pray for the money. By chance he knelt next to a man
who was praying for $100 to pay an urgent debt.
The businessman took out his wallet and pressed $100 into the other man's
hand. Overjoyed, the man got up and left the church. The businessman
then closed his eyes and prayed, "And now, Lord, that I have your
undivided attention..."

[prayer]

Nehemiah 6:15

First construction worker: "I still don't understand how the ancient
Israelites managed to build the walls of Jerusalem in fifty-two days."
Second construction worker: "They probably didn't take coffee breaks!"

[coffee, work]

Nehemiah 8:1-8

An Israelite, writing to a friend back in Persia about the great revival they
were experiencing, said, "We are having a great rebible here."

[revival]

ESTHER

Esther 1:1

Description of person with name altered by one letter:
XEROXES — Persian photocopy king.

[names]

Esther 6:1

A coincidence is a small miracle where God prefers to remain anonymous.

[miracle, sovereignty]

Esther 8:3

QUESTION: What is the greatest water power known to man?
ANSWER: A woman's tears.

[crying, emotion, woman]

Esther 9:22

Short summary of every Jewish Holiday: "They tried to kill us, we won, let's eat."

[food, holidays]

JOB

Job 1:13–2:9

Asked to describe the sufferings of Job, a little girl declared: "Job had one trouble after another. First he lost his cattle, then he lost his children, and then he had to go and live in the desert with his wife."

[marriage, suffering]

Job 1:19

When Job's only remaining servant staggered in to tell him about the death of all Job's sons and daughters, he watched silently as Job sobbed and tore his robes. Finally he said, "It could have been worse, you know."
"What do you mean it could have been worse?" cried out Job.
The servant immediately replied, "I could have been killed too."

[death, optimism, suffering]

Job 1:21

"I wish ministers wouldn't keep saying that we come into this world with nothing and we take nothing with us when we leave. It always sounds as if the first thing St. Peter does, is frisk you!"

[heaven, possessions]

Job 1:21

I came from nowhere and I will return to nowhere. I live in Jersey.

[geography]

Job 1:22

See James 5:11.

Job 2:9-10

A man looked up from his hospital bed and said to his wife, "You've always been with me when I have had trouble. When I lost my shirt in a poor investment, you were there. When I had the car accident, you were with me. I got fired, and you were there. I've now come to the conclusion that you're bad luck!"

[marriage, suffering]

Job 2:9-10

A skeptic called on a rabbi to challenge him on a point the doubter considered an inconsistency in the Bible. "It puzzles me," he said, "when God tested Job, He took everything from him but left him his wife. Why?"

"The answer is simple," said the rabbi. "After God finished testing Job, He returned to him twice what He had taken away. If Job's wife had also been removed, He would have had to give him two wives. And such a penalty not even God dared to inflict on him."

[judgment, suffering]

Job 2:11

QUESTION: Who is the shortest man in the Bible?
ANSWER: Bildad the Shuhite [shoe-height]
(See also Matthew 26:40.)

[height, size]

Job 2:11

QUESTION: Why was Job always so cold in bed?
ANSWER: He had such poor comforters.

[comfort, sickness, sympathy]

Job 2:13

Job had so many pains and problems that if a new one were to come today, it would be at least two weeks before he'd have time to worry about it.

[suffering, worry]

Job 3:1

When little Margaret returned from Children's Church she asked her father when their new baby would talk. He told her that it probably would not be for two years, since little babies don't talk. "But they did in the Bible," said Margaret. "The teacher told us this morning that Job 'cursed the day he was born.'"

[babies, speech]

Job 3:1

"Did you know that Job spoke when he was a very small baby?"
"Where does it say that?"
"It says, 'Job cursed the day he was born.'"

[babies, speech]

Job 3:3

If I had my life to live over again I'd drop dead.

[death]

Job 3:3

Population control would be more effective, if it could be made retroactive.

[birth control]

Job 7:11

A man joined the priesthood. The order he joined could not speak for seven years. Then they could only say 2 words.

The first seven years passed and they went into a small room. His 2 words were "too cold".

The next seven years passed and they took him back into the small room and his 2 words were "bad food".

The next seven years passed they took him back into the small room and his 2 words were "I quit".

"Good," they said, "all you have done is complain."

[complain]

Job 15:20-24

No matter what happens, there is always someone who knew it would.

[knowledge, prophecy]

Job 16:12

QUESTION: How do we know that Job went to a chiropractor?
ANSWER: Because in Job 16:12 (K.J.V.) we read, "I was at ease, but he hath broken me asunder; he hath also taken me by my neck, and shaken me to pieces ... "

[body, bones, doctors]

Job 18:5

The Scripture reading was from the Book of Job and the minister had just read, "Yea, the light of the wicked shall be put out," when immediately the church was in total darkness.

"Brethren," said the minister with scarcely a moment's pause, "in view of the sudden and startling fulfillment of this prophecy, we will spend a few minutes in silent prayer for the electric lighting company."

[judgment, prayer]

Job 26:1-14

Man: "I will give you a candy bar if you will tell me where God is."
Boy: "I will give you two candy bars if you will tell me where he is not."

[God]

Job 31:35

A journalist assigned to the Jerusalem bureau takes an apartment overlooking the Wailing Wall. Every day when she looks out, she sees an old Jewish man praying vigorously. So, the journalist goes down and introduces herself to the old man.

She asks, "You come every day to the wall. How long have you done that and what are you praying for?"

The old man replies, "I have come here to pray every day for 25 years. In the morning I pray for world peace and then for the brotherhood of man. I go home have a cup of tea and I come back and pray for the eradication of illness and disease from the earth."

The journalist is amazed. "How does it make you feel to come here every day for 25 years and pray for these things?" she asks.

The old man looks at her sadly. "Like I'm talking to a wall."

[prayer]

Job 33:9

A little boy got lost at the YMCA and found himself in the women's locker room. When he was spotted, the room burst into shrieks, with ladies grabbing towels and running for cover. The little boy watched in amazement and then asked, "What's the matter — haven't you ever seen a little boy before?"

[ignorance]

Job 37:10

"It was so cold where we were that the candle froze and we couldn't blow it out."

"That's nothing. Where we were the words came out of our mouth in pieces of ice, and we had to fry them to see what we were talking about."

[speech, weather]

Job 38:32

A theologian and an astronomer were talking together one day. The astronomer said that after reading widely in the field of religion, he had concluded that all religion could be summed up in a single phrase.

"Do unto others as you would have them do unto you," he said, with a bit of smugness, knowing that his field is so much more complex.

After a brief pause, the theologian replied that after reading widely in the area of astronomy he had concluded that all of it could be summed up in a single phrase also.

"Oh, and what is that?" the astronaut inquired.

"Twinkle, twinkle, little star; how I wonder what you are!"

[theology]

Job 40:1

Unless you can create the whole universe in less than a week, perhaps giving advice to God isn't such a good idea!

[advice, God]

Job 40:4

"Silence is often misinterpreted, but never misquoted."

[silence]

Job 41:13

A teacher asked the kindergartners, "Can a bear take his warm overcoat off?"
"No," they answered.
"Why not?"
Finally, after a long silence, a little fellow spoke up. "Because only God knows where the buttons are."

[animals, creation]

Job 42:2-3

A three-year-old girl, named Norah, used to reply to any statement made to her with, "I know."
For example, "The world is round." ("I know."). "People should always tell the truth." ("I know.").
One day the girl's older brother said to her, "You always answer 'I know.'"
"What's wrong with that?" asked the girl.
"Well," said the brother, "only God knows everything!"
The girl replied, "I know."

[attributes of God, knowledge]

PSALMS

Psalm 1:1

Two bums came to rest on the same park bench and struck up a conversation. Eventually they got around to how each of them had come to such dire straits.

One explained, "You are looking at a man who *never* took a word of advice from any man!"

"Isn't that a coincidence?" replied the other. "You are looking at a man who took *all* his friend's advice."

[advice]

Psalm 1:2

Unbiblical meditation: that which makes doing nothing perfectly respectable.

[meditation]

Psalm 1:2

A Children's Church class had been emphasizing the memorization of Scripture. One little seven-year-old was beginning to get into the program. And it seems he was working on his memory work at home.

His dad was inquiring into the whole procedure and asked him what prize or reward he would get if he learned all those verses.

His son eyed him with that simple childlike look and said, "We get to learn more!"

[Bible, memorization, reward]

Psalm 5:3

I hate mornings ... they're so early.

[time]

Psalm 8:3

Teacher: "Which is more important to us—the moon or the sun?"
Timothy: "The moon."
Teacher: "Why?"
Timothy: "The moon gives us light at night when we need it, the sun gives us light only in the day when we don't need it."

[creation, light]

Psalm 8:5

Upon hearing the part of this verse that declares, "For thou hast made man a little lower than the angels," one church member turned to the other and retorted, "And he's been getting a little lower ever since."

[angels, image of God, man]

Psalm 10:7

See Romans 3:14.

Psalm 14:1

A Soviet teacher, trying to prove to her class that God did not exist, emphasized that the Soviet astronauts in orbit did not see him. One seven-year-old suggested, "Maybe they fly too low."

[atheist]

Psalm 14:1

The agnostic is a person who says that he knows nothing about God and, when you agree with him, he becomes angry.

[agnostic]

Psalm 14:1

An atheist is a man who has no invisible means of support.

[atheist]

Psalm 14:1

Did you hear about the son of the atheists who asked his parents: "Do you think God knows we don't believe in Him?"

[atheist, God]

Psalm 14:1

Atheists are really on the spot: They have to sing "Hmmmmmmmm bless America."

[atheist, music]

Psalm 14:1

A man came to a believer and said, "You say that you know God exists. Prove it to me."
The believer said, "Do you have any matches?"
"Yes."
The believer took a napkin, and soaked it in water. "You say that you have matches. Set this napkin on fire."

[atheist, God]

Psalm 14:1

A freshman in college started his first day of classes. His professor was clearly an atheist, and started the day by saying the following: "Students, is there anyone here who can see God? If so, raise your hand.
If there is anyone who can hear God, raise your hand.
If there is anyone who can smell God, raise your hand."
After a short pause, without any response from the students, he concluded, "Since nobody can see, smell, or hear God, there isn't any God."
A student then raised his hand and asked if he could address the class. The student approached the class and asked, "Students, can anyone here see the professor's brain?
Can anyone hear the professor's brain?
Can anyone smell the professor's brain?"
After a short pause he concluded, "Since no one can see, hear, or smell the professor's brain, I conclude that he doesn't have a brain!"

[atheist, education, God]

Psalm 14:1

An atheist complained to a Christian friend, "Christians have their special holidays, such as Christmas and Easter; and Jews celebrate their holidays, such as Passover and Yom Kippur; Muslims have their holidays. EVERY religion has its holidays. But us atheists," he said, "have no recognized holidays. It's an unfair discrimination."
"What do you mean, atheists have no holidays," his friend replied, "People have been observing a special day in your honor for years."
"I don't know what you're talking about," the atheist said, "When is this special day honoring atheists?"
"April first."

[atheist, holidays]

Psalm 19:7-10

Dust on your Bible is not evidence that it is a dry book.

[Bible]

Psalm 19:7-11

How wise are Thy commandments, O Lord. Each one of them applies to somebody or other I know.

[commandments, pride]

Psalm 20:7

In God we trust, all others pay cash!

[God, money, trust]

Psalm 22:10

A Catholic priest, a Baptist minister, a Jewish rabbi, and an Episcopalian vestryman are discussing the question of when life begins.

The Catholic priest states, "Life begins at the moment of conception when the sperm and the egg unite."

The Baptist minister declares, "No, it begins when the fetus is viable, when if it should be born, it would be able to live."

The rabbi insists, "Life does not begin until the very moment of birth."

The Episcopalian vestryman argues, "In my opinion, life begins when the children go off to college and the dog dies."

[enjoyment, life]

Psalm 23

"Now how does the 23rd Psalm begin?" Tom asked *sheepishly*.

[embarrassment]

Psalm 23

The Student's Psalm
The Lord is my shepherd, I shall not flunk;
He keepeth me from lying down when I should be studying.
He leadeth me beside the water cooler for a study break;
He restores my faith in study guides.
He leads me to better study habits
For my grades' sake.
Yea, tho' I walk through the valley of borderline grades,
I will not have a nervous breakdown;
For Thou art with me;
My prayers and my friends, they comfort me.
Thou givest me the answers in moments of blankness;
Thou anointest my head with understanding,
My test paper runneth over with questions I recognize.
Surely passing grades and flying colors shall follow me
All the days of examinations;
And I shall not have to dwell in this university forever!
Amen!

[student]

Psalm 23

For Tech Heads
The Lord is my programmer, I shall not crash.
He installed His software on the hard disk of my heart. All of His commands are user friendly.

His directory guides me to the right choices for His name's sake. Even though I scroll through the problems of life, I will fear no bugs, for He is my back-up.

His password protects me. He prepares a menu before me in the presence of my enemies.

His help is only a keystroke away.

Surely goodness and mercy will follow me all the days of my life and my file will be merged with His and saved forever.

Amen

[computer]

Psalm 23

A Recession Version

The politician is my shepherd ...I am in want;

He maketh me to lie down on park benches,

He leadeth me beside the still factories;

He disturbeth my soul,

Yea, though I walk through the valley of the shadow of depression and recession,

I anticipate no recovery, for he is with me.

He prepareth a reduction in my salary in the presence of my enemies;

He anointeth my small income with great losses;

My expenses runneth over.

Surely unemployment and poverty shall follow me all the days of my life.

And I shall dwell in a mortgaged house forever.

[money]

Psalm 23

Dieter's Psalm

My weight is my shepherd;

I shall not want low calorie foods.

It maketh me to munch on potato chips and bean dip;

It leadeth me into 31 Flavors;

It restoreth my soul food;

It leadeth me in the paths of cream puffs in bakeries.

Yea, though I waddle through the valley of weight watchers,

I will fear no skimmed milk;

For my appetite is with me;

My Hostess Twinkies and Ding Dongs they comfort me;

They anointeth my body with calories;

My scale tippeth over!

Surely chubbiness and contentment shall follow me

All the days of my life.

And I shall dwell in the house of Marie Callender Pies ... forever!

[diet, food]

Psalm 23:1

As they were leaving church one Sunday, a man confided to his friend he was suffering from insomnia. The friend asserted he had no trouble getting to sleep.

"Really?" he inquired. "Do you count sheep?"

"No," was the retort, "I talk to the shepherd."

[worry, sleep]

Psalm 23:1

A Children's Church teacher decided to have her young class memorize one of the most quoted passages in the Bible ... Psalm 23. She gave the youngsters a month to learn the Psalm. Little Bobby was excited about the task, but he just couldn't remember the Psalm. After much practice, he could barely get past the first line.

On the day that the kids were scheduled to recite Psalm 23 in front of the congregation, Bobby was so nervous. When it was his turn, he stepped up to the microphone and said proudly, "The Lord is my shepherd ... and that's all I need to know."

[trust]

Psalm 23:2

The pastor had been disturbed by a person in his congregation who was a fast reader.

"We shall now read the Twenty-third Psalm in unison," he announced.

"Will the person who is always by 'the still waters' while the rest of us are in 'green pastures', please wait a minute until we catch up?"

[worship]

Psalm 23:2

A three-year-old version of Psalm 23:2: " ...He leadeth me beside distilled water."

[water]

Psalm 23:5

The young girl of the house, by way of punishment for some misdemeanor, was compelled to eat her dinner alone at a little table in a corner of the dining room. The rest of the family paid no attention to her presence until they heard her audibly praying over her food with the words, "I thank thee, Lord, for preparing a table before me in the presence of mine enemies."

OR

One day little Jane was seated alone at a small table while her parents sat with their guests at the large table. This greatly displeased Jane. Before eating, Jane's parents thought it would be nice for Jane to be included in the group although she was seated separately, so the father asked her to say the blessing. This was her prayer: "Lord, I thank thee for this table in the presence of mine enemies. Amen."

[enemies, resentment]

Psalm 23:6

A young woman named Murphy was teaching a Children's Church class the Twenty-third Psalm. As the little voices chorused out, she seemed somewhere to detect a false note. She heard the children one by one until at last she came across one little boy who was concluding with the words, "Surely good Miss Murphy shall follow me all the days of my life."

[names]

Psalm 23:6

A pastor was giving a lesson to a group of children on the Twenty-third Psalm. He noticed that one of the little boys seemed disquieted by the phrase "Surely, goodness and mercy will follow me all the days of my life..." "What's wrong with that, Johnny?" the pastor asked.

"Well," answered Johnny, "I understand about having goodness and mercy, for God is good. But I'm not sure I'd like Shirley following me around all the time."

[names]

Psalm 23:6

Timmy was a little five year old boy that his Mom loved very much and, being a worrier, she was concerned about him walking to school when he started Kindergarten. She walked him to school the first couple of days. He came home one day and told his mother that he did not want her walking him to school everyday. He wanted to be like the "big boys." He protested loudly, so she had an idea of how to handle it. She asked a neighbor, Mrs. Goodnest, if she would surreptitiously follow her son to school, at a distance behind him that he would not likely notice, but close enough to keep a watch on him. Mrs. Goodnest said that since she was up early with her toddler anyway, it would be a good way for them to get some exercise as well so she agreed. The next school day, Mrs. Goodnest and her little girl, Marcy, set out following behind Timmy as he walked to school with another neighbor boy he knew. She did this for the whole week. As the boys walked and chatted, kicking stones and twigs, the little friend of Timmy noticed that this same lady was following them as she seemed to do every day all week. Finally, he said to Timmy, "Have you noticed that lady following us all week? Do you know her?" Timmy nonchalantly replied, "Yea, I know who she is." The little friend said, "Well who is she?" "That's just Shirley Goodnest" Timmy said. "Shirley Goodnest? Who the heck is she and why is she following us?" "Well," Timmy explained, "every night my Mom makes me say the 23rd Psalm with my prayers cuz she worries about me so much. And in it, the prayer psalm says, "Shirley Goodnest and Marcy shall follow me all the days of my life." So I guess I'll just have to get used to it."

[names]

Psalm 31:18

Joe Hanover was resting in his usual chair at the barbershop, as young Dr. Armstrong was completing his weekly visit. The conversation among the barbershop friends had turned to the condition of a lawyer they both knew, Benson by name, who had suffered a massive heart attack only a few days earlier.
"He's not doing too well," the young doctor noted solemnly, "In fact, Benson is lying at death's door."
"Now that's something," commented Hanover. "At death's door and still lying!"

[death, lying]

Psalm 32:8-9

Learn from your mistakes and those of others. You can't live long enough to make them all yourself!

[mistakes]

Psalm 37:4

When asked what he needed for his birthday, the little boy said firmly, "I don't want to need, I want to want."

[contentment, desire]

Psalm 37:4

A man was walking along a California beach and was in deep prayer to the Lord. He said, "Lord, you have promised to give me the desires of my heart. Please give a confirmation that you will grant my wish." Suddenly the sky darkened and the Lord, in a booming voice said, "I have searched your heart and determined it to be pure. I think that I can trust that you will not disappoint me. Because you have been faithful to me, I will grant you one wish."
The man said, "I've always wanted to go to Hawaii, but I'm deathly afraid of flying and I get very sea sick in boats. Could you build a bridge to Hawaii, so I can drive there whenever I want?" The Lord laughed and said,

"That's almost impossible! Think of the logistics! How would the supports ever reach the bottom of the Pacific? Think of the concrete and steel! Your request is very materialistic and disappointing. I could do it but it's hard for me to justify. Take a little more time and make another wish, one you think would honor and glorify Me."

After much thought, the man said, "I've been married 3 times. My wives always said that I was insensitive to their needs. So I wish that I could understand women. I want to know how they feel and what they're thinking. I want to know why they cry and how to make them truly happy. That's my wish, Lord." Then, after a few minutes, God said, "You want two lanes or four on that bridge?"

[desire, knowledge, marriage]

Psalm 37:8

Wife to husband: "Seven o'clock, dear. Time to get up and start worrying."

[worry]

Psalm 37:39

Paul came home from Children's Church and his mother asked him if he could repeat the memory verse. "Oh sure," he replied, "it's the verse that says, 'A lie is an abomination unto the Lord, but an ever present help in time of trouble.'"

[lies]

Psalm 40:8

What the world really needs is another hymn: "I Did It Thy Way."

[hymn, obedience]

Psalm 50:10

Minister before the morning offering: "The Lord owns the cattle on a thousand hills. He only needs cowboys to round them up. Will the ushers please come forward for the offering?"

[offering]

Psalm 50:15

The only person whose troubles are all behind him is a school-bus driver.

[trials]

Psalm 52:3-4

A couple of weeks after hearing a sermon on Psalms 51:2-4 (about knowing my hidden secrets) and Psalms 52:3-4 (about lies and deceit), a man wrote the following letter to the IRS:

"I have been unable to sleep, knowing that I have cheated on my income tax. I understated my taxable income, and have enclosed a check for $150.00. If I still can't sleep, I will send the rest."

[sleep, taxes]

Psalm 53:1

An atheist complained to a Christian, "You Christians have all the holidays: Christmas, Good Friday, Easter, Ascension, Pentecost, Thanksgiving, and others."

The Christian retorted, "You can have April first."

[atheist, fool, holidays]

Psalm 53:1

The chief fault with atheism is that it has no future.

[atheist]

Psalm 53:1

Sign on a tomb of an atheist: HERE LIES AN ATHEIST, ALL DRESSED UP AND NO PLACE TO GO.

[atheist]

Psalm 56:1

A verse that our pastor refuses to let his daughter post on her bedroom door — "Be merciful to me, O God, for men hotly pursue me; all day long they press their attack." (NIV)

[dating, men]

Psalm 68:14

A little girl in southern California was having her first glimpse of snow. "Oh, mama, what is it?" she asked excitedly.

"Why, that's snow, Penny. What did you think it was?"

"It looks like popped rain."

[weather]

Psalm 70:1

A church congregation sat enthralled while a young, very pregnant woman rose in the choir and sang, "O Lord make haste and deliver me."

[song, pregnant]

Psalm 81:10

My cousin, who had just opened his dental practice, was dismayed when his mother told him she was embroidering a Bible verse to hang on the wall of his waiting room. "Mom, you don't just put Bible verses in dentist's offices," he groaned. His mother assured him that he would like it.

He did. The verse his mother had chosen was Psalm 81:10: "... open thy mouth wide, and I will fill it."

[Bible, context]

Psalm 89:9

Does the Bible mention the microwave?
Well maybe not specifically but what about the implications of Psalm 89:9:
"When the Lord stills the waves, there are not even microwaves left?"

[calm, cooking]

Psalm 90:10

If forty is the old age of youth then I'd say fifty is the youth of old age!

[age]

Psalm 90:10

A reporter, interviewing a man who had reached his 99th birthday, said, "I certainly hope I can come back next year and see you reach 100."
"Can't see why not, young feller," the old-timer replied, "you look healthy enough to me."

[age, confidence]

Psalm 90:10

A pious man, who had reached the age of 105, suddenly stopped going to synagogue. Alarmed by the old fellow's absence after so many years of faithful attendance, the Rabbi went to see him. He found him in excellent health, so the Rabbi asked, "How come after all these years we don't see you at services anymore?"
The old man lowered his voice. "I'll tell you, Rabbi," he whispered. "When I got to be 90, I expected God to take me any day. But then I got to be 95, then 100, then 105. So, I figured that God is very busy and must've forgotten about me, and I don't want to remind Him!"

[age, death]

Psalm 90:10

God created the mule, and told him, 'you will be the mule, working constantly from dusk to dawn, carrying heavy loads on your back. You will eat grass and you lack intelligence. You will live for 50 years.
The mule answered: 'To live like this for 50 years is too much. Please, give me no more than 20.' And it was so.
Then God created the dog, and told him, 'you will hold vigilance over the dwellings of Man, to whom you will be his greatest companion. You will eat his table scraps and live for 25 years.
And the dog responded, 'Lord, to live 25 years as a dog is too much. Please, no more than 10 years.' And it was so.
God then created the monkey, and told him, 'You are Monkey. You shall swing from tree to tree, acting like an idiot. You will be funny, and you shall live for 20 years.'

And the monkey responded, 'Lord, to live 20 years as the clown of the world is too much. Please, Lord, give me no more than 10 years.' And it was so.

Finally, God created Man and told him, 'You are Man, the only rational being that walks the earth. You will use your intelligence to have mastery over the creatures of the world. You will dominate the earth and live for 20 years.

'And the man responded, 'Lord, to be Man for only 20 years is too little. Please, Lord, give me the 20 years the mule refused, the 15 years the dog refused, and the ten years the monkey rejected.' And it was so.

And so God made Man to live 20 years as a man, then marry and live 20 years like a mule working and carrying heavy loads on his back. Then, he's to have children and live 15 years as a dog, guarding his house and eating the leftovers after they empty the pantry; then, in his old age, to live 10 years as a monkey, acting like a clown to amuse his grandchildren.

[age, contentment, time]

Psalm 103:1

A minister was baptizing some new church members. As the first woman came up out of the water, she joyously exclaimed to the congregation, "Bless the Lord, O my soul."

The next new member shouted, "The LORD is my shepherd!"

A third quoted, "I can do all things through Christ, who strengthens me."

The fourth to be baptized was a fellow with little knowledge of the Bible. He also was timid in front of a group. As he came up out of the water, he gave a wide grin to the congregation and exclaimed, "Merry Christmas, everyone!"

[Christmas, Scripture, strength]

Psalm 119:9

The most fortunate thing about small boys is that they're washable.

[boys, wash]

Psalm 119:99

Education covers a lot of ground, but it doesn't necessarily cultivate it.

[education, wisdom]

Psalm 127:2

The trouble with being punctual is that there's nobody there to appreciate it.

[appreciation, time]

Psalm 127:3

A mother thanked God in a testimony service for the "blessing" of her four, healthy, lively sons. Then she added, "And a prayer request that I have, is that God might give me the patience to endure my blessings."

[blessings, boys, prayer]

Psalm 127:3

Little Brother was gazing into the crib at his new baby sister, who lay, wailing at the top of her voice.

"Has she come from heaven?" inquired Little Brother tenderly.

"Yes," replied his mother.

"Well," said Little Brother, "it's no wonder they put her out."

[crying, heaven]

Psalm 127:3

I asked Mom if I was a gifted child ... she said they certainly wouldn't have paid for me.

[children, gift]

Psalm 127:4

Woman to the pastor's wife: "We have four children already but my husband wants more and he keeps quoting to me the verse, 'Like arrows in the hand of a warrior, so are the children of one's youth. How blessed is the man whose quiver is full of them.' What can I say to him?"

Pastor's wife: "Tell him 'How blessed is the man who knows the size of a quiver!'"

[children, family]

Psalm 127:4

QUESTION: Who do you think is more satisfied — a man with a million dollars or a man with eight sons?

ANSWER: The man with eight sons is more satisfied because a man with a million dollars would want more!

[contentment, family, fertility]

Psalm 127:5

Having children is hereditary, if your parents didn't, you won't either.

[family, heredity]

Psalm 127:5

The bride brought her new husband up to meet Granny at the family picnic. The old woman looked the young man over carefully and then said to him, "Young man, do you desire to have children?"

He was a bit startled by her candid approach. "Well, yes, as a matter of fact, I do," he managed to say.

She looked at him scornfully and then surveyed the very large clan gathered around a dozen picnic tables and said, "Well, try to control it."

[fertility, population control]

Psalm 128:3

Children and wives have terrible memories. They remember everything you promise them.

[memory, promise]

Psalm 128:5,6

Apparently, unlike the Israelites, today when all the children have grown up, married and moved away, most parents experience a strange new emotion. It's called ecstasy.

[children, emotion, joy]

Psalm 133:1

Christians may not always see eye-to-eye, but they can walk arm-in-arm.

[unity]

Psalm 136

First disappointed but polite church member: "I thought the sermon was divine. It reminded me of the peace of God. It passed all understanding."
Second, less impressed church member: "I thought it reminded me of the mercies of God. I thought it would endure forever."

[mercy, peace, sermon)

Psalm 137:1

A minister was completing a sermon about the evils of drinking alcohol. With great expression he said, "If I had all the beer in the world, I'd take it and pour it into the river."
With even greater emphasis he said, "And if I had all the wine in the world, I'd take it and pour it into the river."
And then finally, he said, "And if I had all the whiskey in the world, I'd take it and pour it into the river."
Sermon complete, he then sat down.
The song leader stood very cautiously and announced with a smile, "For our closing song, let us sing Hymn #365: 'Shall We Gather at the River'".

[drinking, hymn, sermon]

Psalm 139:7-12

A Children's Church teacher was explaining the omnipresence of God to his students, and ended by telling them that He was everywhere.
Whereupon a red-headed boy asked: "Is he in my pocket?"

The teacher replied that the question was rather silly maybe even profane but he would answer. "Yes, he is in your pocket."

"I've got you there," said the boy, "I ain't got no pocket."

[attributes, God, impossibility]

Psalm 139:13

A protestant minister, a catholic priest and a rabbi were discussing when life begins. The catholic priest said that life begins with conception, while the pastor believed that life began at birth.

Then the rabbi, after pondering on this question for a while looked up and said, "Life begins when the kids move out and the dog is dead!"

[Catholic, children, fetus, life]

Psalm 139:13

There is a big controversy these days concerning when life begins. In Jewish tradition the fetus is not considered a viable human being until after graduation from either law or medical school.

[career, fetus]

Psalm 139:13,14

The mother was explaining the facts of life to her daughter. The youngster listened attentively as her mother told her about the birds and bees, then, with amazement in her voice the girl asked softly, "Does God know about this?"

[God, sex]

Psalm 139:14

One night a wife found her husband standing over their newborn baby's crib. Silently she watched him. As he stood looking down at the sleeping infant, she saw on his face a mixture of emotions: disbelief, doubt, delight, amazement, enchantment, skepticism.

Touched by this unusual display and the deep emotions it aroused, with eyes glistening she slipped her arms around her husband.

"A penny for your thoughts," she whispered in his ear.

"It's amazing!" he replied. "I just can't see how anybody can make a crib like that for only $46.50!"

[fathers, money]

Psalm 139:14

Grandpa and granddaughter were sitting talking when she asked, "Did God make you, Grandpa?"

"Yes, God made me," the grandfather answered.

A few minutes later, the little girl asked him, "Did God make me too?"

"Yes, He did," the old man answered.

For a few minutes, the little girl seemed to be studying her grandpa, as well as her own reflection in the mirror, while her grandfather wondered what was running through her mind. At last she spoke up. "You know, Grandpa," she said, "God's doing a lot better job lately."

OR

Little Juliet was sitting on her grandfather's lap as he read her a bedtime story.
From time to time, she would take her eyes off the book and reach up to touch his wrinkled cheek. She was alternately stroking her own cheek, then his again. Finally she spoke up, "Grandpa, did God make you?" "Yes, sweetheart," he answered, "God made me a long time ago."
"Oh," she paused, "Grandpa, did God make me too?" "Yes, indeed, honey," he said, "God made you just a little while ago." Feeling their respective faces again, she observed, "God's getting better at it, isn't he?"

[creation, grandparents]

Psalm 146:4

Where is a flat tire mentioned in the Bible?
You need to know the Hebrew language to answer this question because Psalms 146:4 "His spirit departs, he returns to the earth" can be translated from the Hebrew as "Its air went out and returned to the earth"

[transportation]

Psalm 150:3

Lyre—A biblical instrument that masqueraded as a harp.

[lying, music]

PROVERBS

Proverbs 1:7

A Vermonter had seventeen children, all boys. When they came of age, they voted uniformly for the Republican ticket—all except one boy. The father was asked to explain this terrible fall from family grace.

"Well," he said. "I've tried to bring them boys up right, in the fear of the Lord and Republicans to the bone, but John, the ornery cuss, got to readin.'"

[education , politics]

Proverbs 1:7-9

Learn from the skillful: He who teaches himself has a fool for a master.

[education, foolishness]

Proverbs 2:3-5

Some students drink from the fountain of knowledge, while others merely gargle.

[education, knowledge]

Proverbs 3:1-5

One teenager to another: "The trouble with my father is that he remembers what it's like to be young!"

[fathers, youth]

Proverbs 5:3

Never let a fool kiss you and never let a kiss fool you.

[discernment]

Proverbs 5:3

Son: How do they catch lunatics, Dad?
Dad: With lipstick, beautiful dresses, and pretty smiles.

[dating]

Proverbs 5:7

Young man, consult your father. He's often as old as you are, and sometimes knows as much too.

[fathers, wisdom]

Proverbs 5:18

The bonds of matrimony are a good investment only when the interest is kept up.

[marriage]

Proverbs 6:6

Do ants have brains?" asked little Saul.

"Of, course," declared Ben. "How else could they figure out where you're having a picnic?"

[insects]

Proverbs 6:6

Doctor: "You've got to have more diversion and relaxation."

Patient: "But I'm too busy."

Doctor: "Nonsense. The ants are hardworking creatures but they have time to attend all the picnics."

[rest]

Proverbs 6:6

Despite what the Bible says about the ant being no sluggard, I can't help but notice that it always finds time to go to picnics!

[rest]

Proverbs 6:9-10

You can never make your dreams come true by oversleeping.

[laziness, sleep, work]

Proverbs 6:29

King David and King Solomon lived merry, merry lives,

With many, many lady friends and many, many wives.

But when old age crept over them, with many, many qualms

King Solomon wrote the Proverbs, and King David wrote the Psalms.

[experience]

Proverbs 9:10

Fear of jail is the beginning of wisdom. (Nigerian proverb)

[wisdom]

Proverbs 10:4

The trouble with opportunity is that it always comes disguised as hard work.

[work]

Proverbs 10:4

The new sales manager had called the sales force together and was laying down the law. "There's going to be a new regime around here—all work. And," he concluded, "from now on I want you out of here and calling on your customers at the stroke of 9."

The salesman who was always the wise guy, piped up, "The first stroke of 9 or the last stroke, sir?"

[business, smart-alecky]

Proverbs 10:5

He who rolls up sleeves seldom loses shirt.

[laziness, work]

Proverbs 10:18

Jeremiah, a grape farmer, was brought in to testify in a slander suit involving two of his neighbors. "Tell me the exact conversation," said the judge.

"I can't remember it all," answered the witness, "'cept each one was callin' the other what they both is."

[slander, truth]

Proverbs 10:19

A closed mouth gathers no foot.

[discernment, speech]

Proverbs 10:19

Talk is cheap because the supply is greater than the demand.

[speech]

Proverbs 10:19

To avoid trouble, breathe through your nose, and keep your mouth shut.

[discernment, speech]

Proverbs 10:19

Youngster: "Why do they call it the 'mother tongue'?"
Dad (cryptically): "Who uses it most?"

[speech]

Proverbs 10:19

When there is a gap in the conversation, don't put your foot in it!

[discernment, speech]

Proverbs 11:13

Secret: Something that is hushed about from place to place.

[gossip]

Proverbs 11:17

A troublemaker is a guy who rocks the boat then persuades everyone else there is a storm at sea.

[trouble]

Proverbs 12:4

First husband: "My wife's a real angel"
Second Husband: "I know what you mean, mine's always up in the air harpin' about something too."

[angels, wife]

Proverbs 12:4

See Ephesians 5:23.

Proverbs 12:5

Thinking occurs when your mouth stays shut and your head keeps talking to itself.

[contemplation, speech]

Proverbs 12:11

If you must kill time, work it to death!

[time , work]

Proverbs 12:15

First woman: "Does your husband ever take advice?"
Second woman: "Occasionally, when nobody is looking."

[advice, husbands]

Proverbs 12:17

Savanna and her sister are close, and that allows them to be honest with each other. One evening as Savanna prepared for a date, she remarked, "I'm fat."
"No, you're not," her sister scolded.
"My hair is awful," she said.
"It's lovely," her sister encouraged.
"I've never looked worse," Savanna whined.
And then her sister said, "Yes, you have."

[honesty]

Proverbs 13:1

One of Mark Twain's best known remarks is worth repeating:
"When I was a boy of fourteen, my father was so ignorant I could hardly stand to have the old man around. But when I got to be twenty-one, I was astonished at how much the old man had learned in seven years."

[experience]

Proverbs 13:3

He who has a sharp tongue usually cuts own throat.

[speech]

Proverbs 13:22

A miser isn't much fun to live with, but he sure makes a wonderful ancestor.

[selfish]

Proverbs 13:22

The easiest way to teach children the value of money is to borrow some from them.

[children, money]

Proverbs 13:24

The behavior of some children suggests that their parents embarked on the sea of matrimony without a paddle.

[discipline, parents]

Proverbs 13:24

When my father found me on the wrong track, he always provided switching facilities.

[discipline, father]

Proverbs 13:24

Son: "Dad, the Bible says if you don't let me have the car, you hate me."
Father: "Where does it say that?"
Son: "Proverbs 13:24 — 'He that spareth his 'rod'[hot rod] hateth his son.'"

[discipline, transportation]

Proverbs 13:24

In the words of a wise man using the metric system: Spare the 5.03 meters and spoil the child.

[discipline]

Proverbs 13:24

The only advice I get about raising children is to be consistent. But how can I be consistent? They never do the same thing twice.

[children, parents]

Proverbs 13:24

Boy (about to be spanked): "Dad, did grandpa spank you when you were little?"
Father: "Yes, son."
"And did grandpa's father spank him, too?"

"Yes, son."
"Well, don't you think it's about time to stop this inherited brutality?"

[discipline, heredity]

Proverbs 13:24

Whack—whack—whack went the strap. "I hope you see I'm doing this for your own good," the father said.
"Sorry, Pop," bawled Herman. "My eyesight ain't that good."

[discipline]

Proverbs 13:25

See 1 Corinthians 6:12.

Proverbs 14:17

You can't save face if you lose your head.

[self-control]

Proverbs 14:29

Poise is the act of raising your eyebrows instead of the roof.

[self-control]

Proverbs 14:29

Funny thing about temper: You can't get rid of it by losing it.

[anger, self-control]

Proverbs 15:1

Teacher: "Billy, what did you do when Ed called you a liar?"
Billy: "I remembered what you told me: 'A soft answer turns away anger.'"
Teacher: "Very good, Billy. What answer did you give him?"
Billy: "I answered him with a big soft tomato in the face."

[revenge, speech]

Proverbs 15:1

Some neighbors of my grandparents gave them a pumpkin pie as a gift. As lovely as the gesture was, it was clear from the first bite that the pie tasted bad. It was so inedible that my grandmother had to throw it away.
Ever gracious and tactful, my grandmother still felt obliged to send the neighbors a note. It read, "Thank you very much for the pumpkin pie. Something like that doesn't last very long in our house."

[honesty]

Proverbs 15:14

Some students never let studying interfere with their "education."

[education, study]

Proverbs 15:28

A gossip is just a fool with a keen sense of rumor.

[gossip]

Proverbs 15:31

If you're not big enough to stand some criticism, you're too small to be praised.

[criticism, pride]

Proverbs 16:18

The foolish and dead alone never change their opinion — James Russell Lowell.

[foolishness, stubborn]

Proverbs 16:18,19

Isn't it a shame that when success turns someone's head it doesn't wring his neck at the same time!

[pride, success]

Proverbs 16:24

A pastor was preaching on Proverbs 16:24: "Pleasant words are as a honeycomb, sweet to the soul, and health to the bones." The minister then added, "You know, you catch more flies with honey than you do with vinegar."

The deacon's wife leaned over, put her head on her husbands shoulder and whispered in his ear, "I just love to watch your muscles ripple when you take out the garbage."

[compliment, motivation]

Proverbs 16:25

Learn from other people's mistakes. It is a big time-saver.

[mistakes]

Proverbs 16:28

People who gossip usually end up in their own mouth traps.

[gossip]

Proverbs 16:32

That's what I like about you ... when your golf ball goes into the rough, you don't swear," stated the head deacon to his minister.

"That may be," responded the minister, "but where I spit, the grass dies!"

[anger, sports]

Proverbs 16:32

The prudent man does not let his temper boil over lest he get into hot water.

[anger, consequences]

Proverbs 17:6

Some grandchildren are a double blessing. They're a blessing when they come, and they're a blessing when they go.

[blessing, grandchildren]

Proverbs 17:6

It is true that children are a comfort to parents in their old age; and very often children help them reach it faster, too.

[children, comfort]

Proverbs 17:22

A smile is God's cosmetic. Besides, why not wear a smile? It's just about the only thing you can wear that isn't taxed!

[joy, smile, taxes]

Proverbs 17:22

Doctors claim that cheerful people resist diseases much better than glum ones. So remember, "The surly bird always catches the germ."

[sickness, joy]

Proverbs 17:28

Better to keep your mouth shut and be thought a fool, than to open it and remove all doubt!

[self-control, speech]

Proverbs 18:8

A preacher overheard this talk between two men in the church hallway: "Listen carefully, because I can only tell this once. I promised not to repeat it."

[gossip]

Proverbs 18:9

He who does nothing is seldom without helpers.

[laziness]

Proverbs 18:13

We wouldn't necessarily call him a liar. Let's just say he lives on the wrong side of the facts.

[lies, truth]

Proverbs 18:22

When William Jennings Bryan went to call on the father of his prospective wife and seek the hand of his daughter in marriage, knowing the strong religious feeling of the father, he thought to strengthen his case by a quotation from the Bible, and quoted the proverb of Solomon: "Whoso findeth a wife findeth a good thing." But to his surprise the father replied with a citation from Paul to the effect that he that marrieth doeth well, but he that marrieth not doeth better. The young suitor was for a moment confounded. Then with a happy inspiration he replied that Paul had no wife and Solomon had seven hundred, and Solomon, therefore, ought to be the better judge as to marriage.

[context, marriage]

Proverbs 19:6

"If you can't think of any other way to flatter a man, tell him he's the kind who can't be flattered."

[flattery]

Proverbs 19:11

Speak when you are angry and you'll make the best speech you'll ever regret.

[anger, speech]

Proverbs 19:15

She keeps asking her husband to show her his birth certificate. She wants proof that he's alive.

[boredom, husband]

Proverbs 19:15

Getting up in the morning is simple—just a question of mind over mattress.

[self- control, sleep]

Proverbs 19:18

Permissiveness believes in letting your child do whatever he likes on the premise that if he gets killed doing it, he won't do it again. — Sam Levenson

[parenting]

Proverbs 20:10, 13

See Micah 6:11

Proverbs 20:11

On the first day of school, a first grader handed his teacher a note from his mother. The note read, "The opinions expressed by this child are not necessarily those of his parents."

[children, school]

Proverbs 20:13

Some people who think they are dreamers are just sleepers!

[dreams, sleep]

Proverbs 20:13

A dollar may not go as far as it used to, but what it lacks in distance it makes up in speed!

[money]

Proverbs 20:13

The best way to hear money jingle in your pocket is to "shake a leg."

[money, work]

Proverbs 20:19

It's all right to hold a conversation, but you should let go of it now and then.

[self-control, speech]

Proverbs 20:21

A little girl says, "Grandpa, can I sit on your lap?"
"Why sure you can." Her grandfather replied.
As she is sitting on grand dad's lap she says, "Grandpa, can you make a sound like a frog?"
"A sound like a frog? Well, sure Grandpa can make a sound like a frog."
The girl says, "Grandpa, will you please, please MAKE a sound like a frog?"
Perplexed, her granddad says, "Sweetheart, why do you want me to make a sound like a frog?"
And the little girl says, "'Cause Daddy said that when you croak, we're going to Florida!"

[death, grandparents, grandchildren]

Proverbs 21:9

Horse sense shows itself when a fellow knows enough to stay away from a nag.

[common sense, nag]

Proverbs 21:9

Nag: a woman with no horse sense.

[nag, woman]

Proverbs 21:9

First wife: "My husband is an efficiency expert in a large company."
Second wife: "What does an efficiency expert do?"

First Wife: "Well, the best I can make out, if we women did it, they'd call it nagging."

[nag, woman, work]

Proverbs 21:9

The news media featured a convict's daring daylight escape from prison and his voluntary return and surrender later that evening. When reporters asked him why he'd come back, he said, "The minute I sneaked home to see my wife, the first thing she said was, 'Where have you been? You escaped eight hours ago!'"

[marriage, nag]

Proverbs 21:16

Thousands of nuts hold a car together — but one can scatter it all over the road.

[stupidity, transportation]

Proverbs 21:23

When you're in deep water, be sure to keep your mouth shut.

[silence, speech]

Proverbs 21:23

As the mama whale said to the baby whale, "It's only when you're spouting that you get harpooned."

[animals, pride]

Proverbs 21:23

The best way to save face is to keep the lower part shut.

[humility, silence]

Proverbs 22:1

So live that when death comes the mourners will outnumber the cheering section.

[character, death]

Proverbs 22:1

Some men wake up to find themselves famous; others stay up all night and become notorious.

[character, fame, shame]

Proverbs 22:6

It was a wise school principle who said to the parents, "I cannot control your child in the High School, if you haven't controlled him in the High Chair."

[parenting]

Proverbs 22:6

Children are growing up when they start asking questions parents can answer.

[parenting, questions]

Proverbs 22:6

Two teenagers were walking down the street.
"You know," said one, "I'm really worried."
"What's the problem? His friend inquired."
"Well, last night I was talking with my parents, and I'm beginning to see and believe my parent's point of view."

[parents, teenagers]

Proverbs 22:8

See Galatians 6:7.

Proverbs 22:15

Sometimes bending a child over has a strange way of straightening him out!

[discipline, parenting]

Proverbs 22:15

David, if you had more spunk you would stand better in your classes. Do you know what spunk is?" asked his father.
David (recalling past experiences): "Oh, yes, Dad. It's the past tense of spank."

[discipline, parenting]

Proverbs 22:26, 27

There are two times in an Israelite's life when he should not put up security for debts: when he can't afford it, and when he can.

[debt]

Proverbs 23:2

More people commit suicide with a fork than with any other weapon.

[death, eating]

Proverbs 23:4, 5

By the time a man discovers that money doesn't grow on trees, he's already out on a limb.

[debt, money}

Proverbs 23:13

One parent to another: "Do you believe in spanking children?"

Other parent: "Certainly not. But what I have found to be effective is patting them on the back every once in awhile — often enough, low enough, and hard enough."

[discipline, parenting]

Proverbs 23:13 ,14

A pat on the back develops character, if it is administered young enough, often enough, and low enough.

[discipline, parenting]

Proverbs 23:13, 14

Father: "Now remember, Son, I'm spanking you because I love you."
Whimpering Son: "I just wish I were big enough to return your love."

[discipline, love]

Proverbs 23:22

A woman reported the disappearance of her husband to the police.
The officer looked at the guy's photograph, questioned her, and then asked if she wanted to give her husband any message if they found him.
"Yes, please" she replied. "Tell him his mother didn't come after all."

[mother-in-law]

Proverbs 23:23

There are some people so addicted to exaggeration that they can't tell the truth without lying.

[exaggeration, lying]

Proverbs 23:24

The subject for discussion in class was proverbs.
"Can anyone give me a proverb about parents?" asked the teacher. "How about a proverb about fathers?"
Little Clarissa raised her hand. "My mommy has a proverb about my daddy," she informed the class. "There's no fool like an old fool."

[foolishness, husbands, proverb]

Proverbs 23:31, 33

Wife to husband with a hangover: "I don't see why your head should hurt this morning — you certainly didn't use it last night."

[drinking, self-control,]

Proverbs 24:10

Adversity sometimes is the only diet that will reduce a fat head!

[adversity, diet, pride]

Proverbs 25:17

Some people stay longer in an hour than others can in a week.

[hospitality, visitors]

Proverbs 25:17

Social tact is making your company feel at home even though you wish they were.

[hospitality, lying]

Proverbs 25:17

It's nice to see people with plenty of get-up-and-go, especially if some of them are visiting you.

[hospitality, visitors]

Proverbs 25:17

After a long evening where a guest had made no move to leave though it was late, the host finally said, "I'm also rather good at imitations. I can imitate almost any bird you can name."

[hospitality, visitors]

Proverbs 25:24

See Proverbs 21:9.

Proverbs 26:11

Grandpa," said young Joshua, "why do people say 'There's no fool like an old fool?"

"I guess," replied the old man, "it's because folks know you just can't beat experience."

[experience, foolishness]

Proverbs 26:12

As a rule the fellow who toots his own horn the loudest, is in the biggest fog.

[boasting, pride]

Proverbs 26:16

A patient told his doctor, "If there's anything wrong with me, Doctor, just tell me in plain English."

"Well," replied the doctor hesitatingly, "to be perfectly frank, you're just plain lazy."

"Thanks, Doctor," muttered the patient, "Now I would appreciate it if you would give me the scientific name so I can tell my family."

[doctors, laziness]

Proverbs 26:20

Some people will believe anything if they happen to overhear it.

[gossip]

Proverbs 26:22

Gossip seems to travel faster over sour grapevines.

[discontentment, gossip]

Proverbs 27:1

The greatest laborsaving device for some people is tomorrow.

[procrastination]

Proverbs 27:2

A ferocious lion killed and ate a bull. Afterward he felt so proud he just roared and roared. A hunter heard him roar and came and shot him. Moral: When you're full of bull, you'd better keep your mouth shut.

[consequences, pride]

Proverbs 27:2

An egotist is a person who is me-deep in conversation.

[pride]

Proverbs 27:2

Did you hear about the French-horn player whose toupee fell into the bell of his horn? He spent the rest of the night blowing his top!

[anger, music]

Proverbs 27:6

Most of us would rather be ruined by praise than saved by criticism.

[criticism, praise]

Proverbs 27:10

A college student wrote to his father: "Dear father, I am broke and have no friends. What shall I do?"
His father's ANSWER: "Make friends at once."

[debt, friends]

Proverbs 27:15

Wife: Scientists claim that the average person speaks 10,000 words a day.
Husband: Yes, dear, but remember, you are far above average.

[talk, women]

Proverbs 27:15

My wife suffers in silence louder than anyone I know.

[silence, suffering]

Proverbs 27:21

The human body is very sensitive. Pat a man on the back and his head swells.

[pride]

Proverbs 27:23,24

The only time most of us hear money talking is when it's saying "Good-bye".

[money]

Proverbs 28:1

Israelite man: "It says here, 'The wicked flee when no man pursueth.'"
Prophet: "Yes, that is true, but they make much better time when somebody is after them."

[judgment, prophet, wicked]

Proverbs 28:1

Teacher?"
"Yes, Jay."
"Is there a Christian flea?"
"What on earth ever put that idea into your head?"
"The preacher read it today from the Bible: 'The wicked flee, when no man pursueth.'"
"Why, Jay, that means that the wicked men flee."
"Oh, Then is there a wicked woman flea?"
"No, no. It means that the wicked flee, runs away."
"Why do they run?"
"Who?"
"The wicked fleas."
"No, no! Don't you see? The wicked man runs away when no man is after him."
"Oh. Is there a woman after him?"
"Jay, we have no more time today. Please go home!"

[context, misunderstanding]

Proverbs 28:1

What are the 2 smallest insects in the Bible? (The widow's mite [Mark 12:42] and the wicked flea [Proverbs 28:1])

[insects, size]

Proverbs 28:7

Mother: Johnny, what is all the racket from the pantry?
Johnny: I'm busy fighting temptation.

[temptation]

Proverbs 29:3

"Dad"
"Yes, son."
"Is it true that a man is known by the company he keeps?"
"Yes, son."

"Well, if a man keeps company with a bad man, is the good man bad because he keeps company with the bad man, or is the bad man good because he keeps company with the good man?"

[friends]

Proverbs 29:9

The only people who listen to both sides of the argument are the neighbors.

[argument, neighbors]

Proverbs 29:9

An argument usually occurs when two people try to get the last word in first.

[argument]

Proverbs 29:11

Epitaph on the gravestone of an army mule: Here lies Maggie, who in her time kicked two captains, four lieutenants, ten sergeants, fifty privates, and one bomb.

[anger, stubborn]

Proverbs 29:15

Benjamin, the precocious son of a couple from the line of Levi, was acting in a manner that met the displeasure of his parents.

"That will be quite enough, Benjamin," his mother reproved. "I am weary of your juvenility."

"Well," said little Ben, in one of his rebellious moods, "there are times when I get fed up with your adultery."

[adultery, rebellion]

Proverbs 29:15

A permissive mother said to her wild son, "Sit down and stop making so much noise."

"No, I won't ... so there!" said the boy in an impudent tone.

"Stand up, then ... I will be obeyed!"

[disobedience, obedience, rebellion]

Proverbs 29:15

One reason there are so many juvenile delinquents today is that their dads didn't burn their britches behind them.

[discipline]

Proverbs 29:17

A father was admonishing his complaining and failing son: "Son, all you need is encouragement and a swift kick in the seat of your can'ts."

[discipline, encouragement]

Proverbs 29:15

See Proverbs 13:24.

Proverbs 29:23

The man who claims to be a self-made man has relieved God of an embarrassing responsibility. He usually is a horrible example of unskilled labor.

[pride]

Proverbs 30:11

"Mommy, we want a hamster," the children wailed.

"You can't have a hamster. You won't take care of it. It will end up being my responsibility," Mom replied.

"We'll take care of it," they protested. "We promise."

So Mom relented. She bought them a hamster, and they named it "Danny." Two months later, though, when Mom found herself responsible for cleaning and feeding the creature, she located a prospective new home for Danny the hamster.

When she told the children the news of Danny's imminent departure, they took the news quite well, which somewhat surprised her. One of the children remarked, "He's been around here a long time. We'll miss him."

Mom agreed, saying, "Yes, but he's too much work for one person, and since I'm that one person, I say he goes."

Another child offered, "Well, maybe if he wouldn't eat so much and wouldn't be so messy, we could keep him."

But Mom was firm. "It's time to take Danny to his new home now," she insisted. "Go and get his cage."

In tearful outrage the children shouted, "Danny? We thought you said, 'Daddy!'"

[father]

Proverbs 31:16

I have always been confused when I hear the phrase "professional women" — are there any amateurs?

[women]

Proverbs 31:27

Husband: "I know you're having a lot of trouble with the baby, dear, but keep in mind, 'The hand that rocks the cradle is the hand that rules the world.'"

Wife: "How about you taking over the world for a few hours while I go shopping?"

[children, responsibility]

Proverbs 31:27

Top Tips For Cheapskates:
Old telephone directories make ideal personal address books. Simply cross out the names and addresses of people you don't know.
When reading a book, try tearing out the pages as you read them. This saves the expense of buying a bookmark, and the pages can later be used for shopping lists.
Fool other drivers into thinking you have an expensive car phone by holding an old TV or video remote control up to your ear and occasionally swerving across the road and mounting the curb
Drill a one-inch diameter hole in your refrigerator door. This will allow you to check that the light goes off when the door is closed.
Avoid being wheel-clamped by jacking your car up, removing the wheels and locking them safely in the car until you return.
Avoid parking tickets by leaving your windshield wipers to "fast wipe" whenever you leave your car parked illegally.
Take your trash can to the supermarket with you so that you can see which items you have recently run out of.
No time for a bath? Wrap yourself in duct tape and remove the dirt by simply peeling it off.
Expensive hair gels are a con. Marmalade is a much cheaper alternative, but beware of bees in the summer.
Avoid cutting yourself while clumsily slicing vegetables by getting someone else to hold them while you chop away.

[cheap, stupidity]

Proverbs 31:28

A young mother of one asked an older lady who had raised a large family how she thought the virtuous woman of Proverbs could have time to do all she did. "Well," she replied. "When she had one child it took all her time ... so how could any other responsibility make any difference?"

[busy, time]

Proverbs 31:28

A teacher showed her class a magnet and how it drew things to itself. Later to test their listening ability she asked, "My name starts with M and I pick up things. What am I?"
A chorus of children hollered out, "MOTHER!"

[mothers]

Proverbs 31:28

A young boy of five was looking at his parents' wedding pictures in the family album. His father, described the ceremony and tried to explain its meaning.

In a flash, the young boy understood (or thought he did). "I think I've got it," he exclaimed. "That's when Mom came to work for us, right?"

[wedding, work]

Proverbs 31:30

To marry a woman for her beauty is like buying a house for its paint.

[beauty]

Proverbs 31:30

An elderly minister was holding forth at a local bus stop, his small audience enthralled by his interesting monologue. Suddenly he broke off and turned to gaze at a smartly dressed young lady with an eye-catching figure who walked gracefully past. As the girl turned the corner, the spell was finally broken and the minister resumed his talk. "You know," he said, "I just never tire of admiring the work of the Lord."

[beauty, creation]

ECCLESIASTES

Ecclesiastes

I have a new philosophy. I am only going to dread one day at a time." — Charlie Brown

[worry]

Ecclesiastes 1:16

A man could retire nicely in his old age if he could dispose of his experience for what it cost him.

[experience]

Ecclesiastes 3:1

A young girl awoke early and, as she was going downstairs to get something to eat, the grandfather clock struck seven. But it didn't stop there. It went right on striking: 8, 9, 10, 11, 12—and still it didn't stop: 13, 14, 15 and so on. The girl ran back upstairs shouting to the whole family, "Get up! It's later than it ever was!"

[time]

Ecclesiastes 3:1

A purpose for everything? God didn't create anything without a purpose, but mosquitoes and roaches come close.

[creation, purpose]

Ecclesiastes 3:4

"Now, tell me," said the Bible teacher, "what is the opposite of the word 'weep'?"
"'Laugh'," replied the class.
"And the opposite of 'sadness'?"
"'Gladness'," they chorused.
"And the opposite of 'woe'?"
"'Giddap'!" shouted the students.

[opposite]

Ecclesiastes 3:6

It's very reassuring to some people to know that there is biblical support for having a garage sale. In Ecclesiastes 3:6 it states: "a time to keep and a time to throw away."

[business, context]

Ecclesiastes 3:7

Silence is evidence of a superb command of the English language.

[communication, silence]

Ecclesiastes 4:2

In spite of the cost of living, it's still popular.

[life]

Ecclesiastes 4:13

Miss Swenson's fifth grade class was assigned to write a short essay on parents. Samantha Peters' essay read: "The trouble with parents is that when we get them, they are so old that it is very hard to change their habits."

[age, change, parents]

Ecclesiastes 5:1

Minister's prayer: "May the members of my congregation be as free with their money as they are with their advice, and may their minds be as open as their mouths."

[generous]

Ecclesiastes 5:2

Nothing is opened more by mistake than the mouth.

[mistakes, mouth]

Ecclesiastes 5:4

A man is walking along when suddenly he got his foot caught stuck in some railroad tracks. He tried to get it out but it was really stuck in there well. He heard a noise and turned around to see a train coming. He panicked and started to pray, "God, please get my foot out of these tracks and I'll stop drinking!" Nothing happened, it was still stuck, and the train was getting closer! He prayed again, "God, please get my foot out and I'll stop drinking AND swearing!" Still nothing ... and the train was just seconds away! He tried it one last time, "God please, if you get my foot out of the tracks, I'll quit drinking, swearing, and smoking" Suddenly his foot shot out of the tracks and he was able to dive out of the way, just as the train passed! He got up, dusted himself off, looked toward Heaven and said, "Thanks anyway God, I got out myself."

[prayer, thanks]

Ecclesiastes 5:10

Money doesn't always bring happiness. A guy with ten million dollars is no happier than a guy with nine.

[happiness, money]

Ecclesiastes 6:12

Near Perfect Attendance

A pious man who had reached the age of 105 suddenly stopped going to synagogue. Alarmed by the old fellow's absence after so many years of faithful attendance the rabbi went to see him. He found him in excellent health, so the rabbi asked, "How come after all these years we don't see you at services anymore?"

The old man looked around and lowered his voice. I'll tell you, Rabbi," he whispered. "When I got to be 90 I expected God to take me any day. But then I got to be 95, then 100, then 105. So I figured that God is very busy and must have forgotten about me ... and I don't want to remind Him."

[age, God]

Ecclesiastes 9:9

Mrs. Jamison came bursting into her lawyer's office and declared, "I want a divorce."

"But why?" asked the startled lawyer. "Do you have grounds?"

"Sure do! A house in Paramus and a cabin in the Poconos."

"No, what I mean is, do you have some kind of grudge?"

"Not exactly, but there's a carport in front of the house," Mrs. Jamison replied.

"That's not what I mean," said the lawyer, exasperated. "Your husband, does he beat you up or something?"

"Oh, no, I'm the first one up every morning."

"Mrs. Jamison!" yelled the lawyer. "Can you just tell me why you want a divorce?"

"Yes! It's because I just can't carry on a decent conversation with the man!"

[communication, divorce, hearing]

Ecclesiastes 9:9

My wife is an angel. She doesn't have an earthly thing to wear! And, she's always up in the air harping about something!

[angels, wife]

Ecclesiastes 10:2

You may have wondered why it is that Conservatives are called the "right" and Liberals are called the "left." The answer, according to some right-wingers is found in the Bible, in Ecclesiastes 10:2.

"The heart of the wise inclines to the right, but the heart of the fool to the left." (NIV)

[context, politics]

Ecclesiastes 10:18

See Proverbs 19:15.

Ecclesiastes 12:1

Father to teenage son: "Maybe you should start to provide for yourself while you still know everything."

[knowledge, teenagers]

Ecclesiastes 12:1

A group of senior citizens at a retirement home was having a grand old time discussing their various aches, pains and ills. Arthritis, indigestion, ulcers, insomnia, on and on it went. Finally an eighty-five-year-old man said, "Think of it this way, my friends. It just proves that old age isn't for sissies!"

[age, courage]

Ecclesiastes 12:1f

One advantage to advancing years is that you know a lot more about being young than teen-agers know about being old.

[age, knowledge, teenagers]

Ecclesiastes 12:1f

You know you're getting older when:
You sit in a rocking chair and can't get it going.
You burn the midnight oil after 8:00 P.M.
Everything hurts, and what doesn't hurt, doesn't work.
You look forward to a dull evening.
The gleam in your eyes is from the sun hitting your bifocals.
You feel like the morning after, and you haven't been anywhere.
Your little black book contains only names ending in M.D.
You get winded playing chess.
Your children begin to look middle-aged.
You join a health club and don't go.
You decide to procrastinate, but never get around to it.
Your mind makes contracts your body can't meet.
Dialing long-distance wears you out.
You know all the answers, but nobody asks you the questions.
You walk with your head held high, trying to get used to your bifocals.
You're turning out lights for economic rather than romantic reasons.
Your knees buckle and your belt won't.
The best part of your day is over when the alarm goes off.
Your back goes out more than you do.
A fortune teller offers to read your face.

The little gray-haired lady you help across the street is your wife.
You've got too much room in the house and not enough in the medicine cabinet.
You sink your teeth in a steak, and they stay there.

[age]

Ecclesiastes 12:1f

An 80–year–old man went for his annual check up and the doctor said, "Friend, for your age you're in the best shape I've seen." The old man replied, "Yep. It comes from clean living. I know I live a good, clean, spiritual life." The doctor asked, "What makes you say that?" The old man replied, "If I didn't live a good, clean life the Lord wouldn't turn the bathroom light on for me every time I get up in the middle of the night." The doc was concerned. "You mean when you get up in the night to go to the bathroom, the Lord Himself turns on the light for you?" "Yep," the old man said, "whenever I get up to go to the bathroom, the Lord turns the light on for me."
Well, the doctor didn't say anything else, but when the old man's wife came in for her check up, he felt he had to let her know what her husband said. "I just want you to know," the doctor said. "Your husband's in fine physical shape but I'm worried about his mental condition. He told me that every night when he gets up to go to the bathroom, the Lord turns the light on for him." "He what?" she cried. "He said every night when he gets up to go to the bathroom, the Lord turns the light on for him." "A–ha!" she exclaimed. "So he's the one who's been peeing in the refrigerator!"

[aging]

Ecclesiastes 12:3

"How was your game, dear?" asked Jack's wife Tracy.
"Well, I was hitting pretty well, but my eyesight's gotten so bad I couldn't see where the ball went," he answered.
"But you're 75 years old, Jack!" admonished his wife, "Why don't you take my brother Scott along?"
"But he's 85 and doesn't play golf anymore," protested Jack.
"But he's got perfect eyesight. He would watch the ball for you," Tracy pointed out.
The next day Jack teed off with Scott looking on. Jack swung and the ball disappeared down the middle of the fairway.
"Do you see it?" asked Jack.
"Yup," Scott answered.
"Well, where is it?" yelled Jack, peering off into the distance.
"I forget."

[age, forgetfulness]

Ecclesiastes 12:4

Two elderly women were eating breakfast in a restaurant one morning. Ethel noticed something funny about Mabel's ear and she said, '"Mabel, do you know you've got a suppository in your left ear?" Mabel answered, "I have a suppository in my ear?" She pulled it out and stared at it. Then she said, "Ethel, I'm glad you saw this thing. Now I think I know where to find my hearing aid."

[hearing]

Ecclesiastes 12:5

A pastor called on a home one afternoon after school to visit a new family who had come to his church. Suddenly a little boy rushed into the room, exhibiting a mangled, dead rat. As the mother let out a little shriek and shrank away, the little boy reassured her, "Oh, it can't hurt you. It's dead all right. I beat it and beat it and beat it until ..." Then spotting the pastor, his tone changed to one of solemnity, " ... until God called it home."

[cruelty, heaven]

Ecclesiastes 12:12

"What's your son going to be when he graduates?"
"An old man."

[age, student]

Ecclesiastes 12:12

Why study? The more we know, the more we forget. The more we forget, the less we know. The less we know, the less we forget. The less we forget, the more we know. So why study?

[knowledge, students]

Ecclesiastes 12:13

The mother of a religious family was listening to her daughter saying a rather lengthy bedtime prayer. "Dear God" prayed the child, "let me do well in my test tomorrow. Make my friends be nice to me. Tell my brother not to mess up my room. Please get my father to raise my allowance. And ..." The mother interrupted, "Don't bother to give God more instructions. Just report for duty."

[obedience, prayer]

SONG OF SONGS

Song of Solomon

The Song of Solomon is the one book of the Bible dedicated solely to romantic love. Isn't it ironic that its initials are SOS?

Song of Songs 1:2

1. Marriage is not a word. It is a sentence (A life sentence!!!)
2. Marriage is very much like a violin; after the sweet music is over the strings are attached.
3. Marriage is love. Love is blind. Marriage is an institution. Therefore marriage is an institution for the blind.
4. Marriage is an institution in which a man loses his Bachelor's Degree and the woman gets her Masters.
5. Marriage is a thing which puts a ring on a woman's finger and two under the man's eyes.
6. Marriage certificate is just another name for a work permit.
7. Marriage is not just having a wife but also worries inherited forever.
8. Marriage requires a man to prepare 5 types of "RINGS" :
    #1) The Engagement Ring
    #2) The Wedding Ring
    #3) The SufferingRing
    #4) The EnduringRing
    #5) The TorturingRing
9. Married life is full of excitement and frustration:
    -In the first year of marriage, the man speaks and the woman listens.
    -In the second year, the woman speaks and the man listens.
    -In the THIRD year, they both speak and the NEIGHBORS listen.
10. It is true that love is blind but marriage is definitely an eye-opener.
11. Getting married is very much like going to the restaurant with friends...You order what you want, and when you see what the other fellow has, you wish you had ordered that.
12. It's true; all men are born free and equal — but some of them get married.
13. There was this man who muttered a few words in the church and found himself married. A year later he muttered something in his sleep and found himself divorced.

14. A happy marriage is a matter of giving and taking; the husband gives and his wife takes.

15. Son : How much does it cost to get married , Dad?
Dad : I don't know son, I'm still paying for it.

16. There was a man who said, "I never knew what happiness was until I got married ... and then it was too late !!"

17. Love is one long sweet dream, and marriage is the alarm clock.

18. They say that when a man holds a woman's hand before marriage, it is love; after marriage it is self-defense.

19. When a newly married man looks happy, we know why. But when a ten-year married man looks happy, we wonder why.

20. There was this lover who told his love that he would go through hell for her. They got married — and now he is going through HELL !

21. Marriage is like a besieged castle — those on the outside want to get in, and those on the inside want to get out.

22. A man is not complete until he marries — after that he is finished.

23. At the cocktail party, one woman said to another, "Aren't you wearing your wedding ring on the wrong finger?" The other replied, "Yes I am, I married the wrong man."

24. Son : Is it true, Dad, that I heard that in ancient China, a man doesn't know his wife until he marries ?
Dad : That happens everywhere, son. EVERYWHERE.

25. After a quarrel, a wife said to her husband, "You know, I was a fool when I married you." And the husband replied, "Yes, dear, but I was in love and didn't notice it."

26. It doesn't matter how often a married man changes his job, he still ends up with the same boss.

27. A man inserted an 'ad' in the classifieds: "Wife wanted". Next day he received a hundred letters. They all said the same thing: "You can have mine."

28. When a man opens the door of his car for his wife, you can be sure of one thing: either the car is new or the wife.

[marriage]

Song of Songs 1:2

Dear GOD,
I went to this wedding and they kissed right in church. Is that okay?
-Holden

[kissing, wedding]

Song of Songs 1:2

Kissing shortens life—the single life.

[kissing, life]

Song of Songs 1:2

In kissing, two heads are better than one.

[kissing]

Song of Songs 1:2

Kissing—a means for getting two people so close together that they can't see anything wrong with each other.

[kissing]

Song of Songs 1:7

A man usually falls in love with a girl who asks the kind of questions he is able to answer.

[love, men, questions]

Song of Songs 1:15

"Without you everything is dark and dreary. The clouds gather and the wind beats the rain. Then comes the warm sun—you are like a rainbow."
"Is this a proposal or a weather report?"

[communication, weather]

Song of Songs 4:1-7

Sol sat on one end of the sofa, his girl friend on the other. For a long time neither spoke. Finally she said, "Sol, do you think my eyes are beautiful?"
"Uh huh."
"And do you think my hair is the prettiest you ever saw?"
"Uh huh."
"Do you think I have a perfect figure?"
"You bet."
"Do you think my lips are like rubies?"
"Sure."
"Are my teeth like pearls?"
"I'll say."
"Oh, Sol, you say the nicest things!"

[communication]

Song of Songs 4:2

Her teeth were like pearls. They, however, needed restringing badly.

[beauty]

Song of Songs 4:11

Beloved: "Are mine the only lips you have kissed?"
Solomon: "Yes, and they are the sweetest of all."

[kissing]

Song of Songs 5:6

Marriages may be made in heaven, but a lot of the details have to be worked out here on earth.

[marriage]

Song of Songs 5:10-16

A man is never so weak as when some woman is telling him how strong he is.

[man]

Song of Songs 6:5-7

He was wooing her ardently. "Your cheeks are so rosy," he declared.
"My cheeks belong to you," she whispered.
"Your lips are like rubies," he said.
"My lips belong to you, darling — just you," she breathed. "But when you get to my eyelids — they're Max Factor's."

[beauty]

Song of Songs 6:6

Romantic Husband: In the moonlight your teeth are like pearls.
Suspicious Wife: And when were you in the moonlight with Pearl?

[jealousy]

Song of Songs 6:8

See 1 Kings 11:3.

The Prophets

Seminary Professor to Students: I'm asking all of you to join me in my new company. It's not a pyramid scheme but it is a prophet-sharing [profit-sharing] company!

[business, prophets, wages]

Minor Prophets are like baseball players, hoping someday to make it into the Majors.

[prophets]

Some think that the Minor Prophets were the wages of men who worked in the stone quarries.

[prophets, wages]

A pastor was preaching on the Minor Prophets...all twelve of them in one sermon. After two hours he was only half-way through his message. Everyone was getting restless. Most had stopped paying attention. After four hours, to everyone's relief, he said "Finally." It was almost over, they thought. Then to their horror, the Pastor said, "Oh my, I forgot about Micah ... what shall we do with Micah?" One old lady sitting right in front could take no more. She stood up and said, "Hey, preacher! Micah can take my seat ... I'm going home!"

[boredom, prophets, sermon]

Atheism is a non-prophet organization.

[prophets]

ISAIAH

Isaiah 2:4

See Micah 4:3.

Isaiah 3:9

In the first Freshman English class of the semester, the professor stated "Let us establish some examples about opposites. Mr. Nichols, what is the opposite of joy?"

"Sadness," said the student.

"Fine. And the opposite of depression, Ms. Biggs?"

"Elation," she replied with a smile.

"Very good. And you, Mr. Cates, what is the opposite of woe?"

"I believe that would be 'giddy up'"

[communication]

Isaiah 3:12

Ozark Proverb: Terrible is the fate to have a rooster who is silent and a hen who crows.

[gender]

Isaiah 3:12

"Won't it be strange when women rule the country?"

"Only to the bachelors."

[submission]

Isaiah 3:12

Son: Do you agree with the prediction that women will be ruling the world in the year 2020?

Father: Yes, they will still be at it.

[gender, submission]

Isaiah 3:16

"I wonder why so many women pay more attention to their beauty than they do to their brains."

"Because no matter how stupid a man is, he is seldom blind."

[beauty, woman]

Isaiah 5:11

I hate mornings. They're so early!

[sleep]

Isaiah 6:2

An old lady in a remote part of Ireland said to her unlearned parish priest: "Father, can you tell me what is the difference between Cherubim and Seraphim?"

The priest replied: "Well now, I believe there was a wee difference between them once, but I hear they're the best of friends now."

[angels]

Isaiah 6:5

QUESTION: What was the name of Isaiah's horse?

ANSWER: "Isme," after all Isaiah did say, "Whoa, is me."

[animals, names]

Isaiah 6:8

The closest some believers come to offering themselves to the Lord is expressed in the following commitment, "Lord, Lord, use me in Thy work—but primarily in an advisory capacity."

[commitment, ministry]

Isaiah 7:14

Little boy: "Daddy, what's a virgin?"

Father: "Well, it's usually a kind of forest, son."

[virgin]

Isaiah 7:18

Bees fly thousands of miles to gather enough nectar to make a pound of honey. Then someone comes along and steals it from them. Maybe this explains why bees have such lousy dispositions.

[insects]

Isaiah 8:12

LIFE IN THE HEADLINES
(Biblical headlines as might be written by today's media)

On Red Sea crossing:
WETLANDS TRAMPLED IN LABOR STRIKE
Pursuing Environmentalists Killed

On David vs. Goliath:
HATE CRIME KILLS BELOVED CHAMPION
Psychologist Questions Influence of Rock

On Elijah on Mt. Carmel:

FIRE SENDS RELIGIOUS RIGHT EXTREMIST INTO FRENZY
400 Killed

On the birth of Christ:
HOTELS FULL, ANIMALS LEFT HOMELESS
Animal Rights Activists Enraged by Insensitive Couple

On feeding the 5,000:
PREACHER STEALS CHILD'S LUNCH
Disciples Mystified Over Behavior

On healing the 10 lepers:
LOCAL DOCTOR'S PRACTICE RUINED
"Faith Healer" Causes Bankruptcy

On healing of the Gadarene demoniac:
MADMAN'S FRIEND CAUSES STAMPEDE
Local Farmer's Investment Lost

On raising Lazarus from the dead:
PREACHER RAISES A STINK
Last Will & Testament Reading Delayed

[words]

Isaiah 9:4

What is the rod of affliction?" the Children's Church teacher asked.
"Goldenrod," shouted the little girl whose mother has hay-fever every fall.

[sickness]

Isaiah 9:6

A young minister, ecstatic at the birth of a new baby, sent his mother this
brief email, "Isaiah 9:6," to indicate the gender.
His mother read too much into the message however. Phoning her husband
at his office she excitedly proclaimed, "Our daughter-in-law has had a baby
boy who weighs nine pounds and six ounces, and they've named him
Isaiah!"

[babies, communication, context]

Isaiah 9:6

The Christian Education committee was working on the Christmas
program and had undertaken the making of a large banner to be hung in
the church. They had decided on the material but were to decide that
evening on the text and the dimensions. They had also decided to have it

made in the city and to ask the secretary to ask her husband, who was leaving for the city that same day, to place the order. So the secretary arranged with her husband that she would send him a text-message with the necessary information after the ladies had decided on it.

When he looked at his phone later that morning, and forgetting about the Christmas program his wife was working on, he was extremely surprised to see the following text message: UNTO US A CHILD IS BORN TEN FEET LONG TWO FEET WIDE. YOUR WIFE.

[babies, communication, context]

Isaiah 11:12

A kindergarten teacher asked, "What is the shape of the earth?"
One lil' girl named Kayla spoke up: "According to my Daddy — terrible!"

[world]

Isaiah 13:1

QUESTION: What does the rabbi do during some sermons?
ANSWER: Babylon [babble on].

[Babylon, preaching]

Isaiah 30:15

If silence is golden, not many people can be arrested for hoarding.

[silence]

Isaiah 30:26

The Temperature of Heaven

The temperature of Heaven can be rather accurately computed. Our authority is Isaiah 30:26, "Moreover, the light of the Moon shall be as the light of the Sun and the light of the Sun shall be sevenfold, as the light of seven days." Thus Heaven receives from the Moon as much radiation as we do from the Sun, and in addition 7x7 (49) times as much as the Earth does from the Sun, or 50 times in all. The light we receive from the Moon is one 1/10,000 of the light we receive from the Sun, so we can ignore that. The radiation falling on Heaven will heat it to the point where the heat lost by radiation is just equal to the heat received by radiation, i.e., Heaven loses 50 times as much heat as the Earth by radiation. Using the Stefan-Boltzmann law for radiation, $(H/E)^4 = 50$, where E is the absolute temperature of the earth (-300K), gives H as 798K (525C).

The exact temperature of Hell cannot be computed ... [However] Revelations 21:8 says "But the fearful, and unbelieving ... shall have their part in the lake which burneth with fire and brimstone." A lake of molten brimstone means that its temperature must be at or below the boiling point, 444.6C. We have, then, that Heaven, at 525C is hotter than Hell at 445C.!

[heaven, hell]

Isaiah 38:1

"Am I g-g-going to d-d-die, doctor?'

"My dear, I can assure you that dying is the last thing you'll do!"

[death, fear]

Isaiah 38:5

A middle aged woman has a heart attack and is taken to the hospital. While on the operating table she has a near death experience. During that experience she sees God and ask if this is it.

God says no and explains that she has another 30 years to live.

Upon her recovery she decides to just stay in the hospital and have a face lift, liposuction, breast augmentation, tummy tuck, etc. She even has someone come in and change her hair color. She figures since she's got another 30 years she might as well make the most of it.

She walks out of the hospital after the last operation and is killed by an ambulance speeding up to the hospital.

She arrives in front of God and complains: "I thought you said I had another 30 years.

God replies, "I didn't recognize you."

[beauty, death, God]

Isaiah 40:26

A dense fog halted all flights from the big airport. The lobby soon filled with passengers eager to be on their way. Most of them philosophically accepted the airlines' obvious explanation about the fog. However, one extremely wealthy woman, used to getting her own way refused to be satisfied. Taking a position directly in front of the counter, she rejected all efforts of a young assistant manager to explain the delay. Finally she said, "Young man, I don't believe you know what you are talking about. I insist on speaking to the person responsible for delaying my flight."

In a voice loud enough for everyone to hear, the young man said into his telephone, "Hello, operator, would you connect this party with Extension One in Heaven?"

[flying, pride, weather]

Isaiah 43:18

"But, pastor," lamented the young husband who had come in for counseling, "whenever Anne and I quarrel, she becomes historical."

"You mean, hysterical."

"No, historical. She is always digging up my past."

[history, marriage, memory]

Isaiah 44:6

How can you tell that God is the only one who enters the heavenly Olympics? He is both first and last in the races.

[God, sports]

Isaiah 45:1

An older Christian lady was well-known for her faith in the Lord and her lack of hesitation in talking about her Lord. Every once in a while she would go out on the front porch of her small home and yell, "Praise the Lord!"

Her next door neighbor, an ungodly man would shout back, "There ain't no God!"

During those days, the lady was very poor, so the neighbor decided to prove his point by buying a large bag of groceries and placing it at her door.

The next morning, the older Christian lady went to the porch and, seeing the groceries, shouted, "Praise the Lord!"

The neighbor stepped out from behind a tree and said, "I brought those groceries, and there ain't no God."

The lady, looking heavenward, replied, "Lord, you not only sent me food but you made the devil pay for it."

[devil, faith, food]

Isaiah 49:15

Mark met his old friend Matt and told him that he was in desperate need of five thousand dollars. He begged Matt to loan it to him, but Matt refused.

"Then I have to remind you, then," said Mark, "of what happened twenty-five years ago when we were in Vietnam together. You were lying wounded in the jungle. I crawled out to you, dodging bullets, threw you over my shoulder, and dragged you back. For this, I got the Medal of Honor. But the important thing was, I saved your life. Now, will you let me borrow the five thousand dollars?"

"No," said Matt, unimpressed.

"Let's go back to fifteen years ago," said Mark. "I'd like to remind you who introduced you to your wife. Who set you up with her when you were afraid to ask her out? Who gave the money for your honeymoon, Matt? Me! Now will you let me have the five thousand dollars?"

The response was again, "No."

Still determined, Mark continued. "How about ten years ago," said Mark, "when your daughter was struck by that rare disease and your doctor was desperately trying to find the right blood to give her a transfusion? Whose was it that finally matched? Your pal Mark. I gave her seven blood transfusions, and it pulled her through. You'll let me have the money, won't you, Matt?"

"No, I won't," said Matt.

"Think back to five years ago," urged Mark. "Remember when your back was against the wall and you had to have twenty- seven thousand dollars or the bank would foreclose on your company. Who signed the note that guaranteed your loan? Good old Mark! I saved your business for you then, didn't I, Steve? Now you will find it in your heart to loan me the five thousand dollars!"

Matt still had no problem refusing.

"What kind of friend are you, anyway?" yelled Mark, exasperated. "Twenty-five years ago I saved your life, fifteen years ago I introduced you to your wife, ten years ago I saved your daughter's life, five years ago I saved your business. In light of that, I can't imagine why in the world you won't loan me the five thousand dollars!"

"What have you done for me lately?" asked Matt.

[appreciation, indebtedness, ingratitude]

Isaiah 53:2

A minister was showing a painting of Christ to a child. "It's not really Jesus," he explained, "just an artist's conception of him."

"Well, it sure looks like him," said the child.

[Christ, images, picture]

Isaiah 53:9

See Luke 23:33.

Isaiah 53:12

See Luke 23:32.

Isaiah 60:2

The pastor was preaching from the text, "The darkness shall cover the earth, and gross darkness the people (KJV)."

"Now, brethren," he said, "there may be some of you just don't know what gross darkness means. Well, I'll tell you. It's exactly 144 times darker than dark."

[dark, preaching]

Isaiah 65:20

Patient: How can I live to be a hundred, doctor?

Doctor: Give up cookies, cake, and ice cream. Stop eating red meat, potatoes, and bread. And no soft drinks.

Patient: And if I do that, I will live to be a hundred?

Doctor: Maybe not, but it will certainly seem like it.

[age, food, life]

Isaiah 65:25

A preacher who believed in a future millennial kingdom was visiting a Moscow zoo and was amazed to see a cage marked CO-EXISTENCE NOW, containing a wolf and some lambs.
"How in the world can this be possible in this present age?" the visitor asked. "This is not the millennium yet."
"Nothing to it," replied the Russian zoo keeper. "We just add a fresh lamb now and then."

[animals, millennial, zoo]

Isaiah 65:25

Skeptic: "The lion and the calf shall lie down together, but the calf might not get much sleep."

[animals, millennial, sleep]

JEREMIAH

Jeremiah 1:5

QUESTION: How do we know Jeremiah's parents were good business people?

ANSWER: They both raised a good prophet [profit].

[prophets]

Jeremiah 3:22

"Are you a Christian?" asked the farmer.

"Of course," said the tramp. "Can't you tell? Just look at the knees of my pants. Don't they prove it?"

The farmer and his wife noticed the holes in the knees and promptly gave the man some food.

As the tramp turned to go the farmer asked, "By the way, what made those holes in the seat of your pants?"

"Backsliding," said the tramp.

[backsliding, spiritual battle]

Jeremiah 6:20

A small Israelite boy attended a feast at Jerusalem with his parents. When he knelt to say his prayers before going to bed, he prayed, "Dear Lord, we had such a good time at your house today. I wish you could have been there!"

[God, prayers]

Jeremiah 7:26

It seems that this lady didn't quite make it to the hospital for the birth of her child. In fact, the baby was born on the lawn just outside the main entrance. The poor woman was dreadfully embarrassed and was being consoled by one of the nurses, who said; "Don't worry about it. It could have been worse. Why, two years ago we had a woman who gave birth in the elevator."

The woman cried out, "That was me!" and burst into tears.

[embarrassment]

Jeremiah 8:22

A Jewish demolition expert had as his life verse Jeremiah 8:22, "Is there no bomb [balm] in Gilead?"

[names, weapons]

Jeremiah 9:5

Dylan had poor luck fishing. On his way home, he entered the fish market and asked the dealer, "Just stand over there and throw me five of your biggest trout,"
Dealer: "Throw them? What for?"
Dylan: "So I can tell my friends I caught them. I may be a poor fisherman, but I'm not a liar."

[honesty, liar]

Jeremiah 9:23

"A bore is someone who opens his mouth and puts his feats in it."
- Henry Ford

[boredom, pride]

Jeremiah 15:9

A scientifically and theologically minded young man sat up all night trying to figure where the sun went when it went down. It was morning before it finally dawned on him!

[science, weather]

Jeremiah 15:19

David received a parrot for his birthday. This parrot was fully grown with a bad attitude and worse vocabulary. Every other word was an expletive. Those that weren't expletives were, to say the least, rude.
David tried hard to change the bird's attitude and was constantly saying polite words, playing soft music, anything that came to mind. Nothing worked. He yelled at the bird, the bird got worse. He shook the bird and the bird got madder and ruder.
Finally, in a moment of desperation, David put the parrot in the freezer. For a few moments he heard the bird squawking, kicking and screaming and then, suddenly, all was quiet.
David was frightened that he might have actually hurt the bird and quickly opened the freezer door. The parrot calmly stepped out onto David's extended arm and said: "I'm sorry that I offended you with my language and actions. I ask for your forgiveness. I will try to check my behavior..."
David was astounded at the bird's change in attitude and was about to ask what changed him when the parrot continued, "May I ask what the turkey did?"

[education, profanity]

Jeremiah 16:17

Jesse, middle-aged now but as wild as in his youth, was being scolded by a deacon of his church. "You ought to be ashamed of yourself, drinkin' and fightin' and carousin' around like that. The least you could do, is set an example for the children."

"I don't set no bad example for the kids," protested Jesse in his own defense. "I do all my hell-raisin' at night, when they're sleepin'."

The deacon shook his head sadly. "Oh Jesse, you know that the Lord sees all — day or night."

"Maybe so," Jesse retorted, "but you gotta admit, the Lord don't never talk!"

[example, God, gossip]

Jeremiah 17:9

Ron and Ed, two professors of theology, were walking across the campus of a Theological Seminary when Ron asked Ed, "Do you believe in Original Sin?"

Ed answered, "Yes, I do. We have a child."

"Do you believe in Total Depravity?" asked Ron.

"No, I don't. That's an excess of Calvinistic theology," replied Ed.

Ron looked at his friend and replied, "Well, just wait till you have more children."

[children, sin, theology]

Jeremiah 17:9

The police station had been quiet most of the week. Things were so slow the detectives were playing cards to pass the time. "What a life," grumbled one of the officers. "No fights, no thefts, no riots, nor murders, no nothing'"

"Rest easy, Mike," said the captain. "Things'll break soon. You just gotta have faith in human nature."

[sin]

Jeremiah 20:11

Asked if he had any last words before his sentence of capital punishment was carried out, the criminal replied, "This is sure going to be an everlasting lesson for me."

[capital punishment, eternity, experience]

Jeremiah 20:18

A little girl came over to her neighbor and announced that there was a new baby at her house.

"Has the baby come to stay?" she was asked.

"I think so," she said, "he's taken all his things off."

[babies, naked]

Jeremiah 23:12

A clergyman and one of his elderly parishioners were walking home from church one frosty day when the old gentleman slipped and fell flat on his back. The minister looked at him a moment, and being assured that he was not much hurt, said to him, "Friend, sinners stand on slippery places." The old gentleman looked up as if to assure himself of the fact, and then said, "I see they do; but I can't."

[hypocrisy, sin]

Jeremiah 23:29

A rule of thumb for preachers: If after ten minutes you haven't struck oil, stop boring!

[boredom, preaching]

LAMENTATIONS

Lamentations 3:22

Sign tacked on a tree near a convent: "No trespassing; violators will be prosecuted to the fullest extent of the law — Sisters of Mercy."

[law, mercy]

Lamentations 3:23

"Somebody has well said there are only two kinds of people in the world. There are those who wake up in the morning and say, "Good morning, Lord," and there are those who wake up in the morning and say, "Good Lord, it's morning."

[grammar, gratitude, optimism]

EZEKIEL

Ezekiel 27:31

At a certain time of life a man's hair begins to grow inward. If it strikes gray matter it turns gray. If it doesn't strike anything it disappears.

[age, hair]

Ezekiel 37:3

One skeleton to the other: "If we had any guts, we'd get out of here."

[courage, cowardice]

Ezekiel 43:2

Three men of different occupations looked at the Grand Canyon.
The geologist said: "What a wonder of science!"
The clergyman said: "One of the glories of God!"
The cowboy said: "A heck of a place to lose a cow!"

[nature]

Ezekiel 43:13

QUESTION: What is a cubit?
ANSWER: The language spoken in Cuba.

[places, words]

Ezekiel 47:8

A boy boasting: "You know the Dead Sea? Well, my father killed it."

[boasting, places]

DANIEL

Daniel 1:8

"Butt Prints in the Sand."

One night I had a wondrous dream,
A set of prints on the sand was seen,
The footprints of my precious Lord,
Yet mine were not along the shore.

Then a stranger print appeared,
I asked the Lord, "What have we here?"
"This print is large and round and neat,
But Lord it's just too big for feet."

"My child, He said in somber tones,
"For miles I carried you alone.
I challenged you to seek my face,
Take up your cross and walk in grace."

"You disobeyed; you would not grow.
You would not stand against the flow.
Your neck was stiff; your ears were shut.
So there I dropped you on your butt.

"Because in life there comes a time,
When one must fight, when one must climb,
When one must rise and take a stand,
Or leave one's butt-print in the sand."

Anonymous.

[responsibility]

Daniel 1:17

After Aunt Harriet woke up, she told Uncle Irv, "I just dreamed you gave me a pearl necklace for Valentine's Day. What do you think it means?" "You'll know tonight," he said.

That evening, Uncle Irv came home with a package and gave it to this wife. Delighted, she opened it-to find a book entitled, The Meaning of Dreams.

[disappointment, dreams]

Daniel 3:12,13

A Children's Church teacher was having her class read certain Bible passages aloud. One boy was reading the account of the three Hebrews who had been thrown into the fiery furnace. When he came to the names of Shadrach, Meshach and Abednego, he broke down completely and had to be helped by the teacher.

He bravely continued, but a moment later he stopped dead. "What is the matter?" his teacher asked.

"Shucks," he said, "here are those same three fellows again."

[difficulty, names]

Daniel 3:15

You know what the penalty is for refusing to bow down, don't you?" said Nebuchadnezzar <u>heatedly</u>.

[anger, puns]

Daniel 4:30

Israel Zangwill once remarked about the great George Bernard Shaw: "The way Shaw believes in himself is very refreshing in these atheistic days when so many believe in no God at all."

[pride]

Daniel 4:32

QUESTION: Who was the first drug addict in the Bible?
ANSWER: Nebuchadnezzar. He was on grass for seven years.

[drugs, words]

Daniel 4:33

Who was the first drug addict in the Bible?
Nebuchadnezzar, he was on grass for seven years (others had gotten stoned before this but usually this was a single occurrence!).

[drugs]

Daniel 4:37

A little girl was sitting on her daddy's lap. She gazed up at her father and said, "Daddy, did anyone ever tell you that you're the smartest man in the world?"

Her father, filled with pride said, "Why no, honey, they haven't."

"Then where did you get the idea?" she asked.

[pride]

Daniel 5:5

Today, handwriting on the wall usually means there's a small child in the house.

[children, handwriting]

Daniel 5:20

Did you hear about the pastor who wrote a wonderful sermon on "humility" then filed it away? He wanted to save it for a really big occasion when he could impress a lot of people.

[pride, sermon]

Daniel 5:25

Charles was telling his friend Greg all about the mystery writing he had learned in Children's Church.

"It was in the story of Daniel," Charles said. "And a finger wrote some words on the wall of the palace. The king must not have behaved in church as the message was for him."

"What was the message?" asked Greg.

Happily Charles told him: "Meany, meany, tickle the pastor/parson!"

[handwriting, pastor]

Daniel 6:8

"One man's Mede is another man's Persian."

"Are you Shah?"

"Sultanly."

[names, puns]

Daniel 6:10

Three preachers sat discussing the best positions for prayer while a telephone repairman worked nearby.

"Kneeling is definitely best," claimed one.

"No," another contended. "I get the best results standing with my hands outstretched to Heaven."

"You're both wrong," the third insisted. "The most effective prayer position is lying prostrate, face down on the floor."

The repairman could contain himself no longer. "Hey, fellas, " he interrupted, "the best prayin' I ever did was hangin' upside down from a telephone pole."

[prayer]

Daniel 6:10

Billy: "What are prayers anyway?"

Mother: "They are messages sent to heaven."

Billy: "Well ... do I pray at night because the international rates are cheaper?"

[prayer]

Daniel 6:10

A farmer was in town at noon and went into a restaurant for a hamburger and French fries. When he was served, he quietly bowed his head and gave the Lord thanks for his food.

Some rough-looking fellows at the next table saw him and thought they would give him a hard time. One of them called out, "Hey farmer, does everyone do that where you live?"

"No, son," answered the farmer, "the pigs and donkeys don't."

[courage, insults, prayer]

Daniel 6:16

Children's Church teacher to class of boys who had been brought up with television rather than church: "Who went into the lion's den and came out unhurt?"

The boys in unison: "Tarzan!"

[misunderstanding]

Daniel 6:22

One Persian government official to another, "I've always told you, Daniel is one hard guy to swallow!"

[stubborn]

Daniel 9:21

Preacher to a little boy: "Do you say your prayers at night, Jimmy?"

Jimmy: "Yes, sir."

Preacher: "And do you always say them in the morning too?"

Jimmy: "No, sir. I ain't scared in the daytime."

[fear, prayer]

Daniel 12:2

At a dinner party, the subject of eternal life and future punishment came up for a lengthy discussion.

Mark Twain took no part in it, so the woman seated next to him asked: "Why haven't you said something? Surely you must have some opinion about this."

"Madam, you must excuse me," Twain replied. "I am silent because of necessity. I have friends in both places."

[heaven, hell]

HOSEA

A preacher spoke 20 minutes on Isaiah, 20 minutes on Ezekiel, 20 minutes on Jeremiah, and 20 minutes on Daniel. Then he said, "We now come to the 12 minor prophets. What place will I give Hosea?"
A man in the back of the church said, "I'm leaving. Give Hosea my place."

[boredom, preaching, prophets]

Hosea 7:9

There are three things that happen to you when you grow older. First you begin to lose your eyesight, then you tend to forget, and third — I can't remember.

[age, forgetfulness]

Hosea 10:12

"This picture doesn't do you justice."
"It's not justice I want. It's mercy."

[justice, mercy]

Hosea 13:15

How Hot & Dry will it be in that day??????
The Baptist will be sprinkling,
The Methodist will be using a wet wash cloth,
The Presbyterians will be giving rain checks and,
The Catholics will be turning wine back into water.
Now friends, that is DRY.

[denominations, drought]

JOEL

Joel 1:2

Advantages Of Aging
- In a hostage situation you are likely to be released first.
- No one expects you to run into a burning building.
- People call at 9 p.m. and ask, "Did I wake you?"
- People no longer view you as a hypochondriac.
- There's nothing left to learn the hard way.
- Things you buy now won't wear out.
- Kidnappers are not very interested in you.
- You can eat dinner at 4pm.
- You can't remember the last time you laid on the floor to read a book.
- You consider prune juice one of the most important things in life.
- You really enjoy hearing about other people's operations.
- You get into heated arguments about Social Security.
- You got cable for the Discovery/Health channel.
- You have a party and the neighbors don't even realize it.
- You no longer think of speed limits as a challenge.
- You quit trying to hold your stomach in, no matter who walks into the room.
- You sing along with the elevator music.
- Your ears are hairier than your head.
- Your investment in health insurance is finally beginning to pay off.
- Your joints are more accurate than the National Weather Service.
- Your secrets are safe with your friends because they can't remember them either.

[age]

Joel 2:25

Of course, life doesn't usually begin at 40 if you went like 60 when you were 20!

[age, consequences]

AMOS

Amos 1:1

A little girl who loved to watch the old T.V. reruns, came home all excited after Children's Church . She enthusiastically says to her mother: "Oh, Mother, we've been learning the books of the Bible and there's an Amos in it but no Andy!"

[names, television]

Amos 1:10

QUESTION: Where in Scripture is there burning rubber?
ANSWER: When there was "fire in tire [Tyre]."

[fire, names, puns]

Amos 4:1

A newspaper columnist was found guilty and fined for calling a countess a cow. When the trial ended and the man paid his fine, he asked the judge if, since it was now clear that he could not call a countess a cow, he could call a cow a countess.
The judge said that that was all right to do. Whereupon the newspaperman turned toward the countess in the courtroom, bowed elaborately, and said, "How do you do, Countess."

[insults]

Amos 4:1

Little Johnny was sitting in a classroom and the teacher asked the class, "Can anyone use the word sensuous in a sentence?"
Little Johnny was the first to raise his hand so the teacher called on him. He replied, "My mother used that word last night; she said 'Hubby, sensuous up, get me a glass of water.'"

[puns]

Amos 4:1

Before marriage a man declares that he will be the boss in his home or know the reason why. After marriage he knows the reason why.

[marriage]

Amos 4:1

See Isaiah 3:12.

Amos 4:1

In some cultures there's a new gadget that does all the housework for the woman. It's called a husband.

[husband]

Amos 4:7

Our drought was so bad, that during the time of Noah's flood, we got only 2 1/2 inches of rain in our section of the country.

[drought, weather]

Amos 4:8

They eat dry toast—and wash it down with crackers.

[drought, weather]

Amos 4:8

It's so dry in my home town they have fishes three years old that still haven't learned to swim.

[drought, weather]

Amos 4:12

Old Zach was very close to dying but made a miraculous recovery. The local Levite priest came to visit him and the conversation went like this: "Tell me, Zach, when you were so near death's door, did you feel afraid to meet your Maker?"
"No," said Zach. "It was the other man I was afraid of!"

[death, devil, hell]

Amos 5:13

Sometimes we forget to turn off the sound when our minds go blank.

[silence, speech]

Amos 5:18

The evangelist for a country church high up in the mountains was out visiting prospective members one day. He had spotted a house up in a mountain range that required at least a two-mile walk from the mail box. Out of breath from climbing the hill, he arrived at the front porch. He discovered a man rocking back and forth lazily on the porch.
"Howdy, friend, my name is Evangelist Jones. What's your?"
"Calloway's the name. What can I do for ye?" The minister continued, "Well, I just came up here to talk to you about some things and ask you a few questions."
"Shoot!" replied the mountaineer.
"Well, the first thing I want to know, Mr. Calloway, is, have you made peace with God?"

"Peace with God?" questioned Calloway, "Me and God ain't never had no argument!"

"No, no, no, you don't understand, Mr. Calloway, are you a Christian?"

"Nah, I ain't no Christian, preacher: I just told you my name is Calloway. The Christians live four mountains up the road."

"Mr. Calloway, I'm having a hard time getting through to you. What I really want to know is this—are you lost?"

"Nah, I ain't lost. I've been living here in these parts all my life. I know these mountains like the back of my hand."

"Mr. Calloway, what I really want to know is, are you ready for the judgment day?"

"Judgment Day?" When's it going to be?" The young minister replied, "Well, Mr. Calloway, it could be today, or it could be tomorrow."

"Well, lands sakes alive, parson, don't tell my wife. She'll want to go both days."

[evangelism, judgment, misunderstanding]

Amos 5:19

So you think you're having a bad day? The following is taken from a Florida newspaper:

A man was working on his motorcycle on his patio and his wife was in the house in the kitchen. The man was racing the engine on the motorcycle and somehow, the motorcycle slipped into gear. The man, still holding the handlebars, was dragged through a glass patio door and the motorcycle dumped onto the floor inside the house. The wife, hearing the crash, ran into the dining room, and found her husband laying on the floor, cut and bleeding, the motorcycle laying next to him and the patio door shattered. The wife ran to the phone and summoned an ambulance. Because they lived on a fairly large hill, the wife went down the several flights of long steps to the street to direct the paramedics to her husband. After the ambulance arrived and transported the husband to the hospital, the wife righted the motorcycle and pushed it outside.

Seeing that gas had spilled on the floor, the wife obtained some paper towels, blotted up the gasoline, and threw the towels in the toilet.

The husband was treated at the hospital and was released to come home. After arriving home, he looked at the shattered patio door and the damage done to his motorcycle. He became despondent, went into the bathroom, sat on the toilet and smoked a cigarette. After finishing the cigarette, he flipped it between his legs into the toilet bowl while still seated.

The wife, who was in the kitchen, heard a loud explosion and her husband screaming. She ran into the bathroom and found her husband laying on the floor. His trousers had been blown away and he was suffering burns on the buttocks, the back of his legs and his groin. The wife again ran to the phone and called for an ambulance.

The same ambulance crew was dispatched and the wife met them at the street. The paramedics loaded the husband on the stretcher and began carrying him to the street. While they were going down the stairs to the street accompanied by the wife, one of the paramedics asked the wife how the husband had burned himself. She told them and the paramedics started laughing so hard, one of them tipped the stretcher and dumped the husband out. He fell down the remaining steps and broke his arm.

Now THAT is a bad day.

[misfortune]

Amos 8:5

A lawyer dies in a car accident on his 40th birthday and finds himself greeted at the Pearly Gates by a brass band. Saint Peter runs over, shakes his hand and says "Congratulations!!!"

"Congratulations for what?" asks the lawyer.

"Congratulations for what?!?!?" says Saint Peter. "We're celebrating the fact that you lived to be 160 years old."

"But that's not true," says the lawyer. "I only lived to be forty."

"That's impossible," says Saint Peter. "We've added up your time sheets."

[dishonesty, lawyers]

Amos 8:5

A gorilla walked into a drugstore and ordered a $1.50 chocolate sundae. He put a ten-dollar bill on the counter to pay for it.

The clerk thought, what could a gorilla know about money? So he gave the gorilla a single dollar bill in change. As he did, the clerk said, "You know, we don't get too many gorillas in here."

"No wonder," the gorilla replied, "at nine dollars a sundae."

[cheating]

Amos 9:3

I found another snake today but it was only a baby. I wasn't afraid of it," bragged young Soren.

"How did you know it was only a baby? Asked his father. "You know there are poisonous snakes appearing all over."

"Because this one," Soren said, "had a rattler."

[animals, fear]

Amos 9:8

An officer in a police helicopter spotted a car speeding down the Interstate. He radioed his partner on the ground and the patrol officer in the car stopped the speeder and began writing a citation.

"How in the world did you know I was speeding?" the man asked.
The patrol officer didn't say anything but pointed skyward.
"Aww," the man moaned. "You mean, He's turned against me, too?"

[consequences, God, knowledge]

OBADIAH

Obadiah 1:3

One can't help but wonder if the Edomites had the expression "People living in stone houses shouldn't throw glass."

[races, revenge]

Obadiah 1:5

Catching her in the act, I jokingly confronted a visitor's 3-year-old daughter, "Are you taking your little sister's grapes?"
"No," she innocently replied, "I'm teaching her to share!"

[share, stealing]

Obadiah 1:8

At the conclusion of the sermon, the worshipers filed out of the sanctuary to greet the minister. As one of them left, he shook the minister's hand, thanked him for the sermon and said, "Thanks for the message, Reverend. You know, you must be smarter than Einstein. "Beaming with pride, the minister said, "Why, thank you, brother!"
As the week went by, the minister began to think about the man's compliment. The more he thought, the more he became baffled as to why anyone would deem him smarter than Einstein. So he decided to ask the man the following Sunday.
The next Sunday he asked the parishioner if he remembered the previous Sunday's comment about the sermon. The parishioner replied that he did. The minister asked: "Exactly what did you mean that I must be smarter than Einstein?"
The man replied, "Well, Reverend, they say that Einstein was so smart that only ten people in the entire world could understand him. But Reverend, no one can understand you."

[confusion, knowledge]

JONAH

Jonah 1:3

A Children's Church teacher asked her class, "What do we learn from the story of Jonah?"

An eight-year-old boy put up his hand. "Travel by air," he said.

[lessons, transportation]

Jonah 1:4-5

The minister was out fishing with a hired boatman when suddenly the storm broke, sending waves of tremendous force smashing against the side of the boat.

"I wish I'd been a better man," moaned the seaman.

"And I," said the minister, "wish I'd been a better swimmer."

[ambition, regrets]

Jonah 1:4-5

JONAH'S MOTHER: "That's a nice story. Now tell me where you've really been for the last three days."

[lies, resurrection]

Jonah 1:6

As the storm raged, the captain realized his ship was sinking fast. He called out, "Anyone here know how to pray?"

One man stepped forward, "Aye, Captain, I know how to pray."

"Good," said the captain, "you pray while the rest of us put on our life jackets — we're one short."

[prayer]

Jonah 1:17

Skeptic: "I'd believe but I just can't swallow Jonah."

Believer: "You don't have to. God prepared a fish to do that."

[faith, miracle]

Jonah 1:17

QUESTION: How did the great fish that swallowed Jonah obey the divine law?

ANSWER: Jonah was a stranger, and he took him in.

[hospitality]

Jonah 1:17

Pastor: "Just think of it, Jonah spent three days in the belly of a large fish."
Member: "That's nothing, my husband spent longer than that in the belly of an alligator."
Pastor: "Well, I declare ... just how long was he in there?"
Member: "It's almost four years, now."

[death, miracle]

Jonah 1:17

QUESTION: Why could Jonah be swallowed by the big fish in one gulp?
ANSWER: Jonah was one of the "minor prophets"!

[prophets]

Jonah 2:1

A guest on the speaker's platform was unexpectedly called upon to make a speech. He stammered for a moment, apologized for coming unprepared, then looked at the chairman and quoted what he claimed was Jonah's admonition to the whale: "If you had kept your big mouth closed I wouldn't be in this predicament now."

[speech, unexpected]

Jonah 2:2

QUESTION: How did Jonah feel when the great fish swallowed him?
ANSWER: Down in the mouth.

[discouragement]

Jonah 2:9

QUESTION: What did Jonah do while he was in the whale?
ANSWER: Sing, you always sing when you're in Wales!

[songs]

Jonah 2:10

QUESTION: What does the story of Jonah and the big fish teach us?
ANSWER: It teaches that you can't keep a good man down.

[lessons, optimism]

Jonah 2:10

A lady turned to her young son and said, "Didn't you enjoy the preachers sermon about Jonah and the whale?"
"I guess so," the boy said. "But I feel just like that whale. All that preaching and praying has given me a bellyache."

[preaching, sickness]

Jonah 2:10

Jonah escaped from the whale just because he did not wish to di-gest [die just] yet!

[death, pun]

Jonah 2:10

QUESTION: Who was Jonah's tutor?
ANSWER: The fish that brought him up.

[education, teacher]

Jonah 2:10

Now I'm really washed up," Jonah <u>wailed</u>.

[failure, puns]

Jonah 2:10

QUESTION: Who was the most ambitious man in the Bible?
ANSWER: Jonah — even a whale couldn't keep him down.

[ambition]

Jonah 2:10

Sometimes if you put yourself into the Bible stories they are humorous without making puns out of them. I remember hearing a comedian put himself into the Jonah story:
So you're walking along the beach minding your own business, and all of a sudden this big fish slides himself up on shore, pukes all over, and slides back into the water. Out of the slime and fish parts and seaweed, a man drags himself out, struggles, and stands up — his clothes half digested, a piece of seaweed stuck to the side of his face. He looks at you, coughs up some seawater, clears his throat, and says, "Repent!" What would you do? I know what I'd do: I'd repent!"

[repentance]

Jonah 4:9

Skeptic: "Do you honestly believe that Jonah spent three days and nights in the belly of a whale? How is that possible?"
Preacher: "I don't know, sir, but when I get to heaven I'll ask him."
Skeptic: "But suppose he isn't in heaven? He ended up being pretty angry with God you know."
Preacher: "Then you ask him!"

[heaven, hell, skeptic]

OR

There was a Christian lady that had to do a lot of traveling for her business so she did a lot of flying. Since flying made her nervous, she always took her Bible along with her to read and it helped relax her.

One time she was sitting next to a man. When he saw her pull out her Bible he gave a little chuckle and went back to what he was doing.

After a while he turned to her and asked "You don't really believe all that stuff in there do you?"

The lady replied "Of course I do. It is the Bible."

He said, "well what about that guy that was swallowed by that whale?"

She replied, "Oh, Jonah. Yes I believe that, it is in the Bible."

He asked "Well, how do you suppose he survived all that time inside the whale?"

The lady said "Well I don't really know. I guess when I get to heaven I will ask him."

"What if he isn't in heaven?" the man asked sarcastically.

"Then you can ask him." Replied the lady.

[heaven, hell, skeptic]

Jonah 4:11

After reading the story of Jonah and the whale to her Children's Church class, Miss Martha decided to give them a little quiz.

"What," she asked, "is the moral of this story?" For the answer she called on little Katya.

Katya thought for a minute and then replied, "People make whales throw up."

[lessons]

OR

A Children's Church class was ready for its question and answer session.

"What is it that we learn from the story of Jonah and the whale?" the teacher asked.

A bright kid spoke up and said, "What we learned is that people make whales sick."

[lessons]

MICAH

Micah 4:3

A six year old boy in Children's Church wrote, "My favorite Bible story is the one where the plowshares are turned into Fords."

[transportation]

Micah 4:3

Beating swords into plowshares and spears into pruning hooks has now become only a Senior Citizen's Arts and Crafts activity.

[peace]

Micah 5:2

See Luke 2:1-4.

Micah 6:11

Sign: HONEST SCALES—NO TWO WEIGHS ABOUT IT

[honesty]

NAHUM

Nahum 1:6

A Bible school teacher asked a student in his class, "What is righteous indignation?"
The boy thought for a moment and then said "That's to get real mad and not cuss."

[anger]

HABAKKUK

Habakkuk 1:1

Difficult Teacher: "What can you tell me about the prophet Habakkuk?
Desperate Student: "He's dead."

[death, prophets]

Habakkuk 1:1

QUESTION: Where can you find the first soft drink commercial in the Bible?
ANSWER: In the Book of Hab-a-kkuk ["Have-a-Coke"]

[drink]

Habakkuk 2:20

A Children's Church teacher asked the children, just before she dismissed them to go into big church, "And why is it necessary to be quiet in church?"
Little Johnny jumped up and yelled, "Because people are sleeping!"

[silence, sleep]

Habakkuk 2:20

Six-year old Nicole and her four-year old brother Joel were sitting together in church. Joel giggled, sang and talked out loud. Finally, his big sister had had enough. "You're not supposed to talk out loud in church."
"Why? Who's going to stop me?" Joel asked.
Nicole pointed to the back of the church and said, "See those two men standing by the door?— They're hushers [ushers]."

[silence]

ZEPHANIAH

Zephaniah

The sermon had lasted an hour and a half already — an hour to the major prophets, and the preacher had just got half way through the minor prophets. At last, he paused impressively, and exclaimed: "And Zephaniah — where shall we put him?"

A man rose in the back row, "He can have my seat, Mister."

[long, prophets, sermon]

HAGGAI

Haggai 1:11

It's been so dry lately that the rain that we did get had only 40% moisture.

[weather]

Haggai 1:11

It was so dry that even Baptists had to resort to sprinkling.

[weather, baptism/Baptist]

ZECHARIAH

Zechariah 4:10

The reason some plans die quickly in some people's heads is because they can't stand solitary confinement!

[knowledge, study]

Zechariah 9:16

Me and my father were making a crop back in the 1930s. He was working on one side of the hill, and I was on the other. I started singing, "Will There Be Any Stars in My Crown?" and I heard him singing, "No, Not One." — Virgil Anderson

[hymns, rewards, songs]

MALACHI

Malachi 2:3

While driving in Pennsylvania, a family caught up to an Amish carriage. The owner of the carriage obviously had a sense of humor, because attached to the back of the carriage was a hand printed sign...
"Energy efficient vehicle: Runs on oats and grass.
Caution: Do not step in exhaust."

[caution]

Malachi 3:8

One morning as the offering plate was being passed in church, a five year old removed his tie and put it in the plate. His mother snatched it out and whispered, "What do you think you are doing?"
The boy looked up at her and replied, "Mommy, didn't you hear the minister? He asked for our ties [tithes] and offerings."

[giving]

Malachi 3:8

"How come you have such a nice car and a such big house and I am poor?" said a rabbi to a priest. "Well, whenever people make a donation, I draw a line on the floor and throw the money. Whatever falls to the right side is for God, and whatever fall to the left I keep for myself." Said the priest.
"Wow, what a good idea! I think I will do the same. Thank you very much for the tip" said the rabbi.
A few months later, the priest noticed that the rabbi had became filthy rich. He was driving a Ferrari and had a huge house. "How did you become so rich?" said the priest to the rabbi.
"Remember that tip you gave me a few months ago?" replied the rabbi.
"Well, I came up with a better idea! Whenever people made a donation, I threw the money up in the air. Whatever stays up is for God, and whatever falls down, I keep for myself!"

[giving, greed]

Malachi 3:8-10

Malachi, speaking to some other prophets, was heard saying, "I just don't understand why some people who give the Lord credit are reluctant to give him cash."

[greed, wealth]

The BIBLE — General

The Bible in Fifty Words:

God made, Adam bit, Noah arked, Abraham split, Jacob fooled, Joseph ruled, Bush talked, Moses balked, Pharaoh plagued, People walked, Sea divided, Tablets guided, Promises landed, Saul freaked, David peeked, Prophets warned, Jesus born, God walked, Love talked, Anger crucified, Hope died, Love rose, Spirit flamed, Word spread, God remained. Amen

Old and New Testament

A 6-year-old boy was carrying a heavy Bible across the room when he asked, "Is this the Old Intestine or the New Intestine?"

[Bible, body]

Old and New Testament

Why is there an Old and a New Testament in the Bible?
Because God is so mysterious that he even keeps 2 sets of books.

[Bible]

Old and New Testament

Top 13 ways the Bible would be different if written by college students:
13. Out go the mules, in come the mountain bikes.
12. New edition every two years in order to limit reselling.
11. Last Supper would have been eaten the next morning – cold.
10. Loaves and Fishes replaced by Pizza and Chips.
9. Ten Commandments are actually only five, but because they are double-spaced and written in larger font, they look like ten.
8. Forbidden fruit would have been eaten because it wasn't cafeteria food.
7. Paul's letter to the Romans becomes Paul's e-mail to abuse@romans.gov.
6. Reason Cain killed Abel: They were roommates.
5. The place where the end of the world occurs? Not the Plains of Armageddon; rather, Final Exams.
4. Book of Armaments would be in there somewhere.
3. Reason why Moses and his followers walked in the desert for 40 years: they didn't want to ask directions and look like a Freshman.
2. Tower of Babel blamed for Foreign Language requirements.
1. Instead of God creating the world in six days and resting on the seventh, He would have put it off until the night before it was due and then pulled and all-nighter and hoped no one noticed.

[Bible, commandments]

MATTHEW

Matthew

A young boy came home from church and proudly announced that he'd been asked to read from the Bible that morning. When asked from what book the passage had been taken, he replied: "Oh, the gossip according to Matthew."

[Bible, gossip]

Matthew 1:2

Dear God:
I read the Bible. What does "begat" mean? Nobody will tell me.
Sincerely,
Heidi

[sex]

Matthew 1:18

A mother, concerned over her little son's potential behavior when some Christmas company was scheduled, asked, "Johnny, are you going to be good when Joe and Mary come over later?"
Little Johnny asked in amazement, "Are Jesus' parents coming here?"

[names, parents]

Matthew 1:18

A Children's Church teacher asked her class, "What was Jesus' mother's name?"
One child answered, "Mary."
The teacher then asked, "Who knows what Jesus' father's name was?"
A little kid said, "The Verge."
Confused, the teacher asked, "Where did you get that?"
The kid said, "Well, you know they are always talking about 'the Verge 'n' Mary.'"

[names]

Matthew 1:18

"Give me a sentence about a public servant," said a teacher. The small boy wrote: "The fireman came down the ladder pregnant."
The teacher took the lad aside to correct him. "Don't you know what pregnant means?" she asked.

"Sure," said the young boy confidently. "Means carrying a child."

[pregnant]

Matthew 1:23

The two young girls had been given parts in a Christmas play at school. At dinner that night they got into an argument as to whom had the most important role. Judy aged 11, was very superior.
"Why of course mine's the most difficult part," she told five-year-old Lucy. "Anybody'll tell you it's much harder to be a virgin than an angel."

[angel, virgin]

Matthew 1:23

A ten-year old, under the tutelage of her grandmother, was becoming quite knowledgeable about the Bible. Then one day she floored her grandmother by asking, "Which virgin was the mother of Jesus? The virgin Mary or the King James virgin [version]?"

[virgin]

Matthew 1:25

Advent — A season filled with the sounds of pipers piping, drummers drumming and cash registers ringing.

[holidays]

Matthew 1:25–2:2

A woman takes her 16-year-old daughter to the doctor. The doctor says, "Okay, Mrs. Jones, what's the problem?"
The mother says, "It's my daughter Darla, she keeps getting these cravings, she's putting on weight and is sick most mornings."
The doctor gives Darla a good examination then turns to the mother and says, "Well, I don't know how to tell you this but your Darla is pregnant — about 4 months would be my guess."
The mother says, "Pregnant? She can't be, she has never ever been left alone with a man. Have you Darla?"
Darla says, "No mother! I've never even kissed a man!"
The doctor walked over to the window and just stares out it. About five minutes pass and finally the mother says, "Is there something wrong out there doctor?"
The doctor replies, "No, not really, it's just that the last time anything like this happened, a star appeared in the east and three wise men came over the hill. I'll be darned if I'm going to miss it this time!"

[pregnant]

Matthew 2:1

A little boy excited about his part in the Christmas play came home and said: "I got a part in the Christmas play!"

"What part?" asked his mother.

"I'm one of the three wise guys!" was the reply.

[Christmas, wise]

Matthew 2:1

It's an indictment on our unbiblical society that many businessmen think the Three Wise Men are the guys who got out of the stock market at the right time.

[business, wise]

Matthew 2:1

In a small southern town I saw a wonderful "Nativity Scene," but one feature bothered me. The three wise men were wearing firemen's helmets. Unable to come up with a reason or explanation, I left. At a gas station on the edge of town, I asked the lady behind the counter about the helmets. She exploded into a rage, yelling at me, "You darn Yankees never do read the Bible!"

I assured her that I did, but simply couldn't recall anything about firemen in the Bible.

She jerked her Bible from behind the counter and ruffled through some pages, and finally jabbed her finger at a passage. Sticking it in my face she said, "See, it says right here, 'The three wise men came from afar [a fire].'"

[Christmas]

Matthew 2:1

See Luke 2:34.

Matthew 2:1

What if it had been Three Wise Women instead of Three Wise Men?

They would have:

Asked directions,

Arrived on time,

Helped deliver the baby,

Cleaned the stable,

Made a casserole, and

Brought practical gifts!

[Christmas, gifts]

Matthew 2:2

When it comes to road maps, you can't beat following a star. It's simple, it's clear, and you don't have to refold it!

[directions]

Matthew 2:5

A man went to the local church and asked to join. The preacher said, "Ok, but you have to pass a small Bible test first. The first question is "Where was Jesus born?"
The man answered, "Longview."
The preacher said, "Sorry...you can't join our church."
Soooooo....he went to another church and asked to join. The preacher said, "We would love to have you but you have to pass a Bible test first. Where was Jesus born?"
The man said "Tyler."
The preacher said "Sorry ... you can't join our church."
Soooo ... .he goes to another church and asked to join. The preacher said, "That's great! We welcome you with open arms."
The man said, "I don't have to pass no Bible test first?"
The preacher said, "No."
The man said, "Can I ask you a question?"
The preacher said, "Sure."
The man said, "Where was Jesus born?"
The preacher said, "Palestine."
The man mumbled to himself "I knew it was in East Texas somewhere."

[geography]

Matthew 2:7-8

Some children, all in their early school years, got out of line while putting on a Christmas pageant in church. It was disconcerting.
Thirteen of them were to walk across the stage, each carrying a letter-bearing placard. All together — if they were in correct order and in line — spelled: B-E-T-H-L-E-H-E-H-E-M S-T-A-R.
But the "star" bearers got turned around and went in backwards, so to speak, spelling out: B-E-T-H-L-E-H-E-H-E-M R-A-T-S.

[Christmas, names]

Matthew 2:9

The three wise men were on their way to Bethlehem. Suddenly, one of them ground his camel to a halt: "Now listen, guys," he said to the other two. "Remember, no mentioning how much we paid for the gifts."

[gifts, money]

Matthew 2:10

One wise man turns to another and says: "Typical! The first Christmas and we get to spend it away from home!"

[Christmas, wise]

Matthew 2:11

Teacher: "What did the three wise men bring the Christ child?"
Little girl: "Gold, Frankenstein, and mermaids."

[gifts]

Matthew 2:11

One church is so progressive, it's doing a modernized version of the Christmas story. The three wise men are bringing gift certificates!

[gifts]

Matthew 2:11

In answer to the question, "Who brought gifts to the Infant Jesus?" one little boy piped up, "A Mr. Frankincense and Mr. Goldenmyrrh."

[gifts, names]

Matthew 2:11

A Children's Church was producing the Christmas play. The teacher told her students that if they forgot their lines they should ad-lib instead of just standing there. At the big performance all went well until the three Wise Men made their entrance:
"Baby Jesus, here is your gold," said the first.
"Baby Jesus, here is your frankincense," offered the second.
The third Wise Man forgot the name of his gift and froze. "Say anything," whispered the teacher from the wings.
The boy peered into the manger and exclaimed, "Ooh, doesn't he look just like his dad!"

[Christmas]

Matthew 2:11

Myrrh — The second gift of the Magi, and a great scrabble word when you're out of vowels.

[games, gifts]

Matthew 2:11

At a Christmas three six-year-olds were playing the wise men in the nativity play. As they came up to Mary and Joseph at the stable, the first one handed over his present and said, "Gold." The second presented his gift and said,

"Myrrh." The third one then gave them his treasure and said, "And Frank sent this [frankincense]."

[gifts]

Matthew 2:11

In a cartoon by Guindon, a weary woman shopper is shown resting for a moment with her arms filled with packages. She is in the middle of a very busy department store filled with other Christmas shoppers, and she is explaining the whole Christmas scene to her small son as follows: "No one is quite sure how Christmas worked out like this, dear. Theologians are working very, very hard on that question right now."

[gifts, theology]

Matthew 2:11

See Luke 2:7.

Matthew 2:14

A lad was asked by his children's church leader to draw a picture of the holy family's flight into Egypt. So he pictured father, mother, baby and a third adult all in an airplane.
When asked why he had drawn three adults and why all were in a plane, he responded, "That's Mary and Joseph, Jesus and Pontius the Pilot on their flight to Egypt."

[names, transportation]

Matthew 2:14

A Children's Church teacher asked her class why Joseph and Mary took Jesus with them to Jerusalem. A small child replied: "They couldn't get a baby-sitter."

[baby]

Matthew 3:1

Do you know what Winnie the Pooh and John the Baptist have in common … Their middle name!

[names]

Matthew 3:2

A minister waited in line to have his car filled with gas just before a long holiday weekend. The attendant worked quickly, but there were many cars ahead of him in front of the service station. Finally, the attendant motioned him toward a vacant pump.

"Reverend," said the young man, "sorry about the delay. It seems as if everyone waits until the last minute to get ready for a long trip."
The minister chuckled, "I know what you mean. It's the same in my business."

[anticipation, heaven]

Matthew 3:8

Charity had been misbehaving and was sent to her room. After a while she emerged and informed her mother that she had thought it over and then said a prayer. "Fine," said the pleased mother. "If you ask God to help you not misbehave, He will help you."
"Oh, I didn't ask Him to help me not misbehave," said Charity. "I asked Him to help you put up with me."

[patience, prayer]

Matthew 4:18

Did you know that the disciples first baptized the Mouseketeers?
Peter, and Andrew his brother, cast Annette [a net] into the lake!

[disciples, names]

Matthew 4:19

A little boy was going through a stage where he had to wear what his friend Titus was wearing. His mother used all kinds of creative tactics to persuade him otherwise, but to no avail. One morning his mother blurted out, "Joshua, Jesus is our leader: we follow Him, not our friends!"
After a moment Joshua calmly asked, "Okay, Mom. What's He wearing?"

[clothes, imitation]

Matthew 4:24

See Mark 1:34 (KJV).

Matthew 5:1-12

Beatitudes — Sayings that look nice on a cross-stitched plaque.

[beatitudes]

Matthew 5:1-12

Beatitudes [B — attitudes] — Second-rate attitudes.

[beatitudes, grades]

Matthew 5:1-12

Blessed are the young, for they shall inherit the national debt.

[debt]

Matthew 5:1-12

Then Jesus took his disciples up the mountain and gathering them around him, he taught them saying:

Blessed are the poor in spirit for theirs is the kingdom of heaven.

Blessed are the meek.

Blessed are they that mourn.

Blessed are the merciful.

Blessed are they who thirst justice.

Blessed are you when persecuted.

Blessed are you when you suffer.

Be glad and rejoice for your reward is great in heaven ...

Then Simon Peter said, "Do we have to write this down?"

And Andrew said, "Are we supposed to know this?"

And James said, "Will we have a test on it?"

And Phillip said, "What if we don't know it?"

And Bartholomew said, "Do we have to turn this in?"

And John said, "The other disciples didn't have to learn this."

And Matthew said, "When do we get out of here?"

And Judas said, "What does this have to do with the real life?"

Then one of the Pharisees present asked to see Jesus' Lesson plans and inquired of Jesus his terminal objectives in the cognitive domain ... and Jesus wept.

OR

Why Teachers Weep

Jesus took his disciples up on the mountain and gathered them around Him.

And then He taught them, saying:

Blessed are the poor in spirit,

Blessed are the meek,

Blessed are the merciful,

Blessed are you who thirst for justice,

Blessed are you who are persecuted,

Blessed are the peacemakers.

And Simon Peter said, "Do we have to write this stuff down?"

And Philip said, "Will this be on the test?"

And Andrew said, "John the Baptist's disciples don't have to learn this stuff."

And Matthew said, "Huh?"

And Judas said, "When am I ever going to use this in real life?"

198

Then one of the Pharisees, an expert in law, said, "I don't see any of this in the syllabus. Do you have a lesson plan? Is there an activity for each of the seven intelligences? Where is the study guide? Will there be any authentic assessment? Will remediation and extra credit be provided for those who did not meet class requirements so they can still pass?"

And Thomas, who had missed the sermon, came to Jesus privately and said, "Did we do anything important today?"

AND JESUS WEPT.

[disciples, Pharisee, students, teachers]

Matthew 5:1-12

See Luke 6:20.

Matthew 5:1-11

Christians believe the Bible is a resource for all ages. However a few churches have updated "The Beatitudes" ... originally presented at the "Sermon on the Mount"

* Blessed are the poor in spirit, they are rife consumers for all manner of inspirational products and fair game for the televangelists/marketers

* Blessed are those who mourn, for they too shall spend great sums with regard to various memorials, remembrances and all manner of laminated items. Forget them not on the anniversary of their sorrow; for what profit it a man not to follow-up initial sales and thus forego many years of future purchases

* Blessed are the meek, they complain not concerning low wages or poor working conditions; neither shall they raise their voices in protest over shoddy workmanship or substandard products

* Blessed are those who hunger and thirst, for they are following their "low fat" diets in strict accordance with their physician's wishes

* Blessed are the merciful, for they shall forgive your sexual harassment and file not a discrimination suit; neither shall they contact the EEO or ACLU, nor congregate in demonstrations and protests

* Blessed are the pure in heart, for surely, their cholesterol shall be the lowest in the land; neither shall their arteries clog. Strike fear into their minds, then they will purchase all manner of drugs, herbs and potions so they may maintain their purity

* Blessed are the peacemakers, for the profits from "peace-keeping" armaments shall be ten-fold that of those gun merchants who would wage war

* Blessed are those who are persecuted, their names shall be entered in nomination for political office and even the least among them shall be appointed to positions of authority

* Blessed are you when men revile you and persecute you, for you shall be known as President of the United States, or some governor thereof, whereas citizens of other lands shall be known as despots
* Rejoice and be glad, for verily I say unto you — the Consumer Confidence Index is at an all time high; tax surpluses are everywhere, as far as the eye can see; unemployment is at an all time low and the stock markets are as high as the interest rates are low; again, I say "Rejoice"
* Your reward is great in Heaven ... be ever mindful of the fact that the keepers of the records are compounding daily the interest on the treasures you have stored there
* It is no longer good for anything to be thrown out, be joyful concerning the money-making opportunities in the recycling fervor sweeping all mankind
Let your light so shine before men, this I say unto you, even if you should fail to become a leading merchant among men with profit-margins unforeseen, there is untold wealth and fame for a great multitude of financial advisors, consultants and tax experts.

[beatitudes]

Matthew 5:1

Teacher: "Does anyone know where to find the Beatitudes?"
Boy: "Did you try the Yellow Pages?"

[beatitudes]

Matthew 5:3

A beatitude for young ministers, "Blessed is he who expects nothing, for he shall never be disappointed."

[contentment]

Matthew 5:5

God sure will have to change a few things in the future if business is to survive. After all, if the meek inherit the earth, who's going to collect the bills?

[business]

Matthew 5:5

Kids in Children's Church are often asked to memorize passages from the Sermon on the Mount, and a little girl proudly recited it like this for her family: "Blessed are the poor in spirit, for theirs is the kingdom of heaven. Blessed are they that mourn, for they shall be comforted. Blessed are the meek, for they shall ... they shall ... they shall come home, dragging their tails behind them."

[discouragement]

Matthew 5:6

The three children usually were able to persuade their dad to take them to a fast-food restaurant right after church. One Sunday he protested, "Where does it say in the Bible that you should always get something to eat and drink after church?"

A quick-thinking daughter replied, "Where it says, 'Blessed are those who hunger and thirst after righteousness.'"

[food, hunger]

Matthew 5:7

See John 8:11.

Matthew 5:9

A beatitude posted in a cardiologist's office "Blessed are the pacemakers!"

[doctors]

Matthew 5:9

Blessed are the peace-makers, for they shall never be numbered amongst the unemployed.

[peace]

Matthew 5:12

See 1 Corinthians 3:14.

Matthew 5:22

A very foul-mouthed man met the local pastor on the street one day and said, "Now, where in hell have I seen you? To which the pastor replied, "From where in hell do you come, sir?"

[hell]

Matthew 5:39

At an adult Bible study the leader asked the group to think of everyday ways in which we could practice the Sermon on the Mount. The topic on driving courtesy came up first. "How do you respond to the driver who rudely cuts you off?" the leader asked.

A woman responded, "I turn the other fender!"

[forgiveness, revenge]

Matthew 5:39

A Quaker became exasperated with his cow for kicking over a pail of milk. He warned, "Thou knowest that, because of my religion, I can't punish thee. But if thee doeth that again, I will sell thee to a Baptist preacher and he will kick thee so thee won't be able to kick it over again!"

[consequences, pacifist]

Matthew 5:39

An irate father broke up a fight between his two sons and demanded to know who started it.
"I thought I had made it clear, that I will tolerate no fighting," he shouted. "Now, which one of you started it?"
"He did," replied his firstborn son. "It wasn't a fight until he hit me back."

[fighting]

Matthew 5:39

Turn the other cheek — The rule of thumb when the other guy is bigger.

[revenge]

Matthew 5:48

Preacher: "Does anyone know anyone who is perfect?"
A little man in the back of the church raised his hand.
Preacher: "And who do you know that is perfect?"
Little man: "My wife's first husband."

[perfection]

Matthew 6:2

A hypocrite is a person who pretends to be burying the hatchet when he's only digging up dirt.

[hypocrisy]

Matthew 6:3

A biblical piano player: one whose left hand doesn't know what his right hand is doing.

[music, unaware]

Matthew 6:5

After attending a prayer meeting where everyone prayed very loud a little boy remarked, "If they lived nearer to God they wouldn't have to pray so loud."

[noise, prayer]

Matthew 6:5

It was an exceptionally hot day, and they were having company for dinner.
Mother asked five-year-old Joshua to say the prayer before they ate.
"But what should I say?" asked Joshua.
"Just say what you've heard me say," said his mother.
Little Joshua bowed his head and said, "Dear Lord, why did I ever invite
people over on a hot day like this?"

[complain, prayer]

Matthew 6:5

A man had a habit of grumbling at the food his wife placed before him at
family meals. Then he would ask the blessing. One day after his usual
combination complaint-prayer, his little girl asked, "Daddy, does God hear
us when we pray?"
"Why, of course," he replied. "He hears us every time we pray."
She thought about this for a moment, and then asked, "Does he hear
everything we say the rest of the time?"
"Yes, dear, every word," he replied, encouraged that he had inspired his
daughter to be curious about spiritual matters. However, his pride was
quickly turned to humility when she asked:
"Then which does God believe?"

[hypocrisy, prayer]

Matthew 6:6

Attending church with her mother for the first time, a little girl was awed
by everything. When the congregation knelt, she asked what the people
were doing. "Saying their prayers," her mother whispered.
The child looked around in amazement, then turned again to her mother to
ask: "Saying their prayers with all their clothes on?"

[clothes, prayer]

Matthew 6:6

The child knelt at his bed to say his prayer. Mother, waiting in the hallway,
called, "I can't hear you praying."
"It doesn't matter, Mom," said the little boy. "But I wasn't speaking to you."

[prayer]

Matthew 6:7

Pharisee: "It's terrible for a man like you to make every other word an
oath."
Israelite: "Oh, well, I swear a good deal and you pray a good deal, but we
don't neither of us mean nuthin' by it."

[Pharisee, prayer, swearing]

Matthew 6:9

Too many people who say, "Our Father" on Sunday, spend the rest of the week acting like orphans.

[hypocrisy]

Matthew 6:9

Our Father, Who art in heaven, hello! What be thy name?"

[Father, prayer]

Matthew 6:9

"Pilot to tower ... pilot to tower ... I am 300 miles from land ... 600 feet in the air and running out of gas ... please instruct ... over."
"Tower to pilot ... tower to pilot ... repeat after me ... repeat after me ... 'Our father who art in heaven ...'"

[prayer]

Matthew 6:9

It's no use. Art doesn't listen to me," said the little boy who was praying for a new bike. "Art who?" asked the boy's mother.
"Art in heaven," came the reply.

[prayer]

Matthew 6:9

Our Father, Who are in heaven, Hollywood be Thy name.

[Father]

Matthew 6:9

A mother told her son to get into his bed and to pray before he went to sleep. He came out shortly later because something was puzzling him. He was anxious to find out who Harold was. The mother was also puzzled and asked, "Where did you learn about him?"
The son answered, "In church of course. You know, 'Our Father, Who art in heaven, Harold be his name.'"

[prayer]

Matthew 6:9

A Children's Church teacher began her lesson with a question. "Boys and girls, what do we know about God?"
A hand shot up in the air. "He is an artist!" said the kindergarten boy.
"Really?! How do you know?" the teacher asked.

"You know – 'Our Father, who does art in Heaven ...'"

[art, God]

Matthew 6:9-13

Two lawyers were bosom buddies. Much to the amazement of one, the other decided to go to Seminary. "I bet you don't even know the Lord's Prayer," the first one fumed.

"Everybody knows that," the other replied. "It's 'Now I lay me down to sleep ...'"

"You win," said the first one admiringly. "I didn't know you knew so much about the Bible."

[knowledge, lawyers, prayer]

Matthew 6:10

A lawyer was approached by his priest who wanted a will drawn up. When the work was completed and ready to be picked up, the lawyer couldn't resist sending this brief note to his priest, "Thy Will Be Done."

[lawyers, priest]

Matthew 6:11

Children's Church teacher: "Why in your prayers do you only ask for your daily bread instead of asking enough for a week?"

Boy: "I guess it's so we can get it fresh every day."

[food, prayers]

Matthew 6:11

The wife of an advertising copywriter put her small son to bed and told him. "Now, Chase, say your prayers."

"Oh, Lord," mumbled the little fellow, "please bless mama and daddy, and give us this day our slow-rising, oven-baked, vitamin-enriched bread."

[food, prayers]

Matthew 6:11

Give us this day our daily breath.

[life]

Matthew 6:11

Give us this day our jelly bread.

[food]

Matthew 6:11

During a Papal audience, a business man approached the Pope and made this offer: "Change the last line of the Lord's prayer from "give us this day our daily bread" to "give us this day our daily chicken." And KFC will donate 10 million dollars to Catholic charities."

The Pope declined. 2 weeks later the man approached the Pope again. This time with a 50 million dollar offer. Again the Pope declined. A month later the man offers 100 million, this time the Pope accepts. At a meeting of the Cardinals, The Pope announces his decision in the good news/bad news format. "The good news is ... that we have 100 million dollars for charities. The bad news is that we lost the Wonder Bread account!"

[Catholic, food, greed, prayer]

Matthew 6:11

Mr. Bouncer, an American manufacturer who had obtained an interview with the Pope, was overheard to offer $1,000,000 to the Pope in return for a favor. But the Pope said, "No," with amazement and indignation.

When the American had gone, the Cardinal, thinking that $1,000,000 could achieve a great amount of good, asked the Pope why he had refused.

"Oh," said the Pope, "he wished me to change two words in the Lord's Prayer."

"Only two words?" exclaimed the Cardinal.

"Yes," replied the Pope. "He wanted me to change 'daily bread' to 'Bouncer's Wheat-flakes.'"

[food, prayer]

Matthew 6:12

Sign in lot: CHURCH PARKING ONLY. WE WILL NOT FORGIVE THOSE WHO TRESPASS AGAINST US.

[mercy]

Matthew 6:12

A four-year-old fashioned his prayer after what he thought he heard in church. "And forgive us our trash-baskets as we forgive those who passed trash against us."

[forgiveness, misunderstanding]

Matthew 6:12

A small boy, repeating the Lord's Prayer one evening prayed: "And forgive us our debts as we forgive those who are dead against us."

[death, debts]

Matthew 6:13

Lead us not into creation but deliver us from weevils.

[insects]

Matthew 6:13

"Lead us not into temptation. Just tell us where it is — we'll find it."

[temptation]

Mathew 6:13

A mother was teaching her three-year-old daughter The Lord's Prayer. For several evenings at bedtime, she repeated it after her mother. One night she said she was ready to solo. The mother listened with pride, as she carefully enunciated each word right up to the end.

"And lead us not into temptation", she prayed, "but deliver us some e-mail, Amen."

[prayer]

Matthew 6:13

Temptation — A condition conducive to sinning — for most people, just being conscious.

[sin, temptation]

Matthew 6:13

A driver tucked this note under the windshield wiper of this automobile: "I've circled the block for twenty minutes. I'm late for an appointment, and if I don't park here I'll lose my job. 'Forgive us our trespasses.'"

When he came back he found a parking ticket and this note: "I've circled the block for twenty years, and if I don't give you a ticket, I'll lose my job. 'Lead us not into temptation.'"

[forgiveness, temptation]

Matthew 6:15

Alice and Mildred, two sisters kept up a feud for thirty years. On Mildred's seventieth birthday, Alice, who was seventy-five, felt a pang of remorse, but it passed. Yet later, when she heard Mildred was ill, she felt compelled to visit.

From her sickbed, Mildred looked sternly at her sister. At last she said in a faint voice, "The doctors say I'm seriously ill, Alice. If I pass away, I want you to know you're forgiven. But if I pull through, things stay as they are!"

[bitterness, forgiveness]

Matthew 6:24

See Luke 16:13.

Matthew 6:26

God gives every bird his food, but he doesn't throw it into the nest.

[work]

Matthew 6:28

See Luke 12:27.

Matthew 6:30

See Matthew 25:35.

Matthew 6:34

Today is the tomorrow you worried about yesterday.

[worry]

Matthew 7:1

Moe and Lenny are strolling home from the synagogue one Saturday morning. Suddenly a cab speeds past, and their friend, Irving, is running frantically behind it, flailing his arms wildly.

"Well," said Lenny, "I never imagined our good friend Irving was a Sabbath violator! Look at him running for that taxi."

"Wait a minute," Moe replied. "Didn't you read that book I lent you, 'The Other Side of the Story', about the command to judge other people favorably? I'll bet we can think of hundreds of excuses for Irving's behavior."

"Yeah, like what?"

"Maybe he's sick and needs to go to the hospital."

"Come on! He was running 60 miles an hour after that cab — he's healthier than any athlete."

"Well, maybe his wife's having a baby."

"She had one last week."

"Well, maybe he needs to visit her in the hospital."

"She's home."

"Well, maybe he's running to the hospital to get a doctor."

"He is a doctor."

"Well, maybe he needs supplies from the hospital."

"The hospital is a three minute walk in the opposite direction."

"Well, maybe he forgot that it's the Sabbath!"

"Of course he knows it's Sabbath. Didn't you see his tie? It was his paisley beige 100% silk Giovanni tie from Italy. He never wears it during the week."

"Wow, you're really observant! I didn't even notice he was wearing a tie."
"How could you not notice? Didn't you see how it was caught on the back fender of the taxi?"

[judging, Sabbath]

Matthew 7:3-5

A lady was showing a church friend her neighbor's wash through her back window. "Our neighbor isn't very clean. Look at those streaks on the wash!" Replied her friend, "Those streaks aren't on your neighbor's wash. They're on your window."

[judging]

Matthew 7:5,7

The hypocrite believes that life is what you fake it.

[hypocrisy]

Matthew 7:6

Interrupted by the sound of the bell announcing the end of the class, the professor was annoyed to see the students noisily preparing to leave even though he was in the middle of his lecture. "Just a moment, class," he said, "I have a few more pearls to cast."

[context]

Matthew 7:7

When a pastor was asked to comment on the new Administrative Assistant he had hired, he replied, "She's what one might call a biblical secretary. She uses the 'seek-and-ye-shall-find' method."

[lost]

Matthew 7:12

See Luke 6:31.

Matthew 7:12

The minister had a special filing drawer for his bills. It was labeled: "DUE UNTO OTHERS."

[debts]

Matthew 7:12

Always remember we are here to help others," said a mother as she explained the Golden Rule.
Her little one meditated for a moment and inquired, "Well, what are the others here for?"

[kindness, selfish]

Matthew 7:12

The kids were fighting again and the mother shouted from the kitchen where she was working, "Stop that fighting. Haven't I told you to go by the Golden Rule?"

"Yes," came a voice from the recreation room, "but he did it unto me first."

[revenge]

Matthew 7:12

Dear GOD,
Did you really mean "do unto others as they do unto you"?
Because if you did, then I'm going to fix my brother!
Sincerely,
Tyrone

[revenge]

Matthew 7:12

Sign on a high-rise condominium: "Do under others as you would have them do under you."

[kindness]

Matthew 7:12

A noted astronomer found a bishop seated next to him on an airplane. In the course of conversation, the astronomer said, "I never had much interest in theology. My religion can be summed up in 'Do unto others as you would have them do unto you.'"

The bishop responded, "Well, I've had little time for astronomy. My views about it are summed up in 'Twinkle, twinkle, little star.'"

[simple]

Matthew 7:13

One reason the way of the transgress can sometimes be so hard is because it's so crowded.

[sin]

Matthew 7:13-14

The disappointing thing about going the straight and narrow path is that you so seldom meet anybody you know."

[friends, lonely]

Matthew 7:21

Notice in church bulletin: The church dinner was like Heaven. Many we expected to see were absent.

[heaven]

Matthew 7:21

"I wonder what we'll wear in heaven," a lady said to her next door neighbor.

"I know what I'll wear if we are there together," her friend said.

"What is that?" the first lady asked.

"A surprised look," her friend said.

[clothes, heaven]

Matthew 7:21

A senator and a minister arrived at the pearly gates at the same time. Saint Peter threw open the gates and shouted, "He's here! He's here!" As he led the politician inside, trumpets began to sound, flutes began to play, and a chorus of angels sang a celestial greeting.

In the excitement, the minister was knocked down and the pearly gates slammed in his face. He knocked again. Saint Peter opened the gates, and let him in.

"Saint Peter," cried the minister, "I have served God all my life, and dedicated myself to the salvation of mankind, yet you ignore me and give a great welcome to a politician!"

"Oh, I'm so terribly sorry," explained Peter. "See, we get a great many ministers up here, but this is the first Senator we've ever had!"

[heaven, politics]

Matthew 8:12

An evangelist was exhorting his hearers to flee the wrath to come. "I warn you," he thundered, "that there will be weeping, and wailing and gnashing of teeth!"

At this point an old lady in the balcony stood up. "Sir," she shouted, "I have no teeth."

"Madam," roared the evangelist, "teeth will be provided."

OR

A preacher of the old school was describing the events of Judgment Day and, of course, he used Biblical phraseology whenever he could.

"Oh, my friends," he intoned, "imagine the suffering of the sinners as they find themselves cast into the outer darkness, removed from the presence of the Lord and given to eternal flames. My friends, at such a time there will be weeping, wailing and a great gnashing of teeth!"

At this point, one of the elders of the congregation interrupted to say, "But Reverend, what if one of those hopeless sinners has no teeth?"

The preacher crashed his fist on the pulpit, "My friends, the Lord is not put out by details. Rest assured ... teeth will be provided!"

[hell, judgment]

Matthew 8:14-15

QUESTION: Why do some men think Peter denied Jesus?
ANSWER: Jesus healed his mother-in-law.

[mother-in-law]

Matthew 8:14

You look sad, Fred, what's the trouble?"
"Domestic trouble."
"But you're always bragging that your wife is a pearl!"
"She really is. It's the mother-of-pearl that's giving me trouble!"

[mother-in-law]

Matthew 8:16

A revival was being conducted by a muscular preacher. He was disturbed by several young men who scoffed at everything they saw or heard.

He paused and asked them why they attended the meeting. "We came to see a miracle performed," impudently replied one of them.

Leaving the pulpit and walking quietly down the aisle, the minister seized one after the other by the collar, and as they disappeared out of the door, remarked: "We don't perform miracles here, but we do cast out demons!"

[demon, miracles]

Matthew 8:22

Impatient preacher announced to the congregation "Crying babies and disruptive children, like good intentions, should be carried out immediately."

[babies, intentions]

Matthew 8:32

See Mark 5:13 (KJV).

Matthew 9:9

Remember Matthew the tax collector? They called him Levi for shorts.

[clothes]

Matthew 9:9

According to ancient tradition, the Gospel of Matthew was written by a tax-collector, and if this is true, the clarity and the simplicity of this Gospel comes as a surprise to anyone who reads it. Imagine, a Gospel written by a tax collector! What do you suppose a gospel written by the IRS might sound like today?

[taxes]

Matthew 10:1

Graffiti for the wall of a Christian college — IF GOD HAD WANTED US TO USE THE METRIC SYSTEM, HE WOULD HAVE CHOSEN TEN DISCIPLES.

[disciples, numbers]

Matthew 10:2-4

Jesus, Son of Joseph
Woodcrafters Carpenter Shop
Nazareth 25922
Dear Sir:
Thank you for submitting the resumes of the twelve men you have picked for management positions in your new organization. All of them have now taken our battery of tests; and we have not only run the results through our computer, but have also arranged personal interviews for each of them without psychologist and vocational aptitude consultant.
The profiles of all the tests are included, and you will want to study each of them carefully.
As part of our service and for your guidance, we make some general comments much as an auditor will include some general statements. This is given as a result of staff consultation and comes without any additional fee.
It is the staff opinion that most of your nominees are lacking in background, education and vocational aptitude for the type of enterprise you are undertaking. They do not have the team concept. We would recommend that you continue your search for persons of experience in managerial ability and proven capability.
Simon Peter is emotionally unstable and given to fits of temper. Andrew has absolutely no qualities of leadership. The two brothers, James and John, the sons of Zebedee, place personal interest above company loyalty. Thomas demonstrates a questioning attitude that would tend to undermine morale. We feel that it is our duty to tell you that Matthew has been blacklisted by the Greater Jerusalem Better Business Bureau. James, son of Alpheus, and Thaddeus definitely have radical leanings, and they both registered a high-score on the manic-depressive scale.

One of the candidates, however, shows great potential. He is a man of ability and resourcefulness, meets people well, has a keen business mind and has contacts in high places. He is highly motivated, ambitious, and responsible. We recommend Judas Iscariot as your controller and right-hand man. All of the other profiles are self- explanatory.
We wish you every success in your new venture
Sincerely yours,
Jordan Management Consultant

[disciples]

Matthew 10:6

Why can't missionaries get to sleep at night? They count lost sheep.

[missions, sleep]

Matthew 10:10

Burglar: "One move and you're dead. I'm looking for your money".
Poor Minister: "Hang on, let me get a light and I'll help you".

[ministry, poverty]

Matthew 10:19

A young man was asked to preach just before the morning service at a Bible conference. The regular speaker had not shown up for the service.
This young man was scared to death. He wasn't prepared and didn't know what to say.
He went to the bishop's tent and said, "What will I do? I have no sermon. What will I do?"
The bishop said, "Trust in the Lord, Son, trust in the Lord." The bishop then left for an appointment.
In desperation, he picked up the bishop's Bible and found a nice set of typewriter notes, so he took them and preached the bishop's sermon.
Everyone was amazed. The people crowded around him and told him what a great sermon it was.
Then came the bishop. "Young man," he said, "you preached my sermon — the one I had prepared for tonight. What am I going to do tonight?"
With much dignity, the young man replied, "Trust in the Lord, bishop, just trust in the Lord."

[hypocrisy, trust]

Matthew 10:28

A minister in Florida lamented that it was difficult to get his message across to his congregation: "It's so beautiful here in the winter," he said, "that heaven doesn't interest them."

"And it's so hot here in the summer that hell doesn't scare them."

[heaven, hell]

Matthew 10:30

Child: "Mother, what number is this hair I pulled out?"
Mother: "Child, I don't know."
Child: "Well, the Bible says that the hairs of your head are all numbered."

[hair, numbers]

Matthew 11:19 (KJV)

The seventh grade lesson dealt with the publican and the sinner. Asked the teacher, "What is a publican?"
Answered one of his wiser students: "The opposite of a democrat."

[politics]

Matthew 11:19

Jews don't recognize Jesus as the Son of God.
Protestants don't recognize the pope as the Ruler of the Church.
Baptists don't recognize each other in a liquor store.

[denominations]

Matthew 12:2

A Jew, a Christian and a Muslim were having a discussion about who was the most religious.
"I was riding my camel in the middle of the Sahara," exclaimed the Muslim. "Suddenly a fierce sandstorm appeared from nowhere. I truly thought my end had come as I lay next to my camel while we were being buried deeper and deeper under the sand. But I did not lose my faith in the Almighty Allah, I prayed and prayed and suddenly, for a hundred meters all around me, the storm had stopped. Since that day I am a devout Muslim and am now learning to recite the Koran by memory."
"One day while fishing," started the Christian, "I was in my little dinghy in the middle of the ocean. Suddenly a fierce storm appeared from nowhere. I truly thought my end had come as my little dinghy was tossed up and down in the rough ocean. But I did not lose my faith in Jesus Christ, I prayed and prayed and suddenly, for 300 meters all around me, the storm had stopped. Since that day I am a devout Christian and am now teaching young children about Him."
"One day I was walking down the road," explained the Jew, "I was in my most expensive designer outfit in the middle of New York city. Suddenly I saw a black bag on the ground in front of me appear from nowhere. I put my hand inside and found a million dollars in cash. I truly thought my end

had come as it was a Saturday and we are not allowed to handle money on Saturdays. But I did not lose my faith in Yahweh, I prayed and prayed and suddenly, for 500 meters all around me, it was Tuesday!"

[denominations]

Matthew 12:13

The number of times the average man says "No" to temptation is once weakly.

[temptation]

Matthew 12:25

You must admit though, a house divided does bring in more rent.

[division, money]

Matthew 12:34

Be careful of your thoughts — they may break into words at any time!

[speech]

Matthew 12:36

Dear GOD,
Is it true my father won't get in Heaven if he uses his bowling words in the house?
Sincerely,
Anita

[swearing]

Matthew 12:38

So it seems that these four rabbis had a series of theological arguments, and three were always in accord against the fourth. One day, the odd rabbi out, after the usual "3 to 1, majority rules" statement that signified that he had lost again, decided to appeal to a higher authority.
"Oh, God!" he cried. "I know in my heart that I am right and they are wrong! Please give me a sign to prove it to them!"
It was a beautiful, sunny day. As soon as the rabbi finished his prayer, a storm cloud moved across the sky above the four. It rumbled once and dissolved. "A sign from God! See, I'm right, I knew it!" But the other three disagreed, pointing out that storm clouds form on hot days.
So the rabbi prayed again: "Oh, God, I need a bigger sign to show that I am right and they are wrong. So please, God, a bigger sign!" This time four storm clouds appeared, rushed toward each other to form one big cloud, and a bolt of lightning slammed into a tree on a nearby hill.

"I told you I was right!" cried the rabbi, but his friends insisted that nothing had happened that could not be explained by natural causes.

The rabbi was getting ready to ask for a "very big" sign, but just as he said, "Oh God ... ," the sky turned pitch black, the earth shook, and a deep, booming voice intoned, "HEEEEEEEE'S RIIIIIIGHT!"

The rabbi put his hands on his hips, turned to the other three, and said, "Well?"

"So," shrugged one of the other rabbis, "now it's 3 to 2."

[frustration]

Matthew 12:38

See Mark 16:17.
See Luke 11:16.

Matthew 12:39

The Bible College president had just dedicated an expensive sign for the campus entrance, which was immediately stolen by the senior class and hidden away. After searching for several days, the president found the sign and hid it elsewhere. Then he informed the senior class that unless the sign was returned by that Saturday night, they would lose all their privileges. That Sunday, he appeared in chapel before the glum and unsuccessful seniors and read the morning's text: "A wicked adulterous generation seeketh for a sign and there shall be none given unto them."

[signs, students]

Matthew 12:44

New Christian: What happens if you don't pay your exorcist?
Newer Christian: You get repossessed.

[devil]

Matthew 13:10

QUESTION: How do we know that Jesus raised cattle?
ANSWER: Because he used a pair 'o' bulls (Parables).

[parables]

Matthew 13:31

QUESTION: Who is the shortest person in the Bible?
ANSWER: Bildad the Shuhite! ... or ...
ANSWER: Knee High Miah! ... or ...
ANSWER: Peter (when he slept on his watch) ... or ...
ANSWER: Jesus (when He spoke on a mustard seed)

[size]

Matthew 13:42

The chilly weather made her think of her poor dead husband. He was always cold. Poor man, he used to wonder if ever he would get warmed through. He was so miserable when he was cold. But it gives her great comfort to know that he is hot and happy now.

[hell]

Matthew 14:10

"I never thought Salome would do it," mused John the Baptist <u>absentmind</u>edly.

[puns]

Matthew 14:6-8

A denominational Church Superintendent visited a church to help the new pastor administer communion for his first time. The Pastor, a young progressive, approved a liturgical dance during the service and the Superintendent was not advised. During the dance a young lady in flowing robes floated across the sanctuary and in the middle of the dance she presented the Superintendent with a rose. He was thoroughly embarrassed. As she continued her dance the Superintendent leaned over to the Pastor and whispered: "You know of course that if she asks for your head — she will get it."

[embarrassment]

Matthew 14:6-10

During an ethics class, the lesson centered on the problem of King Herod offering up half his kingdom to see the daughter of Herodias dance.
"Now, what if you had this problem and you made the offer of anything she wanted and the girl came to you asking for the head of John the Baptist, and you didn't want to give her the head of John. What would you do?" asked the teacher.
Soon a hand was raised, "I tell her," said one student, "that the head of John the Baptist was not in the half of the kingdom I was offering to her."

[wisdom]

Matthew 14:13-21

See Mark 6:32-44.
See John 6:9.

Matthew 14:25

Two laymen took their pastor on a fishing trip to their favorite fishing place. Upon rowing out to where they wanted to fish one discovered he had left his bait ashore. Unperturbed he stepped carefully out of the boat and walked across the water to get it. The pastor looked on with amazement but since the second laymen didn't seem to express any amazement he kept quiet. Shortly after the first had come back the second discovered he needed new line and also stepped out of the boat and walked to shore to get some more. Well, upon his return, the pastor wanting to demonstrate to his laymen that he too had faith as strong as theirs announced he too would walk on water to go get some refreshment for them. But upon stepping out of the boat, he immediately sank. The two laymen looked at each other and one finally said, "Perhaps we should have told him where the rocks are?"

[faith]

Matthew 14:25

Josh had heard a family rumor that his father, his grandfather and even his great-grandfather, all "walked on water" on their 21st birthday. Well today was his 21st birthday and if they could do it, so could he.

So, off he went in a boat with his friend Jake on calm, mid-July morning. When he got out in the middle of the lake, he got up and stepped out of the boat ... and nearly drowned.

The next day, Josh asked his grandmother why he wasn't given the same gift as the others in his family. The grandmother told him that his father, grandfather and great-grandfather had all been born up north, in February.

[faith, misunderstanding]

Matthew 14:25

Heard some two thousand years ago at the Sea of Galilee from the lips of an irreligious fisherman: "I don't care who your father is! You're not going to walk where I'm fishing!"

[frustration]

Matthew 14:30

Little Dennis began falling out of a tree and remembering his Bible verse of the week cried, "Lord, save me!"

There was a pause and then he said, "Never mind, Lord, my pants just caught on a branch."

[faith, prayer]

Matthew 14:30

A man named Smith was sitting on his roof during a flood, and the water was up to his feet. Before long a fellow in a canoe paddled past and shouted, "Can I give you a lift to higher ground?"

"No, thanks," said Smith. "I have faith in the Lord and he will save me."

A short while later a rowboat came by and again the man was offered a ride to dry land but once again he turned it down declaring his faith in the Lord. Later a helicopter flew by, and Smith was now standing on the roof with water up to his neck. "Grab the rope," yelled the pilot. "I'll pull you up." "No, thanks," said Smith. "I have faith in the Lord and he will save me." But after hours of treading water, poor exhausted? Smith drowned and went to his reward. As he arrived at the Pearly Gates, Smith met his maker and complained about this turn of events. "Tell me, Lord," he said, "I had such faith in you to save me and you let me down. What happened?" To which the Lord replied, "What do you want from me? I sent you two boats and a helicopter!"

[faith, foolishness, heaven]

Matthew 14:30

The way it DIDN'T happen!
Jesus saw Peter get out of the boat and after taking three steps on the water begin to sink into the Sea of Galilee.
"Lord, save me," screamed Peter.
"What seems to be your trouble?' the Lord asked quietly.
"Help! Help! I can't swim!" screamed Peter.
"Well, son, now is your chance to learn," Jesus replied.

[faith, foolishness]

Matthew 15:6

An influential lady had been a member of First Baptist church for twenty-five years. After the service, as she walked toward the pastor who stood waiting at the sanctuary door, it was obvious that she had something on her mind. She complained, "Reverend, if God were alive today, He would be shocked at the changes in this church!"

[tradition]

Matthew 15:7

One Sunday morning during service, a 2,000 member congregation was surprised to see two men enter, both covered from head to toe in black and carrying submachine guns. One of the men proclaimed, "Anyone willing to take a bullet for Christ remain where you are."
Immediately, the choir fled, the deacons fled, and most of the congregation fled. Out of the 2,000 there only remained around 20.
The man who had spoken took off his hood, looked at the preacher and said "Okay Pastor, I got rid of all the hypocrites. Now you may begin your service. Have a nice day!" And the two men turned and walked out.

[hypocrisy]

Matthew 15:19

"Sects! Sects! Sects! Said one monk to another. "Is that all you think about?"

[cults, sex]

Matthew 16:1

A Pharisee asked a disciple what a miracle was. A full explanation did not satisfy the man. Smiling at his fellow Pharisees, he said to the disciple, "Now, won't you give me an example of a miracle?"
"Well," said the disciple, "step before me and I'll see what I can do." As the man did so, the disciple gave him a terrific kick in the middle of his backside.
"Did you feel that?" asked the disciple.
"I sure did," replied the Pharisee.
"Well," said the disciple, "it would have been a miracle if you hadn't."

[disciples, miracle, Pharisee]

Matthew 16:13-16

The pastor of a fundamentalist Christian church was presenting to some children the children's feature in the main service before they were dismissed to their own service. He decided to enliven things up a bit by posing them a riddle: "What is it that collects nuts for winter, climbs trees, and has a bushy tail?"
An eager youngster waved her hand. The pastor called on her. "Well," she said, "I know the answers supposed to be Jesus, but it sure sounds like a squirrel to me!"

[animals, Jesus]

Matthew 16:23

One day a boy came walking home from school. On the way home he saw a creek. He quickly jumped in, clothes and all to have a little swim. When he arrived home completely soaked his dad asked, "Son what happened?"
"I jumped in that creek down the road."
"Why did you do that?"
"I dunno. Just because I guess I just wanted to swim for a while."
His dad was very angry and said, "If you jump in that creek again, just because, I'm gonna tan your hide — just because! Is that clear?"
"Yes dad." Replies his son.
The next day, the boy came home walking from school, and sure enough when he saw that creek, he jumped right on in.
When he went home, his dad knew what had happened and asked, "Didn't I tell you not to jump in that creek again?"
"Yes dad, but Satan told me to do it!"

His dad, being somewhat religious, decided to give his son the benefit of the doubt and tells him, "Next time Satan tells you to do something like that, say 'Satan get thee behind me in the name of Jesus'."

"Ok dad." Replied the son.

Well the next day after school, the boy was walking across the bridge, and well you know the rest. He came home again soaked.

His dad said, "I thought I told you what to say when you came to that creek!"

"I said what you told me dad, and when I did, Satan pushed me in!"

[Satan, temptation]

Matthew 16:23

See Mark 8:33.

Matthew 16:24

Mommy," said little Sarah, "did you ever read in the Bible about a cross-eyed bear?"

"Why no, Sarah," chuckled her mother, "but why do you ask?"

"Well, in church this morning, we sang a song about 'Gladly, the cross I'd bear'."

[Bible, hymns]

Matthew 17:2

Transfiguration of Christ — When Scotty used the wrong coordinates and almost beamed up Jesus.

[television]

Matthew 17:20

Faith is telling a mountain to move and being shocked only if it doesn't.

[faith]

Matthew 17:16

One Sunday morning a priest and a choirboy were getting the church ready for mass in a Roman Catholic church. The minister prepared his sermon while the choirboy filled the holy water fountain.

Suddenly, the choirboy burst into the minister's room and yelled, "Father, Father, I just saw the most amazing thing! I filled the holy water fountain. Then a man came in on crutches. He moved to the fountain, dipped his left hand in the holy water, blessed himself and threw away his left crutch. Then he dipped his right hand in the holy water, blessed himself and threw away his right crutch. Then he turned to me ... and he took a step forward"!

The minister was awe struck by what he just heard. "My boy," he said, "you just witnessed a miracle from God! Where's this man now?"
The Choirboy replies, "Flat on his face in front of the holy water fountain"!

[miracle]

Matthew 17:20

Two nuns were driving in the country when their car ran out of gas. Hiking to the nearest farm, they found a farmer who agreed to give them a free gallon. His only problem was he couldn't find anything clean and free of rust to put it in except an old bedpan. The nuns were grateful and headed back to their car whereupon they began to pour the gas from the bedpan into the car. Just then a Baptist preacher drove by and upon seeing what they were doing, stopped and said to the two nuns, "I may disagree with your theology but I sure do admire your faith!"

[denominations, faith, nuns]

Matthew 17:20

The substitute Children's Church teacher was struggling to open a combination lock on the supply cabinet. She had been told the combination, but couldn't quite remember it. Finally she went to the pastor's study and asked for help.
The pastor came into the room and began to turn the dial. After the first two numbers he paused and stared blankly for a moment.
Finally he look serenely heavenward and his lips moved silently.
Then he looked back at the lock, and quickly turned to the final number, and opened the lock.
The teacher was amazed. "I'm in awe at your faith, pastor," she said.
"It's really nothing," he answered somewhat embarrassed. "The number is on a piece of tape on the ceiling."

[faith, prayer]

Matthew 17:20

My wife tells me that in this day and age, nothing is impossible ... except some people.

[impossibility]

Matthew 18:9

One gratifying impression we get from modern theological discussions is that hell is not as hot as it was forty years ago — Toledo Blade.

[hell, theology]

Matthew 18:19

The minister asked his son, "Do you think the congregation reacted favorably to my sermon this morning?"

Son: "Yes, I'm sure they did, Dad. I saw several of them nodding all through your message."

[sermon, sleep]

Matthew 18:20

A woman who "enjoyed her religion" visited a very staid and formal church. "Amen" she said, as the preacher brought out a point with which she agreed.

"Madam," said the usher standing nearby, "Please try and restrain yourself. We don't allow that in this church."

In a few moments she was so carried away by the sermon that she shouted, "Amen, praise the Lord, hallelujah!"

The usher rushed to her side: "Madam! You must quiet down immediately or leave!"

"I didn't mean to disturb ... but I am just so happy since I found the Lord," she explained.

"You may have found the Lord," retorted the usher severely, "but I am quite sure you didn't find him here!"

[tradition]

Matthew 18:23-35

The kingdom of heaven is like a department chair checking on the progress of the graduate students. She came to a graduate student who was supposed to turn in his thesis that week, but had procrastinated and hadn't started to analyze data yet. The department chair reminded him that there was no more funding for him after this term. The grad student pleaded with her. "Be patient with me," he begged, "and I will finish the thesis by the deadline."

The department chair took pity on him, and told him she would let him re-enroll and would find money somewhere for another term. But when the graduate student went out, he ran into one of the undergraduates in the course he was grading. He yelled at the student, "Where is your homework? It's a day late!" The undergraduate begged him, "Be patient with me, and I will turn it in tomorrow." But the grad student refused and said, "No. I'm giving you a zero and you're failing the course!" When the other students saw what had happened, they were greatly distressed and went and told the department chair everything that had happened.

Then the chair called the graduate student in. "You wicked student," she said, "I forgave you for procrastinating on your thesis because you begged me. Shouldn't you have had mercy on the undergraduate just as I had on you?" In anger the chair expelled him from the department, to find a job until he could finish his thesis. This is how the heavenly Father will treat each of us unless we forgive our brothers from the heart.

[forgiveness]

Matthew 19:6

What a cry would ensue if people had to pay the minister as much to marry them as they have to pay a lawyer to get a divorce.

[divorce, marriage, money]

Matthew 19:6

The divorce rate would be lower if, instead of marrying for better or worse, people would marry for good.

[divorce]

Matthew 19:9

She married him because he was such a "dominating man;"
She divorced him because he was such a "dominating male."
He married her because she was so "fragile and petite;"
He divorces her because she was so "weak and helpless."
She married him because "he knows how to provide a good living;"
She divorced him because "all he thinks about is business."
He married her because "she reminds me of my mother;"
He divorced her because "she's getting more like her mother every day."
She married him because he was "happy and romantic;"
She divorced him because he was "shiftless and fun-loving."
He married her because she was "steady and sensible;"
He divorced her because she was "boring and dull."
She married him because he was "the life of the party;"
She divorced him because "he never wants to come home from a party."

[divorce, marriage]

Matthew 19:14

Advice for the day: If you have a lot of tension and you get a headache, do what it says on the aspirin bottle:
"Take two aspirin" and "Keep away from children."

[children, head]

Matthew 19:23

It's hard for a rich man to enter the kingdom of heaven, but in some churches it's still easy for him to get on the church board of trustees.

[leaders, money]

Matthew 19:24

Eye of the needle — The analogy that provides a strong incentive for rich men to breed tiny camels.

[difficulty, rich]

Matthew 19:24

See Genesis 7:9 re. Camels.

Matthew 21:8

It was Palm Sunday, and Starr's three year old son had to stay home from church because of strep throat. When the family returned home carrying palm branches, he asked what they were for. His mother explained, "People held them over Jesus' head as he walked by."
"Wouldn't you know it," the boy fumed. "The one Sunday I don't go, Jesus shows up!"

[Easter, Jesus]

Matthew 21:12

See John 2:15.

Matthew 21:22

During the minister's prayer one Sunday, there was a loud whistle from one of the back pews. Gary's mother was horrified. She pinched him into silence, and after church, asked: "Gary, whatever made you do such a thing?" Gary answered soberly: "I asked God to teach me to whistle ... And He did just then!"

[confusion, instruction, prayer]

Matthew 21:45

An editor, weary of the abuse following his editorials, decided to run the Ten Commandments in his editorial column.
A few days later came a letter: "Cancel my subscription. You're getting too personal."

[commandments, conviction]

Matthew 22:21

A preacher announced the offering. As the ushers marched forward to get the plates, the preacher commented, "Let us remember — that which we render unto God is deductible from that which we render unto Caesar."

[giving, government, honesty]

Matthew 22:23

See Mark 12:18.

Matthew 22:38

A Children's Church teacher was trying to teach her three year old age class some simple Bible truths. "What did Jesus say," she asked, "was the first and greatest commandment — the one that is the most important of all?" A three year old who had just started nursery school, puffed up himself proudly and announced, "Keep your hands to yourself."

[commandments, fighting]

Matthew 23:3

The question of the day: Is a minister rehearsing his sermon really practicing what he preaches?

[hypocrisy, sermon,]

Matthew 23:14

Poor Israelite: "There are thousands of ways of making money, but only one honest way."
Rich Pharisee: "What's that?"
Poor Israelite: "Ah-ha, I knew you wouldn't know."

[honesty, money, Pharisee]

Matthew 23:14

Children's Church teacher: "Juliet, who were the Pharisees?"
Juliet: "The Pharisees were people who fasted in public but in secret devoured widows' houses."

[Pharisee, hypocrisy]

Matthew 23:23

At the end of a wonderful service the Pastor stood outside to say goodbye to his congregation. As Mrs. McKenzie approached him he remarked; "I am sorry Mrs. McKenzie but I noticed that little Jimmy was crying throughout the service. Is he alright?". "Sure" said Mrs. McKenzie, "He's just teething". "I see" said the Pastor, "and what about your husband? I noticed he was also crying throughout the service". "He's fine" said Mrs. McKenzie, "He's just tithing."

[giving]

Matthew 23:24

A lady asked a student in the Children's Church , "What was the sin of the Pharisees?"

"Eating camels, ma'am," was the quick reply.

She had just read, of course, that the Pharisees "strained at gnats and swallowed camels!"

[animals, Pharisee, sin]

Matthew 23:28

See Galatians 2:13.

Matthew 23:33

A minister was preaching on the subject of future punishment. "Yes, my brethren," said he, "there is a hell; but," (looking at his watch) "we shall not go into that just now."

[hell]

Matthew 24:7

"There will be thunder, lighting, floods, fires and earthquakes!" roared the preacher, describing Judgment Day.

Wide-eyed, a little boy in the congregation tugged at his mother's sleeve and asked, "Will I get out of school?"

[Day of the Lord, judgment]

Matthew 25:2

The conservative, cultural society was organizing a group to be comprised strictly of virgins, when a young lady carrying a baby appeared.

"But, madam," protested the president, "that is evidence that you are not eligible for this society. Why do you think you will be able to join?"

"I was only foolin' around when this happened," she explained. "So I thought I could get in as one of those foolish virgins."

[foolish, virgin]

Matthew 25:32

A small boy was discussing with one of his buddies the minister's sermon that had been on the story of the sheep and the goats. Lamented the boy, "Me, I don't know which I am. Mother calls me her 'lamb', and Father calls me his 'kid'."

[animals, children, division]

Matthew 25:35

The con man argued that he should not be jailed because he only did as he was instructed to do in the Scriptures. The judge, unbelieving, asked the man how he could justify his crime through biblical injunction. The con man replied: "I saw the stranger, and I took him in."

[context, deceit, dishonesty]

Matthew 25:35

See Jonah 1:17.

Matthew 25:35

The proprietor of a country store, who professedly ran his business strictly on biblical principles, would always quote a Scripture verse whenever he rang up a sale on the cash register. For example, if a little boy bought some candy, the owner would say, "Mark 10:14 'Suffer the little children to come unto me and forbid them not'." If he sold a customer an article of clothing, he would say, "Matthew 6:30 'Shall he not much more clothe you, O ye of little faith?'"

One day a stranger came in, looking for a particular kind of hat. When the stranger asked if he had a more expensive hat, the owner produced a hat, which, though really the same price, he said was twenty-five dollars more. When the owner rang up the sale, and the customer departed, bystanders in the store wondered how the owner would fit this shady deal with Scripture. Finally he said, "Matthew 25:35 'He was a stranger, and I took him in.'"

OR

The owner of an old-fashioned corner grocery store in a small country town was fond of quoting a scripture after each sale. He had three old friends that would sit around a pot-bellied stove, playing checkers on a faded board. His ability to produce a scripture for all occasions never ceased to amuse the old timers, and they would listen to see what verse he would come up with relevant to the sale made.

A lady purchased some material and he said, "She seeketh wool, and flax, and worketh willingly with her hands."

A man bought a sack of flour; he said "Man does not live by bread alone, but every word that proceedeth out of the mouth of God."

A little boy bought some candy and as he rung it up he quoted, "Suffer the little children to come unto Me."

It was nearly closing time when the chimes over the door jangled loudly. A well dressed young man, obviously a stranger from one of the larger towns down the road, entered.

"Help you?" offered the proprietor.

"I need a blanket for my horse," said the man. "He's out in his trailer and it's too cold for just one. Bring me the nicest one you've got!"

The store owner went in the back store room and came back with a brown blanket. "That'll be five dollars."

"Five dollars? You've got to be kidding!' said the man. "This horse is a thoroughbred. He gets only the best! He wouldn't stand still for an old five dollar blanket."

Without comment, the store owner took back the blanket, then merely selected a different color and brought it out. "This one's $25 dollars."

"Now, look," said the young man. "Perhaps I didn't make myself plain. This isn't just any old horse! He's worth thousands! Now I want the best, most expensive blanket you've got! Comprende?"

The owner once more went into the store room, pulled out another color of the same material and brought it back. "This is the only one left, and it's $100."

"Now that's more like it!" enthused the fellow as he paid. Throwing the five dollar blanket over his shoulder, he left.

The old timers stared silently at the shopkeeper as they waited to see what possible scripture he could come up with for that sale! Going behind the register, he rung up the hundred dollars and said, "He was a stranger, and I took him in."

[deceit, dishonesty, context]

Matthew 25:41-43

A boy in the back of a crowded elevator yelled to the weary elevator operator, "Suppose the elevator cable broke — would we go up or down?"

The operator answered, "That depends entirely upon a certain decision that you have made, or not made, up to now."

[heaven, hell, judgment]

Matthew 26:20

Jesus was having dinner with his disciples one time and as they gathered reverentially about him, more or less in the attitudes since immortalized by Leonardo da Vinci, he looked about at them.

There, on one direction, he saw Judas Iscariot, who, he well knew, would betray him to the authorities before three hours had passed.

On the other side was Peter, the prince of the disciples, who, as he well knew, would deny him thrice ere the cock crowed.

And almost immediately opposite him was Thomas, who, on a crucial occasion, would express doubts.

There seemed only one thing to do. Jesus called over the head-waiter. "Max," he said, "separate checks."

[business, character, discernment]

Matthew 26:26

Have you heard about the new low-fat communion bread?
It's called "I Can't Believe It's Not Jesus"!

[communion, diet, Jesus]

Matthew 26:27

A young pastor, performing his first baptism by immersion, forgot the
verse he planned to quote as he immersed the candidate in the water.
Having just celebrated communion he quoted the only verse that came to
mind, "Drink ye all of it." [KJV].

[baptism, context]

Matthew 26:30

QUESTION: What were the last words spoken at the Last Supper?
ANSWER: Everyone who wants to be in the picture must get on this side of
the table!

[communion, photography]

Matthew 26:40

QUESTION: Who is the smallest man in the Bible?
ANSWER: Some people believe it was Nehemiah [Knee-high-am-I-ah], or
Bildad, the Shuhite [shoe-height]. But in reality it was Peter, the disciple —
he slept on his watch!

[height, size]

Matthew 26:41

An intrepid photographer went to a haunted castle determined to get a
picture of a ghost which was said to appear in a physical form only once in
a hundred years. Not wanting to frighten off the ghost, the photographer
sat in the dark until midnight when the apparition became visible. The
ghost turned out to be friendly and consented to pose for one snapshot. The
happy photographer popped a bulb into his camera and took the picture.
After dashing into his studio, the photographer developed the negative and
groaned. It was underexposed and completely blank. "The spirit was
willing, but the flash was weak!"

[photography, spirits]

Matthew 26:41

Middle age is when you start having a lot of kidney problems. The spirit is
willing but the flush is weak.

[sickness, spirits]

Matthew 26:52

A clever thief devoted himself to robbing the houses of religious people because he felt that they would not be moved to violence over the loss of worldly goods. One night however, he met his match. The sounds of his ransacking the living room aroused the old Quaker whose house it was. The old man got out of bed, picked up his hunting rifle, and made his way downstairs, where he confronted the thief.

"My friend," he said, "not for anything would I do thee harm, but thee are standing where I am about to shoot."

[pacifist, stealing, violence]

Matthew 26:64

See Mark 16:19.

Matthew 27:1

Youth Pastor: "Who can tell us something about Good Friday?"

Unchurched student: "Wasn't he the fellow who helped Robinson Crusoe?"

[Easter]

Matthew 27:2

Teacher: "Who was the first person to fly an airplane?"

Children's Church Student: "Pontius Pilot!"

[names, transportation]

Matthew 27:5

See John 13:27.

Matthew 27:38

See Luke 23:32.

Matthew 28:2

See Mark 16:4.

Matthew 28:19

Three small siblings had a pet sparrow, which, to everyone's disappointment, died. The children were very sad, and they decided to give the dead bird a really good burial service. Their families were faithful members of the church, so the children had some ideas of how to go about it.

The first step was to dig the grave in a carefully chosen spot in a corner of the yard. Then they solemnly prepared for the actual interment. One child held the sparrow over the grave, and another recited, "In the name of the Father, the Son, and in the hole he goes."

[burial, Holy Spirit, Trinity]

Matthew 28:19

There was a boy riding on his bike outside a church. The priest saw him and asked him to come into the church for a moment but the boy said, "But somebody will steal my bike while I'm inside."

The priest explained how the Holy Spirit would take care of it, so they went inside.

Before heading up the center aisle, the priest showed the boy how to make the sign of the cross and told the boy to repeat, "In the name of the Father, the Son, and the Holy Spirit. Amen."

The boy made the sign of the cross and then said, "In the name of the Father, and the Son. Amen."

The priest asked him, "What about the Holy Spirit?"

The boy replied, "He better be outside taking care of my bike!"

[Holy Spirit, stealing, Trinity, trust]

Matthew 28:19

A sister and brother in a rather religious and patriotic family were playing together, and their words were overheard by their parents. The boy recited at the end of a mock church service, "In the name of the Father, the Son, and the Holy Ghost—"

The girl continued in a strong voice, "and the Republic for which it stands."

[government, Trinity]

Matthew 28:20

A conference speaker was met at the airport by the host pastor. Noticing the speaker looked rather relieved to be on the ground again, the pastor asked him why he couldn't trust God to take care of him when he flew.

"I'm not sure God intended preachers to fly," he said. "After all Matthew 28:20 says, 'Lo[w], I am with you always.'"

[transportation, trust]

Matthew 28:20

Late one night, a burglar broke into a house that he thought was empty. He tiptoed through the living room but suddenly he froze in his tracks when he heard a loud voice say, "Jesus is watching you."

Silence returned to the house, so the burglar crept forward again. "Jesus is watching you," the voice boomed again. The burglar stopped dead again.

233

He was frightened. Frantically, he looked all around. In a dark corner, he spotted a bird cage and in the cage was a parrot.

He asked the parrot, "Was that you who said Jesus is watching me?" "Yes," said the parrot.

The burglar breathed a sigh of relief, then he asked the parrot, "What's your name?" "Clarence," said the bird.

"That's a dumb name for a parrot," sneered the burglar. "What idiot named you Clarence?"

The parrot replied, "The same idiot who named the Rottweiler behind you 'Jesus.'"

[animals, Jesus, stealing]

Matthew 28:20

A preacher drove like a madman. One of his parishioners who often rode with him finally said to him, "Pastor, you must be more careful in your driving."

But the pastor replied, "It's OK, the Lord has told me he will be with me always."

At that the terrified parishioner replied, "I've got news for you. The Lord told me that he just got out at that last stop light."

[presumption]

MARK

Mark 1:8

The drought in Georgia has begun to affect our different communities of faith in different ways. The Baptists have taken up sprinkling ...the Methodists are using damp cloths to baptize ... and the Presbyterians are giving out rain-checks.

[baptism, denominations, weather]

Mark 1:10

The teacher asked her class of five-year-olds, "Do any of you remember who Matthew, Mark, Luke, and John were?" There was silence in the classroom. "Can you tell me who Paul was?" she asked.
No response.
"Well, then," the teacher said, becoming impatient, "surely you should be able to tell me who Peter was?"
A tiny voice from the back squeaked, "I fink he was a wabbit."

[disciples, names]

Mark 1:34

Explaining the verse in the Gospels about Jesus healing "sick people taken with divers diseases (KJV)," a preacher shouted, "There's a regular epidemic of divers diseases among us. Some dive for the TV set at the Sunday evening service hour. Some dive for the car for a weekend trip, while others dive for their dimes and nickels to put into the offering. It takes the Lord and a love for the church to cure DIVERS DISEASES!"

[giving, healing, sickness]

Mark 1:34

Two sisters were discussing a question suggested by a Bible passage. It was occasioned when they heard the words of the King James Version that Jesus healed the sick "of divers diseases."
"I don't understand that part. What are 'divers diseases'?" asked the younger girl.
"What do you care what they are?" replied the more learned sister, "You can't even swim."

[sickness, sports]

Mark 1:38

The new minister found only one person at his first rural Sunday night service. "What do you think we should do about the service," he asked the man, "inasmuch as we have such a small congregation?"

The man replied, "Well, sir, I have never been to school very much. I don't have much education and I don't know much about the Bible, but this one thing I know, that when I promise my cows a load of hay, I always keep my promise."

"Well, come in then, and we will have a service," said the minister. The minister was long-winded, and it was an exceptionally lengthy service. Afterwards the minister asked the farmer, "What did you think of the service?"

"Well," he said, "I have never been to school, I'm not educated, and I don't know much about the Bible, but this one thing I know, when I promise my cows a load of hay and only one shows up, I never give it the whole load."

[long, sermons,]

Mark 5:13

QUESTION: Where was deviled ham mentioned in the Bible?
ANSWER: When the evil spirits entered the swine (KJV).

[animals, food, spirits]

Mark 5:13

"Wherever did the swine go?" asked the demoniac dispiritedly.

[demon, puns, spirits]

Mark 5:30-31

A church service is always much more meaningful and interesting when the sermon and music go together. Too many times they appear to be separate services, with no apparent connection. One preacher was very enthusiastic about having the music supplement the Scripture text, and usually he and the music director had the program definitely harmonized and planned in advance.

However on one occasion they neglected to do this. In this situation, the preacher chose for his text the beautiful story of an ailing woman of great faith, who was healed merely by touching the garment of the Master as he passed by. The preacher closed with the words of Jesus, "Who touched me?" From the choir loft came the refrain, "Search Me, O God."

[healing, hymns, sermon, touch]

Mark 6:32-44

Two Pharisees, talking together after seeing Jesus' miraculous feeding of the five thousand but still feeling critical of him, were heard to comment, "It wasn't bad, but there was no lemon to go with the fish, and no butter for the loaves."

[food, miracle, Pharisees]

Mark 6:32-44

A preacher forgot his notes for the sermon he was going to deliver. In the midst of the sermon he got a few things twisted when he said that the Lord took 4000 barley loaves and 6000 fishes and fed 24 people, and had plenty left over.

Someone in the congregation called out, "Anybody could do that."

"Could you?" asked the minister.

"Certainly I could."

After the service, when the minister complained about the heckler's conduct, he was told of his error by a deacon.

"Well, next week I will not forget my notes. I'll fix that character."

The next week the minister stepped forward confidently and began his sermon. In the course of it, he brought up again the miracle of the loaves and fishes. He told how the five barley loaves and two fishes had fed the multitudes of probably 24,000 people. He then pointed to the heckler from the previous Sunday and asked, "Could you do that?"

"I sure could," said the heckler.

"And just how would you do that?" asked the minister.

"With the loaves and fishes leftover from last Sunday."

OR

A young minister delivering his first sermon to a new congregation quoted the parable of the loaves and the fishes. "Now," he said dramatically, "consider the scene where the Master with 5,000 loaves and 2,000 fishes fed five people." A murmur of amusement ran through the church and one old man up in front laughed out loud.

The poor young minister was so humiliated that the following Sunday he decided to regain the ground he'd lost by using the same parable in another sermon. "Now consider the scene where the Master with five loaves and two fishes fed 5,000 people," he said. Then, having regained his confidence, he leaned over the pulpit and spoke to the old man who had laughed at him, "You couldn't do that, brother."

"Oh, yes I could," said the old gentleman, "if I had what was left over from last week!"

[food, miracle, skeptic]

Mark 6:38

See John 6:9.

Mark 6:48

A Scotsman, planning a trip to the Holy Land, was aghast when he found it would cost fifty Euro an hour to rent a boat on the Sea of Galilee.
"Hoot mon," he said, "in Scotland it wouldna ha been more than 20 Euro."
"That might be true," said the travel agent, "but you have to take into account that the Sea of Galilee is water on which our Lord himself walked."
"Well, at 50 Euro/hour for a boat," said the Scotsman, "it's no wonder he walked."

[cheap, miracle]

Mark 8:31

See Luke 9:22.

Mark 8:33

Despite a severely limited budget, the wife of a frugal pastor bought herself a pretty dress for Easter.
Her husband rebuked her: "When you were tempted to buy it, you should have said, 'Get thee behind me Satan.'"
"That's what I did say," the minister's wife replied, "and I heard Satan whisper, 'It looks very nice from the back too.'"

[frugal, Satan, temptation]

Mark 8:33

Last week my wife was in her usual hurry to drive home from work. She tailgated one particularly slow car for some distance, mumbling some unflattering comments under her breath the whole time. Suddenly her attention was drawn to the license plate on the car. It was one of those vanity plates people pay extra money for and it read "MARK 8 33". Not familiar with that particular verse my wife didn't immediately understand its significance, but it stuck in her mind, as she continued cursing and tailgating the car down the road.
Finally getting home, my wife sat and relaxed for a minute, thinking about that verse and wondering what it was that the driver of the car was trying to say with that plate. Reaching for her KJV Bible it only took her a minute to locate Mark 8:33 and read, "And Jesus answered and said unto him, Get

thee behind me, Satan..."

[Satan]

Mark 9:24

A man fell from the edge of a precipice, but checked his fall by grabbing the branch of a scrub oak growing from the side of the canyon. He could not make his way back. Dangling in space, he shouted in desperate prayer, "Help! Is there anyone up there?"
From the sky came a majestic voice: "Yes, I am here. Do you believe and trust me my son?"
"I do, I do," cried the man. "I believe and trust you, Lord, please save me!"
"Let go of the branch, my son, if you really trust me."
"I trust you! I trust you!"
"Let go of the branch."
A silence followed. Then the man spoke again, "Is there someone else up there I can talk to?"

OR

A man accidentally falls over a high cliff, and on the way down he grabs onto the only branch within reach or sight. In a few moments he summons enough strength to move again, and he cries upward, "Help! Is there anyone up there who can help me?"
A moment passes without event, and he again cries, "Help; can anyone hear me? I need help!"
After another moment a booming voice answers, "THIS IS THE VOICE OF GOD. BELIEVE IN ME. HAVE FAITH. SAY A PROPER PRAYER AND LET GO OF THE BRANCH. YOU WILL FLOAT SLOWLY TO THE SAND, UNHARMED. JUST LET GO."
Looking down at the jagged rocks and the pounding surf, the man thinks for a second, and then calls up, "Is there anyone ELSE up there?"

[faith]

Mark 9:47

A motorist was picked up unconscious after a smash, and was being carried to a nearby gas station. Upon opening his eyes on route, he began to kick and struggle desperately to get away. Afterward he explained that the first thing he saw was a "Shell" sign and somebody was standing in front of the "S!"

[hell]

Mark 10:14

See Matthew 25:35.

Mark 10:16

Blessed are the young, for they shall inherit the national debt.

[beatitudes, debt]

Mark 10:21-22

The title of the Children's Church lesson was, "The Rich Young Man," and the golden text was, "One thing you lack." The teacher, an attractive but older woman, asked a little boy to repeat the title and text. Looking earnestly into the lady's face, the child said, "One thing you lack — a rich young man."

[singleness]

Mark 10:25

See Genesis 7:9 re. Camels.

Mark 10:27

The impossible: what nobody can do until somebody does.

[impossibility]

Mark 10:44

The Pope has come to visit New York. It was a long and uneventful plane ride. At the airport the Pope sees the limo that has come to pick him up. "Oh" he says to the driver, "this is a beautiful car, may I drive it?"
"Uh," begins the confused driver.
"Please?" says the Pope, "They never let me drive."
"Well okay," says the driver. "How can I say no to the Pope?"
So the Pope gets behind the wheel, and boy, does he SPEED! He hits the gas, going 90 in a school zone. Well, it isn't long before a cop sees the speeding limo and pulls it over. The rookie cop comes up to the window and says:
"Could you please roll down your window?"
When the Pope rolls down the window, the officer immediately recognizes him, being a devout Catholic.
"Excuse me your Holiness," he says, then goes to his patrol car and radios the Chief.
"Chief," the cop says "I got a problem"
"What is it?"
"Well I pulled someone REALLY important over for speeding, and-"
"Important like what? The Mayor?"

"MUCH MORE important!"

"Important like the President?"

"More."

"Who's more important than the president?"

"I don't know, but he's got the Pope, DRIVING for him!"

[Catholic, humility]

Mark 10:44

A young preacher said to an older pastor, "I want to be a great man. What is the first thing I should do?"

The master answered, "Forget about being a great man."

[humility]

Mark 11:15

See John 2:15.

Mark 12:18

When the Sadducees heard that Jewish people were believing that Jesus rose from the dead, they were really 'sad-you-see.'

[Sadducees]

Mark 12:30

Has the heaviness of your old-fashioned church got you weighted down? Try us! We are the New and Improved Lite Church of the Valley. Studies have shown we have 24% fewer commitments than other churches. We guarantee to trim off guilt, because we are Low-Cal., Low-Calvin, that is. We are the home of the 7.5% tithe. We promise 35-minute worship services, with 7-minute sermons. Next Sunday's exciting text is the story of the Feeding of the 500. We have only 6 Commandments — Your choice! We use just 3 gospels in our contemporary New Testament "Good Sound Bites for Modern Human Beings." We take the offering every other week, all major credit cards accepted, of course. We are looking forward with great anticipation to our 800-year Millennium. Yes, the New and Improved Lite Church of the Valley could be just what you are looking for. We are everything you want in a church... and less!

[church]

Mark 12:42

What are the 2 smallest insects in the Bible? (The widow's mite [Mark 12:42] and the wicked flea [Proverbs 28:1])

[insects, size]

Mark 13:37 (KJV)

Little eight-year-old Tyrone wanted a watch so badly that he wearied the whole family with his begging. His father promised him a watch when he was older, and forbade him to mention the topic again. "I don't want you pestering me about a watch any more," he declared with finality.
Next Sunday during devotions at the breakfast table the children, as was their custom, repeated Bible verses. Little Tyrone astonished them all by quoting Mark 13:37: "And what I say unto you, I say unto you all, Watch!"

[context, persistence]

Mark 15:27

See Luke 23:32.

Mark 15:42

A minister was standing behind a lady in line at the bank when there was a commotion at the counter in front of him. The customer was obviously quite distressed, and began exclaiming, "Where will I put my money? I have all my money and my mortgage here. What will happen to my mortgage?"
The minister stepped forward to see if he could be of any help. It turned out that she had misunderstood a small sign on the counter. The sign read, WE WILL BE CLOSED FOR GOOD FRIDAY.
Apparently Easter was not uppermost in her mind, because she thought that the bank was going to close "for good" that coming Friday!

[Easter, holidays]

Mark 16:1-8

Three stupid guys just died and are at the pearly gates of heaven. St. Peter tells them that they can enter the gates if they can answer one simple question.
St. Peter asks the first man, "WHAT IS EASTER?"
The man replies, "Oh, that's easy, it's the holiday in November when everybody gets together, eats turkey, and is thankful..."
"WRONG," replies St. Peter, and proceeds to ask the second man the same question, "WHAT IS EASTER?"
The second man replies, "No, Easter is the holiday in December when we put up a nice tree, exchange presents, and celebrate the birth of Jesus."
St. Peter looks at the second man, shakes his head in disgust, looks at the third man and asks, "WHAT IS EASTER?"
The third man smiles and looks St. Pete in the eye.
"I know what Easter is. Easter is the Christian holiday that coincides with the Jewish celebration of Passover. Jesus and his disciples were eating at the last supper and He was later deceived and turned over to the Romans by

one of his disciples. The Romans took Him to be crucified and was stabbed in the side, made Him wear a crown of thorns, and He was hung on a cross. He was buried in a nearby cave that was sealed off by a large boulder. Every year the boulder is moved aside so that Jesus can come out, and if He sees his shadow there will be six more weeks of winter."

[Easter, holidays, knowledge, resurrection]

Mark 16:4

On the third day, Jesus rose, rolled back the stone which acted as the door of his tomb, and walked again on earth.

As he was leaving, a passer-by pointed at the doorway Jesus had left open. "What's the matter with you?" he said. "Born in a barn?"

[Jesus, resurrection]

Mark 16:15

When a Children's Church teacher requested each of her pupils to quote one favorite verse of Scripture, one small boy recited: "Go ye into all the world and spread the gossip."

[gospel, gossip]

Mark 16:16

The following notice was printed in the bulletin's announcements, THE SERMON NEXT SUNDAY WILL BE UPON THE VERSE "HE THAT BELIEVETH AND IS BAPTIZED SHALL BE SAVED AND HE THAT BELIEVETH NOT SHALL BE DAMNED" AT BOTH THE 9:30 AND 11:00 SERVICES.

[judgment, misunderstanding]

Mark 16:16

A mother decided it was time that her three sons get baptized. So, after weeks of suitable instruction one bright Sunday morning they were on their way to church where the three boys, 8, 10, and 13, would, as their particular church taught, have their sins washed away. The 10 year old was particularly pensive that day, and when the mother asked him what he was thinking about. His reply was in the form of a question.

"Mom, can I go first?"

"Why?"

"Because, I don't want to be baptized in water that has all of my brother's sins floating around in it."

[baptism, sin]

Mark 16:17

See Matthew 8:16

Mark 16:17-18

A preacher was quoting a verse about healing the sick, raising the dead, and casting out devils. He got a little mixed up and said, "The Bible admonishes us to cast out the sick, ... heal the dead, ... and raise the devil."

[context, mistakes]

Mark 16:18

A Baptist preacher and his wife decided to get a new dog. Ever mindful of the congregation, they knew the dog must also be a Baptist. They visited kennel after kennel and explained their needs. Finally, they found a kennel whose owner assured them he had just the dog they wanted. The owner brought the dog to meet the pastor and his wife.

"Fetch the Bible," he commanded. The dog bounded to the bookshelf, scrutinized the books, located the Bible, and brought it to the owner. "Now find Psalm 23," he commanded. The dog dropped the Bible to the floor and showing marvelous dexterity with his paws, leafed through and finding the correct passage, pointed to it with his paw. The pastor and his wife were very impressed and purchased the dog.

That evening, a group of church members came to visit. The pastor and his wife began to show off the dog, having him locate several Bible verses. The visitors were very impressed. One man asked, "Can he do regular dog tricks, too?"

"I haven't tried yet," the pastor replied. He pointed his finger at the dog. "HEEL!" the pastor commanded. The dog immediately jumped on a chair, placed one paw on the pastor's forehead and began to howl.

The pastor looked at his wife in shock and exclaimed, "Good Lord! He's Pentecostal!"

[denominations, healing]

Mark 16:19

A grandmother and her five-year-old grandson were taking a walk in the country just after the first heavy frost of the season had dyed the foliage and given it a brilliantly-colored crazy quilt appearance.

"Just think," the grandmother marveled, gazing at the scarlet and gold hillside, "God painted all that."

"Yes," the grandson agreed. "And He even did it with his left hand."

"What do you mean He did it with his left hand?" she asked, somewhat puzzled by the remark.

"Well," the boy replied, "at Children's Church they told us that Jesus is sitting on the right hand of God. (KJV)"

[God, Jesus, misunderstanding]

Mark 16:19

See Hebrews 1:3.

LUKE

Luke

QUESTION: How do you study the Bible?
ANSWER: You Luke [look] into it.

[study]

Luke 1:3

I think we should name this colt Theophilus," a trainer said to the colt's owner, a famous preacher.
"Why?" asked the owner. "Does he remind you of the recipient of the book of Luke and Acts?"
"Not really," said the trainer. "Rather, he's just the Theophilus [the awfullest] horse I ever seen run."

[names, puns]

Luke 1:28

There has long been a rumor that W. R. Grace Co. was going to buy the Fuller Brush Co. and Mary Kay Cosmetics and then merge with the Hale Business Systems. This would result in the new mega-corporate entity known as ... "Hale Mary Fuller Grace."

[grace, names]

Luke 2:1

Teacher: "Now, who decreed that all the world should be taxed?"
Student: "Must have been the Democrats."

[politics, taxes]

Luke 2:1-4

Bethlehem — Where Mary and Joseph had to come to their census [senses].

[geography, puns]

Luke 2:4

When a child in a suburban Philadelphia Children's Church was asked where Jesus was born, he answered, "Philadelphia."
The teacher said, "No, try again."
The child said, "Pittsburgh."

When the teacher again indicated a wrong answer the child asked, "Where was it, then?"

"Bethlehem," replied the teacher.

"Oh," retorted the child, "I knew it was somewhere in Pennsylvania."

[names, geography]

Luke 2:6

Definition of Christmas — the celebration of the birth of Christ, which invariably falls during the busiest shopping season of the year.

[Christmas]

Luke 2:6

The commercialization of Christmas is getting worse all the time. Nowadays the only time you hear someone mention Jesus is when they stick their finger in a Christmas light socket.

[Christmas, swearing]

Luke 2:7

Twelve-year-old Norton was bitterly disappointed at not being cast as Joseph in the church school Nativity pageant. He was given the minor role of the innkeeper instead. Throughout the weeks of rehearsal he brooded on how he could avenge himself on his little brother, Wayne, who had been awarded the part of Joseph. On the day of the performance, Wayne (as Joseph) and his sister Kelly (as Mary) made their entrance and knocked on the door of the inn. Norton (the innkeeper) opened it a fraction and eyed them with suspicion.

Joseph implored, "Can you give us board and lodging for the night?" He then stood back awaiting the expected rejection. But Norton had not plotted all those weeks for nothing. He flung the door wide, smiled, and shouted, "Come in, come in! You shall have the best room in the hotel." There was a long pause. Then with great presence of mind, Wayne turned and said to Kelly, "Hold on. I'll take a look inside first." He peered past the innkeeper, shook his head firmly and said, "I'm not taking my wife into a filthy place like this. Come on, Mary, I'd rather sleep in a stable."

The pageant was back on course.

[Christmas]

Luke 2:7

Two sisters were looking at a book of religious pictures and came across a painting of Mary and the baby Jesus. "See there," said the older sister, "that's Jesus, and that's his mother."

"Where," the younger girl wanted to know, "is his father?"

Her sister thought for a moment, then explained, "Oh, he's taking the picture."

[photography, picture]

Luke 2:7

City kids have a difficult time understanding the Christmas story. When I said Mary and Joseph had to spend the night in a stable, my daughter asked, "What's a stable?" I said, "Picture your room without your flat-screen or computer!"

[Christmas, mess]

Luke 2:7

QUESTION: Why was baby Jesus born in a stable?
ANSWER: His parents were in ObamaCare.

[birth, Christmas]

Luke 2:7

And Joseph went up from Galilee to Bethlehem with Mary, his espoused wife, who was great with child. And she brought forth a son and wrapped him in swaddling clothes and laid him in a manger because there was no room for them in the inn. And the angel of the Lord spoke to the shepherds and said, "I bring you tidings of great joy. Unto you is born a Savior, which is Christ the Lord."

"There's a problem with the angel," said a Pharisee who happened to be strolling by. As he explained to Joseph, angels are widely regarded as religious symbols, and the stable was on public property where such symbols were not allowed to land or even hover.

"And I have to tell you, this whole thing looks to me very much like a Nativity scene," he said sadly. "That's a no-no, too." Joseph had a bright idea. "What if I put a couple of reindeer over there near the ox and ass?" he said, eager to avoid sectarian strife.

"That would definitely help," said the Pharisee, who knew as well as anyone that whenever a savior appeared, judges usually liked to be on the safe side and surround it with deer or woodland creatures of some sort. "Just to clinch it, throw in a candy cane and a couple of elves and snowmen, too," he said. "No court can resist that."

Mary asked, "What does my son's birth have to do with snowmen?"

"Snowpersons," cried a young woman, changing the subject before it veered dangerously toward religion.

Off to the side of the crowd, a Philistine was painting the Nativity scene. Mary complained that she and Joseph looked too tattered and worn in the picture. "Artistic license," he said. "I've got to show the plight of the haggard homeless in a greedy, uncaring society in winter," he quipped. "We're not haggard or homeless. The inn was just full," said Mary. "Whatever," said the painter.

Two women began to argue fiercely. One said she objected to Jesus' birth "because it privileged motherhood." The other scoffed at virgin births, but said that if they encouraged more attention to diversity in family forms and the rights of single mothers, well, then, she was all for them. "I'm not a single mother," Mary started to say, but she was cut off by a third woman who insisted that swaddling clothes are a form of child abuse, since they restrict the natural movement of babies. With the arrival of 10 child advocates, all trained to spot infant abuse and manger rash, Mary and Joseph were pushed to the edge of the crowd, where arguments were breaking out over how many reindeer (or what mix of reindeer and seasonal sprites) had to be installed to compensate for the infant's unfortunate religious character.

An older man bustled up, bowling over two merchants, who had been busy debating whether an elf is the same as a fairy and whether the elf/fairy should be shaking hands with Jesus in the crib or merely standing to the side, jumping around like a sports mascot. "I'd hold off on the reindeer," the man said, explaining that the use of asses and oxen as picturesque backdrops for Nativity scenes carries the subliminal message of human dominance. He passed out two leaflets, one denouncing manger births as invasions of animal space, the other arguing that stables are "penned environments" where animals are incarcerated against their will. He had no opinion about elves or candy canes.

Signs declaring "Free the Bethlehem 2" began to appear, referring to the obviously exploited ass and ox. Someone said the halo on Jesus' head was elitist. Mary was exasperated. "And what about you, old mother?" she said sharply to an elderly woman. "Are you here to attack the shepherds as prison guards for excluded species, maybe to complain that singing in Latin identifies us with our Roman oppressors, or just to say that I should have skipped patriarchal religiosity and joined some dumb new-age goddess religion?" "None of the above," said the woman, "I just wanted to tell you that the Magi are here."

Sure enough, the three wise men rode up. The crowd gasped, "They're all male!" And "Not very multicultural!" "Balthazar here is black," said one of the Magi. "Yes, but how many of you are gay or disabled?" someone shouted. A committee was quickly formed to find an impoverished lesbian wise-person among the halt and lame of Bethlehem. A calm voice said, "Be of good cheer, Mary, you have done well and your son will change the world." At last, a sane person, Mary thought. She turned to see a radiant and confident female face. The woman spoke again: "There is one thing, though. Religious holidays are important, but can't we learn to celebrate them in ways that unite, not divide? For instance, instead of all this business about 'Gloria in Excelsis Deo,' why not just 'Season's Greetings'?" Mary said, "You mean my son has entered human history to deliver the message, 'Hello, it's winter'?" "That's harsh, Mary," said the woman. "Remember, your son could make it big in midwinter festivals, if he doesn't push the religion thing too far. Centuries from now, in nations yet unborn, people will give each other pricey gifts and have big office parties on his birthday. That's not chopped liver." "Let me get back to you," Mary said.

By John Leo, US News & World Report columnist & author of a new book, "Two Steps Ahead of the Thought Police."

[politically correct]

Luke 2:8

Child to Children's Church teacher: "Why do shepherds wash their socks at night?"

[clothes]

Luke 2:8

After the family sang some carols, four-year-old Billy commented, "Wasn't it good of the shepherds to put on clean clothes when they went to see baby Jesus?"
Mother inquired, "What do you mean?"
Billy explained, "We just sang, 'While Shepherds Washed Their Socks by Night'."

[clothes]

Luke 2:10

A five-year-old had one line in a Christmas pageant. Appearing in angel's garb, he was to say, "Behold, I bring you good tidings!" After practice the little boy asked his mother what "tidings" meant. She explained that it meant news.
At the performance, momentarily forgetting his line, he recovered in time to shout out, "Boy, do I got news for you!"

[Christmas]

Luke 2:13

On one Christmas, a church bulletin gave exciting ecclesiastical authority to "Sing, choirs of angels, <u>sin</u> in exultation."

[Christmas, music]

Luke 2:14

The way to sing a Christmas carol during a drought —"Joy to the world, the Savior rains [reigns]"

[hymns, weather]

Luke 2:14

What three phrases best sum up the Christmas season?
"Peace on Earth," "Good will to all," and "Batteries not included."

[Christmas]

Luke 2:16

A kindergarten Children's Church teacher had her class draw a nativity scene. One youngster had done a very fine job in drawing the baby in a manger, with Mary and Joseph and the animals; but the teacher noticed with anxiety that he had drawn a little fat man right beside the manger. She asked, "Jimmy, that isn't Santa, is it? Jimmy answered indignantly, "Of course not, that's Round John Virgin."

[Christmas, virgin]

Luke 2:20

"Angels we have heard on high, sweetly singing o'er the plane [plain]."

[music, transportation]

Luke 2:34

A woman, who apparently has a lot to learn, was riding on a city bus when she noticed the slogan, "Put Christ Back Into Christmas," on a sign. "Gee," she exclaimed to her companion, "even the churches are sticking their noses into Christmas now!"

[Christmas]

Luke 2:41

Children's Church teacher asked: "Why did Mary and Joseph take Jesus with them to Jerusalem?"
A little girl named Haleigh shifted in her seat and said shyly, "I guess they couldn't get a babysitter."

[baby, babysitter, misunderstanding]

Luke 2:47

Teacher: "Why did Jesus know the Scriptures so well?"
Student: "Oh, that's easy. His Daddy wrote them."

[Bible, father, Jesus]

Luke 3:23

QUESTION: Do you know what Jesus and today's young adults have in common?
ANSWER: They live off their parents till they're thirty, and when they do something it's a miracle.

[miracle, parenting]

Luke 4:8

A mother had insisted that Jackie not go swimming. When he came home with his hair wet she knew he had disobeyed.
Mother: "Jackie, shame on you! You've disobeyed me! Didn't I tell you that if Satan tempted you to disobey me that you should tell him to get behind you?"
Jackie: "But Mommy that's what I did. I was standing there on the river bank, and when I was tempted to go swimming I told Satan to get behind me ... and when he got behind me, he just pushed me right into the water!"

[Satan, temptation]

Luke 4:8

See Mark 8:33.

Luke 4:12

Little Johnny desperately wanted a bike for Christmas. So one evening just before Christmas, as he was saying his prayers with his mum, he said, "Dear God, if you get me a bike for Christmas, I promise I'll be really, really good for the whole year!" His mum was shocked. "Johnny," she said, "That's not the way to talk to God! You can't try and bribe him into answering your prayers by promising to be good!" "You can't?" Johnny asked. "No!" said his mum. Johnny looked thoughtful. Next night they were going through the bedtime routine again, and this time Johnny prayed, "Dear God, if you don't get me a bike for Christmas, I warn you, I'm going to be so upset and cross that I'll be really, really naughty." "Johnny!" explodes his mum. "That's even worse than last night! You can't threaten God like that. He won't answer prayers like that, you know." "He won't?" Johnny asked. "No!" said his mum. Johnny looked even more thoughtful. Next morning, mum was in the hall when she noticed something odd about the crib. The model animals were there, and the wise men and the shepherds, and Mary and Joseph, but baby Jesus was missing. She looked all round to see where he'd fallen, but she couldn't find him anywhere. A little later she was changing the sheets on Johnny's bed, when she came across a bundle wrapped in a handkerchief under the pillow. She unwrapped it, and out fell the baby Jesus from the crib. With it was a note. "Dear God," it said. "If you want to see your son alive again you'd better get me that bike!"

[bribes, threaten]

Luke 4:40

See Mark 1:34 (KJV).

Luke 6:20

Did you hear about the new beatitude they discovered? It's "Blessed are the flexible for they shall not be bent out of shape!"

[beatitude]

Luke 6:20-22

See Matthew 5:1-12.

Luke 6:23

See 1 Corinthians 3:14.

Luke 6:27

The Bible tells us to love our neighbors and also to love our enemies; probably because they are generally the same people.

[enemies, friends]

Luke 6:27

Speak well of your enemies. Remember, you made them.

[enemies]

Luke 6:31

See Matthew 7:12.

Luke 6:31

A little boy was writing the memory verse for the week on the blackboard and he wrote: "DO ONE TO OTHERS AS OTHERS DO ONE TO YOU."

[revenge]

Luke 6:31

"Honey," scolded the mom, "you shouldn't always keep everything for yourself. I've told you so many times that you should let your brother play with your toys half of the time."

"I've been doing it," the boy said, "I take the sled going downhill, and he takes it going up."

[cooperation]

Luke 6:45

It was that time during the Sunday morning service for "the children's sermon," and all the children were invited to come forward. One little girl was wearing a particularly pretty dress and, as she sat down, the pastor leaned over and said to her, "That is a very pretty dress. Is it your Easter dress?"

The little girl replied, directly into the pastor's clip-on microphone, "Yes, and my Mom says it's a 'real pain' to iron."

[clothes, Easter]

Luke 7:15

A Catholic priest, a Protestant minister, and a rabbi are discussing what they would like people to say after they die and their bodies are on display in open caskets.

Priest: "I would like someone to say, 'He was a righteous man, an honest man, and very generous.'"

Minister: "I would like someone to say, 'He was very kind and fair, and he was very good to his parishioners.'"

Rabbi: "I want someone to say 'LOOK! HE'S MOVING!!'"

[burial, resurrection]

Luke 7:33

A man lost two buttons from his shirt and put them in his pants pocket. But the pocket had a hole, so the buttons fell into his shoe. Unfortunately, the shoe sole also had a hole, so he lost the buttons. Since pockets with holes, holes without buttons, and shoe soles with holes are useless, the man ripped the buttonholes out of his shirt and the pocket from his pants and tossed them in the trash along with the soles of his shoes. After looking in a mirror at the holes in his clothing, he decided to toss his clothes in the trash as well.

A policeman observed all this and asked the man for identification. The man produced a document that he was an ordained minister of the gospel. So, of course, the policeman promptly escorted him to a mental institution. The minister protested violently, asking why he was receiving such unjust treatment.

"Look, it's the best place for you now," the policeman replied, "Anyone claiming to be a preacher, but who doesn't save souls or wear holy clothes has probably lost his buttons."

[crazy, ministry]

Luke 7:47

The pastor was rejoicing with an elderly church member over a relative of hers who had finally seen the light and joined the church after a lifetime of riotous living.

When she wondered if all the oldster's carrying on would be forgiven, the pastor assured her, "Yes, indeed, the greater the sinner the greater the saint."

"Preacher," she mused wistfully, "I wish I had learned this forty years ago."

[forgiveness, sin]

Luke 8:17

A mother was showing her son how to zip up his coat. "The secret," she said, "is to get the left part of the zipper to fit in the other side before you try to zip it up." The boy looked at her quizzically: "Why does it have to be a secret?"

[misunderstanding]

Luke 8:33

See Mark 5:13 (KJV).

Luke 8:52

An irreligious fellow was out in the cemetery reading epitaphs on the tombstones. He came to one that read, "Luke 8:52 — 'Not dead, but sleeping.'"

He shook his head, "Man, you're not fooling anybody but yourself."

[context, death]

Luke 8:52

See 1 Thessalonians 4:14.

Luke 9:10-17

See Mark 6:32-44.
See John 6:9.

Luke 9:16

A Children's Church teacher was reviewing with her fifth graders the events in the life of Jesus that impressed them the most and the happenings they liked best. These were some of the responses: When Jesus raised Lazarus from the dead; when He raised the twelve-year-old girl to life; when He helped the apostles catch so many fish their boat began to sink.

But little Eddie took the prize when he declared: "I like the story about the big crowd that loafs and fishes."

[food, laziness, reality]

Luke 9:22

QUESTION: What's the first sign of soccer in the bible?
ANSWER: Jesus going for the cross.

[crucifixion, sports]

Luke 10:25-37

The dean was speaking at a faculty meeting. One of the professors stood up and asked, "What must I do to get tenure?" The dean replied, "What does the faculty manual say?" The professor answered, "Do good research, teach well, and mentor students." "You have answered correctly," the dean replied. "Do this and you will get tenure."
But the professor wanted to justify himself, so he asked the dean, "What does it mean to mentor students?" In reply the dean said: "One term there was a student who was struggling in his courses. He went to talk about it to the professor of one of his classes, but the professor brushed him off with, "If you can't handle the work, you should drop the course." The student then went to his academic advisor, but she was on her way out the door to the airport and didn't have time to talk. A custodian overheard the conversation, and, seeing the discouragement of the student, invited him out for a cup of coffee. It turned out the student was dealing with the death of a family member, and the stress was affecting his personal life as much as his studies. The custodian walked him to the counseling center and arranged an appointment for him. He called the student several times in the next few weeks to see how things were going, and helped him think through whether to drop the courses or not. Now, which one of these was the true mentor to the student?" The professor replied, "The one who had mercy on him." The dean told him, "Go and do likewise."

[mercy, students, teacher]

Luke 10:27

See John 13:27.

Luke 10:31

Children's Church teacher: Now class, you remember the story of the Good Samaritan. What would you do if you saw a man lying on the ground bleeding to death?
Little girl: I think I'd throw up.

[reality, sickness]

Luke 10:32

Children's Church teacher: "In the story of the Good Samaritan, why did the Levite pass by on the other side?"
Student: "I'm not sure but I'd guess it was because the poor man had already been robbed."

[stealing]

Luke 10:33-34

While on a sightseeing tour of Israel, a guide pointed out an ancient inn, saying, "That's where the Good Samaritan took the wounded traveler."
"But," a New Testament scholar in the group objected, saying, "that wasn't an actual incident. Jesus used it as a parable to illustrate his point."
The guide quickly replied, "Then in your case, this is the inn that he had in mind."

[archeology]

Luke 11:1

You never really learn to pray until your kids start learning to drive!

[driving, pray, teenagers]

Luke 11:3

The small boy was quizzing his father. He asked, "Is it true that the stork brings babies?"
"Yes, son."
"And Christmas presents come from Santa Claus?"
"Yes, son."
"And the Lord gives us our daily bread?"
"Yes, son."
"Then Daddy, why do we need you?"

[father]

Luke 11:4

See Matthew 12:13.

Luke 11:9

"Tina!" said the boss crossly, "I can never find what I want in these files. What system do you use?"
"The Biblical system, sir"
"The Biblical system? What's that?"
"Seek and ye shall find!"

[context]

Luke 11:9

A young girl, dressed in her Sunday best was running as fast as she could to Children's Church . As she ran, she prayed, "Dear Lord, please don't let me be late! Dear Lord, please don't let me be late!" — at which moment she tripped on a curb and fell, getting dirty and tearing her dress.

She got up, brushed herself off and started running again, praying, "Dear Lord, pleased don't let me be late! Dear Lord, please don't let me be late! ... But don't shove me!"

[frustration, prayer]

Luke 11:16

Someone said to a believer, "If God performed a miracle in front of me, I would believe."

The believer held up a blade of grass.

[miracle, skeptic]

Luke 11:16

See Mark 16:17.

Luke 11:30

QUESTION: What did Jesus have in common with the fish that swallowed Jonah?

ANSWER: Jesus had dinner with a sinner, and the fish had a sinner for dinner.

[context, friend]

Luke 11:41

A little girl was in church with her mother when she started feeling ill.

"Mommy," she said, "can we leave now?"

"No," her mother replied.

"Well, I think I have to throw up!"

"Then go out the front door and around to the back of the church and throw up behind a bush."

After about 60 seconds the little girl returned to her seat.

"Did you throw up?" Mom asked.

"Yes."

"How could you have gone all the way to the back of the church and returned so quickly?"

"I didn't have to go out of the church, Mommy. They have a box next to the front door that says, 'For the Sick'."

[sickness]

Luke 12:1

See Galatians 2:13.

Luke 12:5

A preacher had only two hand gestures. For one, his hand would point up, and for the other, his hand would point down.

As he was preaching one day he raised his arm and pointed upward and said, "When the roll is called up yonder."

Then he lowered his arms and pointed down, and said, "I'll be there."

[hell, preaching]

Luke 12:7

See Matthew 10:30.

Luke 12:19

Eat, drink and be merry for tomorrow we diet!"

[diet, food]

Luke 12:20

Two buddies Bob and Dave were two of the biggest baseball fans in America. For their entire adult lives, Bob and Dave discussed baseball history in the winter and they pored over every box score during the season. They went to 60 games a year. They even agreed that whoever died first would try to come back and tell the other if there was baseball in heaven.

One summer night, Bob passed away in his sleep after watching the Yankee victory earlier in the evening. He died happy. A few nights later, his buddy Dave awoke to the sound of Bob's voice from beyond.

"Bob is that you?" Dave asked.

"Of course it's me," Bob replied.

"This is unbelievable!" Dave exclaimed. "So tell me, is there baseball in heaven?"

"Well I have some good news and some bad news for you. Which do you want to hear first?"

"Tell me the good news first."

"Well, the good news is that, yes, there is baseball in heaven, Dave."

"Oh, that is wonderful! So what could possibly be the bad news?"

"You're pitching tomorrow night."

[death, heaven, sports]

Luke 12:20

A guy is at the Pearly Gates, hoping to be admitted, and St. Peter says to the guy, "I can't see that you did anything really good in your life, but you never did anything bad either. I'll tell you what: if you can tell me one REALLY good deed that you did, you're in."

So the guy says, "Once I was driving down the road and saw a gang of bikers assaulting this poor girl. So I pulled over, got out my car, grabbed a tire iron and walked straight up to the gang's leader — a huge ugly guy with a studded leather jacket, bald head but with hair all over his body, and a chain running from his nose to his ear."

"Undaunted, I ripped the chain out of his nose and ear and smashed him over the head with the tire iron. Then I turned around and, wielding my tire iron, yelled to the rest of them, 'You leave this poor, innocent lady alone! You're all a bunch of sick, deranged animals! GO HOME BEFORE I TEACH YOU ALL A LESSON IN PAIN!'"

Impressed, St. Peter says, "Really? When did this happen?"

"Oh, about two minutes ago."

OR

A guy arrives at the pearly gates, waiting to be admitted. St. Peter is reading through the Big Book to see if the guy's name is written in it.

After several minutes, St. Peter closes the book, furrows his brow, and says, "I'm sorry, I don't see your name written in the Book."

"How current is your copy?" he asks.

"I get a download every ten minutes." St. Peter replies, "Why do you ask?"

"I'm embarrassed to admit it, but I was always the stubborn type. It was not until my death was imminent that I cried out to God, so my name probably hasn't arrived to your copy yet."

"I'm glad to hear that, "Pete says, "but while we're waiting for the update to come through, can you tell me about a really good deed that you did in your life?"

The guy thinks for a moment and says, "Hmmm, well there was this one time when I was driving down a road and I saw a group of biker gang members harassing this poor girl. I slowed down, and sure enough, there they were, about 20 of them harassing this poor woman. Infuriated, I got out of my car, grabbed a tire iron out of my trunk, and walked up to the leader of the gang. He was a huge guy; 6-foot-4, 260 pounds, with a studded leather jacket and a chain running from his nose to his ears. As I walked up to the leader, the bikers formed a circle around me and told me to get lost or I'd be next."

"So I ripped the leader's chain out of his face and smashed him over the head with the tire iron. Then I turned around and yelled to the rest of them, 'Leave this poor innocent girl alone! You're all a bunch of SICK, deranged animals! Go home before I really teach you a lesson in PAIN!'"

St. Peter, duly impressed, says "Wow! When did this happen"

"About three minutes ago."

[death, fighting, unexpected]

Luke 12:20

Old Cyrus Barker was the richest man in town. When he became terminally ill, there was much speculation among the villagers concerning the extent of his wealth. And when Cyrus died, one of the town busybodies made it his business to run to the deceased's lawyer and ask, "How much money did old Cyrus leave?"

The lawyer replied, "All of it, my friend, all of it."

[death, money]

Luke 12:20

An artist asked the gallery owner if there had been any interest in his paintings on display at that time.

"I have good news and bad news," the owner replied. "The good news is that a gentleman inquired about your work and wondered if it would appreciate in value after your death. When I told him it would, he bought all 15 of your paintings."

"That's wonderful," the artist exclaimed. "What's the bad news?"

"The guy was your doctor..."

[death]

Luke 12:20

A man who was an avid golfer finally got a once in a lifetime chance for an audience with the Pope. After standing in line for hours, he got to the Pope and said, "Holiness, I have a question that only you can answer. You see, I love golf, and I feel a real need to know if there is a golf course in heaven. Can you tell me if there is?"

The Pope considered for a moment, and replied, "I do not know the answer to your question, my son, but I will talk to God and get back with you."

The next day, the man is called for another audience with the Pope to receive the answer to his question. He stood before the Pope, who said, "My son, I have some good news and some bad news in relation to your question. The good news is that heaven has the most fabulous golf course that you could imagine and is in eternally perfect shape. It puts all courses on earth to shame..."

"The bad news is that you tee-off tomorrow morning."

[death, heaven, sports]

Luke 12:27

The clerk in the unemployment office was surprised by the lady in line who was applying for benefits, especially since she was wearing designer clothes and a huge diamond ring. But he had a job to do. "Occupation?" he asked.
"I toil not," the woman answered. "Neither do I spin."
Grunting in reply, the clerk wrote, "Lily of the field."

[context, laziness]

Luke 12:40

Why do you keep reading your Bible all day long?" a youngster demanded of his aged grandfather.
"Well," he explained, "you might say that I'm cramming for my final examinations."

[grandparents, judgment]

Luke 13:3

The preacher has been working his way in volume and vocabulary to the climax of his sermon. Finally he declared his conclusion: "I'm telling you as members of this church that you must repent or die," thundered the minister.
Whereupon a visitor to the church smiled, wiped his forehead and said, "I'm sure glad I'm not a member of this church."

[death, judgment]

Luke 13:23

You're a minister, huh?"
"Yes, I am."
"What church?"
"Baptist."
"Oh, you're the narrow-minded bunch that believes only their group is going to make it to heaven."
"I'm even more narrow-minded than that. I don't think all of our group is going to make it!"

[death, denominations, heaven]

Luke 14:5

If people would quit digging pits on Saturday night, there wouldn't be so many oxen in the ditch on Sunday morning!

[excuses, hypocrisy, Sunday]

Luke 14:7-11

When you are writing a paper about exciting new data, do not overstate the impact of your result. Someone else may come along later with better data and prove you wrong, and then you will be humiliated and your colleagues will not respect your work. But when you have an exciting new result, be modest about its implications. Then when the review paper comes out, it will say, "This is an important piece of work," and you will be honored in the presence of all your colleagues. For everyone who exalts himself will be humbled, and he who humbles himself will be exalted.

[humility]

Luke 15:2

Years ago, there was a bag lady in New York City who attended a preaching service at a Manhattan Rescue Mission. Afterwards, in the line to receive soup, she mentioned to the preacher she was ready to give her life to the Lord.
She said, "I never knew until today that my name is in the Bible."
The preacher smiled and said, "What's your name?"
She said, "Edith. My name is Edith. And my name is in the Bible."
The preacher said, "I'm sorry ma'am but you must be mistaken. The name Edith never appears in the Bible."
She said, "Oh yes it does, you read it a few minutes ago!" He opened his Bible and she pointed her dirty finger to Luke 15:2. The preacher had been using the King James Version, and it says, "This man receiveth sinners and eateth with them." She said, "There it is! Jesus receiveth sinners and Edith with them!"

[names]

Luke 15:11-32

The Prodigal Son in F
or
A Fugitive Found
Feeling footloose and frisky, a featherbrained fellow
Forced his fond father to fork over the farthings,
And flew to foreign fields
And frittered his fortune feasting fabulously with faithless friends.
Fleeced by his fellows in folly and facing famine,
He found himself a feed-flinger in a filthy farmyard.
Fairly famishing, he fain would've filled his frame
With foraged food from fodder fragments.
"Fooey, my father's flunkies fare far finer,"
The frazzled fugitive forlornly fumbled, frankly facing facts.

Frustrated by failure, and filled with foreboding,
He fled forthwith to his family.
Falling at his father's feet, he forlornly fumbled. "Father, I've flunked And
fruitlessly forfeited family favor."
The far-sighted father, forestalling further flinching,
Frantically flagged the flunkies.
"Fetch a fatling from the flock and fix a feast."
The fugitive's faultfinding brother frowned
On fickle forgiveness of the former folderol.
But the faithful father figured
"Filial fidelity is fine, but the fugitive is found!
What forbids fervent festivity?
Let flags be unfurled! Let fanfares flare!"
Father's forgiveness formed the foundation
For the former fugitive's future fortitude!

[prodigal]

Luke 15:13

Remember this: Cold cash can melt mighty fast when you are having a hot
time.

[money]

Luke 15:13

Many men who leave home to set the world on fire, come back for more
matches!

[ambition]

Luke 15:17

A little boy told the story of the Prodigal Son for his Children's Church
class:
"He sold his coat to buy food.
He sold his shirt to buy food.
He sold his undershirt to buy food, and then he came to himself."

[body, clothes]

Luke 15:20

A father was sitting in church beside his son while the minister delivered a
sermon based on the timeless story of the prodigal son. When he got to the
point where the father sees his son returning and races out to meet him, the
minister said, "Throwing wide his arms, the father said..." at which point
the younger boy leaned over to his father and whispered "YOU'RE
GROUNDED!"

[forgiveness, judgment]

Luke 15:20

Harry, one day, attended Children's Church where the class read together the parable of the Prodigal Son, and had a lesson about it.

"And what happened when the Prodigal Son returned?" asked the teacher when question time came.

"His father went to meet him and hurt himself," replied one of the class.

"Hurt himself?" said the teacher. "Wherever did you learn that?"

"From the Bible, sir," replied Harry. "It says his father ran to meet him and fell on his neck."

[forgiveness, injury]

Luke 15:23

I'd like to hear a sermon done
On the general theme of the prodigal son.
But slanted anew
From the point of view,
And on behalf
Of the fatted calf.

[forgiveness, sacrifice]

Luke 15:28

The Children's Church class was studying the story of the return of the Prodigal Son and the jealousy of his brother.

"Now let me see how well you've paid attention to this story, " the teacher said. "At the feast that was given to celebrate the return of the Prodigal, there was someone to whom the whole party brought no joy, only resentment and bitterness and disappointment. Who was this?"

A small boy raised his hand and said, "I'd say it was probably the fatted calf"

[forgiveness, judgment]

Luke 16:13

A Mormon acquaintance once pushed Mark Twain into an argument on the issue of polygamy. After long and tedious expositions justifying the practice, the Mormon demanded that Twain cite any passage of scripture expressly forbidding polygamy.

"Nothing easier," Twain replied. "No man can serve two masters."

[bigamy, context, marriage]

Luke 16:21

QUESTION: Where in Scripture do we have a dog with a name and what is the name?
ANSWER: The dog's name is "Moreover." In Luke 16:21 (KJV) it says, "Moreover, the dog came and licked his sores."

[animal, names]

Luke 16:22

Roasted at the 1989 annual banquet of the Religious News Writers Association because of his fund-raising efforts, Dr. Jerry Falwell responded by recalling a letter proposing that his tombstone be inscribed with these words from Luke 16:22, "And it came to pass, that the beggar died."

[death, frugal]

Luke 16:23

A dear old lady knew her time of final departure was approaching.
"Soon, I'll be rocking in the bosom of Moses," she told her pastor.
"No, dear," said the pastor, "the Bible says the bosom of Abraham."
"At my age, you don't care too much whose bosom it is!" she responded.

[death, unconcerned]

Luke 16:23

A man was traveling to go to Florida for a mini-vacation. His wife was due to meet him later after a business trip of her own. When he got to the Miami hotel he decided to e-mail her to let her know the specifics of their weekend accommodations. He tried to remember her e-mail address but sent the message with one address letter misplaced.
Instead, the letter went to a widow of a Baptist minister who had just passed on the day before. She happened to look at her e-mail message before going on to the funeral. She read it and fainted dead away.
When her sons and daughters came into the room to investigate the noise, they read the e-mail from wrong husband in the Miami hotel.
It read, "Hi Honey — Just Arrived — I'm busy making preparations for your arrival tomorrow ... P.S. Boy is it hot down here!

[hell]

Luke 17:4

A woman with fourteen children, ages one through fourteen, sued her husband for divorce on the grounds of desertion.
"When did he desert you?" the judge asked.
"Thirteen years ago," she replied.
"If he left thirteen years ago, where did all these children come from?"

"Oh," said the woman, "he kept coming back to say he was sorry."

[birth control, divorce, forgiveness]

Luke 17:17

Why did only one cleansed leper return to thank Jesus? The following are nine suggested reasons why the nine did not return:
One waited to see if the cure was real.
One waited to see if it would last.
One said he would see Jesus later.
One decided that he had never had leprosy.
One said he would have gotten well anyway.
One gave the glory to the priests.
One said, "O, well, Jesus didn't really do anything."
One said, "Any rabbi could have done it."
One said, "I was already much improved."

[thankfulness]

Luke 18:1

Little Timmy was saying his prayers one night and as his mother walked by his room she heard this heartfelt plea.
"And please make Johnny stop throwing things at me. By the way, I've mentioned this before."

[persistence, prayer]

Luke 18:2-8

In a certain department there was a chairman who neither feared God nor cared about students. There was a student in that department who kept coming to him with the plea, "Grant me justice in my petition." For some time he refused, but finally he said to himself, "Even though I don't fear God or care about students, yet because this student keeps bothering me, I will see that she gets justice, so that she won't eventually wear me out with her coming!" Listen to what the unjust department chair says. "Will not God bring about justice for his chosen ones, who cry out to him day and night? Will he keep putting them off? I tell you he will see that they get justice, and quickly."

[justice]

Luke 18:11

See 1 Timothy 5:19.

Luke 18:25

See Genesis 7:9 re. Camels.

Luke 19: 3

I wish everyone would quit standing in front of me," said Zacchaeus *shortly*.

[puns, size]

Luke 19:45

See John 2:15.

Luke 20:27

See Mark 12:18.

Luke 20:47

QUESTION: How does a lawyer resemble a scribe?
ANSWER: Lawyers also study the law and the profits [prophets].

[lawyers, prophets]

Luke 21:7

A local priest and rabbi were fishing on the side of the road. They thoughtfully made a sign saying, "The End is Near! Turn yourself around now before it's too late!" and showed it to each passing car.
One driver that drove by didn't appreciate the sign and shouted at them: "Leave us alone, you religious nuts!"
All of a sudden they heard a big splash. They looked at each other and the priest said to the rabbi, "You think we should just put up a sign that says 'Bridge Out' instead?"

[warning]

Luke 21:9

A lecturer announced to his audience that the world would probably end in seven billion years.
"How long did you say?" came a horrified voice from the rear.
"Seven billion years."
"Thank goodness!" said the voice. "I thought for a moment you had said seven million."

[fear, future, time]

Luke 22:13-14

Every time a new Pope is elected, there's a whole lot of rituals and ceremonies that have to be gone through, in accordance with tradition. Well there's one tradition that very few people know about. Shortly after the new Pope is enthroned, the Chief Rabbi seeks an audience. He is shown into the Pope's presence, whereupon he presents him with a silver tray bearing a velvet cushion. On top of the cushion is an ancient, shriveled parchment envelope. The Pope symbolically stretches out his arm in a gesture of rejection. The Chief Rabbi then retires, taking the envelope with him and does not return until the next Pope is elected.

John Paul II was intrigued by this ritual whose origins were unknown to him. He instructed the best scholars of the Vatican to research it, but they came up with nothing. When the time came and the Chief Rabbi was shown into his presence, he faithfully enacted the ritual rejection but, as the Chief Rabbi turned to leave, he called him back. "My brother," the Holy Father whispered, "I must confess that we Catholics are ignorant of the meaning of this ritual enacted for centuries between us and you, the representative of the Jewish people. I have to ask you, what is it all about?" The Chief Rabbi shrugs and replies: "But we have no more idea than you do. The origin of the ceremony is lost in the mists of ancient history." The Pope said: "Let us retire to my private chambers and enjoy a glass of wine together, then, with your agreement, we shall open the envelope and discover at last the secret." The Chief Rabbi agreed.

Fortified in their resolve by the wine, they gingerly pried open the curling parchment envelope and with trembling fingers, the Chief Rabbi reached inside and extracted a folded sheet of similarly ancient paper. As the Pope peered over his shoulder, he slowly opened it. They both gasped with shock. It was the check for the Last Supper.

[Catholic, debt, denominations, Judaism]

Luke 22:36

A missionary carried a gun and a Bible. The gun was for tigers who either couldn't read or weren't Presbyterian.

[evangelism]

Luke 22:40

What makes resisting temptation difficult, for most people, is that they don't want to discourage it completely.

[compromise, temptation]

Luke 22:40

Now that there's no more praying in school, the kids may have to go to motels just to read the Bible.

[Bible, prayer]

Luke 23:3

A Catholic priest and a Rabbi are talking about job prospects:
"Well," says the priest, "there's a good chance that I'll be the next bishop — maybe within the next couple of years."

"Bishop!" marvels the Rabbi, "very nice. And after that?"

"Oh, I don't know, I suppose it's possible I could become Archbishop ... given luck and God's blessing."

"Very nice, very nice; and after Archbishop?"

"Ha! Well, you know, it's Cardinal after that, but it's really very unlikely. But in theory, I could become a Cardinal."

"Lovely!" enthuses the Rabbi, "the scarlet would suit your complexion. So what's after Cardinal?"

The priest smiles: "After Cardinal? Well, it's Pope — but I'm hardly likely to become ... hmmm, oh I suppose it's just possible. If a Pole why not an Englishman again? Yes, I could just become Pope."

"Splendid! And after Pope?"

The priest looks at him in surprise: "After Pope? There's nothing after Pope! I mean, there's just God above the Pope — I can't become God."

"Why not? One of our boys made it."

[Catholic, Judaism]

Luke 23:32

The old preacher was dying at home in his bed. He realized his time was short, so he sent for his doctor and his lawyer to come to his home. When they arrived, they were ushered up to his bedroom.

As they entered the room, the preacher held out his hands and motioned for them to sit on each side of the bed.

For the longest time, no one said a word. Finally, the doctor spoke up and said, "Preacher, you're not long for this old world, you'd better tell us why you asked us to come."

The old preacher mustered up all his strength and in a strained voice said, "Well, Jesus died between two thieves and that's how I wanted to die."

[crucifixion, doctor, lawyer]

Luke 23:33

A church group touring the Near East pulled into a stop. It was mid afternoon. "Why are we stopping here?" asked one of the group.

"This is where the Romans crucified their victims," replied the group leader.

"When did that happen?" asked a man.

Thinking of the early days of the Christian church the tour guide replied "I think up to one ten [AD]."

Looking at his watch, the tour member turned to his wife and said, "We missed by an hour and a half."

[crucifixion, time]

Luke 23:34

An elderly preacher advised his young preacher friend that if he ever forgot the marriage ceremony to start quoting Scriptures until he remembered. The second wedding, sure enough, the young preacher forgot, and the only Scripture he could remember on the spot was, "Father, forgive them, for they know not what they do!"

[context, forgiveness, marriage]

Luke 23:43

Paradise: two ivory cubes with dots all over them.

[gambling, paradise]

Luke 23:43

See Luke 12:20.

Luke 24:2

See Mark 16:4.

Luke 24:6

The youngster came home from Children's Church on Easter Sunday and told his mother he could understand about Christ but not about the roses. So he asked his mom, "Why was Christ a rose [arose]?"

[resurrection]

Luke 24:30

The Children's Church Teacher asks, "Now, Johnny, tell me frankly do you say prayers before eating?"

"No sir," Little Johnny replies, "I don't have to, my mom is a good cook!"

[food, prayer]

JOHN

John 1:14

A group of schoolchildren in the US put on their own nativity play which they'd written themselves. As it began, the audience was surprised to see no sign of Mary. Then they heard moaning and groaning from behind some bales of straw, and moments later a doctor came out with a white coat on and carrying a black bag, and disappeared behind the bales with Joseph. A little later he reappeared with a smile on his face and a doll in his arms, announcing to the audience, "It's a GOD!"

[incarnation]

John 1:46

Two skeptical Pharisees from Jerusalem were visiting Nazareth and asked an old man the question, "Ever had any big men born in this town?"
"No," responded the old man slowly. "Best we can do is babies. Different in the big city, I suppose."

[birth, Pharisee]

John 1:46

An aged woman, born and nurtured in the South, was endeavoring to impress upon her nephews and nieces the beauties of the South and its people, when one of the young men spoke up.
"Auntie," he asked, "do you think that all the virtues originated and have been preserved by the Southern people?"
"No, not all, but most of them," she replied.
"Do you think that Jesus Christ was a Southerner?" Asked the young man.
The old lady hesitated a moment and then said: "He was good enough to be a Southerner!"

[Jesus, pride]

John 2:9

A Baptist minister is driving to New York for a weekend away, and he's stopped for speeding.
The state trooper smells alcohol on his breath and he says, "Sir, have you been drinking?"
The minister says, "Just water."
The sheriff says, "Then why do I smell wine?"

The minister looks down at the bottle and says, "Good Lord, He's done it again!"

[Baptist, drinking, miracle]

John 2:15

QUESTION: What's the first sign of the high jump in the bible?
ANSWER: Jesus cleared the temple.

OR

QUESTION: Who holds the high jump record in the Bible?
ANSWER: Jesus, when he cleared the temple!

[sports]

John 2:15

Christ was like a bull in a shekinah [china] shop.

[anger, temple]

John 2:15

Did you know that Jesus had an automobile?
He drove them from the temple in a Fury!

[anger, temple]

John 2:15

Phil Brown, the trial lawyer, came dragging in after a hard day at work. "It was a terrible day in court," he told his wife. "I exhibited moral outrage when I meant to show righteous indignation."

[anger]

John 2:17

As a child Theodore Roosevelt was called "Teedie." His mother Mittie had found he was so afraid of the Madison Square Church that he refused to set foot inside if he was alone. So she pressed him to tell her why. He was terrified, she discovered, of something called the "zeal." He had heard the minister read about it from the Bible. Using a concordance she read him those particular passages containing the word "zeal" until suddenly, very excited, he told her to stop. The line was from John 2:17 (KJV): "And his disciples remembered that it was written, 'The zeal of thine house hath eaten me up.'"

[fear, temple]

John 3:1

QUESTION: What Bible character may have only been a foot tall?
ANSWER: Nicodemus — he was a ruler.

[size]

John 3:8

Did you hear about the observant chap who claims to have discovered the color of the wind? He went out and found it blew [blue].

[weather]

John 3:16

Dear GOD,
I bet it is very hard for You to love all of everybody in the whole world. There are only 4 people in our family and I can never do it.
Sincerely,
Harper

[love]

John 3:16

Children's Church teacher: "Do you remember your memory verse?"
Student: "I sure do. I even remember the zip code ...John 3:16."

[mail]

John 3:16

God so loved the world that he did not leave it in the hands of a committee.

[God, love]

John 3:18

See Mark 16:16.

John 4:7

QUESTION: Who is the largest woman in the bible?
ANSWER: The woman of Some area [Samaria].

[geography, size]

John 4:11

"Tell me more about the living waters," Tom said *thirstily*.

[puns, water]

John 4:18

A couple was arranging for their wedding, and asked the bakery to inscribe the wedding cake with the statement found in 1 John 4:18 which reads "There is no fear in love, but perfect love casts out fear."
The bakery evidently lost, smudged or otherwise misread the noted reference, and beautifully inscribed on the cake John 4:18 "for you have had five husbands, and the man you have now is not your husband."

[context, misunderstanding, wedding]

John 4:18

A widow recently married a widower. Soon after the marriage she was accosted by a friend who laughingly remarked, "I suppose, like all men who have been married before, your husband sometimes talks about his first wife?"
"Oh, not any more, he doesn't," the other replied.
"What stopped him?"
"I started talking about my next husband."

[husbands]

John 4:44

Expert: An ordinary guy who is a long way from home.

[distance, expert]

John 5:37

A little girl named Marlow was struggling with her art assignment. While the rest of the children handed in beautiful drawings, Marlow turned in a blank piece of paper. Confused, the teacher said, "Marlow dear, the assignment was to submit a drawing of some sort. All you have given me is a blank sheet of paper."
Marlow answered, "I did draw something — it's a picture of God!"
Again confused, the teacher responded, "But darling, God has no form. We don't know what God looks like."
To which Marlow responded, "So you are going to give me an 'A' then?"

[art, God]

John 6:1-13

See Mark 6:32-44.

John 6:9

See Luke 9:16.

John 6:9

QUESTION: Why did the boy in the story of the miracle of the feeding of the 5,000 have so much food all for himself in the first place?
ANSWER: Like most boys, he was just an appetite with a skin pulled over it.

[hunger]

John 6:9

Among the five thousand who were fed with the two fish and the five loaves of bread were doubtless several who complained about the bones the fish contained.

[complain]

John 6:19

A mother was watching her four-year-old child playing outside in a small plastic pool half filled with water. He was happily walking back and forth across the pool, making big splashes. Suddenly, he stopped, stepped out of the pool, and began to scoop water out of the pool with a pail.
"Why are you pouring the water out, Johnny?" the mother asked.
"'Cause my teacher said Jesus walked on water, and this water won't work," the boy replied.

[miracle, water]

John 6:19-20

One summer evening during a violent thunderstorm a mother was tucking her small boy into bed. She was about to turn off the light when he asked with a tremor in his voice, "Mommy, will you sleep with me tonight?" The mother smiled and gave him a reassuring hug. "I can't, dear," she said. "I have to sleep in Daddy's room."
A long silence was broken at last by his shaky little voice: "The big sissy."

[father, fear]

John 6:66

I bet it was really tough being an Apostle of Jesus. What if you wanted a day off? So you call up Jesus and say, "Jesus, I'm sick today, running a little fever and feeling congested so I won't be able to make it to today's sermon ... What? ... Say that again? ... I'm cured?"

[disciple, healing]

John 8:11

A pastor in rural Vermont tells the story of the parishioner who volunteered to paint the church. He was given a considerable supply of good-quality paint and so he decided to dilute it a little so he could paint his barn as well.

Before dawn the day after he finished, it rained. He woke up to see the paint streaming off his barn. Horrified, he ran to the church. The paint job was ruined there too. He fell to his knees, looked up, and cried, "What shall I do?" A voice answered, "Repaint, repaint, and thin no more!"

[repentance, sin]

John 8:11

A minister was given a parking ticket. In police court, the judge asked if he had anything to say.

"Yes," the minister replied hoping to influence the judge by the use of Scripture, "Blessed are the merciful for they shall obtain mercy."

The judge, a Bible believing person himself, fined him fifty dollars and admonished him, "Go thou and sin no more."

OR

A minister was stopped by a traffic cop for speeding. Just as the cop was about to write the ticket, the minister said to him in a very solemn voice, "Blessed are the merciful, for they shall obtain mercy."

The cop handed the minister the ticket and said brightly, "Go thou and sin no more."

[mercy, sin]

John 8:12

A little boy named Justin forgot his lines in a Children's Church presentation. His mother was in the front row to prompt him. She gestured and formed the words silently with her lips, but it did not help. Her son's memory was blank.

Finally, she leaned forward and whispered the cue, "I am the light of the world."

The child beamed and with great feeling and a loud clear voice said, "My mother is the light of the world."

[light, mother]

John 11:38-39

"That's where we buried Lazarus," said Martha <u>grave</u>ly.

[burial, puns]

John 11:44

A 77-year-old man wrote, "I seem to be in good health, though getting out of bed in the morning makes the raising of Lazarus look like a cheap trick."

[aging, resurrection]

John 12:4-6

Agnostic: If those Christians would stop building such large and fancy buildings and give the money to the poor, it would be more to their credit.
Christian: I've heard that remark before.
Agnostic: Indeed, And by whom, may I ask?
Christian: Judas Iscariot.

[greed]

John 12:6

The minister of a small congregation in Arkansas disappeared one night with the entire church treasury, and the local constable set out to capture him. This he did, dragging the culprit back by the collar a week later. "Here's the varmint, folks," announced the constable grimly. "I'm sorry to say he's already squandered our money, but I drug him back so we can make him preach it out."

[preaching, stealing]

John 12:12-19

Coach Forest Evashevski's housekeeper at Iowa was a devoutly religious woman. After a Rose Bowl victory, Hawkeye fans presented Coach Ev with a new car. He drove it home, pulled up in front of his house, and strolled to the front porch.
"What do you think?" Ev asked the housekeeper.
The good woman appraised him silently, then said, "Just remember the same people who praised Jesus also crucified Him."

[honor, traitor]

John 12:21

A drunk stumbles along a baptismal service on Sunday afternoon down by the river. He proceeds to walk down into the water and stand next to the Preacher. The minister turns and notices the old drunk and says, "Mister, Are you ready to find Jesus?" The drunk looks back and says, "Yes, Preacher I sure am." The minister then dunks the fellow under the water and pulls him right back up. Have you found Jesus?" the preacher asked. "No, I didn't!" said the drunk. The preacher then dunks him under for quite a bit longer, brings him up and says, "Now, brother, have you found Jesus?" "Noooo, I did not Reverend." The preacher in disgust holds the man under for at least 30 seconds this time, brings him out of the water and says in a harsh tone, "My good man, have you found Jesus yet?" The old drunk wipes his eyes and says to the preacher, "Are you sure this is where he fell in?"

[baptism]

John 12:47

Jesus and Satan have an argument as to who is the better programmer. This goes on for a few hours until they agree to hold a contest with God as the judge.

They set themselves before their computers and begin. They type furiously for several hours, lines of code streaming up the screen.

Seconds before the end of the competition, a bolt of lightning strikes, taking out the electricity. Moments later, the power is restored, and God announces that the contest is over. He asks Satan to show what he has come up with.

Satan is visibly upset, and cries, "I have nothing! I lost it all when the power went out."

"Very well, then," says God, "let us see if Jesus fared any better."

Jesus enters a command, and the screen comes to life in vivid display, the voices of an angelic choir pour forth from the speakers. Satan is astonished. He stutters, "But how! I lost everything, yet Jesus' program is intact! How did he do it?"

God chuckles, "Jesus saves."

[computer, Jesus, salvation]

John 13:23-24

A male Children's Church class teacher, who had difficulty remembering names of Bible characters in his lessons, was advised to write those names on paper and pin the paper on the inside of his coat jacket. Next Sunday, trying to recall the names of Jesus' inner disciples, he looked down inside his jacket, and exclaimed, "Hart, Schaffner & Marx."

[disciples, names]

John 13:27

He was in the habit of opening his Bible at random and taking the first thing his eyes fell on as something that he should obey.

One day the verse he read was Matthew 27:5, "... he went away and hanged himself."

Not thinking that quite suitable, he shut the Bible and opened it again at another place. The verse his eyes fell on this time was Luke 10:27, "... go and do the same."

Worried now, he quickly closed and opened his Bible again to read in horror John 13:27, "... what you do, do quickly."

[context]

John 14:2

If you wish to dwell in the house of many mansions, you must make your reservation in advance.

[heaven, salvation]

John 14:2

There is the story of the Children's Church teacher who asked a little boy if he knew where Jesus dwelt at the present time, confidently expecting that he would ANSWER: "In heaven."
"In the bathroom at my house," replied the child.
"Why do you say that?" inquired the shocked teacher.
"Because every morning my daddy pounds on the door and says, 'My lord, are you still in there?"

[heaven, Jesus]

John 14:3

A preacher who suffered extremely strained relations with his congregation was finally appointed chaplain at the state prison. Elated to be rid of him so easily, the people came in great numbers to hear his farewell discourse. The preacher chose as his text, "I go and prepare a place for you ... that where I am, there ye may be also." (John 14:3)

[context, judgment, prison]

John 14:5

Graffiti found at a theological seminary: Underneath the question, "Where will you spend eternity?" some had scrawled, "The way things look now, in the course Hebrew 101."

[education, eternity, persistence]

John 14:6

An exasperated mother, whose son was always getting into mischief, finally asked him, "How do you expect to get into heaven?"
The boy thought it over and said, "Well, I'll just run in and out and keep slamming the door until St. Peter says what you always say, 'For heaven's sake, come in or stay out!'"

[heaven, salvation]

John 14:16 (KJV)

"Mamma, when is God going to send us a blanket?" asked seven-year-old Silas one day.

"Why do you think God is going to send us a blanket? Asked his mother.

"Because," replied the young son, "our Children's Church teacher said God promised a comforter when Jesus went back to heaven. And Jesus has been in heaven a long time."

[gift, Holy Spirit]

John 14:26-27

A mother didn't feel well one Sunday so she sent her little girl to church and told her to be sure to remember the text of the sermon. When she came home, the little girl said, "The minister said, 'Don't be scared, you'll get your quilt.'"

The mother was perplexed. Finally she phoned the preacher. He explained that his text was, "Fear not, thy comforter will come."

[comfort, Holy Spirit, words]

John 15:13

After hearing a youth talk on the verse, "Greater love hath no man than this, that a man lay down his life for a friend," a girl decided to test her boyfriend. "Do you love me," she asked.

"Yes, dear." He replied.

"Would you die for me?" she asked.

"No," said the boy with a twinkle in his eye, "mine is an undying love."

[death, friend, love]

John 15:14

A minister, having served the same church for many years, decided to leave and take a similar position in another church. Without telling anyone he had made this decision or writing a letter to the congregation, he waited until Sunday morning to announce his resignation in church. When he spoke to the congregation he said, "The same Jesus that called me to this church many years ago has now called upon me to leave and serve another church."

The congregation all stood and then sang the closing hymn that had been previously chosen, "What a Friend We Have in Jesus."

[friend, hymn]

John 16:6-7

See John 14:46-47

John 16:8

The average man's idea of a good sermon is one that goes over his head—
and hits one of his neighbors.

[hypocrisy]

John 16:13

Titus, the minister's son, was watching his father labor over Sunday's
sermon.
"Daddy, I thought you said God tells you what to say every Sunday."
"He does, son," replied his father.
"Then how come," asked his confused son, "you cross so much of it out?"

[preaching]

John 18:28-29

A Children's Church teacher asked her students to draw a picture of the
Holy Family. After the pictures were brought to her, she saw that some of
the youngsters had drawn the conventional pictures — the Holy Family and
the manger, the Holy Family riding on the mule, etc.
But she called up one little boy to ask him to explain his drawing, which
showed an airplane with four heads sticking out of the plane windows.
She said, "I can understand you drew three of the heads to show Joseph,
Mary and Jesus. But who's the fourth head?"
"Oh," answered the boy, "that's Pontius the pilot!"

[transportation]

John 19:18

See Luke 23:32.

John 19:18

A Children's Church teacher was teaching the children about the meaning
of Good Friday and asked the group if any of them knew what happened to
Jesus on that day. "Sure," piped up a little boy, "he got hammered!"

[crucifixion, Easter]

John 19:38-42

The morning after Jesus was buried in Joseph's tomb, Joseph was walking
toward the local synagogue where he met a couple of old friends. Hiram,
one of the friends greeted Joseph warmly and said, "Joseph it was so kind of
you to give your tomb up to that man that was punished yesterday when he
had nowhere to be laid." Joel chimed in, "We know you put a good deal of
money into that tomb as a fitting resting place for your body. This kind
action will be long remembered of you."

Hiram and Joel, without time to waste, continued on their way.
Joseph turned around as they were walking off and said, "Gentlemen, you don't understand. I'm not as generous as you have credited me. I only had to loan it to him for the weekend."

[Easter, generous, resurrection]

John 20:1

See Mark 16:4.

John 20:2

Often the male disciples are criticized because the women came to the tomb first. What many Christians don't realize is that an alternative reading in the Greek of this verse indicates it was Daylight Savings weekend. The disciples came "late" only because these disciples merely forgot to set their watches ahead one hour!

[resurrection, time]

John 20:4

QUESTION: Why did John outrun Peter when they went to Jesus' empty grave?
ANSWER: Because Peter's bike only had 1st and 2nd [1 & 2 Peter] while John had 1st 2nd and 3rd [1, 2, & 3 John].

[Bible, disciples, names]

John 21:3

Even if you've been fishing for 3 hours and haven't gotten anything except poison ivy and a sunburn, you're still better off than the worm."

[optimist]

ACTS

Acts

Student in Bible College: "Ever heard of the resolutions of the disciples?"
Fellow student: "No, but I've heard a great deal about the Acts of the Apostles."

[work]

Acts

Some uninformed Christians think that the Acts of the Apostles are either: 1. Phony motions to the wallet made by the Apostles when the check arrived for the Last Supper, OR 2. Christ's touring company that knocked 'em dead in Samaria, Thessalonica, Damascus, etc.

[names]

Acts

See Ephesians 6:17.

Acts 1:1

When he was born his father chose to call him "Theophilus" (Acts 1:1). When friends asked him why that name, the father's reply was, "He's got 'the awful-ess' face I've ever seen."

[name]

Acts 1:1

See Luke 1:3.

Acts 1:3

Ascension of Christ — Jesus rose into heaven forty days after Passover — an indication of how tough it is to get a table up there.

[heaven, resurrection]

Acts 1:8

Silence is golden except when it comes to witnessing — then it's just plain yellow.

[courage, evangelism, silence]

Acts 2:1

QUESTION: What kind of motor vehicle did the early Christians drive?
ANSWER: Honda, because the apostles were all in one Accord (KJV).

[cars, unity]

Acts 2:3

When trying to motivate Christians, Billy Sunday used to speak graphically of the well-known village atheist, who was seen running vigorously to a burning church building, intent on joining with others in subduing the flames. A neighbor, observing him, exclaimed facetiously, "This is something new for you! I never saw you going to church before." "Well," the atheist replied, "this is the first time I have ever seen a church on fire."

[atheist, enthusiasm]

Acts 2:8

There was a missionary going to the Philippines and his wife had a cat with which she could not part and so it was taken along on the missionary journey. There was a small hole in the wall of the house that they moved into in Manila. A mouse lived there and the cat loved to chase it.

Every day the cat would chase the mouse but he couldn't catch it, and the mouse would laugh at him. One day, the cat almost caught the mouse. On that day the cat waited outside of the mouse hole. The mouse was very scared because he could hear the cat outside of the hole meowing. The cat sat there continuing to meow — meow, meow.

Eventually the meowing stopped and all the mouse could hear was the barking of a dog —ruff, ruff, ruff. The mouse, full of joy, ran out of his house knowing that he had been saved. As the mouse came out of his hole, the cat pounced on him and gobbled him up, and walked away smiling saying to himself, it pays to be bilingual.

[speech, tongues]

Acts 2:38

An elderly woman had just returned to her home from an evening church service when she was startled by an intruder. As she caught the man in the act of robbing her home of its valuables, she remembered her pastor's admonition to quote Scripture aloud whenever a believer found herself alone and afraid so she yelled, "Stop! Acts 2:38!" [...turn from your sin...] The burglar stopped dead in his tracks. The woman calmly called the police and explained what she had done. As the officer cuffed the man to take him in, he asked the burglar, "Why did you just stand there? All the old lady did was yell a Bible reference at you."

"Bible?" replied the burglar, "She said she had an AXE and two 38's!"

[context, stealing]

Acts 2:38

A church that practiced baptismal regeneration took their latest convert out behind the rural church for his baptismal service. The preacher announced:

"I'm going to baptize you in this stream and take away every bit of sin that
you got."

After taking one look at the stream, the convert replied, "In that li'l shallow
crick?"

[baptism]

Acts 3:8

A very dignified pastor was visiting a lady in a nursing home who was
confined to a wheelchair. As he stood to leave, the lady asked him to have a
word of prayer. He gently took her hand and prayed that God would be
with her to bring her comfort, strength and healing.

When he finished praying, her face began to glow. She said softly, "Pastor,
would you help me to my feet?"

Not knowing what else to do, he helped her up.

At first, she took a few uncertain steps. Then she began to jump up and
down, then to dance and shout and cry with happiness until the whole
nursing home was aroused.

After she was quieted, the solemn pastor hurried out to his car, closed the
door, grabbed hold of the steering wheel and prayed this little prayer:
"Lord, don't you ever do that to me again!"

[embarrassment, healing]

Acts 3:38

See Mark 16:16.

Acts 4:7

A minister pulled into a service station on the start of the Fourth of July
weekend and found it really crowded. The busy attendant finally got to the
clergyman, who had been waiting a long time. He apologized, saying,
"Seems like everybody waits until the last minute to get ready for a long
trip."

The clergyman smiled and said, "I know what you mean. I have the same
problem in my line of work."

[holiday, procrastination,]

Acts 4:8

The pastor was greeting folks at the door after the service. A woman said,
"Pastor, that was a very good sermon." The pastor says, "Oh, I have to give
the credit to the Holy Spirit." "Oh," she immediately responded, "It wasn't
THAT good!"

[Holy Spirit, sermon]

Acts 4:19

Aubrey Meek was brought before the court on the charge of refusing to obey a police officer. "Why did you refuse to move on when asked to do so by the officer?" the judge inquired, obviously wondering what unexplained force could have given such a man strength to buck a strong authority of the law.

"It's like this, your honor," explained Meek. "My wife said I was to meet her at exactly twelve noon at that spot — and I was forced to choose between man's law and wife's law."

[government, law, wife]

Acts 4:35

Two fellows are talking religion. One says to the other, "Sometimes I'd like to ask God why he allows poverty, famine and injustice when he could do something about it."

"What's stopping you from asking?" asks the second.

The first replies, "I'm afraid God might ask me the same question."

[giving, questions]

Acts 5:17

See Mark 12:18.

Acts 6:2

The retiring usher was instructing his youthful successor in the details of his office. "And remember, my boy, that we have nothing but good, kind Christians in this church ... until you try to put someone else in their pew."

[kindness, selfish, usher]

Acts 7:56

A very old man lay dying in his bed. In death's doorway, he suddenly smelled the aroma of his favorite chocolate chip cookies, wafting up the stairs. He gathered his remaining strength and lifted himself from the bed. Leaning against the wall, he slowly made his way out of the bedroom, and with even greater effort, forced himself down the stairs, gripping the railing with both hands.

With labored breath, he leaned against the doorframe, gazing into the kitchen. Were it not for death's agony, he would have thought himself already in heaven. There, spread out on newspapers on the kitchen table, were literally hundreds of his favorite chocolate chip cookies. Was it heaven? Or was it one final act of devotion from his wife, seeing to it that he left this world a happy man?

Mustering one great final effort, he threw himself toward the table. The aged and withered hand shook, as it made its way to a cookie at the edge of the table, when he was suddenly smacked with a spatula by his wife. "Stay out of those," she said. "They're for the funeral."

[funeral]

Acts 8:4

The old lady went to church and heard a young minister preach. When she got out, somebody asked her what she thought of his preaching.
She said, "He spoke in true apostolic style. He took a text and went everywhere preaching the gospel."

[apostles, preaching]

Acts 8:36

The mayor off a tough border town was about to engage a preacher for the new church.
"Pastor, you aren't by any chance a Baptist, are you?"
"No I'm not. Why?"
"Well, I was just going to say that we have to haul our water twelve miles."

[Baptist]

Acts 8:38

A little boy was trying to make a good Baptist out of the family cat by immersing him in the bathtub. After the first splash, the cat started yowling, and the little boy finally said, "All right — be a Methodist then," and he let the candidate go.

[Baptist, denominations]

Acts 8:38

Early in the ministry of an older pastor at a rural church, a woman came to the front during the decision time at the end of a morning service, wanting to be baptized. After sharing the scriptures with her the pastor took her down to the "baptizing hole" at the creek and baptized her.
One of the elders came up to him afterwards and expressed his concern over her immersion. When the pastor asked what he was concerned about he said that he had noticed that the pastor did not totally get all of her under the water. When the pastor asked what part did not get immersed, he motioned toward his stomach. The woman he was talking about was eight months pregnant. The pastor, a strong believer in adult baptism only responded, "She is OK, because we don't practice infant baptism in our church."

[babies, baptism]

Acts 8:38

A drunk stumbles along a baptismal service on Sunday afternoon down by the river. He proceeds to walk down into the water and stand next to the Preacher.

The minister turns and notices the old drunk and says, "Mister, Are you ready to find Jesus?"

The drunk looks back and says, "Yessss, Preacher, I sure am."

The minister then dunks the fellow under the water and pulls him right back up. "Have you found Jesus?" the preacher asked.

"Nooo, I didn't!" said the drunk.

The preacher then dunks him under for quite a bit longer, brings him up and says, "Now, brother, have you found Jesus?"

"Noooo, I did not Reverend."

The preacher in disgust holds the man under for at least 30 seconds this time, brings him out of the water and says in a harsh tone, "My Good man, have you found Jesus yet?"

The ole drunk wipes his eyes and says to the preacher... "Are you sure this is where he fell in?"

[baptism, Jesus]

Acts 8:39

The pastor was teaching a class of boys. His lesson was more like a sermon. The story was about Philip and the Ethiopian treasurer. Anxious to impress the boys with the joy of becoming a Christian, he asked, "Why did the eunuch go on his way rejoicing?"

One boy answered promptly, "Because Philip quit preaching."

[joy, preaching]

Acts 9:1

The preacher was wired for sound with a lapel mike, and as he preached, he moved briskly about the platform, jerking the mike cord as he went. Then he moved to one side, getting wound up in the cord and nearly tripping before jerking it again. After several circles and jerks, a little girl in the third pew leaned toward her mother and whispered, "If he gets loose, will he hurt us?"

[danger, preaching]

Acts 10:42 (KJV)

"Quick and the dead" ... in our modern world of cars and trucks all around us, the quick are the ones who had time to get out of the way; the dead are the ones who didn't.

[dead]

Acts 11:19

Children's Church teacher: "What were the Phoenicians famous for?"
Student: "Blinds."

[names]

Acts 11:26

Ben Hur is one story of the early Christians. The believers in Antioch of
Syria is another great story about early Christians. Today we still have early
Christians. They're the ones who get to sit in the back of the church!

[laziness, names]

Acts 11:26

Christians are people who follow Jesus, although they disagree on which
way He went.

[conflicts, division]

Acts 12:4 (KJV)

An unlearned seminary student thought Easter Sunday was Billy Sunday's
sister!

[Easter, holidays]

Acts 13:3

After a special exhortation for support of foreign missions, the basket was
passed. When it was presented to one man, he said to the holder of the
basket, "I don't believe in missions."
"In that case," whispered the deacon, "take something out — it is for the
heathen."

[giving, missions]

Acts 13:10

QUESTION: Did you hear about the dyslexic Devil Worshipper?
ANSWER: He sold his soul to Santa!

[devil, Satan]

Acts 13:38

"Freddie," said the Children's Church teacher, "can you tell me what we
must do before we can expect forgiveness of sin?"
"Yeah, sir," replied the boy, "We must sin."

[forgiveness, sin]

Acts 15:5

The Law is still trying to be kept today. In fact, the reason that you cannot
walk on the mosaics at archeological sites in Israel is because of the Mosaic
Law.

[archaeology, law]

Acts 16:1

Paul to Timothy: I don't care if your house wall is cracking. Please stop telling everyone you come from a broken home.

[family, home]

Acts 16:12

QUESTION: When was the Apostle Paul a baker?
ANSWER: When he went to Philippi [fill-a-pie].

[apostles, names]

Acts 16:30

How would a word processor message concerning saving your work before quitting differ if written by adherents of some different Christian denominations? —
Non-sectarian: Do you wish to Save your work?
Roman Catholic: Registry indicates user is Female; only Males are able to Save.
Anglican: Your work may or may not be Saved.
Lutheran: If you don't follow the instruction manual, don't expect your work to be Saved.
Mennonite: Document contains the word "dancing"; it cannot be Saved.
Jehovah Witness: You are user number 144,001; your work cannot be Saved.
Mormon: Could we interest you in Saving your work?
Millenarian: It is almost too late to Save your work.
Southern Baptist: If your work was not Saved, it is because you are evil.
TV Preacher: This program has made mistakes in the past, but it will try to Save *this* file.
Faith healers: If you believe your work will be Saved, it will be Saved.
Born-again: Before Saving your work, this program will erase all existing data; Proceed?

[computer, denominations, salvation]

Acts 16:33

A father was in church with three of his young children, including his five-year-old daughter. As usual, they sat in the very front row so that the children could see and hear the service.
During this particular service, the minister was performing the baptism of a tiny infant. The five-year-old girl was fascinated, watching intently as the minister uttered the words and poured water over the infant's head.
With a quizzical look on her face, the little girl turned to her father and asked, "Daddy, why is he brainwashing that baby?"

[baptism]

Acts 17:34

Greek names in the Bible are often hard to pronounce. In fact, as proof of this the following story can be told. A Greek professor took his torn trousers to a tailor with a Greek name. The tailor looked at the slacks and asked, "Euripides [you ripped these]?"

"Yes," replied the professor, "Eumenides [you mend these]?"

[clothes, names]

Acts 18:10

A fellow was in a jewelry store one midnight attempting to burglarize it. While trying to find the jewel case in the dark, he suddenly heard a large dog growling, and it almost scared him to death. In desperation, he turned his flashlight into the corner of the room and there sat a large German police dog, poised and ready to attack.

The burglar reasoned, "If I yell for help the police will come and help me, but I'll go to jail for burglary. But if I don't yell, that dog will jump me and either kill me or put me in the hospital completely disfigured. What am I going to do?"

Just then, a voice came from the ceiling, "Jesus is with you and Jesus is watching you!"

"Great!" he thought, "Now I have some help." He turned his flashlight to the ceiling, and saw a large parrot, suspended in a cage. "Jesus is with you and Jesus is watching you!" the parrot repeated.

In anger, the burglar said, "Can't you say anything else?"

The parrot said, "Sic him, Jesus!"

[animals, stealing]

Acts 20:7

One day a little girl was visiting a Children's Church when the teacher asked her to which denomination her relatives belonged.

The little girl replied, "I think they are six-day atheists."

[atheist, denominations]

Acts 20:7

A man walked out of a hall where a speaker was addressing a meeting. Someone in the corridor asked him if the speaker had finished his speech. He replied, "Yes, he finished it shortly after he started, but he hasn't stopped talking yet."

[boredom, talk]

Acts 20:9

As her husband droned on and on in the pulpit, the pastor's wife became more and more exasperated as she thought of her roast at home. Finally, she picked up and threw her hymnbook at him but missed and hit a dear old man in the choir. Just before he lapsed into unconsciousness, he was heard to whisper, "Hit me again, I can still hear him."

[boredom, preaching]

Acts 20:9

Pastor: "What do we learn from the story of Eutychus, the young man who, while listening to the preaching of the Apostle Paul, fell asleep and, after falling out of a window, was taken up dead?"
Member: "Ministers should learn not to preach too long sermons."

[preaching, sermon]

Acts 20:9

Then there is the preacher who keeps bragging that his sermons are well timed. The congregation keeps looking at their watches.

[preaching, time]

Acts 20:9

The last thing I knew, I was dozing off," said Eutychus <u>brokenly</u>.

[puns, sleep]

Acts 20:9

See Habakkuk 2:20.

Acts 20:9

One Sunday morning, the pastor noticed little Johnny was standing and staring up at the large plaque that hung in the foyer of the church. The young man of seven had been staring at the plaque for some time, so the pastor walked up and stood beside him. Gazing up at the plaque, too, he said quietly, "Good morning son."
"Good morning pastor" replied the young man, not taking his eyes off the plaque.
"Sir, what is this?" Johnny asked.
"Well son, these are all the people who have died in the service," replied the pastor.
Soberly, they stood together staring up at the large plaque.
Little Johnny's voice barely broke the silence when he asked quietly, "Which one sir, the 8:30 or the 10:30 service?"

[church, death]

Acts 20:9

A pastor got carried away in his sermon and preached for two hours, with no sign of ending.

One of the members got up to leave and the pastor said, "Brother Smith, where are you going?"

"I'm going to get a haircut," Brother Smith replied.

The pastor said, "Why didn't you get one before you came?"

"I didn't need one then," replied Brother Smith.

[preaching, time]

Acts 20:9

I hope you didn't take it personally, Reverend," an apologetic woman said after a church service, "when my husband walked out during your sermon."

"I did find it rather disconcerting," replied the preacher.

"It's not a reflection on you, sir," insisted the churchgoer. "Ralph has been sleepwalking ever since he was a child."

[preaching, sleep]

Acts 20:9

Our church should be air-conditioned," snapped Mrs. Smith. "It is unhealthy for people to sleep in a stuffy room."

[church, sleep]

Acts 20:9

A sermon can help people in different ways. Some rise from a sermon greatly strengthened; others wake from it delightfully refreshed.

[sermon, sleep]

Acts 20:9

Greg: We call our pastor Reverend. What do you call yours?

Fred: We call ours Neverend.

[preaching]

Acts 20:9

A preacher who was popular with his congregation explained his success as the result of a silent prayer which he offered each time he took the pulpit. It ran thus: "Lord, fill my mouth with worthwhile stuff. And nudge me when I've said enough."

[prayer, preaching]

Acts 20:9

See 1 Corinthians 14:16.

Acts 20:9

Two friends, a Baptist and a Catholic, decided to sample each other's church services. First up was Mass at Patrick's parish. And his friend, Jim Bob, was full of questions.

Every few minutes, Patrick felt an elbow in his ribs: (thump) "What's he saying?" (thump) "What's he carrying?" (thump) "What are the candles for?" (thump) "Why is everyone standing up?"

Being a good catechism student, Patrick was able to answer every question. But his ribs were getting sore. He was looking forward to next Sunday at Jim Bob's church, so he could do some elbowing of his own.

Well, as you may know, there is almost no liturgy at a Baptist church. Nearly everything is straightforward; everything is explained. Patrick's elbow was getting itchy — until the pastor stepped up to the pulpit and made a show of ceremoniously removing his watch, then laying it next to his sermon notes.

This was Patrick's big chance. Drawing back his elbow, he drove it home into his friend's side. (thump) "What does that mean?" Patrick asked.

Jim Bob only looked at him with weary eyes: "Believe me — that doesn't mean a thing."

[denominations, sermons, time]

Acts 20:9

A Children's Church teacher asked her little children, as they were on the way to the big church service, "And why is it necessary to be quiet in church?"

One bright little girl replied, "Because so many people are sleeping."

[church, sleep]

Acts 20:9

In the worship service was a fidgety six-year old boy. He continually made various sounds until about 5 minutes from the end of the service and then he kept quiet. After the service the pastor greeted the mother at the door of the church and mentioned how he appreciated that she had settled her boy down before the pastor gave the serious conclusion. The mother sheepishly explained to the pastor that she had finally leaned over and whispered to her son, 'If you don't be quiet, the pastor is going to lose his place and will have to start his sermon all over again!'"

[church, sermon]

Acts 20:9

A rich man went to his pastor and said, "I want you and your wife to take a three-month trip to the Holy Land at my expense. When you come back, I'll have a surprise for you".

The pastor accepted the offer, and he and his wife went off to the Middle East.

Three months later they returned home and were met by the wealthy parishioner, who told them that while they were gone, he had had a new church built. "It's the finest building money can buy, pastor," said the man. "No expense was spared."

And he was right. It was a magnificent edifice both inside and out. But there was one striking feature. There was only one pew, and it was at the very back.

"A church with only one pew?" asked the vicar.

"You just wait until Sunday," the rich man said.

When the time came for the Sunday service, the early arrivals entered the church, filed onto the one pew and sat down. When the pew was full, a switch clicked silently, a circuit closed, the gears meshed, a belt moved and, automatically, the rear pew began to move forward. When it reached the front of the church, it came to a stop. At the same time, another empty pew came up from below at the back and more people sat down.

And so it continued, pews filling and moving forwards until finally the church was full, from front to back.

"Wonderful!" said the vicar, "Marvelous!"

The service began, and the vicar started to preach his sermon. He launched into his text and, when 12 o'clock came, he was still going strong, with no end in sight. Suddenly a bell rang, and a trap door in the floor behind the pulpit dropped open.

"Wonderful!" said the congregation, "Marvelous!"

[church]

Acts 20:9

He had chosen as his subject that Sunday morning, "The Immortality of the Soul." Waxing eloquent he came to the climax of his sermon: "Behold the mountains, how they reach up toward the eternal heavens. Their grandeur, vastness, beauty and might o'erwhelms us. Some day, after millions and millions of years, these mountains will have all crumpled to dust but I never will. Behold the great oceans in their immensity, vastness, power and great depths. Yet someday, after millions and millions of years, even the oceans will have dried up—but I never will!"

[church, sermon]

Acts 20:10

The preacher was in the middle of his sermon when a man all of a sudden had a heart attack. They called the ambulance and made sure everyone remained where they were as they waited. The paramedics came and enter the sanctuary and went to half the congregation before they actually found the man that was really dead.

[dead, church life]

Acts 20:10

A woman by the name of Gladys Dunne was visiting a church for the first time. After the service, as the congregation was exchanging greetings, she extended her hand to a parishioner and said, "Hi, I'm Gladys Dunn." The parishioner says, "I'm glad he's done, too!"

[names, sermon]

Acts 20:10

The definition of a good sermon: It should have a good beginning. It should have a good ending. And they should be as close together as possible.

[sermon]

Acts 20:10

A man fell asleep in the congregation of a church. The preacher stopped and asked a young boy sitting beside the man to wake him up. The boy replied, "Wake him up yourself — you put him to sleep."

[sermon, sleep]

Acts 20:11

Several churches now serve coffee after the sermons. Maybe this is to make sure they are fully awake before driving home.

[sermon. sleep]

Acts 20:16

The minister, who had forty minutes worth of sermon and only twenty-five minutes in which to deliver it, said, "I feel like the Egyptian mummy—pressed for time."

[sermon, time]

Acts 20:17

Did you hear the one about the ministers who formed a bowling team? Called themselves the Holy Rollers?

[sports]

Acts 20:28

An American preacher, visiting a church in Germany, was asked by the local pastor to say a few words of greeting. When finished, he said, "Now I'll turn you back to your German shepherd."

[animals, pastor]

Acts 20:28

QUESTION: What do they call pastors in Germany?
ANSWER: German Shepherds.

[animals, names, pastor]

Acts 20:28

The pastor had just come to a new church. He was talking to one of the deacons and the deacon said, "Pastor, we have been talking among ourselves about what to call you."
The pastor said, "What did you call the last pastor?"
The deacon replied, "We called him the 'Hog Caller.'"
The pastor looked a little surprised and said, "At the last place, they called me the 'Shepherd of the Flock', but of course you know your people here better than I do."

[congregation, names, pastor]

Acts 20:35

Children's Church teacher: "Now, Cory, I want you to memorize today's verse, 'It is more blessed to give than to receive.'"
Cory: "Yes, ma'am, but I know it now. My father says he has always used that as his motto in business."
Teacher: "Oh, how noble of him! And what is his business?"
Cory: "He's a prize-fighter, ma'am."

[giving, sports]

Acts 20:35

A stingy guy who never picks up the dinner check has an impediment in his reach.

[cheap, greed]

Acts 20:35

Christians should live by the words of Christ, "it is more blessed to give than to receive." It's too bad that Internal Revenue has the same message!

[giving, taxes]

Acts 21:2

See Acts 11:19.

Acts 23:3

It was early one morning when the Pastor heard a noise outside his door. When he opened it, he found a donkey standing outside, which immediately fell over dead. Not exactly knowing what to do about the situation, he called the local sheriff and told him about what was laying before him. The sheriff couldn't resist jabbing at the Minister and said, "Pastor, I thought the first duty of the Minister was to bury the dead." Without hesitation, the Pastor said, "No the first duty of the Minister is to notify the next of kin."

[animal, funeral, ministry]

Acts 24:22

Because it was not politically expedient, none of the three judges resolved Paul's case. Felix walked the fence like a "cat," Festus found Paul to be as irritating as a "festering" sore, and Agrippa failed to get a "grip" on the situation!

[justice, names, politics]

Acts 26:28

A minister and an unbeliever were engaged in a public debate.
The minister was declared the winner because, at the end of the debate, the unbeliever declared, "Thank God I'm an atheist!"

[atheist]

Acts 27:25

An airplane flew into a violent thunderstorm and was soon swaying and bumping around the sky. One very nervous lady happened to be sitting beside a clergyman, so she turned to him for comfort.
"Can't you do something?" she demanded forcefully.
"I'm sorry ma'am," said the reverend gently "I'm in sales, not management."

[pastor, weather]

Acts 28:8

A doctor, who was the superintendent of the Children's Church in a small village church, asked one of the boys this question: "Willie, will you tell me what we must do in order to get to heaven?"
Willie replied, "We must die."
"Very true," replied the doctor, "but tell me what we must do before we die."
"We must get sick," said Willie, "and send for you."

[death, doctor]

Acts 28:15

Did you know that the apostles did pub crawls on their journeys?
'They stopped off at the Three Taverns and took Courage'.(RSV)

[apostles]

ROMANS

Romans

They asked me my views about the Scriptures and St. Paul. I told them before I express my opinion about St. Paul I think we should hear from Minneapolis.

OR

A little girl from Minneapolis came home from Children's Church with a frown on her face.
"I'm not going back there anymore," she announced with finality. "I don't like the Bible they keep teaching us."
"Why not?" asked her astonished mother.
"Because," said the little girl, "the Bible is always talking about St. Paul, and it never once mentions Minneapolis."

[apostles, geography, names]

Romans 1:21

A preacher recently announced that there are 726 different kinds of sin. He is now being besieged with requests for the list, mostly from people who think they are missing something.
[sin]

Romans 1:25

Atheist: a guy who doesn't care who wins the Notre Dame–SMU game.

[atheist, sports]

Romans 1:26-27

Man: "I'm going to Texas, where men are men and women are women."
Friend: "You should fit in some place."

[gender]

Romans 1:27

It is true that opposites should marry. That's why there's usually a male and female involved.

[gender, marriage]

Romans 2:2

Pastor: "I was grieved to hear that your husband has gone to his reward."
Widow: "Yes, he has, sir, and I only hope he has gone to where I know he ain't."

[death, heaven, hell]

Romans 3:12

The minister was passing a group of young teens boys sitting on the Church lawn and stopped to ask what they were doing.
"Nothing much, Pastor," replied the one boy. "We are just seeing who is the winner in telling the biggest lie about their sex life."
"Boys! Boys! Boys!" he intoned. "I'm shocked. Why when I was your age, I never even thought about sex at all."
They all replied, pretty much in unison, "You win Pastor!"

[lies, sex]

Romans 3:14

Man: "I have a bitter taste in my mouth."
Friend: "Been biting your tongue?"

[bitterness, speech]

Romans 3:23

You can't get the worm out of the apple by polishing the apple.

[sin]

Romans 3:23

No matter how many new translations of the Bible come out, people still sin the same way.

[Bible, sin]

Romans 3:23

The Maker of all human beings is recalling all units manufactured, regardless of make or year, due to the serious defect in the primary and central component, or heart. This is due to a malfunction in the original prototype units, resulting in the reproduction of the same defect in all subsequent units.
This defect has been technically termed, 'Sub-sequential Internal Non-morality,' or more commonly known as S-I-N, as it is primarily symptomized by loss of moral judgment.
Some other symptoms are:
(a) Loss of direction
(b) Foul vocal emissions

(c) Amnesia of origin

(d) Lack of peace and joy

(e) Selfish, or violent, behavior

(f) Depression or confusion in the mental component

The Manufacturer, who is neither liable or at fault for this defect, is providing factory authorized repair and service, free of charge, to correct the SIN defect, at numerous locations throughout the world.

The number to call for the recall station in your area is: P-R-A-Y-E-R.

Romans 10:13 For whosoever shall call upon the name of the Lord shall be saved.

WARNING: Continuing to operate the human unit without correction voids Manufacturer's warranty, exposing owner to dangers and problems too numerous to list, and will result in the human unit being permanently impounded.

For free emergency service, kneel and call on the name of J-E-S-U-S for prompt assistance at any location worldwide.

[computer, sin, salvation]

Romans 3:23

The lesson was on getting victory over sin.

"Now, Billy," the teacher questioned, "tell me what must we do before we can expect forgiveness of sin?"

There was a moment's thought, then Billy replied, "We gotta sin."

[sin]

Romans 3:24

Two little girls were comparing progress in catechism study. "I've got to original sin," said one. "How far have you got?"

"Me? Oh, I'm way beyond redemption," said the other.

[doctrine, sin]

Romans 4:25

After hearing his dad preach on "Justification," "Sanctification," and all the other "ations," a minister's son was asked if anybody knew what "procrastination" meant. "I'm not sure what it means," he said, "but I know our church believes in it."

[doctrine. procrastination]

Romans 4:26

A little boy came home from Children's Church and asked his mother, "Do you sin with your liver?"

"Why do you ask that?" she replied.

"Well, I asked my teacher if she ever sinned and she said she used to until God delivered [de-liver] her."

[salvation]

Romans 5:1-2

After twenty years of shaving himself every morning, a man in a small Southern town decided he had enough. He told his wife that he intended to let the local barber shave him each day. He put on his hat and coat and went to the barber shop which was owned by the pastor of the town's Baptist church. The barber's wife, Grace, was working, so she performed the task.

Grace shaved him and sprayed him with lilac water and said, "That will be $20."

The man thought the price was a bit high, but he paid the bill and went to work. The next morning the man looked in the mirror, and his face was as smooth as it had been when he left the barber shop the day before. Not bad, he thought. At least I don't need to get a shave every day.

The next morning, the man's face was still smooth. Two weeks later, the man was still unable to find any trace of whiskers on his face. It was more than he could take, so he returned to the barber shop.

"I thought $20 was high for a shave", he told the barber's wife, "but you must have done a great job. It's been two weeks and my whiskers still haven't started growing back."

The expression on her face didn't even change, expecting his comment. She responded, "You were shaved by Grace. Once shaved, always shaved."

[grace, name, salvation]

Romans 5:2

A mechanic who worked out of his home had a dog named Mace. Mace had a bad habit of eating all the grass on the mechanic's lawn, so the mechanic had to keep Mace inside.

The grass eventually became overgrown. One day the mechanic was working on a car in the backyard and dropped his wrench, losing it in the tall grass. He couldn't find it for the life of him, so he decided to call it a day.

That night, Mace escaped from the house and ate all the grass in the backyard. The next morning the mechanic went outside and saw his wrench glinting in the sunlight. Realizing what had happened he looked toward the heavens and proclaimed,

Are you ready?

Are you SURE?

[Okay, you asked for it]

"A grazing Mace, how sweet the hound, that saved a wrench for me!"

[grace, hymns]

Romans 5:12

A Children's Church teacher asked her class who the first man was. A little boy answered, "George Washington," She then informed him that the first man was Adam. The boy responded, "Oh, well, if you are speaking of foreigners, maybe he was."

[Adam, creation, history, prejudice]

Romans 5:12

An old farmer who didn't talk too much came home from church where he had gone alone because his wife was ill in bed.
"Was the sermon good?" inquired his wife.
"Yes."
"What was it about?" persisted his wife.
"Sin."
"Well, what did he say?"
"He was against it."

[sermon, sin]

Romans 5:14

Children's Church teacher: "Now, my little man, can you explain the cause of Adam's fall?"
Little boy: "Yes, sir; 'cause he hadn't any salt to throw on the icy sidewalk."

[Adam, weather]

Romans 6:3

See Acts 8:38

Romans 6:23

Only the wages of sin have no deductions.

[sin, wages]

Romans 6:23

Unauthorized modern version written by a business man — "You must pay for your sins. If you've already paid please ignore this notice."

[sin]

Romans 6:23

These days, the wages of sin depend on what kind of deal you make with the publisher.

[sin, wages]

Romans 6:23

The wages of sin can be very good in today's competitive market. But the benefits are lousy, and the retirement plan is pure hell!

[hell, judgment, wages]

Romans 7:9

New pastor: "What did you think of the sermon on Sunday, Mrs. Jones?"
Church member: "Very good indeed, Reverend. So instructive. We really didn't know what sin was till you came here."

[church, sin]

Romans 7:14

Come to think of it, if everyone obeyed the Ten Commandments there'd be no Eleven O'clock News.

[commandments, sin]

Romans 7:15

Peter: "Should a person be punished for something he hasn't done?"
Teacher: "No, certainly not."
Peter: "That's good, because I haven't done my math."

[justice, math]

Romans 7:15-16

He had been going from church to church, trying to find a friendly congregation, and finally he stopped in a little church just as the congregation was reading aloud with the minister: "We have left undone those things which we ought to have done; and we have done those things that we ought not to have done."
The man slipped into a pew with a sigh of relief. Thank goodness, he thought, I've found my crowd at last.

[church, confession]

Romans 7:19

A little boy was overheard praying: "Lord, if you can't make me a better boy, don't worry about it. I'm having a real good time like I am."

[enjoyment, sin]

Romans 8:22

"I'll make a suit for you," agreed Ben, an overworked tailor, "but it won't be ready for 30 days."

The customer was shocked. "Thirty days," he protested. "Why the good Lord only took 6 days to create the entire world."

"True," the tailor agreed, "but have you taken a good look at it lately?"

[clothes, creation]

Romans 8:26

While walking through the woods one day, I was surprised to hear a child's voice. I followed the sound, trying in vain to understand the child's words. When I spotted a boy perched on a rock, I realized why his words had made no sense: he was repeating the alphabet.

"Why are you saying your ABC's so many times?" I asked him.

The child replied, "I'm saying my prayers."

I couldn't help but laugh. "Prayers? All I hear is the alphabet."

Patiently the child explained, "Well, I don't know all the words, so I give God the letters. He knows what I'm trying to say."

[Holy Spirit, prayer]

Romans 8:29-30

A young preacher when asked what was meant by procrastination got it mixed up with predestination and answered confidently, "I don't know all the details, but I know it's something our church believes in."

[doctrine, procrastination]

Romans 10:3

People are divided into two groups — the righteous and the unrighteous — and the righteous usually try do the dividing.

[division, judgment]

Romans 12:1

The difference between involvement and commitment — when you look at a plate of ham and eggs, you know the chicken was involved. But the pig was committed.

OR

The chicken and the pig were walking past the church one day and discussing the problems of world hunger. The chicken suggested that between her species and the pig's they could provide everyone in the world with a good breakfast of bacon and eggs every morning. The pig thought long and hard before replying, "That's OK for you to say, because from you that's only a contribution — from me that's total commitment!"

[animals, commitment, food]

Romans 12:1

"Dad," the boy asked his father, "what is a necessary evil?"
"Well son," replied the father, "its one we like so much we don't want to abolish it."

[sin]

Romans 12:1

The only trouble about a living sacrifice is that it keeps trying to crawl off the altar!

[commitment, sacrifice]

Romans 12:3

When he meets another egotist, it's an I-for-an-I. Really, they are both I-sores [eyesore].

[pride]

Romans 12:6

A lot of church members who are singing "Standing on the Promises" are just sitting on the premises.

[service]

Romans 12:8

The doctor sent a note to his minister, "Sorry I haven't tithed for three months. But, you know, there's a lot of that going around."

[giving, sickness]

Romans 12:8

When the usher came up the aisle with the basket at the offertory, a four-year-old boy in the pew in front turned to his father and said loudly and excitedly, "Daddy, here comes the penny-man!"

[giving]

Romans 12:8

There was a pious old gentleman of an earlier generation who used to get up regularly at prayer meeting in his church to pray: "Use me, O Lord, use me — in some advisory capacity!"

[prayer, service]

Romans 12:12

A child defined impatience as "waiting in a hurry."

[patience]

Romans 12:16

What is the difference between a church worship leader and a steel I-beam. The steel I-beam is a little more flexible.

[choir, church, music]

Romans 12:17

Honesty may be the best policy—but there are some people who don't seem to think they can afford the best.

[honesty]

Romans 12:19

Did you hear about the man who burned the farmer's sugarcane field because he wanted sweet revenge?

[revenge]

Romans 12:19

A motorcycle cop was rushed to the hospital with an inflamed appendix. The doctors operated and advised him that all was well. However, the patrolman kept feeling something pulling at the hairs on his chest. Worried that it might be a second surgery the doctors hadn't told him about, he finally got enough energy to pull his hospital gown down enough so he could look at what was making him so uncomfortable.
Taped firmly across his hairy chest were three wide strips of adhesive tape, the ultra sticky kind. Written in large black letters was the sentence, "Get well soon! Luv, from the nurse you gave a ticket to last week!"

[revenge]

Romans 13:1

See Revelation 12:9.

Romans 13:4

A traffic cop flagged down a young driver, got his name, then snarled, "Oh, so you're a preacher, hey? Now don't go telling me you didn't see that stop sign."
The minister, hoping an alibi would get him out of trouble, explained, "Oh, to be sure I saw the sign, officer. The point is — I didn't see you."

[driving, excuse]

Romans 13:6

Psychiatrist to patient: "When did you first discover that you enjoyed paying your income tax?"

[taxes]

Romans 13:6

It seems a little silly now, but this great country of America was founded as a protest against high taxes.

[taxes]

Romans 13:6

A businessman on his deathbed called his friend and said, "Bill, I want you to promise me that when I die you will have my remains cremated."
"And what," his friend asked, "do you want me to do with your ashes?"
The dying businessman said, "Just put them in an envelope and mail them to the Internal Revenue Service and write on the envelope, 'Now you have everything.'"

[death, taxes]

Romans 13:7

Everybody should pay their taxes with a smile. I tried it but they wanted cash.

[taxes]

Romans 13:8

She: "It's isn't my fault I get so deep in debt."
He: "No, it's all owing to other people."

[debt]

Romans 13:8

Jones: "How do you spend your income?"
Smith: "About 30% for shelter, 30% for clothing, 40% for food and 20% for entertainment."
Jones: "But that adds up to 120%."
Smith: "That's right, now you know my problem with living."

[debt, life]

Romans 14:5

"You've been convicted of the same offense fourteen times. Aren't you ashamed of yourself?"
"No, sir. I don't think one ought to be ashamed of his convictions."

[conviction, law, shame]

Romans 15:6

The unchurched child was asked a traditional catechism question, "What is the chief end of man?"
And he answered, "The end with the head on."

[doctrine]

Romans 16:16

See 1 Corinthians 14:39

1 CORINTHIANS

Corinthians

I must sharpen my quill before writing to the Corinthians," said Paul <u>pensively</u>.

[puns, writing]

Corinthians

Paul's Chain Letter to the Corinthians

1. The Chain Letter of Paul the Apostle to the Corinthians. With love all things are possible. This epistle comes to you from Philippi. Grace be to you and peace. Spiritual gifts will be delivered unto you within four days of receiving this letter — providing you in turn send it on.

2. This is no joke. Send copies to whomsoever among the Gentiles or superstitious peoples of other denominations you would comfort in all their tribulation. Do not send material things. Love vaunteth not itself, is not puffed up.

3. While visiting the household of Stephanas, a Macedonian proconsul received the epistle and was greeted by his brethren by a holy kiss. But he broke the chain, and now he has become as sounding brass or a tinkling cymbal.

4. Gaius bestowed all his goods to feed the poor, and gave his body to be burned, but it profited him nothing. He failed to circulate the letter. However, before his death, he received the unleavened bread of sincerity and truth.

5. Do note the following: Crispus had the gift of prophecy, and understood all mysteries, and all knowledge, and had all faith, so that he could remove mountains. But he forgot that the epistle had to leave his hands within 96 hours, and now he is nothing.

6. In AD 37, the epistle was received by a young Galatian woman who put it aside to copy and send out later. She was plagued by various problems: thrice she was beaten with rods, once she was stoned, and thrice suffered shipwreck. On the last day of these occasions, she spent a night and day in the deep. Finally, she copied the letter. A trumpet sounded, and she was raised incorruptible.

7. Remember: Believeth all things, hopeth all things. The chain never faileth.
St. Paul

[Bible]

1 Corinthians 1:2

Two men are standing on the front lawn of a church. One man is leaning on the church's sign and the other is looking at it from the front.
The sign reads:
WATER BROOK Bible Believing, Hand Clapping, Foot Stomping, Hemlines-Below-the-Knee, Tie Wearing, Blood Washed, Coffee-And-Donuts-During-Sunday-School Eating, Council of Nicaea Appreciating, Non-Denominational CHURCH
The man leaning on the sign says, "When you don't believe in written creeds, you have to squeeze a lot of doctrine into your name."

[denominations, doctrine]

1 Corinthians 1:10

A man was stranded on the proverbial deserted Pacific island for years. Finally one day a boat comes sailing into view, and the man frantically waves and draws the skipper's attention. The boat comes near the island and the sailor gets out and greets the stranded man.
After awhile the sailor asks, "What are those three huts you have here?"
"Well, that's my house there."
"What's that next hut?" asks the sailor.
"I built that hut to be my church."
"What about the other hut?"
"Oh, that's where I used to go to church."

[denominations]

1 Corinthians 1:10

I was walking across a bridge one day, and I saw a man standing on the edge, about to jump off. I immediately ran over and said, "Stop! Don't do it!"
"Why shouldn't I?" he said.
I said, "Well, there's so much to live for!"
"Like what?"
"Well ... are you religious or atheist?"
"Religious."
"Me too! Are you Christian or Jewish?"
"Christian."
"Me too! Are you Catholic or Protestant?"

"Protestant."

"Me too! Are you Episcopalian or Baptist?"

"Baptist."

"Wow! Me too! Are you Baptist Church of God or Baptist Church of the Lord?"

"Baptist Church of God."

"Me too! Are you Original Baptist Church of God, or are you Reformed Baptist Church of God?"

"Reformed Baptist Church of God."

"Me too! Are you Reformed Baptist Church of God, Reformation of 1879, or Reformed Baptist Church of God, Reformation of 1915?"

"Reformed Baptist Church of God, Reformation of 1915!"

To which I said, "Die, heretic scum!" and pushed him off.

[denominations]

1 Corinthians 1:12

A woman goes to the post office to buy stamps for her Christmas cards. She says to the clerk, "May I have 50 Christmas stamps?"

The clerk says, "What denomination?"

The woman says, "O my God. Has it come to this? Give me 6 Catholic, 12 Methodist, 32 Baptists.

[denomination]

1 Corinthians 1:12-13

1. How many Pentecostals does it take to change a light bulb?

One to change the bulb and nine to pray against the spirit of darkness.

2. How many Calvinists does it take to change a light bulb?

None. God has predestined when the light will be on. Calvinists do not change light bulbs. They simply read the instructions and pray the light bulb will be one that has been chosen to be changed.

3. How many Baptists does it take to change a light bulb?

Change??? Who said anything about change?

4. How many neo-orthodox does it take to change a light bulb?

No one knows. They can't tell the difference between light and darkness.

5. How many TV evangelists does it take to change a light bulb?

One. But for the message of light to continue, send in your donation today.

6. How many independent fundamentalists does it take to change a light bulb?

Only one, because any more might result in too much cooperation.

7. How many liberals does it take to change a light bulb?

At least ten, as they need to hold a debate on whether or not the light bulb exists. Even if they can agree upon the existence of the light bulb, they still might not change it, to keep from alienating those who might use other forms of light.

8. How many Catholics does it take to change a light bulb?
None. They always use candles.

9. How many worship leaders who use guitars does it take to change a light bulb?
One. But soon all those around can warm up to its glowing.

10. How many members of an established Bible teaching church that is over 20 years old does it take to change a light bulb?
One to actually change the bulb, and nine to say how much they liked the old one.

11. How many United Methodists does it take to change a light bulb?
This statement was issued: "We choose not to make a statement either in favor of or against the need for a light bulb. However, if in your own journey you have found that a light bulb works for you, that is fine. You are invited to write a poem or compose a modern dance about your personal relationship with your light bulb (or light source, or non-dark resource), and present it next month at our annual light bulb Sunday service, in which we will explore a number of light bulb traditions, including incandescent, fluorescent, three-way, long-life, and tinted — all of which are equally valid paths to luminescence."

12. How many Church of Christ folks does it take to change a light bulb?
None. Light bulbs are not mentioned in the New Testament; therefore, it would be unscriptural to change one, or anything else for that matter. Besides, the bulb has to be immersed first, which shorts it out.

13. How many Charismatics does it take to change a light bulb?
One. Their hands are in the air anyway.

14. How many Amish does it take to change a light bulb?
"What's a light bulb?"

15. How many youth pastors does it take to change a light bulb?
Youth pastors aren't around long enough for a light bulb to burn out.

16. How many Southern Baptists does it take to change a light bulb?
109 — Seven on the Light Bulb Task Force Sub-committee, who report to the 12 on the Light Bulb Task Force, appointed by the 15 on the Trustee Board. Their recommendation is reviewed by the Finance Executive Committee of 5, who place it on the agenda of the 18 member Finance Committee. If they approve, they bring a motion to the 27 member church Board, who appoint another 12 member review committee. If they recommend that the Church Board proceed, a resolution is brought to the Convention floor. They appoint another 8 member review committee. If their report to the next Convention supports the changing of a light bulb, and the Convention votes in favor, the responsibility to carry out the light bulb change is passed on to the Trustee

Board, who in turn appoints a 7 member committee to find the best price in new light bulbs. Their recommendation of which hardware has the best buy must then be reviewed by the 23 member Ethics Committee to make certain that this hardware store has no connection to Disney. They report back to the Trustee Board who, then commissions the Trustee in charge of the Janitor to ask him to make the change. By then the janitor discovers that one more light bulb had burned out.

[church, denominations]

1 Corinthians 1:13

A 4-year-old named Ruth was conducting the baptismal service. She held a cat over a barrel of water. Trying to be as solemn as the pastor, she repeated the phrase she had heard many times: "I baptize you in the name of the Father, the Son, and in the hole you go!"

[animals, baptism]

1 Corinthians 1:16

Notice of defective pastor

It has come to our attention that the pastor you received was shipped with a slight defect: he is not psychic. This defect necessitates certain special procedures to ensure optimum performance of your unit.

1. It is necessary to inform him of any members who are hospitalized.

2. It is necessary to inform him of any members who should be added to the "shut-in" list.

3. If someone you know is sick or otherwise in need of the pastor's prayers, or if you know of someone who should be included in the prayers on Sunday morning, the pastor must be told, or he won't know.

4. If you are in need of a pastoral visit or some other service from the pastor, you will get best results if you ask him.

We regret any inconvenience this may cause. If these special procedures create an undue burden, please feel free to send the unit back, and one with full psychic abilities will be shipped as soon as one becomes available.

[pastor, unaware]

1 Corinthians 1:22

See Matthew 12:38.

1 Corinthians 2:1

A boy was watching his father, a pastor, write out his sermon.

" How do you know what to say?" he asked.

"Why, God tells me," his father piously replied.

"Oh, then why do you keep crossing things out?"

[Holy Spirit, imagination]

1 Corinthians 3:8

Cooperate! Remember the banana. Every time it leaves the bunch it gets skinned.

[cooperation]

1 Corinthians 3:12-13

Remember, even a mosquito doesn't get a slap on the back until he starts to work!

[insects, work]

1 Corinthians 3:13

A very rich and very wicked old man was dying. He seemed so worried that his family asked the pastor to come and comfort him.

"I won't mind dying so much," the old man said, "if I could take my money with me and keep it safe."

"Don't worry about that," the preacher responded. "It'll all be burned up anyway."

[death, hell, money]

1 Corinthians 3:14

Working for the Lord may not pay well, but the Retirement Plan is the greatest.

[retirement]

1 Corinthians 3:13-14

A Children's Church teacher was explaining the concept of Judgment Day to her class. She went on at great length and great depth trying to impress on her young class the idea that we would all be rewarded or punished according to our deeds here on earth and that those of us who make it will wear crowns of glory.

"Now," she asked, "who will wear the biggest crown of glory?"

The class thought about it for a minute, and little Sally came up with a childlike logical answer. "The ones with the biggest heads."

[judgment, pride, reward]

1 Corinthians 3:15

"Mommy, don't men ever go to Heaven?" asked a small boy.

His mother reassured him, "Of course they do! What makes you ask?"

"Because I never saw any pictures of men with halos and with whiskers."

"Oh, that's because most men who go to Heaven get there by a close shave!"
[heaven, salvation]

1 Corinthians 3:15

A person waiting in line to fill up his car with gas turns and says to the minister dressed in his liturgical collar who was also waiting, "They wait until the last minute even though the trip was planned a year ago."
The preacher replies, "Works the same in my business, too."
[procrastination]

1 Corinthians 4:4

All too often a clear conscience is merely the result of a bad memory.

OR

It's easy to have a clear conscience. All it takes is a fuzzy memory.
[conscience, forgetfulness]

1 Corinthians 4:5

A man who hadn't lived the best kind of life, even though he had gone to church, passed away. At his funeral the pastor gave a nice description of the man, praised his good deeds, and told what a good husband and father he had been.
After listening for a while, the wife leaned over to her daughter and whispered, "Go over there and see if that's your father in that coffin."
[funerals, hypocrisy]

1 Corinthians 4:5

See 3 John 1:10

1 Corinthians 5:1-5

Unlike the apostle Paul who confronted sin boldly, a cautious preacher, worried about possible lawsuits, concluded his sermon to his TV educated audience with the words: "The sinners referred to in my sermon are fictitious. Any similarity to members of this congregation is strictly coincidental!"
[revenge, sermon]

1 Corinthians 5:4

A Children's Church teacher challenged her children to take some time on Sunday afternoon to write a letter to God. They were to bring back their letter the following Sunday. One little boy wrote, "Dear God, We had an interesting time at church today. Wish you could have been there."

[church, God]

1 Corinthians 5:6

A Seminary professor was discussing the merits of the Bible as literature. "Take 1 Corinthians 5:6, for example," he said. "'A little leaven leaveneth the whole lump' (KJV). I challenge anyone here to put that thought in a more concise statement."

"That's easy," replied a student. "How about, 'a little dab'll do ya?'"

[communication]

1 Corinthians 6:10

A speeding, very drunk motorist lost control of his car and collided with a telephone pole. He awoke to find himself grasping a bunch of wires. He smiled and murmured, "Thank goodness. It's a harp"

[driving, drunkenness, heaven]

1 Corinthians 6:11-12

A woman was at work when she received a phone call that her daughter was very sick with a fever. She left her work and stopped by the pharmacy to get some medication. She got back to her car and found that she had locked her keys in the car.

She didn't know what to do, so she called home and told the baby sitter what had happened. The baby sitter told her that the fever was getting worse. She said, "You might find a coat hanger and use that to open the door."

The woman looked around and found an old rusty coat hanger that had been thrown down on the ground, possibly by someone else who at some time or other had locked their keys in their car. Then she looked at the hanger and said, "I don't know how to use this."

So she bowed her head and asked God to send her some help. Within five minutes an old rusty car pulled up, with a dirty, greasy, bearded man who was wearing an old biker skull rag on his head. The woman thought, "This is what you sent to help me?" But, she was desperate, so she was also very thankful.

The man got out of his car and asked her if he could help. She said, "Yes, my daughter is very sick. I stopped to get her some medication and I locked my keys in my car. I must get home to her. Please, can you use this hanger to unlock my car?"

He said, "Sure". He walked over to the car, and immediately the car was opened. She hugged the man and through her tears she said, "Thank You So Much! You are a very nice man."

The man replied, "Lady, I am not a nice man. I just got out of prison today. I was in prison for car theft and have only been out for about an hour."

The woman hugged the man again and with sobbing tears cried out loud, "Oh, Thank you God! You even sent me a Professional!"

[prayer, prison]

1 Corinthians 6:12

A pastor had a sweet tooth, so his wife knew the chocolate chip cookies she'd just baked might disappear before she returned from running errands.

To discourage him from eating the cookies before dinner time, the wife taped a verse on the wrapped goodies: "'Everything is permissible for me' — but not everything is beneficial." (1 Cor. 6:12).

When she returned she found half the cookies gone and another verse attached: "The righteous eat to their heart's content, but the stomach of the wicked goes hungry" (Prov. 13:25).

[context, food]

1 Corinthians 7:1

The Pope dies, and, naturally goes to heaven. He's met by the reception committee, and after a whirlwind tour he is told that he can enjoy any of the myriad of recreations available.

He decides that he wants to read all of the ancient original text of the Holy Scriptures, so he spends the next eon or so learning the languages.

After becoming a linguistic master, he sits down in the library and begins to pour over every version of the Bible, working back from the most recent "Easy Reading" to the original script. All of a sudden there is a scream in the library.

The Angels come running in only to find the Pope huddled in his chair, crying to himself, and muttering, "An 'R'! The scribes left out the 'R.'"

A particularly concerned Angel takes him aside, offering comfort, and asks him what the problem is and what does he mean. After collecting his wits, the Pope sobs again, "It's the letter 'R.' They left out the 'R.' The word was supposed to be CELEBRATE!" [not celibate]

OR

A monk his entire adult life, Brother Andrew, was responsible for training new scribes in the art of copying by hand — word for word — the holy writs. One day an eager new scribe, Brother Johnathan, asked if anyone had ever made a mistake.

"Oh no." said Brother Andrew. "These words have always been correctly copied from generation to generation." Skeptical, Brother Johnathan asked Brother Andrew how he knew. "My son," said Brother Andrew as he shuffled off towards the monastery's library, "let me get you the first volume ever written, and you will see it is just as correct today as it was then."

Many hours had passed. Finally Brother Johnathan decided to check on the elderly monk. At the library, he spotted Brother Andrew sitting alone in a candle-lit corner, tears running down his wrinkled cheeks. "What's the matter?" Brother Johnathan asked.

"I can't believe it." Brother Andrew responded, his voice quivering with emotion. "The word in 1 Corinthians 7 is not celibate. It's C-e-l-e-Brate!"

[marriage, priests, sex]

1 Corinthians 7:1

If Paul was writing Corinthians today he would not refer to someone being single or a virgin. They would be romantically challenged.

[politically correct, singleness]

1 Corinthians 7:2

The pastor's morning prayer ended, "O, Lord, give us clean hearts, give us pure hearts, give us all sweet hearts," and every girl in the congregation fervently responded, "Ah-men!"

[dating, prayer]

1 Corinthians 7:8

She prays every night: "Dear Lord, I don't ask a thing for myself. Just send my parents a son-in-law."

[generous, prayer]

1 Corinthians 7:8

See Proverbs 18:22.

1 Corinthians 7:8

Definition of Celibacy — A clever comeback used by single men and women to explain why they don't have a date for Saturday night.

[dating, singleness]

1 Corinthians 7:8

"Ever been struck by lightning?"

"After ten years of married life, I don't remember trifles like that."

[marriage]

1 Corinthians 7:8

TOP 10 LINES CHRISTIAN WOMEN USE TO BREAK-UP

10. "I'm sorry, I've found someone more spiritual."
9. "I'm sorry, it's just not God's will."
8. "I feel called to the ministry very soon and very far from you as soon as possible."
7. "I'm sorry, it could never work. I'm a sanguine and you're a phlegmatic."
6. "God loves me and must have a better plan for my life."
5. "You know, I feel like I'm dating my brother."
4. "At least I got a lot out of our Bible studies together."
3. "You need someone with lower standards."
2. "I think we should just be prayer partners."
1. "I do love you, but it's just agape now."

[dating, excuses]

1 Corinthians 7:9

A high school senior said to his girl friend, "Darling, I'm burning with desire for you."

"Don't make fuel [fool] of yourself," she wisely replied.

[dating, foolishness, puns, sex]

1 Corinthians 7:9

He was married, you might say, at an early urge [age].

[age, marriage]

1 Corinthians 7:9

Anxious young lady: "What excuse have you for not being married?"

Slow young man: "I don't know except I was born that way."

[single]

1 Corinthians 7:9

"I have an announcement to make this morning," said the minister of a large church. "If any of you are contemplating matrimony, we will be organizing a special seminar. Would you kindly see me after the singing of our closing hymn, 'Mistaken Souls That Dream of Heaven.'"

[hymns, marriage, singleness]

1 Corinthians 7:9

A minister was planning a wedding at the close of the Sunday morning service.

After the benediction he had planned to call the couple down to be married for a brief ceremony before the congregation.

For the life of him, he couldn't think of the names of those who were to be married.

"Will those wanting to get married please come to the front?" he requested. Immediately, nine single ladies, three widows, four widowers, and six single men stepped to the front.

[church, marriage]

1 Corinthians 7:11

Too many couples marry for better or for worse, but not for good.

[marriage]

1 Corinthians 7:24

A bachelor is someone who thinks that the only thoroughly justified marriage was the one that produced him.

[bachelor]

1 Corinthians 7:26

Spinster — the most singular of women.

[singleness]

1 Corinthians 7:27

See Proverbs 18:22.

1 Corinthians 7:28

Although St. Paul might not agree, some women think it is better to have loved a short man than never to have loved a tall.

[marriage, size]

1 Corinthians 7:28

Girl: "When are you thinking about getting married?"
Girlfriend: "Constantly."

[marriage, singleness]

1 Corinthians 7:32

A bachelor is a guy who doesn't have anyone to share the troubles he doesn't have.

[bachelor]

1 Corinthians 7:32

A bachelor is one who never Mrs [misses] a girl.

[bachelor]

1 Corinthians 7:33

Why a man wants a wife is a mystery. Why a man wants two wives is a bigamystery.

[bigamy]

1 Corinthians 7:35

A bachelor is one who can be miss-led only so far.

[bachelor]

1 Corinthians 7:36

Bachelor: "Let's get married!"
Female friend: "Good heavens! Who'd have us?"

[bachelor, marriage]

1 Corinthians 7:36

Guy: "I've been asked to get married lots of times."
Friend: "Who asked you?"
Guy: "Mother and father."

[marriage]

1 Corinthian 7:39

She's mine till breath do us part.

[death, marriage]

1 Corinthians 7:39

Martha had a troubled marriage. She sought the advice of one of those phone-in psychics. The psychic told her, "Prepare yourself for widowhood. Your husband is about to die a violent death."
Martha sighed deeply and then slowly asked, "Will I be acquitted?"

[marriage, murder]

1 Corinthians 7:39

When we are married or dead, it's for a long time.

[eternity]

1 Corinthians 7:39

"I am" is reportedly the shortest sentence in the English language.

Could it be that "I do" is the longest sentence?

[marriage]

1 Corinthians 7:40

They tell me the spinster died quite happily."
"Yes — she heard the pastor say that marriages are made in heaven."

[marriage, singleness]

1 Corinthians 8:7

Young lady: "I've been misbehaving and my conscience is bothering me."
Pastor: "Should I give you something to strengthen your will power?"
Young Lady: "No, what I was really hoping for was that you could give me something to weaken my conscience."

[conscience, temptation]

1 Corinthians 9:11

A church looking for a minister often has this in mind: he must have the humility of a saint, the administrative skills of an executive, the speaking ability of a spellbinder, the counseling know-how of a psychiatrist, and the wage requirements of an elephant — he has to work for peanuts.

[church, wages]

1 Corinthians 9:26

Did you hear about the efficiency expert who walked in his sleep so he could get his rest and exercise at the same time?

[exercise, rest]

1 Corinthians 10:11

A man's wife had died, and as the mourners were on the way to the cemetery one of the pallbearers tripped over a rock. This shook the casket and revived the woman. She lived another seven years and died again. They were on the way to the cemetery again, and as they approached the same spot the husband shouted out to the pallbearers, "Watch out for that rock!"

[death, funerals]

1 Corinthians 10:11

Cecil B. DeMille was once asked why he made so many Biblical motion pictures. He answered, "Why let two thousand years of publicity go to waste?"

[history, movie]

1 Corinthians 10:13

When you flee from temptation through God's means of escape, be sure you don't leave a forwarding address.

[temptation]

1 Corinthians 10:13

Opportunity may knock once, but temptation bangs on your front door forever.

[temptation]

1 Corinthians 10:13

A young nun is in a monastery and is plagued with thoughts of men. She decides that she can no longer stand life with these thoughts and goes to the Mother Superior. She says, "Oh, Mother, I am being stricken by impure thoughts about men." The mother just smiles and says, "It happens to all the young ones, sister. To relieve yourself of this, every time you have an unclean thought go to a mirror, make your hand into a gun and shoot your reflection."

The young nun is a little skeptical of this but thanks the Mother Superior and leaves. Down the hall a little bit she begins to have an unclean thought. She promptly runs to a mirror and makes her hand into a gun, points it at the reflection, and goes "BANG!" The unclean thought vanishes immediately. This makes the young nun happy and she goes about her routine again.

She has an unclean thought every once in a while but she promptly gets rid of it. One day the young nun rises from bed and gets ready for breakfast when she is plagued by one of those thoughts. So she points at her reflection and goes "BANG" and it goes away. She finishes getting ready and it comes back. She goes to the mirror and goes "BANG" and it goes away. She leaves for breakfast and it comes back so she runs to the hall mirror and goes "BANG" but it comes right back. She goes "BANG" again and it comes back. She goes "BANG, BANG, BANG, BANG" but it is no use because the thought keeps coming back. Panic stricken she runs to the Mother Superiors room throws the door open only to find the Mother Superior in front of her mirror going "Rat tat tat tat tat tat!"

[persistence, temptation, victory]

1 Corinthians 11:4

Two bees ran into each other. One asked the other how things were going. "Really bad," said the second bee, "the weather has been really wet and damp and there aren't any flowers or pollen, so I can't make any honey."

"No problem," said the first bee, "Just fly down five blocks and turn left and keep going until you see all the cars. There's a Bar Mitzvah going on and there are all kinds of fresh flowers and fresh fruit."

"Thanks for the tip" said the second bee and flew away.

A few hours later the two bees ran into each other again and the first bee asked, "How'd it go?"

"Fine," said the second bee, "It was everything you said it would be."

"Uh, what's that thing on your head?" asked the first bee.

"That's my yarmulke," said the second bee, "I didn't want them to think I was a wasp."

[prejudice]

1 Corinthians 11:5

In churches where women still wear hats it's interesting to notice that they're all different. I guess no one wants to make the same mistake twice.

[dress]

1 Corinthians 11:5

"I felt sorry for your wife in church this morning," said the young minister, "when she had a terrific attack of coughing and every one turned to look at her."

"You needn't worry about that," said the husband. "She was wearing a new spring hat."

[dress]

1 Corinthians 11:5

"Aren't some of the hats women wear absurd?" said one woman.

"Yes," said another "and yet when some people put them on they do look so appropriate."

[dress]

1 Corinthians 11:11

She: "A man definitely needs a woman as much as a woman needs a man!"

He: "What do men need women for anyway?"

She: "If there were no women in the world, who'd sew the buttons on your pants?"

He: "If there were no women in the world, who'd need pants?"

[clothes, gender]

1 Corinthians 11:14

A young man had just got his driver's permit and inquired of his father, a preacher, if they could discuss the use of the car. His father took him to the study and said to the boy, "I'll make a deal with you, son. You bring your grades up from a C to a B-average, study your Bible a little, and get your hair cut and we'll talk about the car."

Well, the boy thought about that for a moment and decided that he'd best settle for the offer, and they agreed.

After about six weeks the boy came back and again asked his father about the car. Again they went to the study where his father said, "Son, I've been real proud of you. You've brought your grades up, and I've observed that you've been studying your Bible and participating a lot more in the Bible study class on Sunday morning. But I'm real disappointed seeing as you haven't got your hair cut."

The young man paused a moment and then said, "You know, Dad, I've been thinking about that, and I've noticed in my studies of the Bible that Samson had long hair, John the Baptist had long hair, and there's even strong argument that Jesus Himself had long hair."

To which his father replied, "You're right, son. Did you also notice that they all WALKED everywhere they went?"

[driving, hair]

1 Corinthians 11:16

On vacation with her family in Montana, a mother drove her van past a church in a small town and pointing to it, told the children that it was St. Francis' Church.

"It must be a franchise," her eight-year-old son said. "We've got one of those in our town too."

[denominations, names]

1 Corinthians 11:17ff

One Sunday in church the minister was about to celebrate Communion. Just before he did, during the children's sermon, the minister was talking about Communion and what it represents.

"The Bible talks of Holy Communion being a 'joyful feast.' What does that mean? Well, 'joyful' means happy, right? And a feast is a meal. So a 'joyful feast' is a happy meal. And what are the three things we need for a happy meal?"

One little boy spoke up loudly and said, "Hamburger, fries, and a regular soft drink!"

[communion, food, joy]

1 Corinthians 11:21

"This communion grape juice has fermented!" Tom whined.

[communion, puns]

327

1 Corinthians 11:23ff

The young pastor was on two "honeymoons." He had just married, and he and his new bride had moved to their first pastorate. Their first home was the parsonage located next door to the church building.

The deacons announced, "Pastor, on your first Sunday night as our pastor we have planned to have the Lord's Supper." It was his responsibility to prepare the elements for the Lord's Supper service, so on Sunday afternoon, he and his wife poured the grape juice into the little cups and prepared the unleavened bread for what would be his first experience of administering the Lord's Supper.

It was an unusually large crowd that night. As the deacons served the juice, the young pastor stood reverently at the front of the church observing the congregation. Suddenly, it occurred to him that the crowd was larger than the number of juice containers.

He leaned over the front row and whispered to his wife, "We are going to run out of grape juice!"

"What do you want me to do?" asked his anxious bride.

"Run next door to the parsonage and get that bottle of grape juice out of the refrigerator. If you run fast enough, you can be back here by the time the deacons get back down the aisle."

The pastor's wife bolted out the side door of the church into the kitchen of the parsonage next door. She didn't bother to switch on the lights. She rushed to the refrigerator, reached in, and got what she thought was a bottle of grape juice. It was a bottle of lemon juice!

In the midst of the emergency, neither she nor her husband bothered to read the label. Frantically, she handed the bottle to her young husband/pastor. He uncapped it and poured its contents into the small juice containers for himself and the deacons.

It was like clockwork! Just as he had finished filling the cups for himself and the deacons, the deacons were reverently marching down the aisle with empty trays after having served the congregation.

The pastor picked up the tray of juice glasses and slowly served his deacons. Then, he led the whole congregation in drinking the juice.

Suddenly strange things began to happen. The young pastor's lips began to pucker. He knew he was in trouble.

Turning to the deacon on his right, he wheezed, "Deacon Jones, will you please lead us in the closing prayer?"

Deacon Jones was having his own problems with the lemon juice. He smacked his lips and barely managed to say, "Pastor, please excuse me!"

The pastor turned then to his left and asked Deacon Smith to lead in the closing prayer. Deacon Smith made some funny noises through his puckered lips and shook his head.

The young pastor finally turned to the bewildered congregation, motioned for them to stand, and wheezed out, "Friends, let's all stand, whistle the Doxology, and go home!"

[communion]

1 Corinthians 11:24

The Children's Church Teacher asks, "Now, Johnny, tell me frankly do you say prayers before eating?"

"No sir," little Johnny replies, "I don't have to. My Mom is a good cook."

[prayer]

1 Corinthians 11:26

One communion Sunday, a disgruntled deacon prepared communion with an unusual amount of care and secrecy. When it came time for the pastor to uncover the elements the grape juice looked darker than usual.

Nevertheless the pastor began to serve the communion cups. Promptly upon receiving a cup, each recipient's face had a peculiar, stunned look. When it came time for the pastor to drink he discovered why the strange looks. The juice was prune juice!

Later one parishioner stated, "Perhaps this is a Divine commentary on our spirituality ... we need a little loosening up!"

[church, communion]

1 Corinthians 12:12

Do you know how many members of the Tate family belong to your church?

There is old man Dic Tate who wants to run everything, while Uncle Ro Tate tries to change everything. Their sister Agi Tate stirs up plenty of trouble, with help from her husband, Irri Tate.

Whenever new projects are suggested, Hesi Tate and his wife, Vege Tate, want to wait until next year Then there is Aunt Imi Tate, who wants our church to be like all the others. Devas Tate provides the voice of doom, while Poten Tate wants to be a big shot.

But not all members of the family are bad. Brother Facili Tate is quite helpful in church matters. And a delightful, happy member of the family is Miss Felici Tate. Cousins Cogi Tate and Medi Tate always think things over and lend helpful, steady hands. And of course there is the black sheep of the family, Ampu Tate, who has completely cut himself off from the church.

[church]

1 Corinthians 12:28

After the family's return from church one Sunday, the small boy announced he was going to be a prophet when he grew up.

"What made you decide you want to be a prophet?" his mother inquired.

"Well," said the boy thoughtfully, "I'll have to go to church on Sunday anyway, and I think it would be more fun to stand up and yell than to sit down and listen."

[church, prophets]

1 Corinthians 13 (KJV)

Definition of Charity: 1. What you call your trash when you give it to the Salvation Army Thrift Store. 2 The only theological virtue that pays off every April 15th.

[giving, taxes]

1 Corinthians 13:11

ADULT: A person who has stopped growing at both ends and is now growing in the middle.

[size]

1 Corinthians 13:13 (KJV)

There's nothing wrong with our church policies that faith, hope and clarity couldn't cure.

[church]

1 Corinthians 14:15

In many churches nowadays, whatever is not worth saying is sung.

[music]

1 Corinthians 14:16

A newcomer asked, "Why do you always sing 'Amen' at the end of your songs and not 'Awomen'?"

To which his friend replied, "I guess it's because we sing hymns [hims] not hers."

[gender, hymns]

1 Corinthians 14:16

Amen — The only part of a prayer everyone knows.

[prayer]

1 Corinthians 14:16

The new priest was trying to institute some liturgical reform in his very old-fashioned parish by teaching his parishioners the new responses. He said to them, "When I say, 'The Lord be with you,' you will reply all together, 'And with you also.' Then I will say, 'Let us pray.'"

The day came for the introduction of the new liturgy. Something happened to the microphone, and the priest, trying to adjust it, said in a loud voice, "There is something wrong with this microphone."

The congregation responded with one loud voice, "And with you also!"

[liturgy, prayer]

1 Corinthians 14:16

During the children's sermon, a pastor asked the children what "Amen" meant.

A little boy raised his hand and said, "It means 'Tha-tha-tha-that's all folks'!"

[prayer]

1 Corinthians 14:16

The sermon was not well prepared, extremely disjointed, and went on and on and on. At last the minister paused and asked, "What more, my friends, can I say?"

In the back of the church a voice offered earnestly: "Amen!"

[sermon]

1 Corinthians 14:39

A teenager's misquotation for dating purposes:

"Greet one another with a holy kiss, and forbid not the use of tongues."

[dating kissing]

1 Corinthians 15:4

A pastor received a letter from a long-time parishioner that read, "Dear pastor: If Jesus knew what you are doing to our church, he would turn over in his grave."

Reading the letter to his board, the pastor commented, "It makes me wonder what her theological position will be — come Easter!"

[criticism, Easter, resurrection]

1 Corinthians 15:12

George went on a vacation to the Middle East with most of his family including his mother-in-law. During their vacation and while they were visiting Jerusalem, George's mother-in-law died.

With the death certificate in hand, George went to the Australian Consulate Office to make arrangements to send the body back to Australia for proper burial.

The Consul, after hearing of the death of the mother-in-law told George that the sending of a body back to Australia for burial is very, very expensive. It could cost as much as $5,000.00. The Consul continues, in most cases the person responsible for the remains normally decides to bury the body here. This would only cost $150.00.

George thinks for some time and answers, "I don't care how much it will cost to send the body back; that's what I want to do."

The Consul, after hearing this, says "You must have loved your mother-in-law very much considering the difference in price."

"No, it's not that," says George. "You see, I know of a case many years ago of a person that was buried here in Jerusalem. On the third day he arose from the dead." "I just can't take that chance."

[mother-in-law, resurrection]

1 Corinthians 15:22-23

A Texan was always bragging about Texas being the biggest in everything, so his friends decided to get even with him.

So they put some knockout drops in his coffee. They put on him a white robe, and placed him in a coffin, in a graveyard by a freshly dug grave.

He awakened about sunrise, sat up, and looked at the golden sunrise.

He looked around and then exclaimed, "Praise the Lord! It's resurrection morning and a Texan is the first one resurrected!"

[pride, resurrection]

1 Corinthians 15:35

After an atheist died, a fellow atheist looked at him in the casket, shook his head, and remarked, "All dressed up and no place to go."

[atheist]

1 Corinthians 15:42-44

A young preacher came to one of the distant settlements and started in to reform the natives. Among other things to which he objected was smoking by women. He stopped one day at Old Nancy's cabin and found her enjoying an after-dinner smoke on her corncob pipe.

"Aunt Nancy," he said, "when your time comes to go and you apply for admission at the gate of Heaven, do you expect that St. Peter will let you in if he detects the odor of tobacco on your breath?"

The old woman took the pipe out of her mouth and said: "Young man, when I go to Heaven I expect to leave my breath behind."

[heaven, smoking]

1 Corinthians 15:44

A young minister, in the first days of his first parish, was obliged to call upon the widow of an eccentric man who had just died. Standing before the open casket and consoling the widow, he said, "I know this must be a very hard blow, Mrs. Brown. But we must remember that what we see here is the husk only, the shell. The inside, the nut, has gone to heaven."

[death, funeral]

1 Corinthians 15:51

In an effort to make their new church building as 'biblical ' as possible, one deacon suggested they place the text of 1 Corinthians 15:51 over their nursery door, "Behold, I show you a mystery; We, shall not all sleep but we shall all be changed (KJV)."

[babies, Bible]

1 Corinthians 15:52

Preaching a funeral one afternoon, the minister couldn't seem to find a stopping place on his topic of resurrection. The funeral director grew concerned about the lateness of the hour and stepped over to a member of the church.

"Does your pastor always speak this long at a funeral?" he whispered.

"That's a fine sermon, isn't it?" nodded a loyal church member.

Somewhat embarrassed, the funeral director agreed, but he continued to look at his watch every few minutes. After a while, the church member tugged at his sleeve.

"What's the matter with you?" he demanded. "Don't you believe in the resurrection?"

"I sure do," the funeral director answered. "But I'm afraid we won't get this man buried in time for it."

[funeral, resurrection]

1 Corinthians 15:55

The pastor of the fundamentalist church, in a burst of passionate eloquence in a denunciation of the world's wickedness declared, "Hell is full of cocktails, highballs, short skirts and bikini bathing suits!"

A voice from the balcony where the backslidden young boys sat came softly in the quiet of the church, "Oh, death, where is thy sting?"

[death, hell]

1 Corinthians 15:55

Definition for death:

Death is life's way of telling you you've been fired.

Death is Nature's way of saying "slow down."

[death]

1 Corinthians 16:1

The visiting preacher was really getting the congregation moving. Near the end of his sermon he declared that this church has really got to start to walk — to which someone in the back yelled, "let her walk preacher."

The preacher then said if this church is going to go it's got to get up and run to which someone again yelled with gusto, "let her run preacher."

Feeling the surge of the church, the preacher then said with even louder gusto, "if this church is going to go it's got to really fly" and once again with ever greater gusto, someone yelled, "let her fly preacher, let her fly."

The preacher then seized the moment and stated with even greater gusto, "if this church is really going to fly it's going to need money" to which someone in the back yelled, "let her walk preacher, let her walk."

[generosity, giving]

1 Corinthians 16:2

A greedy man had to decide how much he would give his church. So he decided he would do it this way. On cashing his paycheck he would throw the bills into the air and say, "Lord, you take what's yours, and whatever comes down will be mine."

[giving]

1 Corinthians 16:2

A very old lady and a very small boy were seated together in the pew. As the collection plate approached, the little boy noticed the lady searching through her purse with an alarmed expression. Leaning over, he whispered, "Here, take my dime. I can hide under the pew."

[giving]

1 Corinthians 16:2

A little girl became restless as the preacher's sermon dragged on and on. Finally, she leaned over to her mother and whispered, "Mommy, if we give him the money now, will he let us go?"

[giving, preaching]

1 Corinthians 16:8-9

The trouble with opportunity is that it's always more recognizable going than coming.

[experience]

2 CORINTHIANS

2 Corinthians 4:2

A preacher's young daughter noticed that her father always bowed his head and closed his eyes for a few seconds before he went to the pulpit to preach. When she asked him why he did that, he explained, "I'm asking God to help me preach a good sermon." His daughter thought about it for a minute and said, "Well daddy, why doesn't he do it?"

[preaching]

2 Corinthians 4:8

QUESTION: What kind of motor vehicle did the Apostle Paul drive?
ANSWER: 2 Corinthians 4:8 describes going out for a missionary trip in a Volkswagen Beetle — "We are pressed in every way, but not cramped beyond movement."

[transportation]

2 Corinthians 5:8

The car in which the elderly couple was riding went over the cliff. It was an awful wreck. "Where am I?" moaned the woman when she opened her eyes. "In heaven?" she wondered aloud.
"No," said her dazed husband. "I'm still with you."

[heaven, marriage]

2 Corinthians 5:8

The teacher smiled at her Children's Church class and exclaimed, "All right, class, all those who want to go to Heaven raise your hands."
Everybody in the class had a hand raised, except one boy.
"Don't you want to go to heaven?" asked the teacher.
"I can't, ma'am. My mom wants me to come straight home from church."

[heaven]

2 Corinthians 5:8

"Be an angel," she said, "and let me drive."
She did, and he is.

[driving]

2 Corinthians 5:10

A local newspaper had a very difficult time in reporting the death of one of the town well-known members.

The first report said, "Brother Scott has gone to rust." They tried to correct the misprint the next day and it came out, "Brother Scott has gone to roost."

Finally they tried a third time and the report stated, "Brother Scott has gone to roast."

[death, hell]

2 Corinthians 5:17

A woman testified to the transformation in her life that had resulted through her experience in conversion. She declared, "I'm so glad I got religion. I have an uncle I used to hate so much I vowed I'd never go to his funeral. But now, why, I'd be happy to go to it any time."

[funeral, hatred]

2 Corinthians 5:20

Two preachers were having lunch at a farm during the progress of a certain church anniversary celebration. The farmer's wife cooked a couple of chickens, saying that the family could dine on the remains after the visitors had gone. But the hungry preachers wolfed down the entire two chickens. Later the farmer was conducting his guests round the farm, when an old rooster commenced to crow and crow. "Seems mighty proud of himself," said one of the guests.

"No wonder," growled the farmer, "he's got two sons in the ministry."

[eating, ministry]

2 Corinthians 6:3

Tact is both the ability to put your best foot forward without stepping on anyone's toes while at the same time shutting your mouth before someone else wants to.

[speech, wisdom]

2 Corinthians 6:14

If you are a child of God, and you marry a child of the devil, you are surely going to have trouble with your father-in-law!

[devil, marriage]

2 Corinthians 8–9

A pastor was on a plane, flying from Chicago to California, when the plane ran into some very severe turbulence. As it got worse, the passengers

became more and more alarmed, and finally even the flight attendants began to look concerned. Finally, one of them, having seen my ticket with the Reverend in front of my name, came over to me and said, "Reverend, this is really frightening. Do you suppose you could... I don't know... 'Do something religious?"
So he took up a collection.

[offering, travel]

2 Corinthians 8:2

The trouble with some folks who give until it hurts is that they are so sensitive to pain.

[giving]

2 Corinthians 8:4

The minister was addressing the Children's Church. In his most expressive tones, he was saying: "And now, children, let me tell you a very sad fact. In Africa, there are ten million square miles of territory and hardly any Children's Churches where little boys and girls can spend their Sundays. Now, what should we all try to save up our money to do?"
"Go to Africa!" was the unanimous reply.

[giving, missions]

2 Corinthians 8:12

When the family returned from the Sunday morning service, the father criticized the sermon, the daughter thought the choir's singing was off key, and the mother found fault with the organist's playing. The subject had to be dropped when the small son, having observed what his parents had put into the collection plate said, "Not a bad show for a buck, don't you think Dad?"

[complain, giving]

2 Corinthians 8:21

Once upon a time there was a greedy who decided to open a tea-room. She picked a good location and at first she prospered. Then she decided to cut corners and make some real money.
The greedy woman found that if she saved used teabags and used them over and over again, no one seemed to notice. Before long the greedy old woman was using the same tea-bags over and over and over again.
First her business dwindled. Then it faltered, and soon she was bankrupt.
Moral of this story: Honest tea [honesty] is the best policy.

[honesty]

2 Corinthians 9:1-5

A young mother was quite alarmed when her young son swallowed a coin.
"Hurry, send for the doctor," she urged her husband.
"No, I think we should send for the preacher," replied the father.
"The preacher? Why, you don't think he is going to die, do you? Exclaimed the mother.
"Oh, no," the husband replied quickly. "But you know our preacher — he can get money out of anybody!"

[money, pastor]

2 Corinthians 9:2

Gentle persuasion is when you take the felt out of the collection plates and ask for a silent offering!

[offering]

2 Corinthians 9:2-3

A member of the Internal Revenue Service telephoned a pastor one day and said, "I am reviewing the tax return of one of your church members. He listed a donation of two thousand dollars to your church. Can you tell me if he made the contribution?"
The minister replied, "I don't have those records in front of me, but if he didn't, he will."

[giving, taxes]

2 Corinthians 9:3

The pastor stood before the congregation and said, "I have bad news, I have good news, and I have more bad news." The congregation got quiet.
"The bad news is – the church needs a new roof!" the pastor said. The congregation groaned.
"The good news is – we have enough money for the new roof." A sigh of relief was heard rippling through the gathered group.
"The final bad news is – it's still in your pockets"

[giving]

2 Corinthians 9:4

A paraphrase of Paul's concern: "Protect us from members who, when it comes to giving, stop at nothing."

[giving, sacrifice]

2 Corinthians 9:5

Having a little trouble getting enough money in the offering at your church? You may want to try a new approach. There was a minister who told everyone to stand during the offertory at which time he instructed everyone to reach forward to the person standing in front of him and get his pocketbook or wallet. There he added, "Now open it and give as you always wanted to, but felt you couldn't afford!"

[offering]

2 Corinthians 9:6

The little church was badly in need of repairs, so the pastor was making a fervent appeal for funds before the congregation. To everyone's surprise, the town miser stood up and pledged $100. As he sat back down in the stunned silence, a piece of plaster fell from above and landed on his head. "Guess I'd better make that two hundred," the miser announced. From the back of the hall came a lone voice: "Hit him again, Lord!"

[offering]

2 Corinthians 9:6

A one-dollar bill met a twenty-dollar bill and said, "Hey, where have you been? I haven't seen you around here much."

The twenty answered, "I've been hanging out at the casinos, went on a cruise and did the rounds of the ship, back to the United States for a while, went to a couple of baseball games, to the mall, that kind of stuff. How about you?"

The one-dollar bill said, "You know, same old stuff — church, church, church."

OR

There was this $20 dollar bill and a $1 dollar bill on the conveyor belt at the downtown Federal Reserve Building.

As they were lying there side by side the $1 dollar bill said to the $20 dollar bill, "Hey mannnnnn, where have you been. I haven't seen you in a long time ?"

The $20 dollar bill replied, "Man I have been having a ball! I been traveling to distant countries, going to the finest restaurants, to the biggest and best casinos, numerous boutiques, the mall uptown, the mall downtown, the mall across town and even a mall that I just newly built.

"In fact, just this week I've been to Europe, a professional NBA game, Rodeo Drive, the all-day retreat spa, the top-notch hair salon and the new casino! I have done it all!!!"

After describing his great travels, the $20 dollar bill asked the $1 dollar bill, "What about you? Where have you been?"

The $1 dollar replied, "Well, I've been to the Baptist church, the Methodist church, the Presbyterian church, the Episcopalian church, the Church of God in Christ, the Catholic church, the Mormon church, the church of the Latter Day Saints, the A.M.E. church, the Disciple of Christ church, the..."

"WAIT A MINUTE! WAIT A MINUTE!!" shouted the $20 dollar bill to the $1 dollar bill.

"What's a church?"

[church, money]

2 Corinthians 9:6

A little boy fumbled around noisily in his pocket at offering time. His irritated mother asked, "Whatever are you looking for? You have your dime in your hand now."

"I'm looking for a quarter," said the little boy. "If God is as good as the preacher said He is, then I'm raising His allowance right now!"

[God, offering]

2 Corinthians 9:6

"Give till it hurts."

"Here's a dollar."

"You can't stand much pain."

[offering]

2 Corinthians 9:6

Old man Fielding, the miser, at last went to his reward and presented himself at the Pearly Gates. St. Peter greeted him with appropriate solemnity and escorted him to his new abode. Walking past numerous elegant mansions finally they arrived at a dilapidated shack at the end of the street.

Fielding, much taken aback, began, "Why am I left with a rundown shack when all of these others have fine mansions?"

"Well, sir," replied St. Peter, "we did the best we could with the money you sent us!"

[giving]

2 Corinthians 9:6

"Be grateful for all that the good Lord has done for you," the minister told his flock. "Surely each of us should give one-tenth of all we earn to the Lord."

"Amen!" shouted a particularly fervent church member. "I say let's raise it to one-twentieth."

[offering]

2 Corinthians 9:7

On Sunday morning a father gave his son a fifty-cent piece and a dollar.
"Put the dollar in the offering," the father said. "Then you can have the fifty cents for ice cream."
When the boy came home he still had the dollar.
"Why didn't you put the dollar in the offering?" his father asked.
"Well, it was like this," the boy answered. "The preacher said God loves a cheerful giver. I could give the fifty-cent piece a lot more cheerfully than I could the dollar."

[generous, offering]

2 Corinthians 9:7

The Lord loves a cheerful giver. He also accepts from a grouch.

[giving]

2 Corinthians 9:7

A rookie police officer was asked the following question on his examination paper: "How would you go about dispersing a crowd?"
He answered: "Take up an offering. That does it every time."

[offering]

2 Corinthians 9:7

The minister was preoccupied with thoughts of how he was going to ask the congregation to come up with more money than they were expecting for repairs to the church building.
Therefore, he was annoyed to find that the regular organist was sick and a substitute had been brought in at the last minute. The substitute wanted to know what to play.
"Here's a copy of the service," he said impatiently. "But you'll have to think of something to play after I make the announcement about the finances."
During the service, the minister paused and said, "Brothers and Sisters, we are in great difficulty; the roof repairs cost twice as much as we expected, and we need $4,000 more. Any of you who can pledge $100 or more, please stand up."
At that moment, the substitute organist played "The Star Spangled Banner."

[music, offering]

2 Corinthians 9:13

"Won't you give a dollar to the Lord?" asked the Salvation Army member.
"How auld are ye?" inquired the Scotsman.
"Nineteen, sir."

"Ah well, I'm past seventy-five. I'll be seein' Him afore ye, so I'll hand it to
Him myself."

[age, giving]

2 Corinthians 11:14-15

A man was going to attend a Halloween party dressed in the costume of the
devil. On his way it began to rain so he darted into a church where a revival
meeting was in progress.
At the sight of his devil's costume, people began to scatter through the
doors and windows.
One lady got her coat sleeve caught on the arm of one of the seats and as
the man came closer, she pleaded, "Satan, I've been a member of this
church for twenty years, but I've really been on your side all the time."

[devil, fear, revival, Satan]

2 Corinthians 12:7

At an ordination examination a young candidate declared he did not
believe in a personal devil. Embarrassingly shifting in their seats, the
ministers were about to vote against ordaining him, although he had given
perfectly orthodox answers in all other areas of doctrine.
Then the oldest pastor present made this comment, "Brethren, I see no
reason for refusing this young man simply because now he does not believe
in a personal devil. This matter will take care of itself. He won't be a pastor
of a church in our denomination long before he changes his mind."

[church, devil, doctrine]

2 Corinthians 12:20

When a gossip approaches you with the inquiry, "What's going on?" your
best reply is, "I am!"

[gossip]

2 Corinthians 13:14

A four-year-old boy was having a deep theological discussion with two of
his peers. When he mentioned Jesus one of his peers quickly corrected him,
saying, "You mean God!"
The other boy chimed right in with "Jesus is God. There's the Father, the
Son, and the Holy Spirit. Three in one."
With a look of shock, the four-year-old boy said, "Gee, they must be
squashed!"

[theology, Trinity]

GALATIANS

Galatians 2:13

A hypocrite is a fellow who just isn't himself on Sundays.

[hypocrisy]

Galatians 2:16

A Jew and a Christian were arguing about the ways of their religion. The Jewish man said, "You people have been taking things from us for thousands of years. The Ten Commandments, for instance."
The Christian replied, "Well, it's true that we took the Ten Commandments from you, but you can't actually say that we've kept them!"

[law, obedience]

Galatians 4:6

A four-year-old girl was at her doctor's office for her checkup. As the doctor looked into her ears, he asked if Big Bird was inside. The little girl was silent.
Then the doctor checked her throat and asked if Cookie Monster was down there. The girl still remained quiet. Finally, the doctor put his stethoscope on her chest to listen to her heart. He asked, "Do you think I'll hear Barney in your heart?"
"Oh, no!" the little girl exclaimed. "Jesus is in my heart. Barney is on my underpants."

[doctors, Jesus, television]

Galatians 5:3

The professor at the Ivy League school was just about to pass out the final exam when a student raised his hand.
"Yes Doug, what is it?"
Doug stood up at his desk and said in a loud demanding voice, "I will not take this test until you give me cakes and ale."
The professor was shocked. Doug had been an excellent student until now. "Doug, you will sit down and take the test or you will flunk the semester."
Doug replied, "No I will not Professor, and the university will back me up. I will not take this test until you give me cakes and ale."
Well, that was it. The professor almost went berserk until Doug whipped out a copy of the school's official code of conduct. The code dated back

several centuries to the original European school and clearly stated that a student taking a test could request cakes and ale.

The professor smiled through his gritted teeth and interpreted cakes and ale as being equivalent to a Big Mac and soda. He sent an aide to McDonald's to fetch the "cakes and ale."

When the student's demands had been met, the professor proceeded to administer the exam.

Two weeks later, after some diligent research by the professor, the student was fined 500 shillings for not wearing a sword to class.

[revenge, teaching]

Galatians 5:13

Your personal liberty ends where my nose begins.

[freedom]

Galatians 5:16

Dear God,

I think you'd be proud of me! So far today I've done all right. I haven't gossiped, lusted, lost my temper, haven't been greedy, grumpy, nasty, selfish or overindulgent. I'm very thankful for that. In a few minutes, though, I'm going to get out of bed. From then on I'm probably going to need a LOT of help. Amen.

[self-control, prayer]

Galatians 5:22

God wants spiritual fruit, not religious nuts!

[character]

Galatians 6:7

Life for some people is to sow wild oats during the week and then go to church on Sunday and pray for crop failure.

[repentance, sin]

Galatians 6:7

The chaplain was passing through the prison factory. "Sewing?" he said to a prisoner who was at work. "No, chaplain," replied the prisoner gloomily, "reaping!"

[consequences, prison, sin]

Galatians 6:7

Whatsoever a man sews will rip.

[consequences, sin]

Galatians 6:7

When a rural Kansas preacher returned after visiting New England, a parishioner met him at the train station.

"How are things out our way, Hiram?" the preacher asked.

"Sad, sir. A cyclone came and wiped out my house."

"Dear, dear," cried the preacher. "Well, I'm not surprised, Hiram. You remember I warned you about the way you have been living. Punishment for sin is inevitable."

"It also destroyed your house, sir," said Hiram.

"It did?" The pastor was horrified. Then he declared, "Ah me, the ways of the Lord are past human understanding."

[consequences, hypocrisy]

Galatians 6:9

Always remember, today's mighty oak is just yesterday's nut that held its ground!

[persistence]

Galatians 6:9

A cardinal ran into the Pope's office and said, "Your Holiness, Jesus just rode into the Vatican on a donkey. What do we do?"

The Pope looked up from his work and replied, "Look busy."

[Catholics, work]

EPHESIANS

Ephesians 1:5

A mother had just brought her newborn triplets home from the hospital. Her older boy, a four-year-old, took his first doubtful look at the new babies and said, "We'd better start calling folks. They're going to be a lot harder to get rid of than kittens."

[babies]

Ephesians 2:8-9

See Romans 5:1-2.

Ephesians 2:8-9

A man dies and goes to heaven. Of course, St. Peter meets him at the pearly gates.

St. Peter says, "Here's how it works. You need 100 points to make it into heaven. You tell me all the good things you've done, and I give you a certain number of points for each item, depending on how good it was. When you reach 100 points, you get in."

"Okay," the man says, "I was married to the same woman for 50 years and never cheated on her, even in my heart."

"That's wonderful," says St. Peter, "that's worth three points!"

"Three points?" he says. "Well, I attended church all my life and supported its ministry with my tithe and service."

"Terrific!" says St. Peter, "that's certainly worth a point."

"One point? Golly. How about this: I started a soup kitchen in my city and worked in a shelter for homeless veterans."

"Fantastic, that's good for two more points, " he says.

"TWO POINTS!!" the man cries, "At this rate the only way I get into heaven is by the grace of God!"

"Come on in!"

[grace, salvation]

Ephesians 2:8-9

A mother was questioning her four-year-old daughter on how a person gets saved. The girl answered that people will be saved by going to her family's church every Sunday and Wednesday.

When the mother told her that going to their church wouldn't save anyone, the girl responded: "Well then, we better find another church to go to!"

[denomination, salvation]

Ephesians 2:8-9

"If I sold my house and my car, had a big garage sale, and gave all my money to the church, would I get into heaven?" the teacher asked the children in her Children's Church class.
"NO!" all the children answered.
"If I cleaned the church every day, mowed the yard, and kept everything neat and tidy, would I get into heaven?"
Again the answer was, "NO!"
"Well," I continued, "then how can I get to heaven?"
A five-year-old boy shouted, "You gotta be dead!"

[death, heaven, salvation]

Ephesians 2:9

"Surely salvation must be earned?" he questioned <u>gracefully</u>.

[grace, puns]

Ephesians 2:10

I'm a self-made man!"
"Well, that relieves the Almighty of a great responsibility."

[pride, responsibility]

Ephesians 2:13

My church welcomes ALL denominations, but really prefers tens and twenties!

[denominations, money]

Ephesians 3:20

Charles Spurgeon's mother said, "Son, I prayed to the Lord that he would make you a Christian. But I didn't ask him to make you a Baptist."
Spurgeon replied: "Mother, that is only typical of the Lord's generosity. He always gives over and above all that we ask or think."

[Baptist, generous]

Ephesians 4:2

Pride is not one of my faults, but if I had one that would be it.

[humility, pride]

Ephesians 4:11-12

After the church service a little boy told the pastor,
"When I grow up, I'm going to give you some money."
"Well, thank you," the pastor replied, "but why?"
"Because my daddy says you're one of the poorest preachers we've ever had."

[giving, pastor, preaching]

Ephesians 4:12

Some church members must believe that a layman is someone who lays in bed Sunday morning instead of going to church and getting involved.

[church, laziness]

Ephesians 4:12

It's too bad when you have to explain to your kids that Daddy hasn't died. He just became chairman of the deacons in your church and no one else will get involved.

[church]

Ephesians 4:14-22

A four-year-old Catholic boy was playing with a four-year-old Protestant girl in a plastic wading pool in the back yard. They splashed a lot of water on each other; their clothes were soaking wet, so they decide to take off the wet clothes. The little boy looked at the little girl and said, "Golly, I didn't know there was that much difference between Catholics and Protestants,"

[denominations, gender]

Ephesians 4:22-24

A new seminary student was taken to court for stealing an item from a store. The man explained to the judge, "Your Honor, it is just recently that I became a Christian. I am now studying my Bible and I've just learnt that I am a whole new man. However, I also have an old nature. Please understand that it was not my new man who did wrong. It was my old man."
The judge responded, "I do understand. Since it was the old man that broke the law, we'll sentence him to 60 days in jail. And since the new man was an accomplice in the theft, we'll give him 30 days too. I therefore sentence you both to 90 days in jail."

[sanctification, stealing]

Ephesians 4:25

Mildred, the church gossip and self-appointed arbiter of the church's morals, kept sticking her nose into other people's business. Several residents were unappreciative of her activities, but feared her enough to maintain their silence. She made a mistake, however, when she accused George, a new member, of being an alcoholic, after she saw his pickup truck parked in front of the town's only bar one afternoon. She commented to George and others that everyone seeing it there would know what he was doing.

George, a man of few words, stared at her for a moment and then just walked away. He didn't explain, defend, or deny. He said nothing.

Later that evening, George quietly parked his pickup in front of Mildred's house ... and left it there all night.

[gossip]

Ephesians 4:26

Remember: Anger is just one letter short of Danger.

[anger, danger]

Ephesians 4:26

In our marriage we made the decision not to go to sleep mad. We haven't slept in three weeks.

[anger, marriage, sleep]

Ephesians 4:26

A man and his wife were having some problems at home and were giving each other the silent treatment.

The next day the man realized that he would need his wife to wake him at 5 am for an early flight to Sydney. Not wanting to be the first to break the silence, he finally wrote on a piece of paper,

"Please wake me at 5 am."

The next morning the man woke up, only to discover it was 9 am, and that he had missed his flight!

Furious, he was about to go and see why his wife hadn't awakened him when he noticed a piece of paper by the bed. It said, "It's 5 am, wake up."

[conflict, marriage, silence]

Ephesians 4:26

A man and his wife had their first quarrel during the fiftieth year of their wedded life. The man tucked a gracious note under his wife's pillow: "My darling bride, let's put off quarreling until after the honeymoon is over. Your devoted husband."

[argument, forgiveness]

Ephesians 4:26

When John and his wife have a few words, they send the kids out to play. Man! Are those kids ever sunburned.

[argument, marriage]

Ephesians 4:26

An applicant for an insurance policy turned in his completed form. The agent looked it over. "This seems in order, Mr. Jones," he said, "except for one thing. When it asks for the relationship of Mrs. Jones to you, you should have said 'wife' not 'strained!'"

[argument, marriage]

Ephesians 4:26-27

Temper gets you into trouble: pride keeps you there.

[pride, temper]

Ephesians 4:28

In the King James Version this verse reads, "Let him that stole steal no more; but rather let him labor, working with his hands the thing that is good ..."
This verse, in the affirmation of the thief in prison, who argued he was incarcerated for doing what God told him to do, should be punctuated in this way: "Let him that stole, steal. No more let him labor, working with his hands ..."

[prison, stealing, work]

Ephesians 4:28

A young man worked for a lumber company. He was a very good man, but he had one bad habit. Each night when he finished work he would put a piece of lumber into his truck. Soon he had a big pile of lumber. Finally his conscience began to bother him. And being Catholic he went to see his priest and confessed everything. Father listened very intently and then said, "Young man, you have done something very, very serious. You're going to have to make a novena. Do you know what a novena is?"
"No, Father," he said, "I sure don't but if you've got the plans, I've got the lumber."

[Catholics, stealing]

Ephesians 4:28

The country's champion horse thief was converted at a camp meeting. The preacher called upon him to tell the group what the Lord had done for him.

The reformed thief stood up and said, "It looks like the Lord done ruined me."

[revival, stealing]

Ephesians 4:29

Time had come for the funeral of a woman who always kept her church and community in an uproar with her gossip. It was a dark, stormy day, and the lights were on in the chapel. The preacher was quietly conducting the service.

Suddenly a bolt of lightning and thunder shook the building and the lights went out. The preacher stopped speaking and, in the sudden stillness, a voice was heard in the audience.

"She got there!"

[funeral, gossip, heaven]

Ephesians 4:29

"You don't seem to think too much of him."

"Let me put it this way. If he had his conscience taken out, it would be a minor operation."

[conscience]

Ephesians 4:31-32

A boy who had said some very cruel and nasty things to his younger brother, refused to apologize. His mother tried to appeal to his better nature, but with little success. Just before bedtime she tried a different approach. "Look, James, how would you feel if your little brother died tonight? I'm sure you would feel terrible about having said these awful things to him, and not having said sorry." This seemed to win the day, for she heard him go through to his brother's bedroom and say, "I'm sorry," but then he added, "But if you are not dead in the morning, I'll thump you."

[forgiveness]

Ephesians 4:32

Some people are kind, polite, and sweet-spirited until you try to take their favorite church parking spot.

[kindness]

Ephesians 4:32

See Genesis 2:24.

Ephesians 5:4

At a banquet, a clumsy waiter dropped a plate of hot soup in the lap of the bishop. The clergyman glanced around with a look of agony and exclaimed, "Will some layman please say something appropriate?"

[pain, swearing]

Ephesians 5:15

After the doctor checked the patient over, he asked, "Have you been living a normal life?"
"Yes, doctor," replied the patient.
"Well, you'll have to cut it out for awhile."

[doctors, sickness]

Ephesians 5:16

If you kill time, you'll bury opportunities.

[death, time]

Ephesians 5:18

A cowboy walks into a bar in Texas, orders three mugs of brew and sits in the back room, drinking a sip out of each one in turn.
When he finishes them, he comes back to the bar and orders three more.
The bartender approaches and tells him, "You know, a mug goes flat after I draw it so it would taste better if you bought just one at a time."
The cowboy replies, "Well, you see, I have two brothers. One is in Australia, the other is in Dublin and I'm in Texas. When we all left home, we promised that we'd drink this way to remember the days we were together. So I drink one for each of my brothers and one for myself."
The bartender admits that this is a nice custom and leaves it there. The cowboy becomes a regular in the bar, and always drinks the same way. He orders three mugs and drinks them in turn.
One day, he comes in and orders only two mugs! All the regulars take notice and fall silent. When he comes back to the bar for the second round, the bartender says, "I don't want to intrude on your grief, but I wanted to offer my condolences on your loss."
The cowboy looks quite puzzled for a moment, then a light dawns and he laughs. "Oh, no, everybody's just fine," he explains.
"It's just that my wife and I joined the Baptist Church and obviously I had to quit drinking. Hasn't affected my brothers though."

[Baptist, drinking]

Ephesians 5:18

See Proverb 23:31,33.

Ephesians 5:19

I could tell it was a "progressive liberal" church when we all stood up to sing the first hymn and it was called, "Fine and Dandy."

[church, hymns]

Ephesians 5:22

The minister was good and worked up by his sermon on the duty of wives to be submissive to their husbands. "I see in our congregation today a woman who has disobeyed her husband," he shouted, picking up his hymnal. "I don't want to mention her name but to point her out to you all, I will now throw this book at her head."
Before he even got his arm over his head, half the women in the congregation had ducked!

[sermon, submission, wife]

Ephesians 5:22

A nervous young bride was counseled by her pastor: "When you enter the church tomorrow, you will once again walk down the aisle you've walked down so many times before. Concentrate on that. And when you get halfway down the aisle, concentrate on the altar, where you and your parents have worshipped for so many years. Concentrate on that. And as you reach the end of the aisle, your groom will be waiting for you. Concentrate on him."
It worked to perfection, and on her wedding day the nervous bride boldly completed her processional. But people in the audience were a bit taken aback to hear her chanting three words, all the way down the aisle, what they understood as "I'll-alter-him."

[wedding]

Ephesians 5:22

"Do you have the book *Man, Master of Women*?" a young man asked the lady librarian.
"Fiction counter to your left," the librarian replied.

[men, woman]

Ephesians 5:23

Husband: "Don't forget that the Bible says that the husband is the head of the wife."
Wife: "And don't you forget that the Bible also says that a virtuous woman is a crown to her husband [Prov 12:4], and the crown is worn on the top of the head."

[context, husbands, marriage, submission, wife]

Ephesians 5:23

A pastor announced an extra collection at the end of his sermon. He asked that "the head of the household" to come forward and deposit the money on the altar. Many husbands rose and came to the front, after getting some money from the wives.

[giving, marriage]

Ephesians 5:23

"Tell me, Steve, who is the boss in your house?"
"Well," said Steve thoughtfully, "My wife assumes command of the children, the servants, and the dog. But I say pretty much what I please to the goldfish."

[husbands, marriage]

Ephesians 5:24

Husband: "But you promised me at the altar to obey me."
New wife: "Of course, I didn't want to make a scene in church."

[obedience, submission]

Ephesians 5:27

A middle-aged church lady goes to the doctor and receives breast implants and a facelift. From there she proceeds to get a "tummy tuck." She continues on to have liposuction performed on her hips and thighs and then goes to her cosmetic representative and buys a ton of skin care products and facial creams.
When questioned by another lady in the church as to how she could justify the expense and pain to remain young looking, the woman replied "I heard our preacher say that Jesus was coming back soon and He's looking for a church filled with people without a spot or wrinkle and I wanted to be included."

[appearance, body, rapture]

Ephesians 5:28

Many a wife manages her husband by simply using a little sigh-chology [psychology]!

[psychology]

Ephesians 5:28

Husband: "Sweetheart, I have a present for the person I love best in all the world."
Depressed wife: "A set of golf clubs for yourself, no doubt."

[selfish]

Ephesians 5:31

Newly married, John had a problem leaving his parents, especially his mother. His wife Beth was hanging up his jacket when she noticed a long gray hair on the shoulder.

"So," Beth screamed at him, "You've been over at your mother's getting sympathy again!"

[mothers, sympathy]

Ephesians 5:31

When a man marries a woman, they become one but the trouble starts when they try to decide which one.

[conflict, marriage, unity]

Ephesians 5:33

Marriage is like twirling a baton, turning a hand-spring, or eating with chopsticks — it looks easy till you try it.

[marriage]

Ephesians 5:33

A friend of mine, Vera, told me about this new Husband Shopping Center where a woman could go to choose from among many men for her husband. It was laid out in five floors, with the men increasing in positive attributes as you ascended up the floors. The only rule was once you opened the door to any floor, you must choose a man from that floor, and if you went up a floor, you couldn't go back down except to leave the place. So, a couple of girlfriends go to the place to find a man as a prospective husband.

First floor, the door had a sign saying : "These men have jobs and love kids." The women read the sign and say "Well that's better than not having jobs, or not loving kids, but I wonder what's further up". So up they go.

Second floor says: "These men have high-paying jobs, love kids, and are extremely good looking" Hmmm, say the girls. But, I wonder what's further up?

Third floor: "These men have high paying jobs, are extremely good looking, love kids and help with the housework." Wow! Say the women. Very tempting, BUT, there's more further up! And up they go.

Fourth floor: "These men have high paying jobs, love kids, are extremely good looking, help with the housework, and have a strong romantic streak." Oh, mercy me. But just think! What must be awaiting us further on! So up to the fifth floor they go.

Fifth floor: The sign on the door said:

"This floor is empty and exists only to prove that women are impossible to please."

[husbands, wives]

Ephesians 5:33

"Have you and your wife ever had any difference of opinion?"
"Yes, but she didn't know it."

[conflict]

Ephesians 5:33

A Children's Church teacher was teaching her class about the difference between right and wrong.
"All right children, let's take another example," she said. "If I were to get into a man's pocket and take his billfold with all his money, what would I be?"
Little Johnny raises his hand, and with a confident smile, he blurts out, "You'd be his wife!"

[money, wife]

Ephesians 6:1

After a spanking, a father returned to his son's room to admonish him. "I didn't want to spank you, but the Bible says that children should obey their parents."
"I know," was the tearful reply. "But the Bible also says, 'Be kind one to another' too."

[context, discipline, obedience]

Ephesians 6:1

Officer to man pacing sidewalk at 2 A. M.: "What are you doing here?"
Gentleman: "I forgot my key, officer, and I'm waiting for my children to come home and let me in."

[parents]

Ephesians 6:1

Adolescence is a period of rapid changes. Between the ages of twelve and seventeen, for example, a child may see his parents age twenty years.

[parents, teenagers]

Ephesians 6:1

The story is told of an introspective five-year-old boy who took an interest in how babies came to be. The father only explained how the mother's body protected the baby and how the circulation of her blood kept it warm and provided nourishment.

At dinner a few evenings later, the boy said, "Daddy, you should know that I really don't need to obey you. Mother is my blood relative, but you're only related to me by marriage!"

[family, obedience]

Ephesians 6:1

One of the first things one notices in a "backward country" is that children are still obeying their parents!

[family, obedience]

Ephesians 6:2

A little boy is watching TV in the den and his father is reading a newspaper in the living room. He hears a tapping on the other side of the paper, and looks to discover his son there.

The boy asks, "Daddy, is it true that the stork brings babies?"

He answers, "Yes son it's true."

Satisfied, the boy returns to the TV.

A few minutes later he hears a tapping again, and sees his son.

The little boy asks, "Is it true that God helps those who help themselves?"

He answers, "Yes son it's true."

Satisfied, the boy returns to the TV.

A few minutes later he hears a tapping a third time, and sees his son yet again.

The little boy asks, "Daddy is it true that God gives us our daily bread?"

He answers, "Yes son it's true."

The little boy looks puzzled, and stands there a minute before he finally asks, "Daddy, what do we need you for?"

[fathers, provision]

Ephesians 6:2

A family talked mother into getting a hamster as long as they took care of the creature. Two months later, when Mother was caring for Danny the hamster, she made some phone calls and found a new home for him. She broke the news to the children, and they took it quite well; but they did offer some comments. One of the children remarked, "He's been around here a long time — we'll miss him." Mom agreed saying, "Yes, but he's too much work for one person, and since I'm that one person, I say he goes." Another child offered, "Well, maybe if he wouldn't eat so much and wouldn't be so messy, we could keep him." But Mom was firm. "It's time to take Danny to his new home now," she insisted. "Go and get his cage."

With one voice and in tearful outrage the children shouted, "Danny? We thought you said 'Daddy'!"

[animals, family, fathers]

Ephesians 6:4

A father rebuked his daughter and put her to bed for being cross and ill tempered throughout the day. After she had been tucked in, the little one commented: "How come it's temper when it's me and nerves when it's you?"

[anger, temper]

Ephesians 6:4

If you have teenagers in your house, you'll find it difficult to understand how farmers could possibly grow a surplus of food.

[food, teenagers]

Ephesians 6:4

Parents, be the soul support of your children!

[parenting]

Ephesians 6:4

The secret of being a good parent is being able to put your foot down without putting it in your mouth.

[discipline, parenting]

Ephesians 6:4

"My father thinks I am very responsible," the boy told his school teacher. "Every time something goes wrong at home he says I am responsible."

[responsibility]

Ephesians 6:4

After a family disturbance one of the little boys closed his bedtime prayer by saying, "And please don't give my dad any more children ... he doesn't know how to treat those he's got now."

[family, prayer]

Ephesians 6:4

After the christening of his baby brother in church, little Johnny sobbed all the way home in the back seat of the car. His father asked him three times what was wrong. Finally, the boy replied, "That preacher said he wanted us brought up in a Christian home, and I wanted to stay with you guys."

[church, family]

Ephesians 6:4

Every couple knows how to raise the neighbor's children, so why not have all families swap children?

[parenting]

Ephesians 6:13

Bert has this friend who always seemed to lean slightly to the left all the time. It used to bother him, so he suggested his buddy Louie should see a doctor, and have his legs checked out.

For years, Louie refused ... told Bert he was crazy. Last week however, Louie finally went, and sure enough, the doctor discovered his left leg was 1/4" shorter than his right.

A quick bit of orthopedic surgery later, Louie was cured, and both legs are exactly the same length now, and he no longer leans.

"So," Bert says, "You didn't believe me when I told you a doctor could fix your leg." Louie just looked at Bert and said, "I stand corrected."

[correction]

Ephesians 6:17

Explaining the various items in the Christian's armor, a Children's Church teacher said, "Another weapon we should carry is the Word of God. Can anyone remember what the apostle Paul called the Word of God?"

When no answer was forthcoming, he added, "It's something very sharp, something that cuts."

One little fellow chirped up, "I know. It's the axe [Acts] of the apostles."

[apostles, Bible]

Ephesians 6:18

With all the problems of prayer in school, teachers are rather nervous. A teacher came into the school gym and found a small group of boys on their knees.

Immediately she asked, "What are you boys doing?"

Shooting the dice, they admitted.

"Thank goodness," the teacher said. "For a minute I thought you were praying."

[gambling, prayer]

Ephesians 6:19

One Sunday in a Midwest city, a young child was "acting up" during the morning worship hour. The parents did their best to maintain some sense of order in the pew but were losing the battle. Finally, the father picked the little fellow up and walked sternly up the aisle on his way out. Just before reaching the safety of the foyer, the little one called loudly to the congregation, "Pray for me! Pray for me!"

[church, parenting, prayer]

PHILIPPIANS

Philippians 1:21

An 85-year-old couple, after being married for almost 60 years, died in a car crash. They had been in good health the last ten years, mainly due to her interest in health food and exercising.

When they reached the Pearly Gates, St. Peter took them to their mansion, which was decked out with a beautiful kitchen, master bath suite and a Jacuzzi.

As they looked around, the old man asked St. Peter how much all this was going to cost.

"It's free," St. Peter replied, "this is Heaven."

Next, they went out in the back yard to survey the championship-style golf course where the home was located. They would have golfing privileges every day, and each week the course changed to a new one representing the great golf courses on earth.

The old man asked, "What are the green fees?"

St. Peter replied, "This is heaven, you play for free."

Next, they went to the club house and saw the lavish buffet lunch with the cuisines of the World laid out.

"How much to eat?" asked the old man.

"Don't you understand yet? This is heaven, it is free!" St. Peter replied, with some exasperation.

"Well, where are the low fat and low cholesterol tables?" the old man asked timidly.

St. Peter lectured, "That's the best part — you can eat as much as you like of whatever you like and you never get fat and you never get sick. This is Heaven."

With that, the old man went into a fit of anger, throwing down his hat and stomping on it, and screaming wildly.

St. Peter and his wife both tried to calm him down, asking him what was wrong. The old man looked at his wife and said, "This is all your fault! If it weren't for your blasted bran muffins, I could have been here ten years ago!"

[food, heaven]

Philippians 1:22

After dying in a car crash, three friends go to Heaven for orientation. They are all asked the same question, "When you're lying in your casket, and friends and family are mourning over you, what would you like to hear them say about you?"
The first guy immediately responds, "I would like to hear them say that I was one of the great doctors of my time, and a great family man."
The second guy says, "I would like to hear that I was a wonderful husband and school teacher who made a huge difference in the children of tomorrow."
The last guy thinks for a moment, and then replies, "I guess I'd like to hear them say, 'Look, he's moving!'"

[funeral, heaven, resurrection]

Philippians 2:4

There are two types of people in the world: those who come into the room and say, "Well, here I am!" and those who come and say, "Ah, there you are!"

[politeness, pride]

Philippians 2:4-5

The man who sits in a swamp all day waiting to shoot a duck but gripes if his wife has dinner ten minutes late, is a miserable soul!

[complain]

Philippians 2:6-7

A little girl in a Children's Church class was asked to describe Jesus. "Jesus," she said, "is God with the skin on."

[incarnation, Jesus,]

Philippians 2:10

In our society, the only time people seem to get on their knees is when looking for a contact lens.

[prayer]

Philippians 2:10

One day at kindergarten a teacher said to the class of 5-year olds, "I'll give $2 to the child who can tell me who was the most famous man who ever lived."
An Irish boy put his hand up and said, "It was St. Patrick."
The teacher said, "Sorry Sean, that's not correct."
Then a Scottish boy put his hand up and said, "It was St. Andrew."

The teacher replied, "I'm sorry, Hamish, that's not right either."

Finally, a Jewish boy raised his hand and said, "It was Jesus Christ."

The teacher said, "That's absolutely right, Marvin, come up here and I'll give you the $2."

As the teacher was giving Marvin his money, she said, "You know Marvin, since you're Jewish, I was very surprised you said Jesus Christ."

Marvin replied, "Yeah. In my heart I knew it was Moses, but business is business!"

[business]

Philippians 2:14

"Whines" are the products of sour grapes.

[complain, puns]

Philippians 2:14

Our forefathers did without sugar until the 13th century; without coal fires until the 14th; without buttered bread until the 16th; without tea or soap until the 17th; without gas, matches or electricity until the 19th; and without cars, canned or frozen foods until the 20th century. Now, what was it you were complaining about?

[complain]

Philippians 2:14

He who growls all day lives a dog's life.

[complain]

Philippians 3:5

QUESTION: What is there in the Bible to indicate that women should not make coffee?

ANSWER: <u>He</u>brews

[drink]

Philippians 4:6

Worry is like a rocking chair. It gives you something to do but it doesn't get you anyplace.

[worry]

Philippians 4:6

Don't tell me that worry doesn't do any good. I know better. Almost all the things I worry about don't happen!

[worry]

Philippians 4:6

One good reason for not worrying is that you feel like a fool when things turn out all right.

[worry]

Philippians 4:6

Actual announcement taken from a church bulletin:
"Don't let worry kill you, let the church help."

[worry]

Philippians 4:6

You get ulcers not from what you eat, but from what is eating you.

[worry]

Philippians 4:6

An older black lady who worked as a housekeeper for a minister's family came to work one day with a tale calculated to awaken pity in the hardest heart.
"Cheer up," said the minister. "There is no room according to the Bible for worrying about it."
But the old black lady held another view. "How come there is no use worrying? She demanded. "When the good Lord sends me tribulation He expects me to tribulate, ain't he?"

[trials, worry]

Philippians 4:6

A famous preacher was asked if he worried. "Oh, of course not," he answered, "Because worry is sin—and if I'm going to sin, I would choose something that's a lot more fun."

[sin, worry]

Philippians 4:7

Looking out into the congregation, the young minister noted that the bishop was in attendance.
After the service was over, the minister was shaking hands as the bishop exited.
"How did you like my sermon, Bishop," the young man asked.
"Young man, it was like the peace and mercy of God," replied the bishop.
"It was like his peace in that it passed all understanding and like his mercy in that I thought it would endure forever."

OR

After an exceptionally long and boring sermon the congregation filed out of the church not saying a word to the pastor. After a while a man shook the pastor's hand and said, "Pastor, that sermon reminded me of the peace and love of God!" The pastor was ecstatic. "No-one has ever said anything like that about one of my sermons before! Tell me, how did it remind you of the peace and love of God?" "Well", said the man, "it reminded me of the peace of God because it passed all human understanding and it reminded me of the love of God because it endured forever!"

[eternity, peace, sermon]

Philippians 4:7
See Psalm 136.

Philippians 4:8
Home from college at semester break, a girl told her mother that she was going to a movie that evening with other college students. Under questioning she admitted that "the movie had some bad parts, but they won't hurt me."
At that moment the mother was making a tossed salad. With her daughter looking on, she quietly fished out a handful of garbage and dumped it into the salad.
Horrified, the girl exclaimed, "Mother why did you do that?"
Came the reply, "Since you don't seem to mind filling your mind with garbage, I thought you wouldn't mind filling your stomach with some too"

[food, sin]

Philippians 4:11
An illustration of contentment: a man who is enjoying the scenery along the detour.

[contentment]

Philippians 4:11
A luxury automatically becomes a necessity when you find you can charge it.

[debt]

Philippians 4:11
"You're always wishing for something you haven't got."
"What else is there to wish for?"

[contentment, desire]

Philippians 4:12

Only Americans have fostered the art of being prosperous, though broke.

[debt, wealth]

Philippians 4:12

A preacher, looking for a discount at a store, said, "I'm only a poor preacher."

Said the clerk, "I know, I heard you last Sunday."

[pastor, poverty]

Philippians 4:12-13

A new convert gave this testimony: "I have a mountain-top experience every day. One day I'm on top of the mountain. Then the next day the mountain is on top of me."

[trials, victory]

Philippians 4:15

Someone, mistaking a preacher who had earned a doctorate in theology for a medical doctor, asked, "What is the most sensitive nerve in the human body?"

The preacher answered, "The one that leads to the pocketbook."

[body, giving]

Philippians 4:18

After coming out of the water, a new member exclaimed, "Good grief, preacher, I forgot to remove my wallet from these trousers. It's dripping wet." "Hallelujah," exulted the preacher, "We could stand more baptized wallets."

[baptism, giving]

COLOSSIANS

Colossians

QUESTION: Where do you find rain gear in the Bible?
ANSWER: In the book of Goloshes. (Colossians).

[weather]

Colossians 1:17

A small boy's prayer: "Dear Jesus, I hope you take care of yourself. 'Cause if anything happens to you, we would all be in a terrible mess."

[Jesus, prayer, providence]

Colossians 2:8

Science is the game you play with God to find out what His rules are.

[creation, science]

Colossians 2:16

A minister walked through the lobby of a hotel one morning and noticed a ballplayer he knew by sight. So he sauntered over to the player and introduced himself and said: "One thing I've always wondered ... why must you play ball on Sunday?"
Well, Reverend," smiled the player, "Sunday is our biggest day ... we get the best crowds ... take in more money ... and, after all, Sunday is your biggest day, too, isn't it?"
There was a nod of understanding, but the minister explained: "Yes, but there's a difference. You see, I'm in the right field."
The player brightened and responded eagerly: "So am I ... and ain't that sun a killer out there?"

[sports, Sunday]

Colossians 2:16

The minister was on his way to church one Sunday morning, when in a field he noticed a young farmer whom he knew.
"Say, John," he asked, "don't you know that the Creator made the world in only six days and that he rested on the seventh?"
"I know all about that," said the farmer as he glanced at the darkening clouds. But he got done and I didn't."

[creation, farming, Sunday]

Colossians 2:16

"You shouldn't play such flippant tunes on Sunday," her pastor told a young girl. "Don't you know the Ten Commandments?"

"I'm not sure, but if you'll whistle a bit of it, maybe it will come to me."

[music, Sunday]

Colossians 2:16

A Scottish minister, asked if he thought it wrong to take a walk in the country on Sunday, said, "Well, as I see it, there's no harm in takin' a walk on the Sawbath, sae long as ye dinna enjoy yourself."

[Sunday]

Colossians 2:16

Dear GOD,

Why is Sunday School on Sunday?

I thought it was supposed to be our day of rest.

-Tom

[church, rest, Sunday]

Colossians 3:1

See Mark 16:19.

Colossians 3:9

A minister wound up the services one morning by saying, "Next Sunday I am going to preach on the subject of liars. And in this connection, as a preparation for my discourse, I would like you all to read the 17th chapter of Mark."

On the following Sunday, the preacher rose to begin, and said, "Now, then all of you who have done as I requested and read the 17th chapter of Mark, please raise your hands." Nearly every hand in the congregation went up. Then said the preacher, "You are the people I want to talk to. There is no 17th chapter of Mark."

[lying]

Colossians 3:17

A computer professional said to a pastor, "I'm tired of wasting my time doing little things for God. I want to do something big and important."

The pastor said, "Tell me how to use a computer."

The professional said, "Well, first you turn it on, then y-"

The pastor interrupted him. "Don't waste my time talking about turning it on. I only want to know the big and important stuff."

[service, time]

Colossians 3:18

Some years ago a Canadian newspaper received this anxious letter from one of its readers: "I read with trepidation that the Church of England is omitting the word 'obey' from the marriage service in their new prayer book. May I ask if this new church law is retroactive?"

[marriage, obedience]

Colossian 3:18

My wife and I have had a very simple relationship down through the years. I rule the roost and she rules the rooster.

[marriage]

Colossians 3:19

Every man feels he needs a wife, because there are many things that go wrong that he can't blame on the government.

[blame, singleness]

Colossians 3:19

NEW CLASSES FOR MEN, TO BE HELD AT YOUR LOCAL ADULT LEARNING CENTER
Due to the complexity & difficulty level, each course will accept a maximum of 8 participants.
Topic 1 — How To Fill Up The Ice Cube Tray — Step By Step, With Slide Presentation.
Topic 2 — Toilet Paper: Does It Grow On The Holder? — Round Table Discussion.
Topic 3 — Fundamental Differences Between The Laundry Hamper And The Floor — Pictures And Explanatory Graphics.
Topic 4 — Dishes And Silverware: Can They Levitate And Fly Into The Sink? — Examples On Video.
Topic 5 — Identity Crisis: Losing The Remote To Your Significant Other — Helpline Support And Support Groups.
Topic 6 — Learning How To Find Things, Looking In The Right Place Instead Of Turning The House Upside Down While Screaming — Open Forum.
Topic 7 — Health Watch: Bringing Her Flowers Is Not Harmful To Your Health — Graphics And Audio Tape.
Topic 8 — Real Men Ask For Directions When Lost. — Real Life Testimonials (may be deleted due to unavailability of any men able to give testimonials)
Topic 9 — Is It Genetically Impossible To Sit Quietly As She Parallel Parks? — Driving Simulation.

Topic 10 — Learning About Life: Basic Differences Between Mother And Your Wife — Online Class And Role Playing.

Topic 11 — Becoming The Ideal Shopping Companion — Exercises, Meditation And Breathing Techniques.

Topic 12 — How To Fight Cerebral Atrophy: Remembering Birthdays, Anniversaries, Other Important Dates And Calling When You're Going To Be Late — Cerebral Shock Therapy Sessions And Full Lobotomies Offered.

[gender, roles]

Colossian 3:22

"My secretary told you I was out," exclaimed the puzzled boss. "How'd you know I was in?"

"Easy," explained the salesman. "Your secretary was working."

[laziness, work]

Colossians 3:24

See 1 Corinthians 3:14.

Colossians 4:5

You can't kill time without injuring eternity.

[eternity, time]

Colossians 4:5-6

About a century or two ago, the Pope decided that all the Jews had to leave Rome. Naturally there was a big uproar from the Jewish community. So the Pope made a deal. He would have a religious debate with a member of the Jewish community. If the Jew won, the Jews could stay. If the Pope won, the Jews would leave.

The Jews realized that they had no choice. They looked around for a champion who could defend their faith, but no one wanted to volunteer. It was too risky. So they finally picked an old man named Moishe who spent his life sweeping up after people to represent them. Being old and poor, he had less to lose, so he agreed. He asked only for one addition to the debate. Not being used to saying very much as he cleaned up around the settlement, he asked that neither side be allowed to talk. The Pope agreed.

The day of the great debate came. Moishe and the Pope sat opposite each other for a full minute before the Pope raised his hand and showed three fingers. Moishe looked back at him and raised one finger. The Pope waved his fingers in a circle around his head. Moishe pointed to the ground where he sat. The Pope pulled out a wafer and a glass of wine. Moishe pulled out an apple. The Pope stood up and said, "I give up. This man is too good. The Jews can stay."

An hour later, the cardinals were all around the Pope asking him what happened. The Pope said, "First I held up three fingers to represent the Trinity. He responded by holding up one finger, to remind me that there was still one God common to both our religions. Then I waved my finger around me to show him, that God was all around us. He responded by pointing to the ground, showing that God was also right here with us. I pulled out the wine and the wafer to show that God absolves us from our sins. He pulled out an apple to remind me of original sin. He had an answer for everything. What could I do?"

Meanwhile, the Jewish community had crowded around Moishe, amazed that this old, almost feeble-minded man had done what all their scholars had insisted was impossible! "What happened?" they asked.

"Well," said Moishe, "first he said to me that the Jews had three days to get out of here. I told him that not one of us was leaving. Then he told me that this whole city would be cleared of Jews. I let him know that we were staying right here."

"And then?" asked a woman.

"I don't know," said Moishe. "He took out his lunch and I took out mine."

[argument, Catholic, Judaism, misunderstanding]

Colossians 4:6

Someone was heard to pray, "Lord, make all of my words gracious and tender today, for tomorrow I may have to eat them."

[prayer, speech]

Colossians 4:6

Corporal Conroy needed to use a pay phone, but didn't have change for a dollar. He saw Private Duncan mopping the base's corridor floors, and asked him, "Soldier, do you have change for a dollar?"

Private Duncan replied, "Sure. "

The Corporal turned red. He said, "That's no way to address a superior officer! Now let's try it again. Private, do you have change for a dollar?"

Private Duncan replied, "No, SIR!"

[respect]

Colossians 4:14

There was this city doctor who started a practice in the countryside. He once had to go to a farm to attend to a sick farmer who lived there. After a few house calls he stopped coming to the farm.

The puzzled farmer finally phoned him to ask what's the matter, "Don't you like me or somethin'?"

The doctor said, "No, its your ducks at the entrance. Every time I enter the farm, they insult me!"

[respect]

Colossians 4:16

Children's Church teacher: "What is an Epistle?"
Student: "I guess it is the wife of an Apostle."

[apostle]

1 THESSALONIANS

1 Thessalonians 1:6

A mother was preparing pancakes for her sons, Timothy, age five and Mark, age three. The boys began to argue over who would get the first pancake. Their mother saw the opportunity for a moral lesson. "If Jesus were sitting here, He would say, 'Let my brother have the first pancake, I can wait.'"

Timothy turned to his younger brother and said, "Mark, you be Jesus!"

[Jesus, selfish]

1 Thessalonians 3:4

The manager of the amphitheater in Rome said to the Emperor Nero, "You know, sir, we aren't making much money this season."

"That's right," said Nero, "it seems as though the lions are eating up all the profits [prophets]."

[persecution, prophets]

1 Thessalonians 4:3

A teenage boy and his grandfather go fishing one day. While fishing, the old man starts talking about how times have changed. The young man picks up on this and starts talking about the various problems and diseases going around.

Teen says, "Grandpa, they didn't have a whole lot of problems with all these diseases when you were young did they?"

Grandpa replies, "Nope."

Teen says, "Well, what did you guys use for safe sex?"

Grandpa replies, "A wedding ring."

[sex]

1 Thessalonians 4:3-5

A great many of our troubles are man-maid [man made].

[gender]

1 Thessalonians 4:7

Conversation between two preachers:

Pastor Woods: "Man, I feel lousy today!"

Pastor Harris: "Well I bet I feel worse than you do. My head is splitting."

Pastor Woods: "I just feel like I have a hole in my head."
Pastor Harris: "Well I feel like I have two holes in my head."
Pastor Woods: "You know that's what I don't like about you. You're always a 'holier than thou' type."

[comparison, holiness]

1 Thessalonians 4:9

A Children's Church teacher was trying to impress his class with the concept of kindness to all God's creatures.
"For example," he said, "if I were to stop a man from beating his mule, what virtue would I be exhibiting?"
"Brotherly love," replied a somewhat confused young Billy in a hopeful tone.

[animals, kindness, love]

1 Thessalonians 4:11-12

Whenever one man gets something without earning it, some other man has to earn something without getting it.

[fairness, work]

1 Thessalonians 4:13

See Luke 8:52.

1 Thessalonians 4:14

"My boy," asked his boss, "do you believe in life after death?"
"Yes, sir."
"Then that makes everything just fine," his employer continued tenderly. "About an hour after you left yesterday to attend your grandfather's funeral, he came in to see you."

[after-death, death, work]

1 Thessalonians 4:15

A gambler died. The funeral was well attended by his professional friends. In the eulogy, the minister asserted: "Spike is not dead. He only sleeps." From the rear of the chapel came the interrupting words: "I got $100 says he's dead!"

[gambling]

1 Thessalonians 4:15

Song title: "When the Roll is Called Up Yonder, Will the Hot Dog Be There?"

[food, songs]

1 Thessalonians 4:16

One pastor said that his church people would be the first to go up in the rapture. He gave this reason: "The Bible says, 'The dead in Christ shall rise first.'"

[dead, rapture]

1 Thessalonians 4:17

A small boy, visiting New York City for the first time, went in an elevator to the top of a very tall building. As he shot past the sixty-second floor at a breathtaking speed, he gulped, turned to his father and asked, "Daddy, does God know we are coming?"

[rapture]

1 Thessalonians 4:17

"Jesus is coming soon — perhaps tomorrow. Send $10 for tapes that explain the second coming of Christ. Allow six weeks for delivery."

[rapture]

1 Thessalonians 5:1

Graffiti on a blackboard at Dallas Theological Seminary —
DISPENSATIONALISM IS NOT FOR THIS AGE

[theology]

1 Thessalonians 5:2

Did you hear about the minister who felt his sermon entitled IT'S LATER THAN YOU THINK was a huge success, because people kept looking at their watches?

[sermon, time]

1 Thessalonians 5:12-13

A priest rushed from church one day to keep a golf date. He was halfway down the first fairway, waiting to hit his second shot, when he heard the familiar "FORE!" and a ball slammed into his back.
Soon the golfer who had made the drive was on the scene to offer his apologies. When the priest assured him that he was all right, the man smiled. "Thank goodness, Father!" he exclaimed. "I've been playing this game for forty years, and now I can finally tell my friends that I've hit my first holy one!"

[holy, sports]

1 Thessalonians 5:14

Willie had an alcohol problem. He had lost his job and apartment and he now resorted to panhandling each day. When he met a kind old lady in the park he decided to tell her his story.

"Yes, ma'am," he said, "I've asked for money, I've begged for money, I've cried for money."

"Have you ever thought of working for it, my man?" she asked.

"No, not yet, ma'am," said Willie. "You see, it's like this, I'm going through the alphabet and I ain't got to 'W' yet."

[work]

1 Thessalonians 5:17

It's too bad but in our world today sometimes the only time some church members pray is on Sunday morning and it's for a place to park their car near the church door!

[church, prayer]

1 Thessalonians 5:17

After a preacher died and went to heaven, he noticed that a New York cab driver had been awarded a higher place than he.

"I don't understand," he complained to Saint Peter. "I devoted my entire life to my congregation."

"Our policy here in Heaven is to reward results," Saint Peter explained. "Now, was your congregation well attuned to you whenever you gave a sermon?"

"Well," the minister had to admit," some in the congregation fell asleep from time to time."

"Exactly," said Saint Peter. "And when people rode in this man's taxi, they not only stayed awake, they even prayed."

[fear, prayer, sermon]

1 Thessalonians 5:18

A four-year-old boy was asked to return thanks before Christmas dinner. The family members bowed their heads in expectation. He began his prayer, thanking God for all his friends, naming them one by one. Then he thanked God for Mommy, Daddy, brother, sister, Grandma, Grandpa, and all his aunts and uncles.

Then he began to thank God for the food. He gave thanks for the turkey, the dressing, the fruit salad, the cranberry sauce, the pies, the cakes, even the Cool Whip. Then he paused, and everyone waited and waited.

After a long silence, the young fellow looked up at his mother and asked, "If I thank God for the broccoli, won't he know that I'm lying?"

[food, lying, thanksgiving]

1 Thessalonians 5:18

Man: "So it's Thanksgiving. What have I to be thankful for? I can't even pay my bills."

Friend: "Be thankful you're not one of your creditors."

[debt, thanksgiving]

1 Thessalonians 5:18

There's this guy who had been lost and walking in the desert for about two weeks. One hot day, he sees the home of a missionary. Tired and weak, he crawls up to the house and collapses on the doorstep.

The missionary finds him and nurses him back to health. Feeling better, the man asks the missionary for directions to the nearest town. On his way out the backdoor, he sees this horse. He goes back into the house and asks the missionary, "Could I borrow your horse and give it back when I reach the town?"

The missionary says, "Sure but there is a special thing about this horse. You have to say 'Thank God' to make it go and 'Amen' to make it stop."

Not paying much attention, the man says, "Sure, ok."

So he gets on the horse and says, "Thank God" and the horse starts walking. Then he says, "Thank God, thank God," and the horse starts trotting. Feeling really brave, the man says, "Thank God, thank God, thank God, thank God, thank God" and the horse just takes off. Pretty soon he sees this cliff coming up and he's doing everything he can to make the horse stop. "Whoa, stop, hold on!!!!"

Finally he remembers, "Amen!!"

The horse stops 4 inches from the cliff. Then the man leans back in the saddle and says, "Thank God."

[animals, prayer, thanksgiving]

1 Thessalonians 5:18

Thanksgiving day was approaching and the family had received a Thanksgiving card with a painting of a pilgrim family on their way to church. Grandma showed the card to her small grandchildren, observing: "The Pilgrim children liked to go to church with their mothers and fathers." "Oh yeah?" her young grandson replied, "So why is their dad carrying that rifle?"

[thanksgiving]

1 Thessalonians 5:18

April 15 should be called tax-giving day.

[taxes]

1 Thessalonians 5:21

Father: "How dare you! What do you mean by hugging my daughter?"
Boy: "I-I-I was just carrying out the spiritual injunction 'Hold fast that which is good (KJV).'"

[context, dating]

1 Thessalonians 5:22

A mother was driving with her three young children one warm summer evening when a woman in the convertible ahead of them stood up and waved. She was stark naked! As the mother was reeling from the shock, she heard my 5-year-old shout from the back seat, "Mom! That lady isn't wearing a seat belt!"

[innocence]

1 Thessalonians 5:22

A distinguished minister and two deacons from his congregation attended an out-of-town meeting that did not finish until rather late. They decided to have something to eat before going home, but unfortunately the only spot open was a seedy bar-and-grill with a questionable reputation.
After being served, one of the deacons asked the minister to say grace. "I'd rather not," the clergyman said. "I don't want Him to know I'm here."

[appearance, prayer]

2 THESSALONIANS

2 Thessalonians 3:6

The counselor asked the employee how long he had been working at the company. He said, "Ever since they tried to fire me."

[laziness, work]

2 Thessalonians 3:6

The man's wife, infuriated by his laziness, declared to her closest friend, "When his time is up, I won't bury him. I'll have him cremated. And when I get his ashes, I'll put them in the hourglass. He never did a lick of work all his life, but I'll have him working for me then!"

[laziness, work]

2 Thessalonians 3:6

A young woman brought her fiancé home to meet her parents. After dinner, her mother told her father to find out about the young man. The father invited the fiancé to his study for a talk.

"So what are your plans?" the father asked the young man.

"I am a biblical scholar," he replied.

"A Biblical scholar. Hmmm," the father said. "Admirable, but what will you do to provide a nice house for my daughter to live in?"

"I will study," the young man replied, "and God will provide for us."

"And how will you buy her a beautiful engagement ring, such as she deserves?" asked the father.

"I will concentrate on my studies," the young man replied, "God will provide for us."

"And children?" asked the father. "How will you support children?"

"Don't worry, sir, God will provide," replied the fiancé.

The conversation proceeded like this, and each time the father questioned, the young idealist insisted that God would provide.

Later, the mother asked, "How did it go, Honey?"

The father answered, "He has no job and no plans, and he thinks I'm God!"

[laziness, provision, work]

2 Thessalonians 3:7

Most of you should never try to make anyone like yourself. You know, and God knows, that one of you is enough.

[image of God, imitation]

2 Thessalonians 3:10

Jesus recently walked into a bar somewhere in the Western World. He approached three sad-faced gentlemen at a table, and greeted the first one: "What's troubling you, brother?" he said.

"My eyes. I keep getting stronger and stronger glasses, and I still can't see." Jesus touched the man, who ran outside to tell the world about his now 20-20 vision.

The next gentleman couldn't hear Jesus' questions, so the Lord just touched his ears, restoring his hearing to perfection. This man, too, ran out the door, probably on his way to the audiologist to get a hearing-aid refund.

The third man leapt from his chair and backed up against the wall, even before Jesus could greet him.

"Don't you come near me, man! Don't touch me!" he screamed. "I'm on disability!"

[healing, laziness, work]

2 Thessalonians 3:10

Modern Maxim. Give a man a fish, and he will eat for a day. Teach him to fish, and he will sit in a boat and drink beer all day.

[laziness]

2 Thessalonians 3:11

A rumor is about as hard to unspread as butter.

[gossip]

1 TIMOTHY

1 Timothy 1:4

"Yes," said the boastful young man, "my family can trace its ancestry back to William the Conqueror."

"I suppose," remarked his friend, "you'll be telling us that your ancestors were in the Ark with Noah?"

"Certainly not," said the other. "My people had a boat of their own."

[ancestors, pride]

1 Timothy 1:12

If it weren't for the optimist, the pessimist would never know how happy he isn't.

[optimist, pessimist]

1 Timothy 1:15

See John 12:47.

1 Timothy 1:17

Dear GOD,

Are you really invisible or is that just a trick?

-Marlow

[attributes, God]

1 Timothy 1:19

Conscience is a playback of the still small voice that told you not to do it in the first place.

[conscience]

1 Timothy 1:19

Conscience: That something which prompts a man to tell his wife before someone else does.

[confession, conscience]

1 Timothy 1:19

Conscience is that still small voice that tells you the Internal Revenue Service might check your return.

[conscience, taxes]

1 Timothy 2:1-2

Politics is becoming a precarious game. One week a politician may appear on the cover of Time, and the next week he may be serving it.

[politics]

1 Timothy 2:9

A very puritanical minister noticed one of the young ladies of his church twisting her hair into curls. "If the Lord," he said sternly, "had intended your hair to be curled, he'd have curled it for you."
"When I was a baby," said the young lady sweetly, "He did. But now that I'm grown up I figure He thinks I can do it for myself."

[beauty, hair, responsibility]

1 Timothy 2:9

Those who censor the modern bathing-suit have scant reason for doing so.

[clothes, modesty]

1 Timothy 2:9

My wife is so modest she blindfolds the rubber duck when she takes a bath.

[modesty]

1 Timothy 2:9

Pastor: someone who still preaches against contemporary dresses even though there's not enough left to talk about.

[clothes, modesty, pastor]

1 Timothy 2:14

Husband to wife, "But you must admit that men have better judgment than women."
"Oh, yes," the wife replied, "you married me and I you."

[judgment, marriage]

1 Timothy 3:1-7

Pastoral Search Committee:
In our search for a suitable pastor, the following scratch sheet was developed for your perusal. Of the candidates investigated by the committee, only one was found to have the necessary qualities. The list contains the names of the candidates and comments on each, should you be interested in investigating them further for future pastoral placements.
Noah: Former pastorate of 120 years with not even one convert. Prone to unrealistic building projects.

Joseph: A big thinker, but a braggart, believes in dream-interpreting and has a prison record.

Moses: A modest and meek man, but a poor communicator, even stuttering at times. Sometimes blows his stack and acts rashly. Some say he left an earlier church over a murder charge.

Abraham: He took off to Egypt during hard times. We heard that he got into trouble with the authorities and then tried to lie his way out.

David: The most promising leader of all until we discovered the affair he had with his neighbor's wife. He might have been considered for minister of music had he not 'fallen.'

Solomon: He has a reputation for wisdom but fails to practice what he preaches.

Elijah: He proved to be inconsistent, and is known to fold under pressure.

Hosea: A tender and loving pastor but our people could never handle his wife's occupation. His family life is in a shambles. Divorced, and remarried to a prostitute.

Jonah: Refused God's call into ministry until he was forced to obey by getting swallowed by a great fish. He told us the fish spit him out on the shore near here. We hung up.

Jeremiah: He is too emotional, alarmist; some say a real pain in the neck.'

Amos: Comes from a farming background. Better off picking figs.

John: Says he is a Baptist, but definitely doesn't dress like one. Would not feel comfortable at a church potluck supper because of his weird diet. Often provokes denominational leaders.

Peter: Has a bad temper, even has been known to curse. Had a big run-in with Paul in Antioch. Aggressive, but a loose cannon.

Paul: We found him to lack tact. He is too harsh, His appearance is contemptible, and he preaches far too long.

Timothy: He has potential, but is much too young for the position.

Jesus: He tends to offend church members with his preaching, especially Bible scholars. He is also too controversial. Has popular times, but once his church grew to 5000 he managed to offend them all, and then it dwindled down to twelve people. He even offended the search committee with his pointed questions. Seldom stays in one place for long. And, of course, he's single.

Judas: He seemed to be very practical, co-operative, good with money, cares for the poor, and dresses well. We all agreed that he is just the man we are looking for to fill the vacancy as our Senior Pastor.

Thank you for all you have done in assisting us with our pastoral search. Sincerely,

The Pastoral Search Committee.

[leaders, pastor, qualifications]

1 Timothy 3:1-7

Recipe for a Staff Member

Select a young and pleasing personality, trim off all mannerisms of voice, dress, or deportment. Pour over it a mixture of equal parts of the wisdom of Solomon, the courage of young Daniel, the strength of Samson, and the patience of Job.

Season with the salt of experience, the pepper of animation, the oil of sympathy, and a dash of humor.

Stew for about four years in an active church, testing occasionally with the fork of criticism thrust by a cantankerous church member.

When done to a turn, garnish with a salary increase and serve hot to another church.

[church, leaders, pastor, qualifications]

1 Timothy 3:1-7

The weekly bulletin from a local church included the following:

The ideal pastor preaches exactly 10 minutes. He condemns sin, but never hurts anyone's feelings. He works from 8AM to midnight, and also serves as the church janitor. He makes $40 a week, wears good clothes, and donates $30 a week to the church. He is 29 years old and has 40 years of experience. He makes 15 house calls a day and is always in his office.

If your pastor does not measure up to these criteria, send this list to six other churches that are also dissatisfied with their pastor. Then, bundle up your pastor and send him to the church at the top of the list. In one week you will receive 1,643 pastors. Surely one of them will be perfect. Have faith in this letter. One church broke the chain and got its old pastor back in three months.

[pastor, qualifications]

1 Timothy 3:2

Son: "Dad, does bigamy mean that a man has one wife too many?"
Father: "Not necessarily, son. A man can have one wife too many and still not be a bigamist."

[bigamy, wife]

1 Timothy 3:2

Definition of a bigamist: A man who has taken one too many.

[bigamy, marriage]

1 Timothy 3:2

A Christian should have only one wife. Some call this monotony.

[bigamy, wife]

1 Timothy 3:2

A golfer was having a bad day on the course. Finally, on the 13th hole he flubbed a two foot putt. That did it. He picked up the ball and threw it as far as he could, broke two clubs, and sat down on the grass, a picture of total frustration.

"I've got to give it up! I've got to give it up! He said to his caddy.

"Give up golf?" asked the caddy.

"No," answered the golfer, "the ministry."

[ministry, temper]

1 Timothy 3:2

A missionary heard about a recent convert who had five wives.

"You are violating a law of God," said the missionary. So you must go and tell four of those women that they can no longer live here with their children, or consider you their husband.

The convert thought for a few minutes, then said, "I'll wait here, YOU tell them."

[bigamy, courage, marriage]

1 Timothy 3:3

There are two kinds of ministers ...those interested in the flock, and those interested in the fleece.

[greed, ministry]

1 Timothy 3:3

A group of ministers and a salesmen's organization were holding conventions in the same hotel. The catering department had to work at top speed serving dinners to both.

The salesmen were having 'Spiked Watermelon" for dessert. But the harassed chef discovered this alcoholic dessert was being served to the ministers by mistake.

"Quick!" he commanded the head waiter. "If they haven't eaten the watermelon, bring it back and we'll give it to the salesmen."

The waiter returned in a minute and reported that it was too late — the ministers were eating the liquor-spiced dessert.

"Well," demanded the distraught chef. "What are they saying? Do they notice anything different?"

"Well," replied the waiter, "let me just say they're collecting the seeds and putting them in their pockets.

[alcohol, pastors]

1 Timothy 3:3

Knowing that the minister was very fond of cherry brandy, one of the church elders offered to present him with a bottle on one consideration — that the pastor acknowledge receipt of the gift in the church paper. "Gladly," responded the good man.

When the church magazine came out a few days later, the elder turned at once to the "appreciation" column. There he read: "The minister extends his thanks to Elder Brown for his gift of fruit and for the spirit in which it was given."

[alcohol]

1 Timothy 3:5

As the missionary said when the cannibals put him into the big pot, "At least they'll get a taste of religion."

[food, religion]

1 Timothy 3:6

Experience is a hard teacher. She gives the test first, and the lesson afterward.

[experience]

1 Timothy 3:6

A recent convert in a church was so enthusiastic that he was constantly asking his pastor for something he could do to help the church. Finally, the pastor told him he was appointed as "Elder of Broken Pledges," and since several people were behind on their pledges, maybe he could do something to encourage them to catch up on their giving. The pastor gave the young man a list of names and addresses of the delinquent contributors. The young man immediately began a letter-writing campaign.

The next Sunday the minister told the congregation that during the week he had received many checks and some letters from his church people. He read a portion of one of the letters: "Dear Reverend, Here is the check that I had failed to send earlier. By the way, you need to inform your new secretary that there is only one 'r' in 'dirty' and there is no 'c' in 'skunk'."

[giving, service]

1 Timothy 3:8

A new teenage boy in the Children's Church class was asked to explain the meaning of a bishop, priest, and deacon.

He answered, "I never saw a bishop, so I don't know. A priest is a man in the Old Testament. A deacon is a thing that sits along the seashore and blinks at night."

[deacon]

1 Timothy 3:10

As the head of any deacons' board will tell you, after all is said and done, there's a lot more said than done.

[deacon, procrastination]

1 Timothy 3:11

Conversation between two kindergartners:
"When I grow up, I'm going to marry a doctor. That way I can be sick for nothing."
"That's nothing. When I grow up, I'm going to marry a minister. Then I can be good for nothing."

[forgiveness, hypocrisy, misunderstanding]

1 Timothy 3:11

A little boy walked down the beach, and as he did, he spied a woman sitting under a beach umbrella on the sand.
He walked up to her and asked, "Are you a Christian?" She said, "Yes."
"Do you read your Bible every day?" She nodded her head, "Yes."
Do you pray often?" the boy asked next, and again she answered, "Yes."
With that he asked his final question, "Will you hold my quarter while I go swimming?"

[honesty, trust]

1 Timothy 3:12

See Genesis 2:24.

1 Timothy 3:13

A pastor who bought a doctor's degree from a diploma mill defended his action by quoting part of 1 Timothy 3:13 (KJV): "They that have used the office of a deacon well purchase to themselves a good degree."

[context, education]

1 Timothy 4:1

During an ecumenical gathering, someone rushed in and shouted, "The building is on fire!" The METHODISTS gathered in a corner and prayed. The BAPTISTS cried, "Where's the water?" The CHRISTIAN SCIENTISTS agreed that there was no fire. The FUNDAMENTALISTS shouted, "It's the vengeance of God!" The LUTHERANS posted a notice on the door declaring fire was not justified. The QUAKERS quietly praised God for the blessing that fire brings. The JEWS posted symbols on the door hoping the fire would pass over. The ROMAN CATHOLICS took up a second collection. The CONGREGATIONALISTS & SOUTHERN BAPTISTS shouted, "Every man for himself!" The PRESBYTERIANS appointed a chairperson who was to appoint a committee to look into the matter. The EPISCOPALIANS formed a procession and marched out in grand style and the UNITARIANS toasted marshmallows!

[denominations]

1 Timothy 4:2

There were two evil brothers. They were rich, and used their money to keep their evil ways from the public eye. They even attended the same church, and appeared to be perfect Christians.

Then, their pastor retired, and a new one was hired. Not only could the new pastor see right through the brothers' deception, but he also spoke well and true, and the church membership grew in numbers. A fund-raising campaign was started to build a new assembly.

All of a sudden, one of the brothers died. The remaining brother sought out the new pastor the day before the funeral and handed him a check for the amount needed to finish paying for the new building. "I have only one condition," he said. "At the funeral, you must say my brother was a saint." The pastor gave his word, and deposited the check.

The next day, at the funeral, the pastor did not hold back. "He was an evil man," he said. "He cheated on his wife and abused his family." After going on like this, he finally concluded, "But, compared to his brother, he was a SAINT."

[honesty, hypocrisy]

1 Timothy 4:3

After the birth of their child, an Episcopal priest, wearing his clerical collar, visited his wife in the hospital. He greeted her with a hug and a kiss, and gave her another hug and kiss when he left.

Later, the wife's roommate commented: "Gee, your pastor is sure a lot friendlier than mine."

[friends, pastor]

1 Timothy 4:3

The priest of a large Italian Catholic congregation stood up one Sunday and issued some pronouncements about birth control.

Suddenly an Italian lady with six kids in her pew stood up and replied: "If you donna playa da game, you donna maka da rules."

[birth control]

1 Timothy 4:7

Believe only half of what you hear, but be sure it's the right half.

[truth]

1 Timothy 4:7

A rumor goes in an ear and out many mouths.

[gossip]

1 Timothy 4:8

Children's Church teacher: "Tommy, what happens to a man who never thinks of his soul, but only of his body?"
Tommy: "I imagine, teacher, that he gets fat."

[body, future]

1 Timothy 4:12

Book Title: I WAS A TEENAGE ELDER STATESMAN.

[wisdom, youth]

1 Timothy 4:13

If all the neglected Bibles in this country were dusted off at the same time, we would suffer the worst dust storm we have experienced in many years.

[Bible, weather]

1 Timothy 4:13

A traveling preacher was trapped by a snowstorm at one of the farms on his circuit. The lady of the house was delighted to have such a distinguished guest and did everything she could think of to make him comfortable. When evening came, she inquired if the preacher would like to read the Bible and pray with them before retiring. He assured his hostess that he would be grateful for the privilege, so she turned to her young son and said, "Go into the parlor, dear, and bring me that big book Mama and Papa are always reading." The boy disappeared for a moment and then returned triumphantly carrying the Sears catalog.

[Bible, priorities]

1 Timothy 4:13

The child was being examined to test her reliability as a witness, "Do you know anything that is in the Bible? The judge asked.

"I know everything," she answered.

"What?" the judge exclaimed in astonishment. "Tell us some of the things that are in there."

She replied, "Well, there's a picture of our family, a four leaf clover, some tree leaves, and an old red rose that's dry and flat."

[Bible, knowledge]

1 Timothy 4:13

TOP TEN SIGNS YOU MAY NOT BE READING YOUR BIBLE ENOUGH:

10) The Preacher announces the sermon is from Galatians ... and you check the table of contents.

9) You think Abraham, Isaac & Jacob may have had a few hit songs during the 60's.

8) You open to the Gospel of Luke and a WWII Savings Bond falls out.

7) Your favorite Old Testament Patriarch is Hercules.

6) A small family of woodchucks has taken up residence in the Psalms of your Bible.

5) You become frustrated because Charlton Heston isn't listed in either the Concordance or the Table of Contents.

4) Catching the kids reading the Song of Solomon, you demand: "Who gave you this stuff?"

3) You think the Minor Prophets worked in the quarries.

2) You keep falling for it every time when Pastor tells you to turn to First Condominiums.

And the number one sign you may not be reading your Bible enough:

1) The kids keep asking too many questions about your usual bedtime story: "Jonah the Shepherd Boy and His Ark of Many Colors."

[Bible]

1 Timothy 4:13

A boy was watching his father, a pastor, write out his sermon. "How do you know what to say?" he asked.

"Why, God tells me."

"Oh, then why do you keep crossing things out?"

[guidance, sermon]

1 Timothy 4:13

A preacher concluded that his church was getting into very serious financial troubles.

While checking the church storeroom, he discovered several cartons of new Bibles that had never been opened and distributed. So at his Sunday sermon, he asked for three volunteers from the congregation who would be willing to sell the Bibles door-to-door for $10 each to raise the desperately needed money for the church.

Jack, Paul and Louie all raised their hands to volunteer for the task.

The minister knew that Jack and Paul earned their living as salesmen and were likely capable of selling some Bibles. But he had serious doubts about Louie who was a local farmer, who had always kept to himself because he was embarrassed by his speech impediment. Poor Louie stuttered badly.

But, not wanting to discourage Louie, the minister decided to let him try anyway. He sent the three of them away with the back seat of their cars stacked with Bibles. He asked them to meet with him and report the results of their door-to-door selling efforts the following Sunday.

Anxious to find out how successful they were, the minister immediately asked Jack, 'Well, Jack, how did you make out selling our Bibles last week?' Proudly handing the minister an envelope, Jack replied, 'Using my sales prowess, I was able to sell 20 Bibles, and here's the $200 I collected on behalf of the church.' 'Fine job, Jack!' The minister said, vigorously shaking his hand. 'You are indeed a fine salesman and the Church is indebted to you.'

Turning to Paul, 'And Paul, how many Bibles did you sell for the church last week?' Paul, smiling and sticking out his chest, confidently replied, 'I am a professional salesman. I sold 28 bibles on behalf of the church, and here's $280 I collected.' The minister responded, 'That's absolutely splendid, Paul. You are truly a professional salesman and the church is indebted to you.'

Apprehensively, the minister turned to Louie and said, 'And Louie, did you manage to sell any Bibles last week?' Louie silently offered the minister a large envelope. The minister opened it and counted the contents.

'What is this?' the minister exclaimed. 'Louie, there's $3200 in here! Are you suggesting that you sold 320 Bibles for the church, door to door, in just one week?' Louie just nodded. 'That's impossible!' both Jack and Paul said in unison. 'We are professional salesmen, yet you claim to have sold 10 times as many Bibles as we could.' 'Yes, this does seem unlikely,' the minister agreed. 'I think you'd better explain how you managed to accomplish this, Louie.'

Louie shrugged. 'I-I-I re-re-really do-do-don't kn-kn-know f-f-f-for sh-sh-sh-sure,' he stammered. Impatiently, Paul interrupted. 'For crying out loud, Louie, just tell us what you said to them when they answered the door!'

'A-a-a-all I-I-I s-s-said wa-wa-was,' Louis replied, 'W-w-w-would y-y-y you l-l-l-like t-t-t-to b-b-b-buy th-th-th-this b-b-b-bible f-f-f-for t-t-t-ten b-b-b-bucks ---o-o-o-or wo-wo-wo-would yo-yo-yo-you j-j-j-just l-l-l-like m-m-me t-t-t-to st-st-st-stand h-h-h-here and r-r-r-read it t-t-t-to y-y-y-you?

[Bible, pride, wise]

1 Timothy 4:17

A Children's Church teacher asked a little girl: "What are the sins of omission?"

After some thought, she answered: "I think they're the sins we ought to have committed but haven't."

[sin]

1 Timothy 5:1

The best substitute for experience is being 16 years of age.

[experience, youth]

1 Timothy 5:1-2

A pastor was giving the children's lesson during a Sunday morning service on the Ten Commandments. After explaining the commandment to "honor they father and thy mother," he asked, "Is there a commandment that teaches us how to treat our brothers and sisters?"

Without missing a beat, one five-year old boy answered loudly, "Thou shalt not kill!"

[commandments, family, murder]

1 Timothy 5:2

Miss Smith, a young, unmarried lady, was invited to chaperon a sleigh ride. The other chaperon was to be the eligible but extremely dedicated minister of a nearby church. As they were racing through the winter night, surrounded by amorous couples, Miss Smith heaved a great sigh.

"Why, whatever is the matter?" asked the minister.

"Oh, it's just that nobody loves me, and besides, my hands are cold."

"Nonsense," replied the minister earnestly, "God loves you, and you can sit on your hands."

[dating, singleness]

1 Timothy 5:2

Father" "When I was your age, I never kissed a girl. Will you be able to tell your children that?"

Son: "Not with a straight face."

[dating, kissing]

I Timothy 5:2

According to a recent survey, men say the first thing they notice about a woman is their eyes, and women say the first thing they notice about men is they're a bunch of liars.

[lying]

1 Timothy 5:3

"Is it true that wives live longer than their husbands?" a listener asked a lecturer.
"Yes," was the answer. "Especially widows."

[age, wives]

1 Timothy 5:6

A woman was trying hard to get the catsup to come out of the jar.
During her struggle the phone rang so she asked her four-year old daughter to answer the phone.
"It's the minister, Mommy," the child said to her mother. Then she turned back to the phone and declared to the pastor, "Mommy can't come to the phone to talk to you right now. She's hitting the bottle."

[alcohol, drinking]

1 Timothy 5:8

An old Chinese man was eating too much rice, especially since he was too frail to work. Because the grandfather had become a burden, the father of the home, his son, determined to get rid of him. He put him in a wheelbarrow, then started up the mountain. The little eight-year-old grandson went along. He was full of questions. His father explained that the grandfather was old and useless and the only thing they could do, was to take him up the mountain and leave him to die. Then the grandson had a bright thought. "I'm glad you brought me along, Father, because when you're old, I'll know where to take you!"

[parenting]

1 Timothy 5:8

Husband: "Now look, Lucy, I don't want to seem harsh, but your mother has been living with us for 20 years now. Don't you think it's time one of your brothers or sisters took her for a while?"
Wife: "My mother? I thought she was your mother!"

[mother-in-law]

1 Timothy 5:8

The local United Way office realized that it had never received a donation from the town's most successful attorney. The volunteer in charge of contributions called to persuade him to contribute.

"Our research shows that out of a yearly income of more than $600,000 you give not a penny to charity. Wouldn't you like to give back to the community in some way?"

The lawyer mulled this over for a moment and then replied, "First, did your research also show that my mother is dying after a long illness, and has medical bills several times her annual income?"

Embarrassed, the United Way rep mumbled, "Um ... No."

Second, that my brother, a disabled veteran, is blind and confined to a wheelchair?

The now stricken United Way rep began to stammer out an apology but was put off.

"Third, that my sister's husband died in a horrific traffic accident," the lawyer's voice now rising in indignation, "leaving her penniless with three children?"

The humiliated United Way rep, completely beaten, said simply, "I had no idea..."

On a roll, the lawyer cut him off once again, "...And I don't give any money to them, so why should I give any to you?"

[stinginess]

1 Timothy 5:8

The prospective father-in-law asked, "Young man, can you support a family?"

The surprised groom-to-be replied, "Well, no. I was just planning to support your daughter. The rest of you will have to fend for yourselves!"

[provision]

1 Timothy 5:12

A man suffered a serious heart attack and had open heart bypass surgery. He awakened from the surgery to find himself in the care of nuns at a Catholic hospital.

As he was recovering, a nun asked him questions regarding how he was going to pay for services. He was asked if he had health insurance. He replied, in a raspy voice, "No health insurance."

The nun asked if he had money in the bank. He replied, "No money in the bank." The nun asked, "Do you have a relative who could help you?" He said, "I only have a spinster sister, who is a nun."

The nun got a little perturbed and announced loudly. "Nuns are not spinsters! Nuns are married to God," The patient replies, "That's right! Send the bill to my brother-in-law."

[Catholic, nun]

1 Timothy 5:13

It isn't hard to make a mountain out of a molehill. Just add a little dirt.

[exaggeration, gossip]

1 Timothy 5:13

A gossip is a person who will never tell a lie if the truth will do as much damage.

[gossip, lying]

1 Timothy 5:13

I think we need to change the morning hymn," said the minister to his song leader. "My topic this morning is 'gossip'. I don't think 'I Love To Tell the Story' would be the best closing hymn."

[gossip, hymns]

1 Timothy 5:13

Two young, excited Southern women were sitting together in the front pew of church listening to a fiery preacher. When this preacher condemned the sin of stealing, these two ladies cried out at the tops of their lungs, "AMEN, BROTHER!"

When the preacher condemned the sin of lust, they yelled again, "PREACH IT, REVEREND!"

And when the preacher condemned the sin of lying, they jumped to their feet and screamed, "RIGHT ON, BROTHER! TELL IT LIKE IT IS ... AMEN!"

But when the preacher condemned the sin of gossip, the two got very quiet, and one turned to the other and said, "He's quit preaching and now he's meddlin.'"

[gossip, preaching]

1 Timothy 5:14

In seeking a model husband, it's wise to be sure he's a working model!

[husband, work]

1 Timothy 5:14

Husband: "I know you're having a lot of trouble with the baby, dear, but keep in mind, 'The hand that rocks the cradle is the hand that rules the world.'"

Wife: "Well, in that case, would you mind taking over the world while I go shopping?"

[parenting]

1 Timothy 5:17

The young couple invited their aged pastor for Sunday dinner.

While they were in the kitchen preparing the meal, the minister asked their young son what they were having.

"Goat," the little boy replied.

"Goat?" replied the startled minister. "Are you sure about that?"

"Yep," said the youngster. "I heard dad say to mom, 'Might as well have the old goat for dinner today as any other day.'"

[food, insult, pastor]

1 Timothy 5:17

A new member of a church is talking to the Pastor: "You have such a small congregation. How can they afford to pay you?"

The Pastor said, "Well, I only earn $60 a week."

The man is dumbfounded. "Pastor, how in the world can you get by on an amount that small?"

"Well, I tell you. If I wasn't such a religious man and didn't fast three days a week, I'd probably starve to death."

[provision, sacrifice]

1 Timothy 5:17

See 1 Timothy 3:1-7.

1 Timothy 5:17

An old, retiring farmer called the church office and stated: "I would like to speak to the 'head hog at the trough.'"

"I'm sorry, who?" replied the church secretary.

"I would like to speak to the 'head hog at the trough.'"

"Well," bristled the church secretary, "if you mean the pastor, then you may refer to him as Pastor or Brother, but you may certainly not refer to him as the 'head hog at the trough!'"

"Well, sure, I was just needing to talk to the boss there because I'm planning to donate $10,000 to the building fund."

The church secretary interrupted, "Hang on, I think the big, fat pig just walked in!"

[names, pastor]

1 Timothy 5:17-18

"He may preach against gambling and cheating," one church member admitted, "but I have nothing but praise for our new pastor."
His neighbor agreed: "Yeah — I noticed that about you when they passed the offering plate."

[gambling, giving, selfish]

1 Timothy 5:19

One church member to another: "I make it a point never to say anything about our pastor unless it is good. Now, let me tell you about the Reverend — and this is good!"

[gossip]

1 Timothy 5:19

An elder of the church came to the pastor and said: "Pastor, my six fellow elders are all too uncommitted to be here at prayer meeting, but I alone have come to worship."
The irritated pastor replied, "You would have been better off to have stayed away if your worship of God consists of accusations against your brethren."

[criticism, gossip]

1 Timothy 5:19

A little old lady got into an argument with her pastor. The pastor thought he would never see her again. However she showed up for the evening service the same Sunday.
"I thought you'd gone for good," he said to her.
"Pastor," she said, "I'm going to be loyal to my church, even if the devil is in the pulpit."

[argument, devil, loyalty, pastor]

1 Timothy 6:2

The pastor was telling his guests a story when his little girl interrupted, "Daddy, is that true," she asked, "or is that preaching?"

[honesty, preaching]

1 Timothy 6:7

No hearse ever has a U-Haul being pulled behind it.

[death]

1 Timothy 6:7
Always be wary of the fella who says you can't take it with you — 'cause he's planning to take yours with him.

[death, deceit, greed]

1 Timothy 6:7
See Job 1:21.

1 Timothy 6:8
Little Raymond returned home from Children's Church in a very joyous mood. "Oh, mother," he exclaimed, "the teacher said something awfully nice about me in his prayer this morning!"
"Isn't that lovely! What did he say?" questioned the mother.
"He said, 'O Lord, we thank thee for our food and Raymond [raiment].'"

[names, prayer]

1 Timothy 6:8
In some parts of Mexico hot springs and cold springs are found side by side-and because of the convenience of this natural phenomenon the women often bring their laundry and boil their clothes in the hot springs and then rinse them in the cold ones. A tourist, who was watching this procedure commented to his Mexican friend and guide: "I imagine that they think old Mother Nature is pretty generous to supply such ample, clean hot and cold water here side by side for their free use?"
The guide replied, "No senior, there is much grumbling because she supplies no soap."

[complaint]

1 Timothy 6:10
A minister at a newly founded church was trying to educate his people about the forms and purposes of various church functions. Just before the offering he stood up and said, "I would like to remind you that what you are about to give is deductible, cannot be taken with you, and the love of which, is considered in the Bible, to be the root of all evil."

[offering]

1 Timothy 6:10
The love of money is also the root of all congressional investigations.

[money]

1 Timothy 6:10

Money brings only misery. But with money you can afford it.

[money, trials]

1 Timothy 6:10

An evangelist called a church and said, "I want to come to your church and preach."
The pastor said, "No, Joe. You are not ready."
Six months later, the evangelist called again and said, "Pastor, I really want to come and preach at your church."
The pastor said, "No, Joe. You are not ready."
Six months later, the evangelist called again and said, "Pastor, I want to come and preach at your church so much that I'll pay my way—no honorarium."
The pastor said, "Okay, Joe. You are ready."

[sacrifice]

1 Timothy 6:17

It is better to give away your money while you're alive. It doesn't take away any great generosity to give it away when you're dead.

[generous, money]

1 Timothy 6:17

The pastor was admonishing his parishioners on the evils of materialism. "Remember, my friends," he said, "there will be no buying or selling in heaven."
A disgruntled old gent in the back row shouted back. "That's not where business is going anyway."

[business, hell]

1 Timothy 6:17

QUESTION: What is the central mantra of prosperity theology?
ANSWER: There is no God but Mammon.

[money, theology]

1 Timothy 6:17

The daughter of a wealthy movie producer was asked at school to write a story about a poor family. Her essay began: "Once upon a time there was a poor family. The mother was poor. The daddy was poor. The children were poor. The butler was poor. The chauffeur was poor. The maid was poor. The gardener was poor. Everybody was poor."

[poverty]

1 Timothy 6:17-18

Sarah had a dollar to buy an ice cream soda.

"Why don't you give your dollar to help the poor?" said the minister who was visiting.

"I thought about that," said Sarah, "but I think I'll buy the ice cream and let the ice cream man give it to the poor."

[poverty]

1 Timothy 6:18

A minister was asked to inform a man with a heart condition that he had just inherited a million dollars. Everyone was afraid the shock would cause a heart attack and the man would die.

The minister went to the man's house and said, "Joe what would you do if you inherited a million dollars?"

Joe responded, "Well, pastor, I think I would give half of it to the church."

And the minister fell over dead.

[death, generous, inheritance]

1 Timothy 6:18

After the service, the minister looked blue and despondent. "What was your sermon subject that it took so much energy out of you?" his wife asked.

He replied, "I tried to tell them that it was the duty of the rich to help the poor."

"And did you convince them?" she pursued.

"Only half, I convinced the poor!"

[poverty, sermon, wealth]

1 Timothy 6:18

The beggar was dirty and hungry and as the old lady passed by she gave him five cents. "Tell me," she said, "how did you get so destitute?"

"Well, ma'am," the old beggar said, "I was like you at one time, always giving vast sums to the poor."

[giving, poverty]

2 TIMOTHY

2 Timothy 1:3

Paul would not agree with the man who defined the conscience as "that still small voice that tells you what other people should do."

[conscience]

2 Timothy 1:3

A man visited a psychiatrist. He explained, "I've been doing wrong, Doctor, and my conscience is bothering me."

The psychiatrist asked, "So you want something that will strengthen your will?"

The fellow replied, "Oh, no, I'd rather get something that would weaken my conscience."

[conscience, sin]

2 Timothy 2:3

At the end of the service the minister was standing at the door of the church shaking hands. He grabbed a man by the hand and pulled him aside and asked him, "Are you a soldier in the Army of the Lord?"

The man replied, "Why, yes I am."

The minister then asked, "Then why do we only see you at Christmas and Easter?"

The man quickly whispered, "I'm in the Secret Service."

[discipleship, evangelism]

2 Timothy 2:12

The 2000 member church was filled to overflowing capacity one Sunday morning. The preacher was ready to start the sermon when two men, dressed in long black coats and black hats entered thru the rear of the church.

One of the two men walked to the middle of the church while the other stayed at the back of the church. They both then reached under their coats and withdrew automatic weapons.

The one in the middle announced, "EVERYONE WILLING TO TAKE A BULLET FOR JESUS STAY IN YOUR SEAT!"

Naturally, the pews emptied, followed by the choir loft.

Even the deacons ran out the door.

After a few moments, there were about 20 people left sitting in the church. The preacher was holding steady in the pulpit.

The men put their weapons away and said, gently, to the preacher, "All right, pastor, the hypocrites are gone now. You may begin the service."

[courage, hypocrisy]

2 Timothy 2:15

Little Soren approached his father and said, "I know the Bible!"

His father replied, "What do you mean you know the Bible?"

Little Soren replied, "I know what the Bible stands for!"

His father said, "So, what does the Bible stand for?"

Little Soren replied, "It stands for Basic Instructions Before Leaving Earth."

[Bible]

2 Timothy 2:15

Germany's Cardinal von Faulhaber of Munich once had a conversation with the renowned mathematician, Albert Einstein.

"Cardinal von Faulhaber," Einstein remarked. "I respect religion, but I believe in mathematics. Probably it is the other way around with you."

"You are mistaken," the Cardinal retorted. "To me, both are merely different expressions of the same divine exactness."

"But, your Eminence, what would you say if mathematical science should some day come to conclusions directly contradictory to religious beliefs?"

"Oh," answered the Cardinal, "I have the highest regard for the competence of mathematicians. I am sure they would never rest until they discovered their mistake."

[apologetics, religion, science]

2 Timothy 2:15

TOP TEN SIGNS YOU MAY NOT BE READING YOUR BIBLE ENOUGH:

10) The Preacher announces the sermon is from Galatians ... and you check the table of contents.

9) You think Abraham, Isaac & Jacob may have had a few hit songs during the 60's.

8) You open to the Gospel of Luke and a WWII Savings Bond falls out.

7) Your favorite Old Testament patriarch is Hercules.

6) A small family of woodchucks has taken up residence in the Psalms of your Bible.

5) You become frustrated because Charlton Heston isn't listed in either the Concordance or the Table of Contents.

4) Catching the kids reading the Song of Solomon, you demand: "Who gave you this stuff?"

3) You think the Minor Prophets worked in the quarries.

2) You keep falling for it every time when Pastor tells you to turn to First Condominiums.

And the number one sign you may not be reading your Bible enough:

1) The kids keep asking too many questions about your usual bedtime story: "Jonah the Shepherd Boy and His Ark of Many Colors."

[Bible, ignorance]

2 Timothy 2:15

Exegeting a stop sign — by Darren Harlow

Suppose you're traveling to work and you see a stop sign. What do you do? That depends on how you exegete the stop sign.

1. A postmodernist deconstructs the sign with his bumper, ending forever the tyranny of the north-south traffic over the east-west traffic.

2. Similarly, a Marxist sees a stop sign as an instrument of class conflict. He concludes that the bourgeoisie use the north-south road and obstruct the progress of the workers on the east-west road.

3. A serious and educated Catholic believes that he cannot understand the stop sign apart from its interpretive community and their tradition. Observing that the interpretive community doesn't take it too seriously, he doesn't feel obligated to take it too seriously either.

4. An average Catholic doesn't bother to read the sign, but he'll stop if the car in front of him does.

5. A fundamentalist, allowing the text to interpret itself, stops at the stop sign and waits for it to tell him to go.

6. A suburban preacher looks up "STOP" in his lexicons of English and discovers that it can mean: 1) something which prevents motion, such as a plug for a drain, or a block of wood that prevents a door from closing; 2) a location where a train or bus lets off passengers. The main point of his sermon the following Sunday on this text is: when you see a stop sign, it is a place where traffic is naturally clogged, so it is a good place to let off passengers from your car.

7. An orthodox Jew does one of two things: 1.) Take another route to work that doesn't have a stop sign so that he doesn't run the risk of disobeying the Law. 2.) Stop at the stop sign, say "Blessed art thou, O Lord our God, king of the universe, who hast given us thy commandment to stop," wait 3 seconds according to his watch, and then proceed. Incidentally, the Talmud has the following comments on this passage: R[abbi] Meir says: He who does not stop shall not live long. R. Hillel says: Cursed is he who does not count to three before proceeding. R. Simon ben Yudah says: Why three?

Because the Holy One, blessed be He, gave us the Law, the Prophets, and the Writings. R. ben Isaac says: Because of the three patriarchs. R. Yehuda says: Why bless the Lord at a stop sign? Because it says: "Be still, and know that I am God." R. Hezekiel says: When Jephthah returned from defeating the Ammonites, the Holy One, blessed be He, knew that a donkey would run out of the house and overtake his daughter; but Jephthah did not stop at the stop sign, and the donkey did not have time to come out. For this reason he saw his daughter first and lost her. Thus he was judged for his transgression at the stop sign. R. Gamaliel says: R. Hillel, when he was a baby, never spoke a word, though his parents tried to teach him by speaking and showing him the words on a scroll. One day his father was driving through town and did not stop at the sign. Young Hillel called out: "Stop, father!" In this way, he began reading and speaking at the same time. Thus it is written: "Out of the mouth of babes." R. ben Jacob says: Where did the stop sign come from? Out of the sky, for it is written: "Forever, O Lord, your word is fixed in the heavens." R. ben Nathan says: When were stop signs created? On the fourth day, for it is written: "let them serve as signs." R. Yeshuah says: ... [continues for three more pages]

8. A Karaite does the same thing as an orthodox Jew, except that he waits 10 seconds instead of 3. He also replaces his brake lights with 1000 watt searchlights and connects his horn so that it is activated whenever he touches the brake pedal.

9. A Unitarian concludes that the passage "STOP" undoubtedly was never uttered by Jesus himself, but belongs entirely to stage III of the gospel tradition, when the church was first confronted by traffic in its parking lot.

10. A divinity professor notices that there is no stop sign on Mark street but there is one on Matthew and Luke streets, and concludes that the ones on Luke and Matthew streets are both copied from a sign on a completely hypothetical street called "Q". There is an excellent 300 page discussion of speculations on the origin of these stop signs and the differences between the stop signs on Matthew and Luke street in the scholar's commentary on the passage. There is an unfortunately omission in the commentary, however; the author apparently forgot to explain what the text means.

11. A tenured divinity professor points out that there are a number of stylistic differences between the first and second half of the passage "STOP". For example, "ST" contains no enclosed areas and 5 line endings, whereas "OP" contains two enclosed areas and only one line termination. He concludes that the author for the second part is different from the author for the first part and probably lived hundreds of years later. Later scholars determine that the second half is itself actually written by two separate authors because of similar stylistic differences between the "O" and the "P."

12. A rival scholar notes in his commentary that the stop sign would fit better into the context three streets back. (Unfortunately, he neglects to explain why in his commentary.) Clearly it was moved to its present location by a later redactor. He thus exegetes the intersection as though the stop sign were not there.

13. Because of the difficulties in interpretation, a later scholar amends the text, changing "T" to "H". "SHOP" is much easier to understand in context than "STOP" because of the multiplicity of stores in the area. The textual corruption probably occurred because "SHOP" is so similar to "STOP" on the sign several streets back that it is a natural mistake for a scribe to make. Thus the sign should be interpreted to announce the existence of a shopping area.

[interpretation]

2 Timothy 2:22

QUESTION: "When temptation rushes at you like a lion, what is better than presence of mind!"
ANSWER: "Absence of body."

[temptation]

2 Timothy 2:22

Johnny's teacher wrote a note home to his mother: "Johnny is a bright boy, but he seems to spend all his time thinking about girls."
Johnny's mother wrote back to the teacher: "If you find a cure, let me know. I'm having the same trouble with his father."

[sex]

2 Timothy 3:1

The way things are going, you feel like a fool buying a five-year calendar.

[foolishness]

2 Timothy 3:2

It had been a long hard day for the little boy's mother. Her patience finally failed. She grabbed the little fellow and shook him and shouted at him, "Okay, now you can do anything you want to. Anything, do you hear me? NOW, LET ME SEE YOU DISOBEY THAT!'"

[disobedience, frustration]

2 Timothy 3:2

"My mother made me say five hundred times 'I'm a disobedient boy.' But I got even with her. When I got to my room I said five hundred times 'No I ain't'"

[disobedience, stubborn]

2 Timothy 3:2-4

The church member had asked his pastor to pray for him the following Sunday, but the pastor was reluctant. "Douglas, I understand this is a serious problem, but we usually don't pray about floating kidneys during the service."

"It's not that much different form the other sick people you prayed for last Sunday, pastor."

"Which sick people?"

"All the ones with loose livers!"

[body, healing, prayer,]

2 Timothy 3:4

A little boy prayed, "Lord, if you can't make me a better boy, don't worry about it. I'm having a real good time like I am!"

[contentment]

2 Timothy 3:5

Two sailors were adrift on a raft in the ocean. They had just about given up hope of rescue. One began to pray, "O Lord, I've led a worthless life. I've been unkind to my wife and I've neglected my children, but if you'll save me, I promise ..."

The other shouted, "Hold it! Don't say anything more. I think I see land."

[prayer, repentance]

2 Timothy 3:5

A man seen entering a nightclub with a Bible under his arm was asked to explain. "They say the show is terrific," he replied. "Gorgeous girls, scanty costumes, low-cut dresses on the singers, etc."

"Then why the Bible?"

"If it's as good as they say it is I'm going to stay over Sunday."

[hypocrisy]

2 Timothy 3:5

In the middle of a forest, there was a hunter who was suddenly confronted with a huge, mean bear. In all his fears, his attempt to shoot the bear was unsuccessful. He turned away and started to run as fast as he could. Finally, he ended up at the edge of a very steep cliff. His hopes were dim. But, he got on his knees, opened his arms and said,

"My God! Please give this bear some religion!"

Then, there was a lightning in the air and the bear stopped just a few feet short of the hunter. The bear was puzzled and looked up in the air and said, "My God! Thank you for the food I am about to receive ..."

[animals, prayer, religion]

2 Timothy 3:5

The missionary was captured by cannibals and placed into a pot to cook when the chief appeared and began to talk to him in perfect English. The chief explained his mastery of the language by relating that he'd gone to Harvard. "You're a Harvard man?" said the missionary. "And yet you still eat your fellow man?"

"Yes," replied the chief. "But now I use a knife and fork."

[manners]

2 Timothy 3:5

The Trinity decides to go on a holiday.

The Holy Spirit suggests: "Let's go to Eden! That's a nice place to stay!" But the Father replies: "Well, you know, that's a sad place for me, it reminds me of the time where Adam and Eve first disobeyed me and, well, I'd rather not go there. Why don't we go to Jerusalem instead? After all, it's the Holy City, we should enjoy it!"

Now Jesus replies: "Father, you know I don't have good memories of Jerusalem. No, sorry, but I don't feel like going back there again, I had too much trouble there. But my suggestion is what about attending a service at that well-known liberal mega-church in America? Surely nothing's wrong about that?"

And the Holy Spirit says: "Hey! That's a good idea! I've never been there!"

[church, Holy Spirit, Trinity]

2 Timothy 3:5

See Matthew 15:19.

2 Timothy 3:16

A Critical Literary Review of the Scriptures:

In this work, the main author (God) gives a construction of the universe and establishes some of its metaphysical properties. He refutes certain propositions claimed by some, while at the same time placing the work of his colleague Christ in proper context. In the final section certain conjectures are made as to the nature of future research.

I recommend publication, subject to certain revisions in the early part, where some unnecessary duplication appears to have taken place (cf. Kings and Chronicles).

[Bible, criticism]

2 Timothy 3:16-17

Definition of a 'modern' evangelical church member: one who believes that the New Testament is a divinely inspired book admirably suited to the spiritual needs of his neighbors.

[Bible, hypocrisy]

2 Timothy 3:16,17

See John 16:13.

2 Timothy 4:1

See Acts 10:42.

2 Timothy 4:2

A minister's son said, "My daddy can take the same text and preach a different sermon every Sunday."
Another minister's son said, "Yeah? That's nothing. My daddy can take a different text every Sunday and preach the same sermon."

[interpretation, sermon]

2 Timothy 4:2

A preacher was called upon to substitute for the regular minister, who had failed to reach the church because he was delayed in a snowstorm. The speaker began by explaining the meaning of substitute.
"If you break a window," he said, "and then place cardboard there instead, that is a substitute."
After the sermon, a woman who had listened intently shook hands with him and wishing to compliment him actually said, "You were no substitute. You were a real pane."

[pastor, puns]

2 Timothy 4:2

One day at an old country church, there was to be a double sermon. First, there was a young preacher boy that would preach his first sermon. After him, an old veteran preacher that was well respected in the community was to preach.
All of the "pre-preaching" things took place. There was good singing and nice specials among other things. These all went very well.

As the time for the young preacher to preach came closer, he realized something very dreadful. He leaned over to the old preacher who was sitting next to him and said, "I forgot my Bible, and all of my notes are in it!"

The veteran preacher seemed cool and calm as he replied, "Don't worry son, God will provide. Here, use my Bible. Just speak what's on your heart, and I'm sure God will bless it."

The young man hesitantly took the old Bible, and made his way to the pulpit. Well, this preacher just started preaching away, and had a great time doing it too. The sermon he preached was so great, that at the end when there was an alter call, nearly the entire church came forward. The boy was relieved as he left the pulpit and made his way to his seat.

During the message, the old preacher started to listen to the sermon closely, as it seemed very familiar. After a few minutes, he realized what had happened. The young preacher found the notes that he was going to use for the sermon that he was about to preach. He got very nervous as the boy came down to him. "Now what am I going to do?"

The young preacher calmly said, "Don't worry. God will provide!"

[provision, sermon, worry]

2 Timothy 4:3

An example of the kind of preaching addressed to rich sinners in some of the upper-class congregations: "Brethren, you must repent, as it were, and be converted in a measure, or you will be damned to some extent."

[compromise, judgment, preaching, repentance]

2 Timothy 4:5

While on his first ocean cruise, a man fell overboard. He was floundering in the water, shouting and waving and trying to get the attention of those on board. Finally a lawyer, a politician, and an evangelist noticed his plight.

The lawyer shouted, "Shall I prepare a suit against the cruise line on your behalf?"

The politician promised that he would press a bill in Congress next term to make sailing safer.

The evangelist said with a smile, "Yes, brother! I see your hand! Now, do I see another?"

[evangelism, lawyer, politics]

2 Timothy 4:7

If you stop at third base to congratulate yourself, you'll never score a home run.

[pride]

2 Timothy 4:7-8

See Luke 12:40.

2 Timothy 4:8

A Bible study group was discussing the unforeseen possibility of their sudden death. The leader of the discussion said," We will all die some day, and none of us really know when, but if we did we would all do a better job of preparing ourselves for that inevitable event."
Everybody shook their heads in agreement with this comment.
Then the leader said to the group, "What would you do if you knew you only had four weeks of life remaining before your death, and then the Great Judgment Day?"
A gentleman said, "I would go out into my community and minister the Gospel to those that have not yet accepted the Lord into their lives."
"Very good!", said the group leader, and all the group members agreed, that would be a very good thing to do.
One lady spoke up and said enthusiastically, "I would dedicate all of my remaining time to serving God, my family, my church, and my fellow man with a greater conviction."
"That's wonderful!" the group leader commented, and all the group members agreed, that would be a very good thing to do.
But one gentleman in the back finally spoke up loudly and said, "I would go to my mother-in-law's house for the four weeks."
Everyone was puzzled by this answer, and the group leader ask, "Why you mother-in-law's home?"
Then the gentleman smiled sarcastically and said, "Because, that would be the longest four weeks of my life!"

[mother-in-law, priorities]

2 Timothy 4:10

"I must admit, in one way I'll be sorry to see Demas leave town when he moves away," said Paul.
"But why? He's been one of your worst critics," stated Timothy.
"I know," replied Paul, "but he's given me lots of illustrative material for a great many sermons!"

[criticism, sermon]

2 Timothy 4:10

A small town had three churches; Presbyterian, Methodist, and Baptist. All three had a serious problem with squirrels in the church. Each church in its own fashion had a meeting to deal with the problem.
The Presbyterians decided that it was predestined that squirrels be in the

church and that they would just have to live with them.

The Methodists decided they should deal with the squirrels lovingly in the style of Charles Wesley. They humanely trapped them and released them in a park at the edge of town. Within 3 days, they were all back in the church.

The Baptists had the best solution. They voted the squirrels in as members. Now they only see them at Christmas and Easter.

[Baptist, membership]

2 Timothy 4:11

I've decided to give Barnabas' nephew [Mark] another try," Paul <u>remarked</u>.

[names, puns]

2 Timothy 4:13

A collector of rare books ran into an acquaintance of his who told him he had just thrown away an old Bible that had been in his family for generations. He happened to mention that Guten ... something had printed it.

"Not Gutenberg?" gasped the book collector.

"Yes, that was the name."

"You idiot! You've thrown away one of the first books ever printed. A copy recently sold at auction for $600,000."

"Mine wouldn't have been worth much," replied the man. "Some clown by the name of Martin Luther had scribbled all over it."

[Bible, names]

TITUS

Titus 1:5

The pastor told the search committee, "If I am voted in as pastor of this church, I will work hard to bring us into the 20th century." Someone spoke up, " Uh, Preacher, don't you mean the 21st century?" The pastor replied, " Let's take it one century at a time."

[change, church]

Titus 1:6

Babysitter (greeting the returning parents): "Don't apologize. I wouldn't be in a hurry to come home either!"

[baby, babysitter, parents, procrastination]

Titus 1:7

Two bellhops were discussing the best tippers in the hotel.
"Watch out for that preacher's convention," cautioned the older bellhop.
"Are they careful with their money?" asked the younger man.
"Let me put it this way," answered the voice of experience. "Last year they showed up with the Ten Commandments in one hand and a ten-dollar bill in the other, and when they left, I don't think they hadn't broken either."

[pastors, stinginess]

Titus 1:7

In the middle of his golf game, the minister drove into a sand trap. He picked up his golf club and broke it but didn't say a word. Then he picked up the golf bag and tore it to shreds but didn't say a word. Then he took out all the golf balls and flung them into the woods but did not say one word. Finally he muttered, "I'm gonna have to give it up."
"Golf?" asked the caddie.
"No," he replied. "The ministry."

[anger, ministry, sports]

Titus 1:8

See 1 Timothy 3:2.

Titus 1:16

See 1 Timothy 3:5.

Titus 2:4

Definition: Joy of motherhood — what a woman experiences when all the kids are in bed.

[mothers, parenting]

Titus 2:4

Marriage counselor: "Do you feel that your role as a mother and homemaker is beneath you?"
Counselee: "No, I feel it's beyond me."

[mothers, parenting]

Titus 2:4-5

A lady, newly converted, told her pastor that God was calling her to preach and teach.
He asked her if she had any children.
"Oh, yes," she replied. "I have a large family. All my children are still at home."
The pastor's face lit up. "Praise the Lord! God has not only called you to preach and teach, but he's given you a congregation as well."

[ministry, mothers]

Titus 2:5

A not-too-tidy housewife attended a woman's weekend retreat and was revived spiritually. Arriving home, she told her husband, "Honey, we're going to sweep the country with these eternal truths!"
With minimum enthusiasm he replied, "I hope you start with the kitchen."

[home, ministry]

Titus 2:5

The modern husband believes a woman's place is in the home — and he expects her to go there immediately after work.

[home, work]

Titus 2:5

Husband: "Let her stay home and wash and iron and cook and clean and take care of the kids. No wife of mine is going to work."

[home, work]

Titus 2:5

Nowadays two can live as cheaply as one if both are working.

[work]

Titus 3:9

See 1 Timothy 1:4.

PHILEMON

Philemon 1:1

"I understand," said a young woman to another, "that at your church you are having very small attendance. Is that so?"

"Yes," answered the other girl, "so small that every time our young pastor uses that Pauline expression, 'Dearly Beloved' you feel as if you had received a proposal!"

[church, embarrassment]

HEBREWS

Hebrews

A man and his wife were having an argument about who should make the coffee each morning.

The wife said, "You should do it, because you get up first, and then we don't have to wait as long to get our coffee."

The husband said, "You are in charge of the cooking around here and you should do it, because that is your job, and I can just wait for my coffee."

Wife replies, "No, you should do it, and besides it is in the Bible that the man should make the coffee."

Husband replies, "I can't believe that, show me."

So she fetched the Bible, and opened the New Testament and showed him at the top of several pages, that it indeed says...... "HEBREWS [he brews]"

[drink, marriage]

Hebrews 1:3

Children's Church teacher: "Who sits at the right hand of God?"
Little student: "Er — Mrs. God?"

[God]

Hebrews 1:3

See Mark 16:19.

Hebrews 1:14

Wife: "Aren't you driving a little too fast, dear?"
Husband: "Don't you believe in a guardian angel? He'll take care of us."
Wife: "Yes, I do. But I'm afraid we left him miles back!"

[angels, driving]

Hebrews 2:14-15

There was a huge nut tree by the cemetery fence. One day two boys filled up a bucketful of nuts and sat down by the tree, out of sight, and began dividing the nuts. "One for you, one for me. One for you, one for me," said one boy. The bucket was so full, several rolled out towards the fence. Cycling down the road by the cemetery was a third boy. As he passed, he thought he heard voices from inside the cemetery. He slowed down to investigate. Sure enough, he heard, "One for you, one for me. One for you."

He knew what it was. "Oh my goodness!" he shuddered, "It's Satan and St. Peter dividing the souls at the cemetery!" He cycled down the road and found an old man with a cane, hobbling along. "Come quick!" he said, "You won't believe what I heard. Satan and St. Peter are down at the cemetery dividing the souls."

The man said, "Shoo, you brat! Can't you see I'm finding it hard to walk as it is!"

After several pleas, the man hobbled to the cemetery and heard, "One for you, one for me. One for you, one..." The old man whispered, "Boy, you's been tellin' the truth! Let's see if we can see the Devil himself."

Shivering with fear, they edged toward the fence, still unable to see anything, but they heard, "One for you, one for me. One for you, one for me. And one last one for you. That's all. Let's go get those nuts by the fence, and we'll be done."

They say the old guy made it to town 10 minutes before the boy!

[death, devil, fear]

Hebrews 3:11

A father sent his two sons into the hills on a cold night to herd sheep. Later he went out to see how they were getting along. He found one son dutifully watching the sheep and asked, "How are you?"

"Fine father, " replied the son, "but my lamp has gone out and I am cold." Whereupon the father saw his second son who was fast asleep under a tree. He woke him up and asked, "How are you?" The boy replied, "I am cold father and need a new wick for my lamp."

The father shook his head and said, "You shall not have it. There is no wick for the rested!"

[laziness, wicked]

Hebrews 3:12

A minister, preaching on the danger of compromise, was condemning the attitude of so many Christians who believe certain things concerning their faith, but in actual practice will say, "Yes, but ... "

At the climax of the sermon, he said, "Yes, there are millions of Christians who are sliding straight to Hell on their buts."

The congregation went into gales of laughter, and the minister promptly closed the service with a benediction.

[compromise, hell]

Hebrews 3:13

A visitation pastor once laid his hand on a man's shoulder and said:
"Friend, do you hear the solemn ticking of that clock? Tick-tock; tick tock.

And oh, friend, do you know what day it inexorably and relentlessly brings nearer?"

"Yes," the working man replied, "pay day."

[eternity, wages, work]

Hebrews 4:1

A mother commented, "If Heaven's a place of rest, my teenage son's going to be practiced up for it."

[rest, teenager]

Hebrews 4:11

A minister waited in line to have his car filled with gas just before a long holiday weekend. The attendant worked quickly, but there were many cars ahead of him in front of the service station. Finally, the attendant motioned him toward a vacant pump.

"Reverend," said the young man, "sorry about the delay. It seems as if everyone waits until the last minute to get ready for a long trip."

The minister chuckled, "I know what you mean. It's the same in my business."

[procrastination]

Hebrews 4:16

QUESTION: How do we know that the author of Hebrews used pest control in his vegetable garden?

ANSWER: Because he said, "Lettuce spray." (Let us pray).

[prayer. vegetables]

Hebrews 4:16

Most of us have now learned to live with voice mail as a necessary part of our lives. Have you ever wondered what it would be like if God decided to install voice mail? Imagine praying and hearing the following:

Thank you for calling heaven.

For English press 1

For Spanish press 2

For all other languages, press 3

Please select one of the following options:

Press 1 for request

Press 2 for thanksgiving

Press 3 for complaints

Press 4 for all others

I am sorry, all our Angels and Saints are busy helping other sinners right now. However, your prayer is important to us and we will answer it in the order it was received. Please stay on the line.
If you would like to speak to:
God, press 1
Jesus, press 2
Holy Spirit, press 3
To find a loved one that has been assigned to heaven press 5, then enter his social security # followed by the pound sign.
(If you receive a negative response, please hang up and dial area code 666)
For reservations to heaven, please enter JOHN followed by the numbers, 3 1 6.
For answers to nagging questions about dinosaurs, life and other planets, please wait until you arrive in heaven for the specifics.
Our computers show that you have already been prayed for today, please hang up and call again tomorrow.
The office is now closed for the weekend to observe a religious holiday.
If you are calling after hours and need emergency assistance, please contact your local pastor.
Thank you and have a heavenly day.

[computer, prayer]

Hebrews 7:22

Definition of the New Covenant — A contract between God and His people — one that the Devil is still trying to take to arbitration.

[devil]

Hebrews 9:27

Did you hear about the undertaker who closed his letters with the words, "Eventually yours?"

[death, funeral]

Hebrews 9:27

On visiting a seriously ill lawyer in the hospital, his friend found him sitting up in bed, frantically leafing through the Bible.
"What are you doing?" asked the friend.
"Looking for loopholes," replied the lawyer.
[death, lawyers]

Hebrews 9:27

A preacher was addressing the people one Sunday, trying to impress upon them the importance of faith. "All you people of this congregation," he cried from the pulpit, "one day you're going to die. Do you hear me? All of you people of this congregation, one day you're going to die."

One little man sitting in the front pew started to laugh, so the preacher asked him, "What's so funny?" The man answered, "I don't belong to this congregation."

[church, death]

Hebrews 9:27

The preacher was dangerously ill and couldn't have visitors. But when an agnostic friend called to pay his respects, the preacher asked that he be sent in anyway.

"I sure appreciate this," said the agnostic. "But why did you ask to see me, when you denied admission to your close friends and church members?"

"That's easy to explain," gasped the dying preacher. "I'm confident of seeing them in Heaven. But this is probably the last chance I'll ever have to see you."

[atheist, death]

Hebrews 9:27

Lately I've been doing a lot of thinking about the hereafter. Several times a day, I'll go into another room to get something, then ask myself "What am I here after?"

OR

An eighty-year-old woman was told by her minister that at her age, she should be giving some thought to what he called "the hereafter". She said to him, "I think about it many times a day."

"Oh really?" said the minister. "That's very wise."

"It's not a matter of wisdom," she replied. "It's when I open a drawer or a closet, I ask myself, 'What am I here after?'"

[forgetfulness]

Hebrews 9:27

"Wouldn't it be neat to know the time and place that you were to die?" asked a frivolous teenage girl.

"What good would that be?" asked her boyfriend.

"I wouldn't show up," she said.

[death]

Hebrews 9:27

Health nuts are going to feel stupid someday, lying in hospitals dying of nothing.

[death, health]

Hebrews 10:14

Teacher: "In our lesson today we have talked about the burnt offerings offered in the Old Testament. Why don't we have burnt offerings today?" Student: "On account of air pollution."

[sacrifice]

Hebrews 10:24-25

THINGS YOU NEVER HEAR IN CHURCH:

Hey! It's MY turn to sit on the front pew!

I was so enthralled, I never noticed your sermon went over time 25 minutes.

Personally, I find witnessing much more enjoyable than golf.

I've decided to give our church the $500.00 a month I used to send to TV evangelists.

I volunteer to be the permanent teacher for the Junior High Children's Church class.

Forget the denominational minimum salary: let's pay our pastor so s/he can live like we do.

I love it when we sing hymns I've never heard before!

Since we're all here, let's start the worship service early!

Pastor, we'd like to send you to this Bible seminar in the Bahamas.

Nothing inspires me and strengthens my commitment like our annual stewardship campaign!

[church]

Hebrews 10:25

Church members, like cars, usually start missing before they quit.

[church, membership]

Hebrews 10:25

Two church members decided to play golf one Sunday but both were playing poorly. One said, "I should have stayed home and gone to church." To which the other replied, "I couldn't have gone to church anyway. My wife is sick in bed."

[church, excuses, hypocrisy, Sunday]

Hebrews 10:25

Mrs. Smith: "Very poor manners, I call it, to phone me during church hours."

Mrs. Jones: "Probably she knows you don't go to church."

Mrs. Smith: "Very likely; but she might have had the decency to assume that I do."

[manners, Sunday]

Hebrews 10:25

The excuses of non-attending parishioners have been classified by clergymen into medical categories.

The cardiac worshipper: "I have it, here in my heart."

The laryngeal worshipper: "I get all choked up by the sermon."

The myopic worshipper: "I don't see all this ritual."

[church, excuses, sickness]

Hebrews 10:25

A pastor, apparently disgusted with the excuses parishioners offered as to why they didn't attend worship services, included "Reasons Why I Never Wash" in the Sunday bulletin:

1. I was forced to as a child.
2. People who make soap are only after your money.
3. I wash on special occasions like Christmas and Easter.
4. People who wash are hypocrites — they think they are cleaner than everyone else.
5. There are so many different kinds of soap, I can't decide which one is best.
6. I used to wash, but it got boring so I stopped.
7. None of my friends wash.
8. The bathroom is never warm enough in the winter or cool enough in the summer.
9. I'll start washing when I get older and dirtier.
10. Washing was invented by people who knew nothing about science.
11. I can't spare the time.
12. I don't like the songs people sing in the bathroom.
13. I can clean myself perfectly well whenever I pass a sink, so I don't need a bathtub.
14. I know how to stay clean without washing.
15. The last time I washed, someone was rude to me.
16. What I do doesn't affect anybody but me.
17. I know someone who washes every day and still smells bad.

18. I don't believe in soap. I sat beside a whole case of it for an hour once, and nothing happened.
19. If people saw me without my makeup, they would laugh at me.
20. I'm so dirty now that if I washed, the drain would clog.
21. Cats, dogs, and chickens never wash, and they are happy all the time.
22. Prehistoric humans were happy all the time until the first soap salesman made them feel guilty.
23. If I start washing again, my friends will think I am trying to conform to middle-class standards.
24. Washing is for women and children.
25. Washing is for people much dirtier than I am.
26. I will wash when I find the bathroom that is exactly right for me.
27. I only believe in things I can see, and I can't see bacteria.
28. Children need to see that it is OK to be different.
29. Children need to see a few bad examples.
30. Washing may have been OK in my grandfather's day, but it's not practical in today's world. I need to look dirty, talk dirty, and fight dirty to survive.
31. I watch other people washing on TV.
32. There are lots of clean people who never wash.
33. We've just moved here six years ago and haven't had a chance.
34. I bought a bad bar of soap once, so I swore I would never wash again!
35. I feel as close to washing on the golf course as I do in the bathroom.
36. I never wash when I have company.
37. Washday is the only day I have to sleep in.
38. My wife washes enough for the whole family
39. I know people who wash but don't act very clean.
40. Washing is the opiate of the masses.

[excuses]

Hebrews 10:25

Some ministers believe that the only way their churches will ever have peak attendance is for a Constitutional amendment to be passed prohibiting attendance!

[law]

Hebrews 10:25

Church-Lite
Has the heaviness of your old fashioned church got you weighted down? Try us! We are the New and Improved Lite Church of the Valley. Studies

have shown we have 24% fewer commitments than other churches. We guarantee to trim off guilt, because we are Low-Cal... low Calvin, that is. We are the home of the 7.5% tithe.

We promise 35 minute worship services, with 7 minute sermons. Next Sunday's exciting text is the story of the Feeding of the 500.

We have only 6 Commandments—Your choice!! We use just 3 gospels in our contemporary New Testament *Good Sound Bites for Modern Human Beings*. We take the offering every other week, all major credit cards accepted, of course. We are looking forward with great anticipation to our 800 year Millennium.

Yes, the New and Improved Lite Church of the Valley could be just what you are looking for. We are everything you want in a church... and less!!!

[church]

Hebrews 10:25

No excuses Sunday

To make it possible for everyone to attend church next Sunday we are going to have a special "No Excuse Sunday."

Cots will be placed in the foyer for those who say "Sunday is my only day to sleep in." We will have steel helmets for those who think the church is too cold, and fans for those who say it is too hot. We will have hearing aids for those who say "The minister talks too softly," and cotton for those who say he preaches too loudly. Score cards for those who wish to list hypocrites present. Some relatives will be in attendance for those who like to go visiting on Sundays. There will be TV dinners for those who can't go to Church and cook dinner also. One section will be devoted to trees and grass for those who like to see God in Nature. Finally the Sanctuary will be decorated with both Christmas poinsettias and Easter Lilies for those who have never seen the church without them.

[excuses, Sunday]

Hebrews 10:25

A Reform Rabbi was so compulsive a golfer that once, on Yom Kippur, he left the house early and went out for a quick nine holes by himself. An angel who happened to be looking on immediately notified his superiors that a grievous sin was being committed on earth.

On the sixth hole, God caused a mighty wind to take the ball directly from the tee to the cup for a miraculous and dramatic hole in one.

The angel was horrified. "Lord," he said, "you call this a punishment?"

"Sure," answered God with a smile. "Who can he tell?"

[Rabbi, sports]

Hebrews 10:25

A couple was having their Sunday morning breakfast when the wife went to get her Sunday church clothes on. When she returned, the husband was still in his bathrobe.

"Aren't you going to church this morning?" asked the wife.

"No, I'm not going this morning. In fact, I'm not going to church anymore at all."

"What do you mean, we've gone to church for years, so why the change?

He responded, "Look, there are people at that church who don't like me, and frankly, there are people at that church that I don't like, and I'M NOT GOING!"

She answered back, "I'll give you two good reasons why you need to go to church. One, you're 42 years old. Two, you gotta go, you're the preacher."

[discouragement, faithfulness, pastor, Sunday]

Hebrews 10:25

To some people religious freedom means the choice of churches from which they may stay away.

[church, freedom]

Hebrews 10:25

The Devil loves it when we skip church on rainy Sundays, 'cause he knows that dry people burn better!

[church, devil, faithfulness, hell]

Hebrews 10:25

Hold this page to your face and blow on it. If it turns:

Green — call your doctor.

Brown — see your dentist.

Purple — consult your psychiatrist.

Red — see your banker.

Yellow — call your lawyer and make a will.

If it remains the same color, you're in good health, and there is no reason on earth why you should not be in church this Sunday.

[church, excuses, Sunday]

Hebrews 10:25

Perturbed over the absenteeism of his parishioners at the worship services, a minister handed his secretary some church stationery and a list of ten members who were absent the most often. He asked her to write each of them a letter concerning their absence.

Within a few days the minister received a letter from a prominent physician who apologized profusely for having been absent so often. He enclosed a check for one thousand dollars to cover contributions he would have made had he been present, promised to be there the following Sunday at church service and, further, to be there every Sunday thereafter unless providentially hindered. The usual complimentary closing with his signature was given.

However, the following note was at the bottom of the page: "P.S. Please tell your secretary there is only one t in dirty and no c in skunk."

[excuses, Sunday]

Hebrews 11:26

You can be sure that if Moses were alive today, he'd be considered a remarkable man.

And he sure ought to be—he'd be more than 3,400 years old.

[age, reputation]

Hebrews 11:27

The psychiatrist's receptionist went to her boss and said, "Doctor, there's a man in the office who thinks he's invisible."

The psychiatrist replied, "Tell him I can't see him."

[invisible]

Hebrews 12:23

Note: the word "assembly" in used in the KJV but in many others it tends to be translated "church."

Working as a cargo handler for a major package delivery company, I came across an express envelope with shipping instructions that puzzled me, particularly the line describing the contents.

I finally realized the parcel contained some kind of manual and was addressed to a church. But at first I thought I was processing one of our company's most momentous pieces of freight.

The description read, "Instructions for the Assembly of God."

[confusion, church, misunderstanding]

Hebrews 12:25-26

Preacher: "Do you want to go to Heaven?"
Unbeliever: "No, Sir."
Preacher: "Surely, you want to go to Heaven when you die."
Unbeliever: "Oh sure, when I die. I thought you were organizing a group to go today."

[evangelism, procrastination]

Hebrews 13:2

Little Hugh had been fascinated about the sermon he had heard on angels. As he was telling a friend about it they got into an argument. The little friend insisted that all angels had wings, but Hugh disagreed.

"It isn't true," insisted Hugh. "Our preacher says that some of them are strangers in underwear."

[angels, hospitality]

Hebrews 13:4

Email to newlyweds: "May you have the wisdom of Solomon, the patience of Job, and the children of Israel."

[children, procreation]

Hebrews 13:4

First girl: My pastor said we could have 16 husbands.
Second girl: Are you sure about that?
First girl: Why, yes. At the last wedding at the church I heard him say, "Four better, four worse, four richer, and four poorer!"

[bigamy, marriage, wedding]

Hebrews 13:8

A profane man and woman get married. They go on their honeymoon and return a week later. As soon as they had time to settle in, the wife told her husband, "honey, sit down, and I'll fix you a wonderful dinner." The man did as he was told, and the woman soon called him. He sat down and was presented with, steak, baked potato, green beans, and apple pie for desert. He thought, "My goodness, I must be the luckiest man in the world."

The next day, the man went to work. When he arrived at home that evening, his wife called to him, "honey, supper's on the table." Again the man could only smile and think to himself, "I really made the right decision in marrying this woman." He sat down and was presented with: steak, baked potato, green beans, and apple pie for desert. He thought, "Well, this is strange, but who am I to complain."

The next day, a similar scene occurred. The man came home, and sat down. In came his wife with two plates on which were (you guessed it): steak, baked potato, green beans, and apple pie for dessert. The man stood up, looked at his wife, and said in a profane voice, "King James Version, Hebrews 13:8." He then stormed out of the room.

His wife thought for a moment, then went to the bookcase, and pulled down the old tattered King James Bible. She opened to Hebrews 13:8 and read, "... the same yesterday, today, forever."

[context, marriage]

Hebrews 13:18

Conscience is a thinking man's filter.

[conscience]

Hebrews 13:20

Definition of "Benediction" — The start of the race to the parking lot.

[church, impatience]

Hebrews 13:25

Chaplain: "My man, I will allow you five minutes of Grace before your execution."
Condemned man: "That's not very long to get to know her, but bring her in."

[grace, names]

JAMES

James 1:1

A conscientious minister who enjoyed reminding himself that he was a servant of God and of the Lord Jesus Christ, decided to get acquainted with a newly married couple in his congregation. After his knock on the door, a lilting voice from within called out, "is that you, Angel?" "No," replied the minister, "but I'm from the same department."

[angel, ministry]

James 1:2

Three people were viewing the Grand Canyon-an artist, a pastor and a cowboy. As they stood on the edge of that massive abyss, each one responded with a cry of exclamation.

"Ah," the artist said, "what a beautiful scene to paint!"

"Glory!" the minister cried. "What a wonderful example of the handiwork of God!"

"Shoot," the cowboy mused, "what a terrible place to lose a cow!"

[creation, nature, optimist, pessimist]

James 1:3-4

First Preacher: How do you preach patience to your people and make it effective?

Second Preacher: By making the sermon so long that they have to practice it while they listen.

[patience, preaching]

James 1:13

A stranger stopping into an open church for a few minutes of contemplation found a purse in the pew in front of him. Since no one else was in the church, a question promptly rose in his mind: Was this a temptation of the Devil, or the answer to a prayer?

[blessing, prayer, temptation]

James 1:13-14

Mother: Johnny, what is all the racket from the pantry?

Johnny: I'm busy fighting temptation.

[temptation]

James 1:19

A closed mouth gathers no feet.

[embarrassment, talk]

James 1:19

A pastor of the parish always asked the children the same questions, and in the same sequence: "What is your name? How old are you? Did you say your prayers? What will happen to you if you don't believe in Jesus? An overly ambitious and proud mother, wanting her boy to show how bright he was, rehearsed her little boy with the answer, and so when the pastor called, the boy beat him to the punch by rattling off: "Tyson MacDonald—5—yes—go to hell."

[children, embarrassment, hell]

James 1:19-20

Some people think they have a dynamic personality if they occasionally explode.

[anger]

James 1:19-20

One Sunday, a priest announced that he'd pass out miniature crosses made out of palm leaves. "Put this cross in the room where your family argues the most," he said, "and when you look at it, the cross will remind you that God is watching."

As people were leaving the church, a woman walked up to the priest, shook his hand and said, "I'll take five."

[anger, argument, family]

James 1:20

Righteous indignation is your own wrath as opposed to the shocking bad temper of others.

[anger, hypocrisy]

James 1:22

A little girl told her mother that her brother had set traps to catch poor, harmless birds. The mother inquired if she had done anything about it. "Oh, yes," the girl replied, "I prayed that the traps might not catch the birds."

"Anything else?" responded the mother.

"Yes, then I prayed that God would keep the birds from getting into the traps," said the girl.

"Was that all?" questioned the mother further.

With a smile on her face the little girl admitted, "Then I went and kicked the traps all to pieces."

[prayer, responsibility, zeal]

James 1:25

Everybody liked the new preacher's first sermon. He kept, however, repeating it Sunday after Sunday.

Finally, the deacon's board met with him and demanded, "Pastor, aren't we ever going to get a new sermon?"

The pastor calmly replied, "Not until I get action on the old one."

[sermon, repetition, obedience]

James 1:27

A deacon was presenting the congregation's gift to a church member who was moving to another city. "He was a man who practiced true religion; he was a diligent visitor among our people," asserted the speaker, "and many homes were happy when he left."

[religion, visitation]

James 2:1-4

A preacher in a church, that catered to only rich and important people was presenting his weekly message to his beautiful congregation, when he saw a street bum walk in the back and sit on the last pew. The preacher continued his message, while he thought how he would deal with the bum. The preacher was concerned that he would lose some of his beautiful congregation if the bum stayed around too long, which of course wouldn't be good for the preacher's pocketbook.

After the sermon was over, the bum immediately came up to the preacher and told him he wanted to join his church. The preacher was prepared for this and told the bum he should go home and pray about it and do what God told him.

The preacher didn't see the bum any more, so he feel relieved. Six months later, the preacher saw the bum on the street. The preacher couldn't resist asking the bum what happened with his prayer.

The bum replied, "I prayed three different times and got the same answer each time, so I did what God said."

The preacher had to know, so he asked, "What did God tell you?"

"Well," the bum said, "God told me not to worry about joining your church. He said he had been trying to get in for 20 years and He hadn't made it yet!"

[membership, prejudice]

431

James 2:10

"Why are you here?" the prison chaplain asked the prisoner.
"Just run through the Ten Commandments," he replied. "I'll tell you if I missed any."

[commandments, prison, sin]

James 2:14

An important meeting of Anglican clergymen convened in London, England. After the bishop had called the meeting to order, the door opened and in came a rector obviously embarrassed by his late arrival. As he entered the room, he pulled out his pocket watch. In a defensive tone and in a loud voice he said to the bishop, "I have perfect faith in my Swiss watch."
The bishop replied in soft voice, "Sir, what you need is not perfect faith in your watch but good works."

[excuses, faith, time]

James 2:14

I'm very much afraid I'll not meet you in heaven, Charlie," said a Children's Church teacher to a mischievous pupil.
"Why," exclaimed the incorrigible youth, "what have you been doing now?"

[disobedience, heaven]

James 2:14

A Catholic and a Protestant were having a debate about faith and works, versus faith which works. Someone looked on, and said, "Everything is subject to debate. There is no core of universal Christian faith."
A believer punched him between the eyes.
"What did you do that for?", he asked.
"My fist looked different to your two eyes. Therefore, I did not hit you."

[argument, faith]

James 2:17

The problem with mainline Christianity is that too many church members are singing "Standing on the Promises," when they are merely sitting on the premises.

[laziness, promises]

James 2:20

Shouted the evangelist: "Adultery is as bad as murder! Isn't that so, Sister Johnson?"
Sister Johnson: "I don't rightly know. I ain't never killed nobody."

432

[adultery, honesty, murder]

James 2:25

Sometime things are just not what they seem as first.

At a personal injury suit in Texas, a man from New York was on the witness stand. While driving from Austin to San Antonio, the New Yorker's car had been struck by a beat-up old pickup truck driven by a local rancher. The New Yorker was attempting to collect damages for his injuries.

"How can you now claim to have all these injuries?" asked the insurance company's lawyer. "I notice in the report of the Texas Ranger who investigated the accident that the very first words you said to him were that you'd never felt better in your life. And yet here we are in court, you've sued my client." He said, "Can you explain that statement?"

The New Yorker replied, "Yes, sir, I think I can. After the rancher's truck hit my car, it ran into a ditch and turned over. Now, there was a mule and a dog in that truck, and they were injured worse than the rancher or me. The Texas Ranger heard the mule braying in pain and saw that it had a broken leg. So the Ranger whipped out his pistol and shot the mule right between the eyes. Then he saw that the dog was in terrible pain, so the Ranger shot him too.

"Then he came over to me and asked me, 'Sir, how are you?' And that's when I said I never felt better in my life!"

[intimidation, lying]

James 3:1

It isn't the things that go in one ear and out the other that hurt as much as the things that go in one ear, get all mixed up, and then slip out the mouth.

[confusion, talk]

James 3:1

A young man dies and goes to Heaven, where he finds he is third in line at the Pearly Gates. St. Peter is taking a much-needed break, so an angel is admitting the newly arrived to Heaven.

The angel tells the three new arrivals that because so many drug dealers and other criminals have managed to sneak into Heaven that St. Peter must now be a little stricter with the screening process. Each person is required to state his former occupation and tell his or her yearly salary.

The first man in line says, "I was an actor, and I earned $1 million last year."

The angel says, "Okay, you may enter." He turns to the woman in line and asks her about her life.

She states, "I earned $150,000 as an attorney." The angel thinks for a moment and then lets her in, too.

He turns to the third one in line and asks, "What have you done with your life?"

The man replies, "I earned $8,000 last year..."

"Oh," the angel interrupts. "What did you teach?"

[teacher, wages]

James 3:2

The person who says the art of conversation is dead has never been delayed at a green light waiting for the person in the car in front to finish talking.

[talk, waiting]

James 3:2

Quit griping about your church; if it was perfect, you couldn't belong.

[perfection]

James 3:2

The minister is repairing the church fence. A boy is standing nearby for a long while.

Finally the minister asks him: "Do you want to speak with me, my son?"

"No, I'm just waiting."

"Waiting for what?"

"I want to know what a preacher says when he hits his finger with a hammer."

[self-control, swearing]

James 3:6

A minister thought he could offset his careless memory of a member of the congregation and, after the amenities, confided that he always had trouble with her name, Was it spelled with an "e" or with an "i"?

"With an 'i'," she exclaimed. "My name is 'Hill'."

[embarrassment, hell, names]

James 3:8

Usually the first screw that gets loose in a person's head is the one that controls the tongue.

[self-control, talk]

James 3:8

Meek, soft voice over the telephone: "Doctor, this is Mr. Henpeck. I'm calling for my wife. She just dislocated her jaw. If you're out this way next week or the week after, you might drop in and see her."

[husband, talk]

James 3:9

He talks in stereophonic style ... out of both sides of his mouth.

[hypocrisy, mouth]

James 3:9

Children seldom misquote us. They usually repeat word for word what we should not have said.

[imitation, repetition]

James 3:10

Be sure your brain is in gear before engaging your mouth.

[mouth]

James 3:10

A loose tongue often gets its owner into a tight place.

[speech, trouble]

James 4:1

Usually, the weaker the argument the stronger the words.

[argument]

James 4:8

Psychiatrist: "Do you have trouble making up your mind?"
Patient: "Well, yes and no."

[confusion, decisions]

James 4:10

People want the front of the bus, the back of the church, and the center of attention.

[pride]

James 4:12

Have you ever noticed, that the one who throws dirt loses ground?

[argument, speech]

James 4:14

Don't put off until tomorrow what you can do today. If you enjoy it, you can do it again tomorrow—if you're young enough.

[age, procrastination]

James 4:14

A group of atomic scientists held a convention at Las Vegas, and one of the professors spent all of his free time at the gambling tables. A couple of his colleagues were discussing their friend's weakness.
"Jonathon gambles as if there were no tomorrow," one said.
"Maybe," commented the other slowly, "he knows something."

[future, gambling]

James 4:14

A life insurance agent was speaking with a would-be client. After a long presentation of the risks of not buying the policy, the man was still a bit hesitant. "I feel that you're trying to frighten me into a hasty decision.
"Oh, no, I would never do such a thing!" the agent assured him. "I'll tell you what — Sleep on it tonight. If you wake in the morning, give me a call then and let me know your decision."

[decisions, future, procrastination]

James 4:15

A Scottish lady invited a gentleman to dinner on a particular day and he accepted with the reservation, "If I am spared and the Lord be not come."
"Well, well," she replied, "if you're dead I'll not expect you, and if the Lord does come don't bother to show because I won't be here."

[Day of the Lord, future]

James 4:15

A farmer was on his way to town to buy a cow. On the way he stopped for a brief visit with his neighbor who was a Christian.
"Where are you going today," the neighbor asked.
"I'm going to town to buy a cow."
Well actually, the Christian neighbor instructed, you ought to say, "the Lord willing, I'm going to town to buy a cow."
"What do you mean, I have the money, they have the cow, I'm going to town to buy a cow."
With that, he resumed his walk. Just before reaching the town, the farmer was mugged, his money stolen, and he was left unconscious by the side of the road. When he finally came to, and realizing all his money was gone, he started to limp back towards home.

The Christian neighbor saw him coming, and hastened to help. After hearing the story, the Christian farmer asked, "So now what are you going to do?"

"Well, the Lord willing, I'm going home."

[God's will, presumption]

James 5:9

No one so thoroughly appreciates the value of constructive criticism as the one who is giving it.

[criticism, enjoyment]

James 5:11

QUESTION: Who was the most successful doctor in the Bible?
ANSWER: Job, because he had the most patience [patients].

[patience]

James 5:12

A linguistics professor was lecturing to his class one day.
"In English," he said, "A double negative forms a positive. In some languages, though, such as Russian, a double negative is still a negative. However, there is no language wherein a double positive can form a negative."
A voice from the back of the room piped up, "Yeah, right."

[speech]

James 5:14

Actual announcement taken from a church bulletin:
"Thursday night, potluck supper. Prayer and medication to follow."

[misunderstanding]

James 5:14

There was a couple, in a small town, who had tried to have children, for several years without success. They had consulted with their local doctor. They went to the big city and consulted a specialist. After an examination and many tests, they were told that there was no reason she couldn't become pregnant.
Returning home they had a conference with their pastor at his place of business.
He was their pastor and also a part-time mechanic. They prayed and cried with him.
The pastor asked them if they were willing for him to anoint her with oil, and pray for her to become pregnant.

The couple agreed. The pastor anointed her with some 3 in one oil, which was at hand.

Nine months later, she gave birth to triplets!!

When the pastor visited her, in the hospital, she said," Pastor, I'm sure glad you didn't anoint me with WD-40!

[anointing, babies, healing]

James 5:16

The man who never makes a mistake works for the man who does.

[mistakes, work]

James 5:16

Definition of Confession for some people — What you bragged about the night before.

[boasting, confession]

James 5:16

Have you heard of the new drive-in confessional? It is called, "Toot and tell."

[confession]

James 5:16

In the middle of a sermon, a man jumped up. "Brethren!" he shouted. "I have been a miserable, contemptible sinner for years, and never knew it before tonight!"

A deacon in the nearby pew announced, "Sit down, Brother. The rest of us knew it all the time."

[confession, conscience]

James 5:16

At a revival meeting, Joe was confessing his sins. He went on for a long time. Finally the preacher stood up and asked, "Joe, Are you confessin' or braggin'?"

[boasting, confession]

1 PETER

1 Peter 1:1

A Children's Church teacher wanted to review the semester's lessons asked the class if anyone could tell him anything about the apostle Peter. A little girl raised her hand much to the gratification of her teacher.

"Come up here, Sally," he said. "I'm glad you remember your Bible lessons so well. Now tell the other boys and girls what you know about Peter."

The little girl was quite willing, and commenced, "Peter, Peter, pumpkineater, had a wife and couldn't keep her; so he put her in a ... " but before she could say "in a pumpkin shell" the Children's Church was in a uproar!

[apostle, names]

1 Peter 1:2

A pastor, teaching a communicants' class, asked a boy, "What is the Trinity?"

The boy who had a weak voice answered somewhat quietly, "Father, Son, and Holy Spirit"

Straining to hear, the pastor said, "I can't quite understand you."

To which the bright young lad replied, "You're not supposed to — it's a mystery."

[mystery, Trinity]

1 Peter 1:6

A pastor was being entertained at dinner. He explained that he was suffering with a boil on the back of his neck, and therefore had worn a soft shirt with no tie and the collar unbuttoned.

In response to his hostess' expression of sympathy, he said: "We must endure such misfortunes with patience. I assume that suffering is inflicted on us at times to try us.

The six-year-old son of the hostess listened to his remarks and then asked earnestly: "Well, if you're supposed to suffer, why don't you button your collar?"

[patience, suffering]

1 Peter 1:9

"At least we were able to save a few of these sinners," the evangelist said <u>win</u>somely.

[evangelism, puns]

1 Peter 1:18

While handing a 25 cent-off coupon to the supermarket clerk at the checkout counter, a woman inadvertently missed her hand, and the coupon slipped beneath the scale and was gone.

The checker looked distressed, so the woman said, "That's Okay, it's in coupon heaven now."

"Coupon heaven?", the checker said.

"Yes", the woman said, "That's where coupons go when they die."

"But only the redeemed ones!" said the checker.

[redemption, salvation]

1 Peter 2:2

The man who samples the Word of God occasionally never acquires much of a taste for it.

[Bible, hunger]

1 Peter 2:2

The Pastor was getting into the habit of preaching longer and longer—55 minutes and even an hour or longer. At the deacon meeting, the chairman tried to be very diplomatic in suggesting that the pastor preach shorter messages.

"But," the pastor explained, "don't you realize I'm giving you the milk of the Word?"

"Yes, Pastor," replied the chairman, "but in the future we suggest you give us condensed milk!"

[Bible, sermon. time]

1 Peter 2:10

For some people their definition of mercy is merely when there is no sermon on a hot Sunday.

[mercy, Sunday, weather]

1 Peter 2:18

Jack: I'm so nearsighted I nearly worked myself to death.

Elmer: What's being nearsighted got to do with working yourself to death?

Jack: I couldn't tell whether the boss was watching me or not, so I had to work all the time."

[laziness, work]

1 Peter 2:21

An indignant parishioner phoned her minister, "I tried to get you yesterday, but I couldn't reach you."
"Monday is my day off," said the minister.
"The devil never takes a day off," she replied.
"Since when," retorted the minister, "is the devil my example?"

[devil, example, vacation]

1 Peter 2:21

A mother was preparing pancakes for her two young sons. The boys began to argue over who would get the first pancake. Their mother saw the opportunity for a moral lesson. "If Jesus were sitting here, He would say, 'Let my brother have the first pancake. I can wait.'"
The older brother turned to his younger brother and said, "Okay, you be Jesus!"

[example, imitation]

1 Peter 3:1

When the traffic cop asked the prostrate man if he got the number of the hit-and-run driver, he said, "No, but I'd recognize my wife's laugh anywhere."

[accident, bitterness, wife]

1 Peter 3:3

A minister had been speaking with some feeling about the use of cosmetics by girls.
"The more experience I have of lipstick," he declared, warmly, "the more distasteful I find it."

[mouth, pastor, youth]

1 Peter 3:3

Little Johnnie watching his Mother put on cold cream asked, "Why do you put that on your face?" The mother replied, " It's to make myself pretty." She said, and then began removing it. Johnnie then said, " What's the matter, you giving up?"

[beauty]

1 Peter 3:3

The story is told that when the German Christian women heard that the American Christian women wore make-up, they were so upset that they cried until their tears ran down their face, off their cigars and into their beer!

[hypocrisy, sanctification]

1 Peter 3:6

She: "In most marriage ceremonies they don't use the word 'obey' anymore."
He: "Too bad, isn't it? It used to lend a little humor to the occasion."

[humor, obedience, wedding]

1 Peter 3:6

This letter-to-the-editor appeared in a local newspaper: I have read recently that the word "obey" is now being omitted from the wedding ceremony. May I ask if you think the new wording for the wedding service is retroactive?

[obedience, wedding]

1 Peter 3:6

A Children's Church teacher took her class on an outing to the zoo. A small boy stopped in front of a deer cage and asked, "What kind of animal is that?"
"What does your mother call your father every morning? Asked the teacher.
"Well, whadda you know. So that's a skunk!" answered the boy.

[animals, father, zoo]

1 Peter 3:7

If a man thinks for one minute that he understands his wife, he has it timed just about right.

[marriage, misunderstanding, time]

1 Peter 3:7

There are two periods in a man's life when he doesn't understand women — before and after the wedding.

[marriage, misunderstanding, time]

1 Peter 3:7

The so-called weaker sex is really the stronger sex because of the weakness of the stronger sex for the weaker sex.

[desire, gender]

1 Peter 3:7

My husband is a do-it-yourself guy. Every time I ask him to do something, he says, "Do it yourself."

[selfish]

1 Peter 3:7

A man walking along a California beach was deep in prayer.
Suddenly the sky clouded above his head and in a booming voice the Lord said,
"Because you have tried to be faithful to me in all ways, I will grant you one wish."
The man said, "Build a bridge to Hawaii so I can drive over anytime I want."
The Lord said, "Your request is very materialistic. Think of the enormous challenges for that kind of undertaking. The supports required to reach the bottom of the Pacific! The concrete and steel it would take! It will nearly exhaust several natural resources. I can do it, but it is hard for me to justify your desire for worldly things. Take a little more time and think of something that would honor and glorify me."
The man thought about it for a long time. Finally he said, "Lord, I wish that I could understand my wife! I want to know how she feels inside, what she's thinking when she gives me the silent treatment, why she cries, what she means when she says 'nothing's wrong', and how I can make a woman truly happy."
The Lord replied, "You want two lanes or four on that bridge?"

[understanding, wife]

1 Peter 3:7

Marriage—an investment that pays you dividends if you pay interest.

[consequences, marriage]

1 Peter 3:7

Tony attended the men's prayer breakfast and heard a visiting psychologist speak on the topic of showing appreciation to the important people in one's life. Tony decided to start with his wife, so after work that night, he went to the shopping mall, where he bought a dozen long-stemmed roses, a box of chocolates, and a pair of earrings. He chortled with self-satisfaction as he contemplated surprising his wife, showing her how much he appreciated her.

He stood at the front door with the roses in his right hand, the gaily wrapped box of candy under his arm, and an open jewelry box displaying the earrings in his left hand. With an elbow he rang the doorbell. His wife came to the door, opened it, and stared at him for a long minute. Suddenly she burst into tears.

"Sweetheart, what's wrong?" asked the bewildered husband.

"It's been the worst day of my life," she answered. "First, Jimmy tried to flush his diaper down the toilet. Then Eric melted his plastic airplane in the oven. Then the dishwasher got clogged and overflowed all over the kitchen floor. Then Brittany came home from school with a note from the teacher saying that she beat up a boy in her class. And now you come home drunk!"

[desire, drinking, husband, marriage]

1 Peter 3:7

One teen-age boy to another: "My Dad had a long talk with me about girls last night. He doesn't know anything about them, either."

[gender, understanding]

1 Peter 3:7

While attending a marriage seminar on communication, Tom and his wife Peg listened to the instructor declare, "It is essential that husbands and wives know the things that are important to each other."

He addressed the men, "Can you describe your wife's favorite flower?"

Tom leaned over, touched his wife's arm gently and whispered, "Pillsbury All-Purpose, isn't it?"

The rest of the story is not pleasant.

[communication, misunderstanding]

1 Peter 3:8

Neighbor: "Why did you get rid of your waterbed?"

Woman: "My husband and I were drifting apart."

[dissatisfaction, divorce]

1 Peter 3:15

Joe: "Say, what do you believe about God?"

Bill: "I believe what my church believes."

Joe: "What does your church believe?"

Bill: "My church believes what I believe."

Joe: "What do you and your church believe?"

Bill: "We both believe the same thing."

[church, doctrine]

1 Peter 3:16

Little girl's definition of conscience: "Something that makes you tell your mother what you did before your brother or sister does."

[conscience]

1 Peter 3:21

The Real Problem With Baptismal Regeneration

A Mother decided it was time that her three sons get baptized. So, after weeks of suitable instruction she felt that it was time. One bright Sunday morning they were on their way to church where the three boys, 8, 9, and 11, were to have their sins washed away.

The mother noticed that her 9 year old seemed to be particularly lost in thought so she asked him what was on his mind.

"Mom, I want to go first." He replied.

"Why do you want to first?" she asked her son with a smile.

"Because," he began with a pause in his voice, "I really don't want to be baptized in water that has all of my brother's sins floating around in it."

[baptism, sin]

1 Peter 4:5

See Acts 10:42.

1 Peter 4:5

On the streets of the modern city there are only 2 kinds of pedestrians—"the quick and the dead." (KJV)

[danger, death, driving]

1 Peter 4:7

I'm always suspicious of any preacher who declares that because of the 'signs of the time' the end is near — then asks you to sign a five-year Building Fund pledge!

[future]

1 Peter 4:9

Our society's two biggest liars: The guest who keeps saying he must be going and the host who asks, "What's your hurry?"

[hospitality, liars]

1 Peter 5:5

After church, a woman shook the pastor's hand at the door and went on and on in her praise. "That sermon," she exclaimed, "was one of the most wonderful I've ever heard!"

The humble pastor couldn't accept such a great compliment. "Oh, it really wasn't me," he said, "It was all the Lord."

"Oh, no," she quickly assured him, "it wasn't THAT good."

[compliment, humility, sermon]

1 Peter 5:6

He strutted on to the platform, totally confident that he would amaze the audience with his powers of oratory, his homiletical genius, plus his mastery of vocabulary and syntax.

But the sermon bounced back in his face. The people were bored and unmoved. He felt humiliated. He came back to the parsonage as low as a snake's belly.

His wife put it this way: "If you went up to the pulpit the way you came down from the pulpit, you would have come down the way you went up."

[humility, preaching]

1 Peter 5:8

A minister of a church gave as his text: "The devil as a roaring lion goeth about seeking those whom he may devour," and then added "I will be visiting Thursday night. Please come and go with me."

[devil, visitation]

1 Peter 5:8

Say what you will about the devil; he sure is a hustler.

[busy, devil]

1 Peter 5:12

The janitor had dropped a box of tacks in front of the pulpit of the church and the pastor noticed.

"Now what if you should miss picking up all of those tacks and I should step on one during my sermon?" the aggravated minister asked.

"Sir," replied the janitor, "I bet that's one point you wouldn't linger on."

[sermon, timing]

2 PETER

2 Peter 1:7

"I'd like to die by poison."

"I'd like to be killed by kindness."

"It's easier to get poison."

[kindness]

2 Peter 1:20

See John 16:13.

2 Peter 1:20

There was a guy who owned his own business. He sold plastics to many different companies. One day one of his warehouses burnt to the ground. This led to many orders being cancelled and a loss of customers. The insurance company was not going to cover the damage. This guy was in real trouble. He could lose everything.

Well, the guy decided to see his minister. He said to the minister, "I need help! My warehouse burnt to the ground, my product is all gone, my customers are leaving, and I am losing everything!"

The minister told him, "You can find all the answers to your problems in the Bible."

The guy asked, "Where should I start?" The minister answered, "If you do not know where to look, just open the book and place your finger on the page, and start right there. Sooner or later you will find your answers."

Well, a few months later the minister ran into the individual. It was obvious the individual had become very successful. He had a new car, new clothes, several rings and chains.

The guy walks over to the minister and says, "Thank you. The answers I found turned my life around!" The minister was curious and said, "In what passage did you find your answers?"

The man says, "I did just what you said. I opened the Bible to a spot, looked down, and found my answer staring me right in the face — Chapter 11."

[guidance, success]

2 Peter 1:21

See The Bible General: Old and New Testament.

2 Peter 2:1

You have to wonder about humans beings, they think God is dead and Elvis is still alive.

[confusion, deception]

2 Peter 2:1

Men do not usually reject the Bible because it contradicts itself, but because it contradicts them.

[conviction, rejection]

2 Peter 2:2

Before performing a child baptism, the pastor approached the young father and said solemnly, "Baptism is a serious step. Are you prepared for it?"
"I think so," the man replied. "My wife has made appetizers and we have a caterer coming to provide plenty of cookies and cakes for all of our guests."
"I don't mean that," the priest responded. "I mean, are you prepared spiritually?"
"Oh, sure," came the reply. "I've got a keg of beer and a case of whiskey."

[baptism, drinking]

2 Peter 2:16

Watching her mother as she tried on her new fur coat, the young daughter said unhappily, "Mom, do you realize some poor dumb beast suffered so you could have that?"
The woman shot her an angry look, "How dare you talk about your father like that!"

[marriage, respect, suffering]

2 Peter 3:8

A man was walking through a forest pondering life. He walked, pondered, walked, and pondered. He felt very close to nature and even close to God. He felt so close to God that he felt if he spoke God would listen.
So he asked, "God, are you listening?"
And God replied, "Yes my son, I am here."
The man stopped and pondered some more.
He looked towards the sky and said, "God, what is a million years to you?"
God replied, "Well my son, a million years to you is like a second to me."
So the man continued to walk and to ponder... walk and ponder... Then he looked to the sky again and said, "God, what is a million dollars to you?"
And God replied, "My son, my son...a penny to me is like a million dollars to you. It means almost nothing to me. It does not even have a value it is so little."

The man looked down, pondered a bit and then looked up to the sky and said, "God, can I have a million dollars?"
And God replied, "In a second."

[God, money, time]

2 Peter 3:9-10

Tactless witness: "Did you hear that God is very angry with the sinfulness of man and is going to destroy all of the wicked? But before he does, he has sent a very special letter to all the good and righteous people. Do you know what the letter says?"
Stunned man: "No, what?"
Tactless witness: "You mean you didn't get one?"

[evangelism, wicked]

2 Peter 3:10

How the Media Will Cover the Apocalypse:
USA Today: WE'RE DEAD.
The Wall Street Journal: DOW JONES PLUMMETS AS WORLD ENDS.
National Enquirer: O.J. AND NICOLE, TOGETHER AGAIN?
Playboy: GIRLS OF THE APOCALYPSE.
Microsoft Systems Journal: APPLE LOSES MARKET SHARE.
Victoria's Secret Catalog: OUR FINAL SALE
Sports Illustrated: GAME OVER.
Wired: THE LAST NEW THING.
Rolling Stone: THE GRATEFUL DEAD REUNION TOUR.
Readers Digest: 'BYE.
Discover Magazine: HOW WILL THE EXTINCTION OF ALL LIFE AS WE KNOW IT AFFECT THE WAY WE VIEW THE COSMOS?
TV Guide: DEATH AND DAMNATION: NIELSON RATINGS SOAR!
Lady's Home Journal: LOSE 10 LBS BY JUDGMENT DAY WITH OUR NEW "ARMAGEDDON" DIET!
America Online: SYSTEM TEMPORARILY DOWN. TRY CALLING BACK IN 15 MINUTES.
Inc. magazine: TEN WAYS YOU CAN PROFIT FROM THE APOCALYPSE.
Microsoft's Web Site: If you didn't experience the rapture, download software patch RAPT777.EXE.

[apocalypse]

2 Peter 3:16

A 7-year old boy proudly tells his father: "I finally know what the Bible means from the first letter to the last!" Surprised the father replied: "What

449

do you mean, you "know" what the Bible means? What does it mean?"
"That's easy, dad ... It stands for Basic Instructions Before Leaving Earth."

[Bible, instruction]

1 JOHN

1 John 1:9

I go to a Congregational church that's so democratic, last week the minister said, "O Lord, we ask Thy forgiveness — 48 to 33 with 12 abstentions!"

[church, denominations, forgiveness]

1 John 1:9

A Children's Church teacher had just concluded her lesson and wanted to make sure she had made her point. She said, "Can anyone tell me what you must do before you can obtain forgiveness of sin?"
There was a short interval of silence and then from the back of the room, a small boy spoke up. "Sin," he said.

[sin]

1 John 2:9

Pious Lydia was kneeling down saying her prayers when her four-year-old brother sneaked up behind her and pulled her hair. "Pardon me, God," said Lydia. "I'll be right back after I kill my brother"

[murder, prayer]

1 John 3:8

The Children's Church girl asked her friend, "Do you really think there's a devil?
The other responded, "It'll probably turn out like Santa Claus — it'll probably be my father."

[deception, devil]

1 John 3:8

A minister, in administering the confirmation rites for an elderly new member, asked, "Do you repent of the devil and all of his ways?"
The member replied, "I'm sorry but in my position, I can't afford to antagonize anyone."

[compromise, doctrine, membership]

1 John 4:18

A lady was getting married and she was very apprehensive about her honeymoon. Some of her friends in the church asked to provide the cake.

They called the bakery and asked them to inscribe the wedding cake with the statement found in 1 John 4:18 which reads "There is no fear in love, but perfect love casts out fear." But the person taking the message didn't hear the 1 before John. At the wedding the cake just read: John 4:18 "For you have had 5 husbands and the one you have now is not your husband ..."

[mistake, wedding]

1 John 5:1

A small boy sat with his mother in church, listening to a sermon titled, "What is a Christian?" The minister punctuated his talk at several key intervals by asking, "What is a Christian?" Each time, he pounded his fist on the pulpit for emphasis.

At one point, the lad whispered to his mother, "Mama, do you know? Do you know what a Christian is?"

"Yes, dear," replied the mother. "Now try to sit still and listen."

As the minister was wrapping up the sermon, once again he thundered, "What is a Christian?" and pounded especially hard on the pulpit. At that, the boy jumped up and cried, "Tell him, Mama, tell him!"

[answer, questions]

1 John 5:7

The Coach's Prayer

Thrilled when his team won the World Cup, the goalie decided to throw a party. And as a special honor, he asked the team's coach to say grace. Clearing his throat, the coach rose and offered a small prayer, which he concluded by saying, "...we thank you, Lord, in the name of the Father, the Son and the goalie host."

[prayer, Trinity]

1 John 5:14

A five-year-old said grace at family dinner one night. "Dear God, thank you for these pancakes." When he concluded, his parents asked him why he thanked God for pancakes when they were having chicken.

He smiled and said, "I thought I'd see if He was paying attention tonight."

[God]

2 JOHN

2 John

At a midnight watch service the pastor was conducting a Bible quiz. He asked the question, "Who are the three Johns in the Scripture?"
One eager ten-year-old volunteered the ANSWER: "First, Second, and Third John."

[names, numbers]

3 JOHN

3 John 1:10

The minister's little six-year-old girl had been so naughty during the week, that her mother decided to give her the worst kind of punishment. She told her she couldn't go to the Children's Church Picnic on Saturday.
When the day came, her mother felt she had been too harsh and changed her mind.
When she told the little girl she could go to the picnic, the child's reaction was one of gloom and unhappiness.
"What's the matter? I thought you'd be glad to go to the picnic." Her mother said.
"It's too late!" the little girl said. "I've already prayed for rain!"

OR

The minister of a church discovered at the last minute that he hadn't invited a long time member, a little old lady, to come to his garden party and called her up and asked her to come.
"Its no use," she informed him. "I've already prayed for rain."

[prayer, revenge, weather]

3 John 1:10

WAYS TO KNOW YOU ARE IN THE WRONG CHURCH
• The staff consists of Senior Pastor, Associate Pastor, and Socio-Pastor.
• They have ATM machines in the lobby.
• No cover charge, but communion is a two drink minimum.
• Services are B.Y.O.S. (Bring Your Own Snakes)
• They have karaoke worship time.
• The guy that takes the minutes in business meeting votes against everything because he can't spell unanimous.
• The only song the church organist knows is Inna-Gadda-Da-Vida.
• The church bus has gun racks.
• The Bible they use is the "Dr. Seuss" version.
• The choir wears leather robes.
• When you go in ushers ask you, "Do you want smoking or non-smoking?"

[church]

3 John 1:12

Two worldly men saw elderly Demetrius coming down the street. One man pointed toward him.
"I'll bet you can't mention anybody that old Demetrius can't find something good to say about."
The other fellow took up the bet.
"Good morning, Demetrius," he said politely. "And what do you think about the devil?"
Demetrius tilted his head to one side. "Well," he answered, "there is one thing about him that I've noticed. He is always on the job."

[devil, encouragement]

3 John 1:15

QUESTION: How do we know that the author of Third John raised vegetables?
ANSWER: Because he said. "Peas be upon you." (Peace be upon you).

[peace, vegetables]

JUDE

Jude 1:9

Bible study leader: "Can anyone tell me what is an archangel?"
New convert: "I guess it was an angel who came out of the ark."

[angels]

Jude 1:23

QUESTION: If you smoke does that mean you'll go to hell?
ANSWER: Not necessarily, though it makes you smell like you've been there!

[hell, smoking]

Jude 1:23

The other day a fellow asked his pastor, "Can I smoke and still get to heaven?"
With a grin on his face the pastor replied, "Sure, and if you smoke you might get there a lot sooner."

[heaven, smoking]

REVELATION

Revelation 1:1

Apocalypse — An important event but one for which Hallmark does not yet have a card.

[apocalypse]

Revelation 1:8

Alpha and Omega — The fraternity that Christ belonged to.

[eternity, fraternity]

Revelation 2:4

See Mark 12:30.

Revelation 2:5

Pastor: "Brethren, we must do something to remedy the status quo."
Deacon: "Pastor, what is 'the status quo.'"
Pastor: "That, brother, is Latin for the mess we're in."

[mess]

Revelation 2:14

See 3 John :10.

Revelation 3:15-16

Did you hear about the Indian chief named Running Water? He has two daughters, Hot and Cold, and a son named Luke.

[names, water]

Revelation 3:16

As the junior high boys in our youth ministry at church were studying the book of Revelation, one of them, having just read about the church of Laodicea, was heard to exclaim "I wonder how warm Luke was."

[names]

Revelation 3:19

It is said that St. Teresa of Avila was crossing an icy stream when her donkey stumbled and pitched her into the water. She complained to God for the manner in which He had treated a friend.

God answered that suffering was given by God only to His friends.

Teresa answered testily, "Well, maybe that's why You have so few."

[friend, God, respect]

Revelation 3:20

See Genesis 3:10.

Revelation 3:25

A minister prayed to God in turmoil over the sinful state of his city, "Lord, most of the people in the city have no interest in following you. And the rest of us are having a hard time holding on!"

God heard the prayer and sent down an angel to investigate the claim. Later the angel reported back that, indeed, things were much worse than the minister indicated. 99% of the city was more sinful than Sodom and Gomorrah, and the remaining faithful 1% were struggling.

God considered what to do for those who were staying true to the faith. Finally God decided to send a letter of encouragement to the faithful few. And do you know what the letter said?

......[pause]

Oh, I'm sorry. Would you like to read my copy?

[faithfulness]

Revelation 4:10

See Zechariah 9:16.

Revelation 5:8

The little girl was impressed by the sermon describing the attractions of heaven. Some time later she told her mother: "I know now that cats go to heaven."

Her mother, however, replied that she was afraid the girl had misunderstood and proceeded to explain that since animals do not have souls they could hardly be expected to go to heaven.

"Then where," the little girl inquired, "do the angels get strings for their harps.

[angels, animals, heaven]

Revelation 5:8

Mary: "Mom, what do the angels do in heaven?"

Mother: "Oh, I guess they sing and play their harps."

Mary: "How come? Don't they have internet or smartphones?"

[angels, entertainment]

Revelation 6:11

The Gown with the Split Down the Back

I was sittin' here mindin' my business,
Kinda lettin' my mind go slack,
When in comes a nurse with a bright, sunny smile.
And a gown that was split down the back.

"Take a shower," she said, "and get ready,
And then jump into this sack."
What she was really talkin' about
Was the gown with the split down the back.

"They're coming to do some tests," she said
They're gonna stretch me out on a rack,
With nothin' twixt me and the cold, cruel world,
But a gown that is split down the back!

It only comes to the knees in the front,
In the sides there is also a lack,
But by far the greatest shortcoming
Is that bloomin' split down the back.

Whoever designed this garment,
For humor had a great knack.
But I fail to see anything funny
'Bout a gown that is split down the back.

I hear them coming to get me,
The wheels going clickety-clack.
I'll ride through the halls on a table,
In a gown with a split down the back!

When I get to Heaven I'll feel great
When my robe is still white and not black
The only thing I will ask is, "Please,
Give me one with no split down the back."

[clothing, heaven]

Revelation 7:1

See Isaiah 11:12.

Revelation 8:1

QUESTION: Are there any preachers in Heaven?
ANSWER: "No because in Revelation it says ... 'there was silence in heaven about the space of half an hour.'"

[heaven, silence]

Revelation 8:1

QUESTION: Are there any women in Heaven?
ANSWER: "... there was silence in heaven about the space of half an hour."

[heaven, silence, women]

Revelation 9:2

There was a certain church where the people engaged in what might be called, "responsive praying." Someone in the congregation would spontaneously respond to each request made in a public prayer.
The pastor stood to pray one morning, caught up in the reality of the judgment day. On the front row, as usual, the church treasurer was sound asleep.
"We're going to pick up the phone and call Paris, and they are going to say, 'It's dark over here!'"
"Lord, deliver us!" cried another deacon.
"Then we're going to pick up the phone and call Moscow, and they are going to say, 'It's dark over here!'"
The church treasurer, silent up until this time, uncontrollably cried, "Lord! Lord! What a phone bill!"

[Day of the Lord, money, prayer]

Revelation 12:9

Two little girls had a violent tussle with each other and the mother of one of them said in reprimand to her daughter: "It was Satan who suggested to you to pull your friend's hair."
"I shouldn't be surprised," said the little girl. "But kicking her in the shins was entirely my own idea."

[fighting, Satan]

Revelation 12:9

Two girls were discussing their fathers. One, boasting, said, "My daddy is a doctor."
"That's nothing," retorted the other. "My daddy is a civil serpent."

[vocation]

Revelation 12:9

See Revelation 20:2.

Revelation 13:18

The Number of the Beast
We all know that 666 is the Number of the Beast. But did you know:

$665.95......................Retail price of the Beast
$699.25......................Price of the Beast plus 5% sales tax
$769.95......................Price of the Beast with all accessories and replacement soul
$656.66......................Wal-Mart price of the Beast
$646.66......................Next week's Wal-Mart price of the Beast
00666.........................Zip code of the Beast
1-666 ....Area code of the Beast
1-900-666-0666 ...... Live Beasts! Call Now! Only $6.66/minute. One-on-one pacts! Call Now! Only 6.66/minute. Over 18 only please.
660.............................Approximate number of the Beast
DCLXVI....................Roman numeral of the Beast
666.0000...................Number of the High Precision Beast
0.666 ....Number of the Millibeast
/ 666 ....Beast Common Denominator
666 ^ (-1).................Imaginary number of the Beast
1010011010.............Binary of the Beast
Phillips 666..............Gasoline of the Beast
666k..........................Retirement plan of the Beast
$6.66 9/10.................Price of a Beast gasoline
Route 666...............Highway of the Beast
666° F....................Oven temperature for roast Beast
66.6° C .... Temperature of the Beast
6.66%.......................5 year CD rate at First Beast National Bank, $666 minimum deposit.
I66686.....................CPU of the Beast
6.6.6 ....Software Version of the Beast
666 .... Dewey call number of the Beast
Hell in A Major (op.66, no.6) ......Etude of the Beast
HL666 .... LC call number of the Beast
666@hell.gov.......... E-mail of the Beast
http://666.hell.org/~beast ....Home page of the beast
666i ....BMW of the Beast
DSM-666..................Diagnostic and Statistical Manual of the Beast
668.............................Next-door neighbor of the Beast

```
666 mg......................Recommended Minimum Daily Requirement of Beast
Lotus 6-6-6...............Spreadsheet of the Beast
Word 6.66...............Word Processor of the Beast
6 h. 66 min..............Beast Standard Time (BST)
6,6,6 .........................Exact fertilizer needed to make the Beast bloom
1666 .........................The Beast "redecorates" London (The year of the great
fire of London)
"thickth, thickth, thickth" .............A person with a lisp referring to the Beast
666 6ᵗʰ AVE #666 .......................... Mailing address of the Beast
Boeing 666.................."A Jet for the Beast Age"
Beverly Hills 666........Beast's favorite TV show
6/6/66..........................Birth date of the Beast
666-66-6666...............Social Security number of the Beast
6666............................PIN of the Beast
25.806975....................Square root of the Beast
660...............................Approximate number of the Beast
Motel 666.....................Beast Western
666 .............................The number that all VCR clocks flash in HELL
6.66% .........................% of fat of "lean" Beast prior to cooking
DCLXVI ......................Roman Numeral of the Beast
1010011010 .................Binary number of the Beast
666 mg .........................Recommended daily requirement of the Beast
1-666 ...........................Area Code of the Beast
Windows 96 ver.666..........OS of the Beast
"Hell" v.6 n.66, pp. 6-66 ...Citation of the Beast
```

[numbers, Satan]

Revelation 14:2

A college bulletin board read: "The end of the world has been postponed until next semester due to a shortage of harps and trumpets."

[future]

Revelation 14:2

Did you hear about the dead angel? He died of harp failure.

[angel]

Revelation 14:13

A young student's version of his nightly prayer:
Now I lay me down to rest, I pray the Lord I pass the test. If I should die before I wake, That's one less test I'll have to take!

[death, student, study]

Revelation 16:13

Frogs have it easy; they can eat what bugs them.

[food, insects]

Revelation 16:16

Ad in newspaper: Armageddon — The Earth's Last War — How and Where It Will Be Fought At the First Baptist Church.

[Baptist, fighting, warning]

Revelation 16:16

As St. John said after his dream, "I'm 'agettin' [Armageddon] out of here!"

[warning]

Revelation 16:16

Armageddon — The last day you can redeem your airline points!

[Day of the Lord, flying]

Revelation 19:20

As a patient came slowly out of the anesthetic he said, "Why are the blinds drawn, doctor?"
The doctor replied calmly, "There's a fire raging across the street and we didn't want you to think the operation was a failure."

[doctor, failure]

Revelation 20:2

QUESTION: Where is constipation mentioned four times in the Bible?
ANSWER: Elijah said, "Nothing will move me"; David is on the throne for 40 years; Moses took 2 tablets; and finally, Satan is bound.

[sickness]

Revelation 20:2

See Revelation 12:9.

Revelation 20:3

Four philosophers were discussing world salvation. Commented one, "Now if we could just eliminate all profanity, this would be a better world."
Opined another, "If we could eliminate all liquor, we would have a better world."
Remarked a third, "If we could get rid of those and all other sinful things, we would have the millennium."

At which point the fourth philosopher growled, "Yes, and then we would have THAT to put up with!"

[pessimist, salvation]

Revelation 20:10

The last labor problem of all time. When Satan gets "fired!"

[fire, Satan, work]

Revelation 20:10

One day while walking down the street a highly successful executive woman was tragically hit by a bus and she died. Her soul arrived up in heaven where she was met at the Pearly Gates by St. Peter himself. "Welcome to Heaven," said St. Peter. "Before you get settled in though, it seems we have a problem. You see, strangely enough, we've never once had an executive make it this far and we're not really sure what to do with you."
"No problem, just let me in." said the woman.
"Well, I'd like to, but I have higher orders. What we're going to do is let you have a day in Hell and a day in Heaven and then you can choose whichever one you want to spend an eternity in."
"Actually, I think I've made up my mind ... I prefer to stay in Heaven", said the woman.
"Sorry, we have rules ..." And with that St. Peter put the executive in an elevator and it went down-down-down to hell. The doors opened and she found herself stepping out onto the putting green of a beautiful golf course. In the distance was a country club and standing in front of her were all her friends — fellow executives that she had worked with and they were all dressed in evening gowns and cheering for her. They ran up and kissed her on both cheeks and they talked about old times. They played an excellent round of golf and at night went to the country club where she enjoyed an excellent steak and lobster dinner. She met the Devil who was actually a really nice guy (kinda cute) and she had a great time telling jokes and dancing. She was having such a good time that before she knew it, it was time to leave. Everybody shook her hand and waved good- bye as she got on the elevator.
The elevator went up-up-up and opened back up at the Pearly Gates and found St. Peter waiting for her. "Now it's time to spend a day in heaven," he said.
So she spent the next 24 hours lounging around on clouds and playing the harp and singing. She had a great time and before she knew it her 24 hours were up and St. Peter came and got her.
"So, you've spent a day in hell and you've spent a day in heaven. Now you must choose your eternity," he said.

The woman paused for a second and then replied, "Well, I never thought I'd say this, I mean, Heaven has been really great and all, but I think I had a better time in Hell."

So St. Peter escorted her to the elevator and again she went down-down-down back to Hell. When the doors of the elevator opened she found herself standing in a desolate wasteland covered in garbage and filth. She saw her friends were dressed in rags and were picking up the garbage and putting it in sacks. The Devil came up to her and put his arm around her. "I don't understand," stammered the woman, "yesterday I was here and there was a golf course and a country club and we ate lobster and we danced and had a great time. Now all there is a wasteland of garbage and all my friends look miserable."

The Devil looked at her and smiled. "Yesterday we were recruiting you; today you're staff."

[heaven, hell, reality]

Revelation 20:10

Satan — An angel who has and will get "fired".

[Satan]

Revelation 20:14

"Wonder if I'll drink in the next world."
"Don't know. But I'm sure you'll smoke."

[drink, hell]

Revelation 20:14

Most Texans don't exactly believe in Heaven or Hell. When they die, they figure they either go to Dallas or Alaska.

[heaven, hell]

Revelation 20:14

"How will you spend eternity — Smoking or Non-smoking?"

[eternity, heaven, hell, smoking]

Revelation 20:14

The Texan was one of those bragging, native-born, "Everything's bigger & better" types. He died, and, arriving at the Pearly Gates, was being given the obligatory celestial tour by none other than St. Peter himself.

St. Peter shows him a magnificent canyon scene with a spectacular sunset view. The Texan says, "Hey, that's nearly as nice as one we've got in the Panhandle of Texas."

"Oh, good grief," exclaims St. Peter, "follow me!" He takes him to a meadow overspread with beautiful wildflowers. "Pretty, says Tex, "almost as pretty as the bluebonnets in South Central Texas in the springtime." Becoming slightly agitated, St. Pete takes him to a forest of tall, stately pine trees. "Ah, I'm starting to feel at home now, these are almost as tall as the ones in East Texas!"

Losing all composure, St. Pete shouts, "All right, that does it! Step over this way!" He takes him to a huge trap door, opens it, and the fires of hell can be seen, roaring loudly; and the stench of sulfur is almost overwhelming. "Now then," he says, "do you have anything like [that] in Texas?"

"Well...no," replies Tex, "but we've got a fella' down in Houston who'll put that out for you."

[boasting, fire, heaven]

Revelation 20:14

At Southampton's fashionable St. Andrew's Dune Church, after a week of steaming hot weather, guest minister Rev. William Henry Wagner told the congregation he would preach the shortest sermon ever. It consisted of the following words: "If you think it's hot here — just wait!"

[sermon, size]

Revelation 20:15

A curious fellow died one day and found himself waiting in the long line of judgment. As he stood there he noticed that some souls were allowed to march right through the pearly gates into heaven. Others, though, were led over to Satan who threw them into the burning pit. But every so often, instead of hurling a poor soul into the fire, Satan would toss a soul off to one side into a small pile.

After watching Satan do this several times, the fellow's curiosity got the best of him. So he strolled over and asked Satan what he was doing.

"Excuse me, Prince of Darkness," he said. "I'm waiting in line for judgment, but I couldn't help wondering, why are you tossing those people aside instead of flinging them into the fires of hell with the others?"

"Ah, those..." Satan said with a groan. "They're all from Seattle, they're too wet to burn."

[Satan, hell]

Revelation 20:15

A college drama group presented a play in which one character would stand on a trapdoor and announce, "I descend into hell!" A stagehand below would then pull a rope, the trapdoor would open, and the character would plunge through. The play was well received.

When the actor playing the part became ill, another actor who was quite overweight took his place. When the new actor announced, "I descend into hell!" the stagehand pulled the rope, and the actor began his plunge, but became hopelessly stuck. No amount of tugging on the rope could make him descend.

Finally one student in the balcony jumped up and yelled:

"Hallelujah! Hell is full!"

[hell]

Revelation 21:4

Looking at my bald head makes me think of heaven — there is no parting there!

[heaven]

Revelation 21:8

A minister who was very fond of pure, hot horseradish always kept a bottle of it on his dining room table. He offered some to a guest, who took a big swallow.

When the guest finally was able to speak, he gasped, "I've heard many preach hellfire, but you are the first one I've met who passed out a sample of it."

[fire, food, hell]

Revelation 21:8

The angel was taunting the devil.

"Hey devil," it said, "we're going to be putting on a great show up here later. Too bad you can't come."

"Yeah?" said the devil. "And where are you gonna get actors and actresses?"

[angel, devil, salvation, vocation]

Revelation 21:8

A small girl was impressed by two things: how difficult it was not to tell a falsehood from time to time, and how many people were always telling her that it's a sin to tell a lie. So she decided to investigate, starting with her father. "Dad," she asked, "have you ever told a lie?"

Dad: "Well it wouldn't be true to say I've never lied."

Girl: "How about Mom?"

Dad: "Well, yes when she felt the truth would hurt, I guess she lied."

Girl: "How about Grandpa?"

Dad: "I guess he's like the rest of us. If pressed he . . "

Girl (interrupting): "Dad, you know, it must be terribly lonesome up in Heaven — with nobody there but God and George Washington."

[lying, salvation]

Revelation 21:9-27

A three-year-old said to his father when it was raining, "I don't think Heaven's such a great place after all."

"Why not?" asked his father.

"Because," he answered, "the floor is all full of holes and lets the water through."

[heaven, weather]

Revelation 21:10-14

Mother: What are you drawing, Junior?

Junior: A picture of heaven.

Mother: But you can't do that. No one knows what heaven looks like.

Junior: They will after I'm finished.

[art, heaven]

Revelation 21:21

There once was a rich man who was near death. He was very grieved because he had worked so hard for his money and he wanted to be able to take it with him to heaven. So he began to pray that he might be able to take some of his wealth with him.

An angel heard his plea and appeared to him. "Sorry, but you can't take your wealth with you."

The man begged the angel to speak to God to see if He might bend the rules. The man continued to pray that his wealth could follow him.

The angel reappeared and informed the man that God had decided to allow him to take one suitcase with him. Overjoyed, the man gathered his largest suitcase and filled it with pure gold bars and placed it beside his bed.

Soon afterward he died and showed up at the Gates of Heaven to greet St. Peter. St. Peter, seeing the suitcase, said, "Hold on, you can't bring that in here!"

The man explained to St. Peter that he had permission and asked him to verify his story with the Lord.

Sure enough, St. Peter checked, came back and said, "You're right. You are allowed one carry-on bag, but I'm supposed to check its contents before letting it through."

St. Peter opened the suitcase to inspect the worldly items that the man found too precious to leave behind and exclaimed, "You brought pavement?"

[heaven, money]

Revelation 21:27

A politician was approached by an irate voter who was known in the community to be a swindler. He insulted the man running for office, "I wouldn't vote for you if you were St. Peter himself."

"If I were St. Peter," snapped back the candidate, "you couldn't vote for me. You wouldn't be in my district!"

[insult, politics]

Revelation 22:14-15

Almost everyone is in favor of going to heaven, but too many people are hoping they'll live long enough to see an easing of the entrance requirements.

[heaven, salvation]

Revelation 22:14-15

See Jude 1:23.

Revelation 22:15

A small country church was having a "baptizing" in a river on a cold January day. A revival meeting had just concluded. The preacher asked one baptismal candidate, "Is the water cold?"

"Naw!" he replied.

One of the deacons hearing this shouted: "Dip him again preacher, he's still lyin'!"

[baptism, lying]

Revelation 22:15

The minister was preaching to the young congregation. "One boy chose the wicked path of crime and ended in a cell — while the other became a great lawyer. Now, what can the difference be between those two brothers who embarked upon life's stormy seas?"

"Easy," said Herman. "One got caught."

[lawyer, prison]

Revelation 22:20

A new preacher had just begun his sermon. He was a little nervous and about ten minutes into the talk his mind went blank. He remembered what they had taught him in seminary when a situation like this would arise—repeat your last point. Often this would help you remember what is coming next. So he thought he would give it a try.

"Behold, I come quickly," he said. Still his mind was blank. He thought he would try it again. "Behold I come quickly." Still nothing.

He tried it one more time with such force he fell forward, knocking the pulpit to one side, tripping over a flower pot and falling into the lap of a little old lady in the front row.

The young preacher apologized and tried to explain what happened.

"That's all right, young man," said the little old lady. "It was my fault. I should have gotten out of the way. You told me three times you were coming!"

[forgetfulness, sermon]

Topical Index

Art Matt 6:9; Luke 2:16; John 5:37; Rev 21:8

Atheist Gen 28:12; Ps 14:1; 53:1; Acts 2:3; 20:7; 26:28; Rom 1:25; 1 Cor 15:35; Heb 9:27

Attributes of God (see also God) Exod 20:4; Deut 6:4; Job 42:2-3; Ps 139:7-12; 1 Tim 1:17

Babies/Baby Gen 1:28; Job 3:1; Isa 9:6; Jer 20:18; Matt 2:14; 8:22; Luke 2:41; Acts 8:38; 1 Cor 15:51; Eph 1:5; Titus 1:6; James 5:14

Babysitter 1 Sam 17:14,23; Luke 2:41; Titus 1:6

Babylon Isa 13:1

Bachelor 1 Cor 7:24,32,35,36

Backsliding Jer 3:22

Baptism Hag 1:1; Matt 26:27; Mark 1:8; 16:16; John 12:21; Acts 2:38; 8:38; 16:33; 1 Cor 1:13; Phil 4:18; 1 Pet 3:21; 2 Pet 2:1; Rev 22:15

Baptist Gen 13:11; Hag 1:1; John 2:9; Acts 8:36,38; Eph 3:20; 5:18; 2 Tim 4:10; Rev 16:16

Beatitudes Matt 5:1-12; 5:1; Mark 10:16; Luke 6:20

Beauty Gen 8:18; Prov 31:30; SofS 4:2; 6:5-7; Isa 3:16; 38:5; 1 Tim 2:9; 1 Pet 3:3

Behavior Gen 8:1

Betting 1 Sam 17:50

Bible/Scripture Deut 17:19; Judg 6:12; Ps 1:2; 19:7-10; 81:10; 103:1; The Bible; Matthew; Matt 16:24; Luke 2:47; 22:40; John 20:4; Rom 3:23; Corinthians; 1 Cor 15:51; Eph 6:17; 1 Tim 4:13; 2 Tim 3:16,16-17; 4:13; 1 Pet 2:2; 2 Pet 3:16

Bigamy (see also Polygamy) Luke 16:13; 1 Cor 7:33; 1 Tim 3:2; 4:13; 2 Tim 2:15; Heb 13:4

Birth Gen 21:2; 25:21-22, 24; Jer 7:26; Luke 2:7; John 1:46

Birth Control Gen 1:28; 5:32; Judg 8:20; Job 3:3; Luke 17:4; 1 Tim 4:3

Bitterness Matt 6:15; Rom 3:14; 1 Pet 3:1

Blame Gen 3:12,24; Josh 1:1-2; Col 3:19

Blessings Ps 127:3; Prov 17:6; James 1:13

Boasting (see also Pride) Gen 6–9; 14:3; Judg 16:17; Prov 26:12; Ezek 47:8; James 5:16; Rev 20:14

Body Gen 3:6; Lev 19:28; Judg 1:6; Job 16:12; The Bible; Luke 15:17; Eph 5:27; Phil 4:15; 1 Tim 4:8; 2 Tim 3:2-4

Books of the Bible 1 & 2 Sam

Bones Job 16:12

Boredom Gen 6:19; Exod 21:6; Prov 19:15; The Prophets; Jer 9:23; 23:29; Hosea; Acts 20:7,9

Boys Ps 119:9; 127:3

Brevity 2 Kgs 2:23-25

Bribes Luke 4:8

Brother Gen 4:2,8

Burial Ruth 1:17; Matt 28:19; Luke 7:15; John 11:38-39

Business Gen 2:25; 3:6,7; 6; 7:23; Num 13:32; 22:21-35; Judg 16:29-30; 1 Sam 17:54; Prov 10:4; Eccl 3:6; The Prophets; Matt 2:1; 5:5; 26:20; Phil 2:10; 1 Tim 6:17

Busy Prov 31:28; 1 Pet 5:8

Calm (see Peace) Ps 89:9

Cannibalism 2 Kgs 8:1

Capital Punishment Gen 9:6; Jer 20:11

Career Ps 139:13

Carpentry Gen 6:14

Cars (see also Transportation) Acts 2:1

Catholics Ps 139:13; Matt 6:11; Mark 10:44; Luke 22:13-14; 23:3; Gal 6:9; Eph 4:28; Col 4:5-6; 1 Tim 5:12

Caution Mal 2:3

Change Eccl 4:13; Titus 1:5

Character 1 Sam 25:3, 25; Prov 22:1; Matt 26:20; Gal 5:22

Cheap Prov 31:27; Mark 6:48; Acts 20:35

Cheating Exod 1:22; Num 32:23; Amos 8:5

Children Gen 17:17; 25:21-22; 29:31-35; Exod 2:2; 14; 15:1; Deut 6:7; Josh 1:1-2; Ps 127:3; 128:5-6; 139:13; Prov 13:22, 24; 17:6; 20:11; 31:27; Jer 17:9; Dan 5:5; Matt 19:14; 25:32; Heb 13:4; James 1:19

Choir 1 Chr 25:1; Rom 12:16

Christ Isa 53:2

Christmas Gen 3:20; Ps 103:1; Matt 2:1; 2:7-8, 10,11; Luke 2:6,7,10,13,14,16,34

Church Mark 12:30; Acts 20:9; Rom 7:9,15-16; 12:16; 1 Cor 1:12-13; 5:4; 7:9; 9:11; 11:26; 12:12,28; 1 Cor 13; 13:13; 2 Cor 9:6; 12:7; Eph 4:12; 5:19; 6:4,19; Col 2:16; 1 Thess 5:17; 1 Tim 3:1-7; 3:5; Titus 1:5; Phile 1:1; Heb9:27; 10:24-25,25; 12:23; Heb 13:18; 1 Pet 3:15; 1 John 1:9; 3 John 1:10

Circumcision Gen 17:12; 34:24, 25

Clothes/Clothing Gen 2:25; 3:7; 37:3; Exod 14:28; Deut 22:5; Josh 1:8; Matt 4:19; 6:6; 7:21; 9:9; Luke 2:8; 6:45; 15:17; Acts 17:34; Rom 8:22; 1 Cor 11:11; 1 Tim 2:9; Rev 6:11

Coffee Exod 3:5; Neh 6:15

Comfort (see also Sympathy) Job 2:11; Prov 17:6

Commandments Exod 20:1f; 20:1-17; 20:4; 32:19; Deut 5:1; 5:6-21; 5:17-19; 5:22; Ps 19:7-10; Eccl 9:9; The Bible; Matt 21:45; 22:38; Rom 7:14; 1 Tim 5:1-2; James 2:10

Commitment Exod 4:10; Isa 6:8; Rom 12:1

Committee Exod 20:1f

Common Sense 1 Kgs 11:2; Prov 21:9

Communication Gen 2:25; Deut 24:1; Judg 16:29-30; 1 Sam 28:7; 2 Sam 8:1; 2 Kgs 2:23-25; Eccl 3:7; SofS 1:15; 4:1-7; Isa 3:9; 9:6; 1 Cor 5:6; 1 Pet 3:7

Communion Matt 26:26,30; 1 Cor 11:17ff,21,23ff,26

Comparison 1 Thess 4:7

Competition 1 Sam 17:51

Complain Num 11:4; Job 7:11; Matt 6:5; John 6:9; 2 Cor 8:12; Phil 2:4-5,14; 1 Tim 6:8

Compliment Prov 16:24; 1 Pet 5:5

Compromise Lev 23:27; Luke 22:40; 2 Tim 4:3; Heb 3:12; 1 John 3:8

Computer Gen 3:6; 22:8; Exod 20:1f; Ps 23; John 12:47; Acts 16:30; Rom 3:23; Heb 4:16

Conception Judg 8:20

Concubine 1 Kgs 11:3

Confession Rom 7:15-16; 1 Tim
1:19; James 5:16
Confidence Ps 90:10
Comfort John 14:46-47
Conflict(s) Acts 11:26; Eph 5:31,33
Confusion Gen 6:13; Obad 1:8;
Matt 21:22; Heb 12:23; James
3:1; 4:1; 2 Pet 2:1
Congregation Acts 20:28
Conscience Gen 42:21; 1 Cor 4:4;
8:7; Eph 4:29; 1 Tim 1:19; 2
Tim 1:3; Heb 13:18; James
5:16; 1 Pet 3:16
Consequences Gen 3:6; 19:26;
Exod 3:4; 9:8-12; Lev 19:23;
Prov 16:32; 27:2; Joel 2:25;
Amos 9:8; Matt 5:39; Gal 6:7;
1 Pet 3:7
Constipation Gen 4:2; 8:13; Exod
24:12; 34:1; 2 Sam 5:4
Contemplation (see Meditation)
Prov 12:5
Contentment Ps 37:4; 90:10; 127:4;
Matt 5:3; 4:11; Phil 4:11; 2
Tim 3:1
Context Ps 81:10; Prov 18:22; 28:1;
Eccl 3:6; 10:2; Isa 9:6; Matt7:6;
Matt 25:35; 26:27; Mark 13:37;
16:17-18; Luke 8:52; 11:9,30;
12:27; 16:13; 23:34; John 4:18;
13:27; 14:3; Acts 2:38; 1 Cor
6:12; Eph 5:23; 6:1; 1 Thess
5:21; 1 Tim 3:13; Heb 13:8
Conviction Matt 21:45; Rom 14:5;
2 Pet 2:1
Cooking Lev 1:1-9; Ps 89:8
Cooperation Gen 2:15; Luke 6:31;
1 Cor 3:8
Correction Eph 6:13
Courage Eccl 12:1; Ezek 37:3; Dan
6:10; Acts 1:8; 1 Tim 3:2; 2
Tim 2:12

Court Judges
Courtship (see Dating)
Covet Exod 20:17
Coward/Cowardice Deut 20:8;
Ezek 37:3
Creation Gen 1:1,3,4,5,16, 25;
2:2,3,7,18,19,21; 3:19; Job
41:13; Ps 8:3; 139:14; Prov
31:30; Eccl 3:1; Rom 5:12;
8:22; Col 2:8,16; James 1:2
Crazy Luke 7:33
Cremation 1 Sam 31:12
Criticism Prov 15:31; 27:6; 1 Cor
15:4; 1 Tim 5:19; 2 Tim 3:16;
4:10; James 5:9
Crucifixion Luke 9:22; 23:32,33;
John 19:18
Cruelty Eccl 12:5
Crying Est 8:3; Ps 127:3
Cults Matt 15:19
Curiosity Gen 3:6; 50:2-3
Dance Judg 16:1
Danger Acts 9:1; Eph 4:26; 1 Pet
4:5
Dark Josh 10:12-13; Isa 60:2
Date Gen 50:2-3
Dating Gen 7:8-91; Exodus; Ruth
2:3; Ps 56:1; Prov 5:3; 1 Cor
7:2,8,9; 14:39; 1 Thess 5:21; 1
Tim 5:2
Daughter Gen 22:14
Day of Atonement Lev 23:27;
23:27-29
Day of the Lord/ Judgment Day
Matt 24:7; James 4:15; Rev 9:2
Deacon 1 Tim 3:8,10
Death/Dead Gen 3:19; 5:27; 50:26;
Deut 34:5, 7; Josh 2:14; Judg
16:30; Ruth 1:17; 1 Sam 31:12;
2 Sam 6:20-22; 12:23; 2 Kgs
20:1; Job 1:19; 3:3; Ps 31:18;
90:10; Prov 20:21; 22:1; 23:2;

Isa 38:1, 5; Amos 4:12; Jonah 1:17; 2:10; Hab 1:1; Matt 6:12; Luke 8:52; 12:20; 13:3,23; 16:22,23; Acts 10:42; 20:9; 28:8; Rom 2:2; 13:6; 1 Cor 3:13; 7:39; 10:11; 15:44,55; 2 Cor 5:10; Eph 2:8-9; 5:16; 1 Thess 4:14,16; 1 Tim 6:7,18; Heb 2:14-15; 9:27; 1 Pet 4:5; Rev 14:13

Debt Prov 22:26-27; 23:4-5; 27:10; Matt 5:1-12; 6:12; 7:12; Mark 10:16; Luke 22:13-14; John 15:13; Rom 13:8; Phil 4:11,12; 1 Thess 5:18

Deceit/Deception Num 32:23; 2 Kgs 4:40; Matt 25:35; 1 Tim 6:7; 2 Pet 2:1; 1 John 3:8

Decisions Josh 24:15; James 4:1,14

Dedication 1 Sam 1:28

Demon (see also Devil, Spirits) Matt 8:16; Mark 5:13

Denominations Gen 13:11; Hosea 13:15; Matt 11:19; 12:2; 17:20; Mark 1:8; 16:18; Luke 13:23; 22:13-14; Acts 8:38; 16:30; 20:7,9; 1 Cor 1:2,10,12,12-13; 11:16; Eph 2:8-9,13; 4:14-22; 1 Tim 4:1; 1 John 1:9

Desire Ps 37:4; Phil 4:11; 1 Pet 3:7

Devil[s] (see also Satan) Isa 45:1; Amos 4:12; Matt 12:44; Acts 13:10; 2 Cor 6:14; 11:14-15; 12:7; 1 Tim 5:19; Heb 2:14-15; Heb 7:22; 10:25; 1 Pet 2:21; 5:8; 1 John 3:8; 3 John 1:12; Rev 21:8

Diet Ps 23; Prov 24:10; Matt 26:26; Luke 12:19

Difference Gen 8:4; Isa 6:2

Difficulty Dan 3:12-13; Matt 19:24

Directions Exod 16:15; 32:34; Num 14:34; Deut 31:3; Matt 2:2

Disappointment 1 Kgs 3:9; Dan 1:17

Disagreement (see Conflict)

Discernment Prov 5:3 10:19; Matt 26:20

Disciples Matt 4:18; 5:1-12; 10:1,2-4; 16:1; Mark 1:10; John 6:66; 13:23-24; 20:4

Discipleship 2 Tim 2:3

Discipline Prov 13:24; 22:15; 23:13; 29:15; 29:17; Eph 6:1,4

Discontentment Prov 26:22

Discouragement Jonah 2:2; Matt 5:5; Heb 10:25

Dishonesty Amos 8:5; Matt 25:35

Disobedience Exod 20:4; 32:19; Lev 23:2-3; 2 Sam 15:4; Prov 9:15; 2 Tim 3:2; James 2:14

Dissatisfaction Gen 19:26; 1 Pet 3:8

Distance John 4:44

Division Matt 12:25; 25:32; Acts 11:26; Rom 10:3

Divorce Deut 24:1; Eccl 9:9; Matt 19:6,9; Luke 17:4; 1 Pet 3:8

Doctors Gen 21:7; 34:24, 25; Job 16:12; Prov 26:16; Matt 5:9; Luke 23:32; Acts 28:8; Gal 4:6; Eph 5:15; Rev 16:16

Doctrine Rom 3:24; 4:25; 8:29-30; 15:6; 1 Cor 1:2; 2 Cor 12:7; 1 Pet 3:15; 1 John 3:8

Dreams Gen 28:12; 37:5-7; Prov 20:13; Dan 1:17

Driving Gen 19:26; Deut 24:3-4; 1 Kgs 18:19; 2 Kgs 9:20; Luke 11:1; Rom 13:4; 1 Cor 6:10; 11:14; 2 Cor 5:8; 1 Pet 4:5

Dress Josh 1:8; 1 Cor 11:5

Drink/Drinking/Drunkenness Gen 14:13; Ps 137:1; Prov 23:31-33; Hab 1:1; John 2:9; John 12:21; 19:18; 1 Cor 6:10; Eph 5:18; Phil 3:5; 1 Tim 5:6; Hebrews; Heb 1:14; 1 Pet 3:7; 2 Pet 2:1; Rev 20:14

Drought 1 Kgs 17:1; Hosea 13:15; Amos 4:7, 8

Drugs 1 Sam 17:49; Dan 4:30

Ears Exod 21:6; 32:2

Easter Matt 21:8; 27:1; Mark 15:42; 16:1-8; Luke 6:45; John 19:18,38-42; Acts 12:4; 1 Cor 15:4

Eating Gen 3:17,24; 2 Kgs 2:24; Prov 23:2; 2 Cor 5:20

Education Num 22:30; Deut 6:7; Ps 14:1; 119:99; Prov 1:7; 1:7-8; 2:3-5; 15:14; Jer 15:19; Jonah 2:10; John 14:5; 1 Tim 3:13

Embarrassment Ps 23; Jer 7:26; Matt 14:6-8; Acts 3:8; Phile 1:1; James 1:19; 3:6

Emotion Est 8:3; Ps 128:5-6

Encouragement Prov 29:17; 3 John 1:10

Enemies Gen 5:27; Ps 23:5; Luke 6:27

Enjoyment Ps 22:10; Rom 7:19; James 5:9

Enthusiasm Acts 2:3

Entertainment Judg 16:30; Rev 5:8

Environment/Ecology Gen 1:1; 6; Exod 5:19-21; 14:10

Evolution Gen 4:8

Eternity Jer 20:11; John 14:5; 1 Cor 7:39; Phil 4:7; Col 4:5; Heb 3:13; Rev 1:8; 20:14

Evangelism (see also Gospel) Amos 5:18; Luke 22:36; Acts 1:8; 2

Tim 2:3; 4:5; Heb 12:25-26; 1 Pet 1:9

Exaggeration Prov 23:23; 1 Tim 5:13

Example Jer 16:17; 1 Pet 2:21

Excuses Gen 3:11-14; Luke 14:5; Rom 13:4; 1 Cor 7:8; Heb 10:25; James 2:14

Exercise 1 Cor 9:26

Experience Gen 6–9; Prov 6:29; 13:1; 26:11; Eccl 1:16; Jer 20:11; 1 Cor 16:8-9; 1 Tim 3:6; 5:1

Expert John 4:44

Failure Gen 2:17; Jonah 2:10; Rev 16:16

Fairness 1 Thess 4:11-12

Faith Isa 45:1; Jonah 1:17; Matt 14:25,30; 17:20; Mark 9:24; James 2:14

Faithfulness Heb 10:25; Rev 3:25

Fame Prov 22:1

Family Ps 127:4, 5; Acts 16:1; Eph 6:1,2,4; 1 Tim 5:1-2; James 1:19-20

Famine Deut 28:38

Farming Gen 1:11; 2:15; 8:1; Col 2:16

Father/Fathers Gen 22:3; Deut 6:7; 32:50; Ps 139:14; Prov 3:1-5; 5:7; 13:24; 30:11; Matt 6:9; Luke 2:47; 11:1; John 6:19-20; Eph 6:2; 1 Pet 3:6

Favoritism Gen 29:30

Fear Gen 25:24; 32:31; 42:21; 43:23; Isa 38:1; Dan 9:21; Amos 9:3; Luke 21:9; John 2:17; 6:19-20; 2 Cor 11:14-15; 1 Thess 5:17; Heb 2:14-15

Feelings Gen 3:24

Fertility Gen 1:11,28; Ps 127:4, 5

Fetus Ps 139:13

Fighting Gen 27:40, 41; 1 Sam 17:49; Matt 5:39; 22:38; Luke 12:20; Rev 12:9; 16:16

Finances (also see Money) Gen 17:17; Exod 2:5, 6

Fire Amos 1:10; Rev 20:3,14; 21:8

Flattery Judg 16:6; Prov 19:6

Flood Gen 6–9

Flying Isa 40:26; Rev 16:16

Food Gen 2:22; 3:1-7; 3:6,7; 7:13; 9:3,15; Exod 12:18; 16:15; 20:12; Num 11:4; Deut 14:8; 28:38; 1 Kgs 17:6; 2 Kgs 4:40; Est 9:22; Ps 23; Isa 65:20; Amos 4:8; Matt 5:6; 6:11; Mark 5:1; 6:32-44; Luke 12:19; 24:30; Rom 12:1; 1 Cor 6:12; 11:17ff; Eph 6:4; Phil 1:21; 4:8; 1 Thess 4:15,18; 1 Tim 3:5; 5:17; Rev 16:13; 21:8

Fool/Foolishness Ps 53:1; Prov 1:7-8; 16:18; 23:24; 26:11; Isa 45:1; Matt 14:30; 25:2; Luke 9:16; 1 Cor 7:9; 2 Tim 3:1

Forgetful(ness) Deut 4:9; Eccl 12:3; Hosea 7:9; 1 Cor 4:4; Heb 9:27; Rev 22:20

Forgiveness Matt 5:39; 6:12,13,15; 18:23-25; Luke 7:47; 15:20,23,28; 17:4; 23:34; Acts 13:38; Eph 4:26,31-32; 1 Tim 3:11; 1 John 1:9

Fraternity Rev 1:8

Freedom Gal 5:13; Heb 10:25

Friend(s) Prov 27:10; 29:3; Matt 7:13-14; Luke 6:27; 11:30; John 15:13,14; 1 Tim 4:3; Rev 3:19

Frugal (see also Cheap) Mark 8:33; Luke 16:22

Frustration Gen 8:6; Exod 23:19; Matt 12:38; 14:25; Luke 11:9; 2 Tim 3:2

Funeral(s) Acts 7:56; 23:3; 1 Cor 4:5; 10:11; 15:44,52; 2 Cor 5:17; Eph 4:29; Phil 1:22; Heb 9:27

Future Luke 21:9; 1 Tim 4:8; James 4:14,15; 1 Pet 4:7; Rev 14:2

Gambling Gen 3:23; Luke 23:43; Eph 6:18; 1 Thess 4:15; 1 Tim 5:17-18; James 4:14

Games Gen 6:16-20; Matt 2:11

Gender Gen 2:18,21,24; 3:12; 30:21; Isa 3:12; Rom 1:26-27,27; 1 Cor 11:11; 14:16; Eph 4:14-22; Col 3:19; 1 Thess 4:3-5; 1 Pet 3:7

Generous/Generosity Eccl 5:1; John 19:38-42; 1 Cor 7:8; 16:1; 2 Cor 9:7; Eph 3:20; 1 Tim 6:17,18

Geography Gen 8:13; 10:5; 14:3; 18:20-21; Judg 16:1; 20:1; Job 1:21; Matt 2:5; Luke 2:1-4; John 4:7; Romans

Giving/Gift(s) Gen 17:17; Deut 14:22; Ezra 6:8; Ps 127:3; Mal 3:8; Matt 2:1,9,11; 22:21; 23:23; Mark 1:34; John 14:16; Acts 4:35; 13:3; 20:35; Rom 12:8; 1 Cor 16:1,2; 2 Cor 8:2,4,12; 9:2-3,3,4,6,7,13; Eph 4:11-12; 5:23; Phil 4:15,18; 1 Tim 3:6; 5:17-18; 6:18

God Gen 1:2; Exod 20:4; 34:14; Deut 6:4; Job 26:1-14; 40: Ps 14:1; 19:7-11; 139:7-12, 13-14; Eccl 6:12; Isa 38:5; 44:6; Jer 6:20; 16:17; Amos 9:8; Matt 6:9; Mark 16:19; John 3:16;

5:37; 1 Cor 5:1-5; 2 Cor 9:6; 1
Tim 1:17; Heb 1:3; 2 Pet 3:8; 1
John 5:14; Rev 3:19

God's Will James 4:15

Golf (see also Sports) Judg 16:20

Gospel (see also Evangelism) Mark
16:15

Gossip Gen 2:25; Lev 19:16; Prov
11:13; 15:28; 16:28; 18:8;
26:20, 22; Jer 16:17; Matthew;
Mark 16:15; 2 Cor 12:20; Eph
4:25,29; 2 Thess 3:11; 1 Tim
4:7; 5:13,19

Government Gen 6–9; Matt 22:21;
28:19; Acts 4:19

Grace Deut 14:8; Luke 1:28; Rom
5:1-2,2; Eph 2:8-9,9; Heb
13:25

Grades Matt 5:1-12

Grammar Lam 3:23

Grandchildren Prov 17:6; 20:21

Grandparents Ps 139:14; Prov
20:21; Luke 12:40

Gratitude (see also Thanks) Lam
3:23

Greed Mal 3:8; 3:8-10; Matt 6:11;
John 12:4-6; Acts 20:35; 1 Tim
3:3; 6:7

Guidance Num 22:21-35; 1 Tim
4:13; 2 Pet 1:20

Hair Gen 27:11; Deut 22:5; Judg
16:17, 19; 2 Sam 18:9; Ezek
27:31; Matt 10:30; 1 Cor 11:14;
1 Tim 2:9

Handwriting Dan 5:5, 25

Happiness Eccl 5:10

Hatred Gen 4:8; 2 Cor 5:17

Healing/Health Mark 1:34; Heb
9:27

Hearing Eccl 9:9; 12:4

Head Judg 4:21; 1 Sam 17:49, 51; 1
Kgs 6:1; Matt 19:14

Healing Mark 5:30-31; 16:18; John
6:66; Acts 3:8; 2 Thess 3:10; 2
Tim 3:2-4; James 5:14

Heaven Job 1:21; Ps 127:3; Eccl
12:5; Isa 30:26; Dan 12:2;
Jonah 4:9; Matt 3:2; 7:21;
10:28; 14:30; 25:41-43; Luke
12:20; 13:23; John 14:2,6; Acts
1:3; Rom 2:2; 1 Cor 3:15; 6:10;
15:42-44; 2 Cor 5:8; Eph 2:8-9;
4:29; Phil 1:21,22; James 2:14;
Jude 1:23; Rev 5:8; 6:11; 8:1;
20:10,14; 21:4,9-27,10-14,21

Height Neh 1:1; Job 2:11; Matt
26:40

Hell Gen 1:1; 28:12; Isa 30:26; Dan
12:2; Amos 4:12; Jonah 4:9;
Matt 5:22; 8:12; 10:28; 13:42;
18:9; 23:33; 25:41-43; Mark
9:47; Luke 12:5; 16:23; Rom
2:2; 6:23; 1 Cor 3:13; 15:55; 2
Cor 5:10; 1 Tim 6:17; Heb
3:12; 10:25; James 1:19; 3:6;
Jude 1:23; Rev 20:10,14,15;
21:8

Heredity Gen 1:26; Ps 127:5; Prov
13:24

History Deut 32:7; Isa 40:18; Rom
5:12; 1 Cor 10:11

Holidays (see also Vacations) Lev
23:27-29; Est 9:22; Ps 14:1;
53:1; Matt 1:25; Mark 15:42;
16:1-8; Acts 4:7; 12:4

Holy/Holiness Exod 3:5; 1 Thess
4:7; 5:12-13

Holy Spirit (see also Trinity) Gen
1:2; Matt 28:19; John 14:16;
Acts 4:8; Rom 8:26; 1 Cor 2:1;
2 Tim 3:5

Home/House Gen 3:6; Acts 16:1;
Titus 2:5

Judging Matt 7:1,3-5

Judgment Exod 7:14ff; 2 Kgs 17:7-23; Job 2:9-10; Job 18:5; Prov 28:1; Amos 5:18; Matt 8:12; 24:7; 25:41-43; Mark 16:16; Luke 12:40; 13:3; 15:20,28; John 14:3; Rom 6:23; 10:3; 1 Tim 2:14; 2 Tim 4:3

Justice Hosea 10:12; Luke 18:2-8; Acts 24:22; Rom 7:15 1 Cor 3:13-14

Kindness Matt 7:12; Acts 6:2; Eph 4:32; 1 Thess 4:9; 2 Pet 1:7

Kissing 1 Cor 14:39; SofS 1:2; 4:11; 1 Tim 5:2

Knowledge Gen 3:1-7; 12:4; 19:26; Job 15:20-24; Job 42:2-3; Ps 37:4; Prov 2:3-5; Eccl 12:1, 12; Amos 9:8; Obad 1:8; Zech 4:10; Matt 6:9-13; Mark 16:1-8; 1 Tim 4:13

Kosher Lev 11:7

Land of Israel Exod 3:8; 17:6; Deut 8:6-9; 31:3; Judg 20:1

Languages Gen 11:8, 9

Laundry (see also Clothes) Gen 1:4

Law Lam 3:22; Acts 4:19; 15:5; Rom 14:5; Gal 2:16; Heb 10:25

Lawyers Gen 8:12; Exod 19:16; Amos 8:5; Matt 6:9-13; 6:10; Luke 20:47; 23:32; 2 Tim 4:5; Heb 9:27; Rev 22:15

Laziness Prov 6:9-10; 10:5; 18:9; 26:16; Luke 9:16; 12:27; Acts 11:26; Eph 4:12; Col 3:22; 2 Thess 3:6,10; Heb 3:11; James 2:17; 1 Pet 2:18

Leaders Gen 41:40-41; Exod 17:4; 32:34; Matt 19:23; 1 Tim 3:1-7

Lent Lev 23:27-29

Lessons Jonah 1:3; 2:10; 4:11

Lies/Liars/Lying 1 Sam 16:18; Ps 31:18; 37:39; 150:3; Prov 18:13; 23:23; 25:17; Jonah 1:4-5; Rom 3:2; Col 3:9; 1 Thess 5:18; 1 Tim 5:2,13; James 2:25; 1 Pet 4:5; Rev 21:8; 22:15

Life Josh 2:14; Ps 22:10; 139:13; Eccl 4:2; SofS 1:2; Isa 65:20; Jer 9:5; Matt 6:11; Rom 13:8

Light Gen 1:3; 6; Ps 8:3; John 8:12

Listening Deut 22:5

Liturgy 1 Cor 14:16

Logical Ex 14; 15:1

Long Josh 10:13-14; Zeph; Mark 1:38

Lonely Matt 7:13-14

Lost Exod 20:1f; Matt7:7

Love Gen 2:25; 1 Kgs 11:2; Prov 23:13-14; SofS 1:7; John 3:16; 15:13; 1 Thess 4:9

Loyalty 1 Tim 5:19

Mail John 3:16

Man/Men Gen 1:1; 2:18,21; 8:18; Num 14:34; Judg 16:6; Ps 8:5; 56:1; SofS 1:7; 5:10-16; Eph 5:22

Manhood Gen 2:10; 3:12

Manners 2 Tim 3:5; Heb 10:25

Marriage Gen 2:24; 22:14; 24:63-67; 25:1; 26:34-35; 29:30; Lev 1:3; Deut 24:1, 3-4; Ruth 2:20; 4:8; 1 Sam 25:3; 28:7; Job 1:13–2:9; Ps 37:4; Prov 5:18; 18:22; 21:9; SofS 1:2; 5:6; Isa 40:18; Amos 4:1; Matt 19:6,9; Luke 16:13; 23:34; Rom 1:27; 1 Cor 7:1,8,9,11,28,36,39,40; 2 Cor 5:8; 6:14; Eph 4:26; 5:23,31,33; Col 3:18; 1 Tim 2:14; 3:2; Hebrews; Heb 13:4,8; 1 Pet 3:7; 2 Pet 2:16

Math Gen 3:6; 6:1; 9:1,7; Rom 7:15

Medicine Gen 1:2; Exod 24:12;
31:18; 2 Kgs 4:41
Meditation Ps 1:2
Men (see Man)
Membership 2 Tim 4:10: Heb
10:25; James 2:1-4
Memorization Ps 1:2
Memory Gen 25:1; Deut 4:9; Ps
128:3; Isa 40:18
Mercy Ps 136; Lam 3:22; Hosea
10:12; Matt 6:12; Luke 10:25-
37; John 8:11; 1 Pet 2:10
Mess Luke 2:7; Rev 2:5
Military Deut 20:7; 8; Judg 7:7
Millennial Isa 65:25
Ministry Isa 6:8; Matt 10:10; Luke
7:33; Acts 23:3; 2 Cor 5:20; 1
Tim 3:2,3; Titus 1:7; 2:4-5,5;
James 1:1
Miracle/Miracles Exod 14; Num
22:30; Josh 10:12; Est 6:1;
Jonah 1:17; Matt 8:16; 16:1;
17:16; Mark 6:32-44,48; Luke
3:23; 11:16; John 2:9; 6:19
Misfortune Amos 5:19
Missions Matt 10:6; Acts 13:3; 2
Cor 8:4
Mistakes Ps32:8-9; Prov 16:25;
Eccl 5:2; Mark 16:17-18;
James 5:16; 1 John 4:18
Misunderstanding Gen 1:28; Exod
13:19; Prov 28:1; Dan 6:18;
Amos 5:18; Obad 1:8; Matt
6:12; 14:25; Mark 16:16,19;
Luke 2:41; 8:17; John 4:18; Col
4:5-6; 1 Tim 3:11; Heb 12:23;
James 5:14; 1 Pet 3:7
Mock/Mockery Gen 4:17; 19:26
Modesty Gen 2:24; 1 Tim 2:9
Money Gen 1:28; 2:22; 7:8; 8:11;
Exod 12:35-36; Ezra 6:8; Ps
19:7-11; Ps 23; 139:14; Prov

13:22; 20:13; 23:4-5; 27:23-24;
Eccl 5:10; Matt 2:9; 12:25;
19:6, 23; 23:14; Luke 12:20;
15:13; 1 Cor 3:13; 2 Cor 9:1-
5;6; Eph 2:13; 5:33; 1 Tim
6:10,17; 2 Pet 3:8; Rev 9:2;
21:21
Morality Josh 24:15
Moses Numbers; Num 11:4; Deut
34:5, 10-12
Mother(s) Exod 20:4; 20:12; Prov
31:28; John 8:12; Eph 5:31;
Titus 2:4,4-5
Mother-in-law 1 Kgs 3:16-27; 11:3;
Prov 23:22; Matt 8:14-15; 1
Cor 15:12; 1 Tim 5:8; 2 Tim
4:8
Motivation Prov 16:24
Mouth Eccl 5:2; James 3:9,10; 1
Pet 3:3
Movie 2 Sam 11:1f; 1 Cor 10:11
Murder Gen 4:2,8; Exod 20:12; Lev
24:17; 1 Cor 7:39; 1 Tim 5:1-2;
James 2:20; 1 John 2:9
Music/Songs (see also Hymns) Gen
1:16; 4:8; 7:17; Exod 20:8-11;
20:15; Deut 5:1; 6:4; 1 Sam
16:18; 17:40; 18:11; Ps 150:3;
Prov 27:2; Matt 6:3; Luke
2:13,20; Rom 12:16; 1 Cor
14:15; 2 Cor 9:7; Col 2:16
Mystery 1 Pet 1:2
Nag Prov 21:9
Naked Gen 3:10; Jer 20:18
Names Gen 2:19,20,23; 3:6,19;
4:1,6-7,8,17; 5:27; 6:3; 7:7,9,13;
8:4; 18:20-21; Exod 2:10; 4:14;
1 Sam 5:4; 17:14,23; Est 1:1; Ps
23:6; Isa 6:5; Jer 8:22; Dan
3:12-13; 6:8; Amos 1:1,10;
Matt 1:18; 2:7-8,11; 3:12:14;
4:18; 27:2; Mark 1:10; Luke

1:3,28; 2:4; 15:2; 16:21; John
13:23-24; 20:4; Acts; Acts 1:1;
11:19,26; 16:12; 17:34;
20:10,28; 24:22; Romans; Rom
5:1-2; 1 Cor 11:16; 1 Tim 5:17;
6:8; 2 Tim 4:11,13; Heb 13:25;
James 3:6; 1 Pet 1:1; 2 John;
Rev 3:15-16,16
Nature Ezek 43:2; James 1:2
Neighbors (see Friends) Deut 8:6-
9; Prov 29:9
New Gen 3:7
Noise Gen 2:22; 4:1; 7:23; 11:9;
Matt 6:5
Nostalgia Gen 1:31
Numbers Gen 1:26; Numbers;
Matt 10:1,30; 2 John; Rev
13:18
Nuns Num 6:3; Matt 17:20; 1 Tim
5:12
Obedience Josh 10:12; Ps 40:8;
Prov 29:15; Eccl 12:13; Gal
2:16; Eph 5:24; 6:1; Col 3:18;
James 1:25; 1 Pet 3:6
Offering(s) (see also giving) Exod
22:29; Ps 50:10; 2 Cor 8-9;
9:2,5,6,7; 1 Tim 6:10
Old see Age/Aging
Optimism Job 1:19; Jonah 2:10; 1
Tim 1:12
Opposite Eccl 3:4
Optimist John 21:3; James 1:2
Ordinary 1 Sam 17:49
Pacifist Matt 5:39; 26:52
Pain (see also Sickness) 2 Cor 8:2;
Eph 5:4
Pairs Gen 7:9
Parents/parenting Gen 2:24; 22:3;
Exod 1:7; 20:12; Num 13:16;
Prov 13:24; 19:18; 22:6, 15;
23:13; Eccl 4:13; Matt 1:18;

Luke 3:23; Eph 6:1,4,19; 1 Tim
5:8,14; Titus 1:6; 2:4
Parable Matt 13:10
Paradise Gen 1:27; 2:25; 3:23;
Luke 23:43
Party Gen 18:20-21
Pastor Dan 5:25; Acts 20:28; 27:25;
1 Cor 1:16; 2 Cor 9:1-5; Eph
4:11-12; Phil 4:12; 1 Tim 2:9;
3:1-7,3; 4:3; 5:17,19; 2 Tim 4:2;
Titus 1:7; Heb 10:25; 1 Pet 3:3
Patience Matt 3:8; Rom 12:12;
James 1:3-4; 5:11; 1 Pet 1:6
Peace Ps 136; Micah 4:3; Matt 5:9;
Phil 4:7; 3 John 1:15
Perfection 1 Sam 25:25; Matt 5:48
Permissive Exod 20:1f
Persecution 1 Thess 3:4
Persistence Mark 13:37; Luke 18:1;
John 14:5; 1 Cor 10:13; Gal 6:9
Pessimist Gen 7:8-9; 1 Tim 1:12;
James 1:2; Rev 20:3
Pharisee Matt 5:1-12; 6:7; 16:1;
23:14,24; Mark 6:32-44; John
1:46
Phone Exod 2:2
Photography Matt 26:30,41; Luke
2:7
Picture Isa 53:2; Luke 2:7
Piercing Lev 19:28
Places Ezek 43:13; 47:8
Poison 2 Sam 6:20-22
Politeness Phil 2:4
Politics Gen 1:2; Exod 3:4; Prov
1:7; Eccl 10:2; Matt 7:21;
11:19; Luke 2:1; Acts 24:22; 1
Tim 2:1-2; 2 Tim 4:5; Rev
21:27
Politically Correct Luke 2:7; 1 Cor
7:1
Polygamy Gen 2:24; 4:19; Exod
1:15

Eph 2:9; Phil 2:14; 2 Tim
4:2,11; 1 Pet 1:9

Purpose Eccl 3:1

Questions Gen 7:9; Prov 22:6; SofS
1:7; Acts 4:35; 1 John 5:1

Qualifications 1 Tim 3:1-7

Rabbi Lev 11:7; Heb 10:25

Race/Races Gen 2:7; 4:21-22;
27:40; Obad 1:3

Rain (see weather)

Rapture Eph 5:27; 1 Thess 4:16,17

Reality Luke 9:16; 10:31; Rev 20:10

Rebellion Prov 29:15

Rebuke 2 Sam 6:20-22

Redemption (see also Salvation) 1
Pet 1:18

Regret Jonah 1:4-5

Reincarnation Deut 18:11

Rejection Gen 3:17,24; 2 Pet 2:1

Rejoice (see Joy)

Religion 1 Tim 3:5; 2 Tim 2:15;
3:5; James 1:27

Repentance Judg 11:30; Jonah
2:10; John 8:11; Gal 6:7; 2 Tim
3:5; 4:4

Repeat/Repetition Deut 32:7;
James 1:25; 3:9

Reputation Heb 11:26

Resentment Ps 23:5

Respect Ruth 2:19; Col 4:6,14; 2
Pet 2:16; Rev 3:19

Responsibility Exod 15:22; Prov
31:27; Dan 1:8; Eph 2:10; 6:4;
1 Tim 2:9; James 1:22

Rest Gen 1:5; 2:2,3,22; Prov 6:6; 1
Cor 9:26; Col 2:16; Heb 4:1

Resurrection 1 Sam 17:49; Jonah
1:4-5; Mark 16:1-8,4; Luke
7:15; 24:6; John 11:44; 19:38-
42; 20:2; 1 Cor 15:4,12,22-
23,52; Phil 1:22

Retaliation Gen 32:31

Retirement 1 Cor 3:13

Revenge Prov 15:1; Obad 1:3; Matt
5:39; 7:12; Luke 6:31; Rom
12:19; 1 Cor 5:1-5; Gal 5:3; 3
John 1:10

Revival Neh 8:1-8; 2 Cor 11:14-15;
Eph 4:28

Reward Ps 1:2; Zech 9:16; 1 Cor
3:13-14

Rich Matt 19:24

Roles (male and female) Gen 1:27;
2 Kgs 21:13; Col 3:19

Sabbath Gen 2:2; Lev 23:2-3; Matt
7:1

Sacred Lev 1:3-5

Sacrifice Gen 4:6-7; 22:7; Lev 1:3;
1:1-9; 1 Kgs 18:33-35; Luke
15:23; Rom 12:1; 2 Cor 9:4; 1
Tim 5:17; 6:10; Heb 10:14

Sadducees Mark 12:18

Salvation John 12:47; 14:2,6; Acts
16:30; Rom 3:23; 4:26; 5:1-2; 1
Cor 3:15; Eph 2:8-9; 1 Pet
1:18; Rev 20:3; 21:8; 22:14-15

Sanctification Eph 4:22-24; 1 Pet
3:3

Satan (see also Devil) Matt 16:23;
Mark 8:33; Luke 4:8; Acts
13:10; 2 Cor 11:14-15; Rev
12:9; 13:18; 20:3,15

School Prov 20:11

Science Gen 1:2; 2:7; 19:26; Jer
15:9; Col 2:8; 2 Tim 2:15

Scripture (see Bible)

Self-control/Self-discipline Prov
13:17; 14:29; 17:28; 19:15;
20:19; 23:31-33; Gal 5:16;
James 3:2,8

Selfish 1 Sam 22:8: Prov 13:22;
Matt 7:12; Acts 6:2; Eph 5:28;
1 Thess 1:6; 1 Tim 5:17-18; 1
Pet 3:7

Sam 17:49, 51; Prov 16:32; Isa 44:6; Mark 1:34; Luke 9:22; 12:20; John 2:15; Acts 20:17; 20:35; Rom 1:25; Col 2:16; 1 Thess 5:12-13; Titus 1:7; Heb 10:25

Steal/Stealing Exod 20:15; Josh 7:1; Obad 1:5; Matt 26:52; 28:19,20; Luke 10:32; John 12:6; Acts 2:38; 18:10; Eph 4:22-24,28

Stinginess (see also Cheap, Greed) 1 Tim 5:8; Titus 1:7

Strength Ps 103:1; SofS 5:10-16

Stubborn Prov 16:18; 29:11; Dan 6:16; 2 Tim 3:2

Stupidity 2 Sam 13:11; Prov 21:16; 31:27

Student/Students Gen 2:2; Deut 5:22; Ps 23; Eccl 12:12; Matt 5:1-12; 12:39; Luke 10:25-37; 2 Pet 1:21; Rev 14:13

Study Prov 15:14; Zech 4:10; Luke; Rev 14:13

Submission Gen 3:16; Isa 3:12; Eph 5:22,23,24

Success Josh 1:8; Prov 16:18,19; 2 Pet 1:20

Suffering Job 1:13–2:9; 1:19; 2:9-10, 13; Prov 27:15; 1 Pet 1:6; 2 Pet 2:16

Sun Josh 10:12-13

Sunday Exod 20:8-11; 20:11; Deut 5:12-14; Luke 14:5; Eph 5:4; Col 2:16; Heb 10:25; 1 Pet 2:10

Sunday School (see Children's Church)

Surprise Gen 21:2,7

Swearing Gen 7:8; Nahum 1:6; Matt 6:7; 12:36; Luke 2:6; James 3:2

Sympathy Job 2:11; Eph 5:31

Tact Prov 15:1

Talk/Talking (see also Speech) Gen 7:17; Prov 27:15; Acts 20:7; James 1:19; 3:1,2,8

Taxes 1 Sam 8:18; Ps 52:3-4; Prov 17:22; Matt 9:9; Luke 2:1; Acts 20:35; Rom 13:6,7; 1 Cor 13; 2 Cor 9:2-3; 1 Thess 5:18; 1 Tim 1:19

Teacher/Teaching Jonah 2:10; Matt 5:1-12; Luke 10:25-37; Gal 5:3; James 3:1

Teenagers (see also Youth) Gen 22:7; Prov 22:6; Eccl 12:1; Luke 11:1; Eph 6:1,4; Heb 4:1

Television Gen 2:20; 3:20; Amos 1:1; Matt 17:2; Gal 4:6

Temper (see also Anger) Eph 4:26-27; 6:4; 1 Tim 3:2

Temple 1 Kgs 6:1; John 2:15,17

Temperature Gen 8:24

Temptation Gen 3:6; Prov 28:7; Matt 6:13; 12:13; 16:23; Mark 8:33; Luke 4:8; 22:40; 1 Cor 8:7; 10:13; 2 Tim 2:22; James 1:13,13-14

Thanks/Thanksgiving Eccl 5:4; Luke 17:17; 1 Thess 5:18

Theology (see also Doctrine) Job 38:32; Jer 17:9; Matt 2:11; 18:9; Rom 3:24; 2 Cor 13:14; 1 Thess 5:1; 1 Tim 6:17

Thinking (see Contemplation)

Threaten Luke 4:12

Tithing (see also Giving) Matt 23:23

Time Gen 2:26; 3:6; Ps 5:3; 90:10; 127:2; Prov 11:12; 31:28; Eccl 3:1; Luke 21:9; 23:33; John 20:2; Acts 20:9,16; Eph 5:16; Col 3:17; 4:5; 1 Thess 5:2;

James 2:14; 1 Pet 2:2; 3:7; 2
Pet 3:8
Timing Gen 2:7; 1 Pet 5:12
Tongues Acts 2:8
Touch Mark 5:30-31
Tradition Matt 15:6; 18:20
Traitor John 12:12-19
Transportation Gen 1:24; 3:24;
50:2-3; Exod 7:10; 14:9; 1 Sam
18:7; 1 Kgs 18:19; Ps 146:4;
Prov 13:24; 21:16; Jonah 1:3;
Micah 4:3; Matt 2:14; 27:2;
28:20; Luke 2:20; John 18:28-
29; 2 Cor 4:8
Travel Gen 3:6; 2 Cor 8-9
Trials Ps 50:15; Phil 4:6,12-13; 1
Tim 6:10
Trinity Gen 1:26; Lev 10:8; Matt
28:19; 2 Cor 13:14; 2 Tim 3:5;
1 Pet 1:2; 1 John 5:7
Trouble/Trouble-maker 2 Sam
15:4; Prov 11:17; James 3:10
Trust Gen 2:22; 7:9; Ps 19:7-11; Ps
23:1; Matt 10:19; 28:19,20; 1
Tim 3:11
Truth Prov 10:18; 18:13; 1 Tim 4:7
*Unaware (see also Ignorance,
Misunderstanding)* Matt 6:3; 1
Cor 1:16
Unconcerned Luke 16:232
Understanding 1 Pet 3:7
Unexpected Jonah 1:17; Luke
12:20
Unisex Deut 22:5
Union Exod 20:11
Unity (see also Peace) Deut 6:4; Ps
133:1; Acts 2:1; Eph 5:31
Usher(s) Acts 6:2
Vacation (see also Holidays) Gen
7:17; 1 Pet 2:21
Value Job 1:19
Vegetables Heb 4:16; 3 John 1:15

Vengeance (see Revenge)
Victory 1 Sam 18:7; 1 Cor 10:13;
Phil 4:12-13
Violence Matt 26:52
Virgin Isa 7:14; Matt 1:23; 25:2;
Luke 2:16
Visit/Visitation/Visitors Gen 3:10;
Prov 25:17; James 1:25; 1 Pet
5:8
Vocation Ezek 43:2; Rev 12:9; 21:8
Vows Judg 11:30
Wages Rom 6:23; 1 Cor 9:11; Heb
3:13; James 3:1
Waiting James 3:2
Warning Luke 21:7; Rev 16:16
Wash Ps 119:9
Water 1 Kgs 17:1; 18:33-35; Ps
23:2; John 4:11; 6:19; Rev
3:15-16
Wealth Josh 3:15; Mal 3:8-10; Phil
4:12; 1 Tim 6:18
Weather Gen 6:17; 7:12,13,17;
8:12; Exod 17:1; 19:16; 1 Kgs
17:1; Job 37:10; Ps 68:14; SofS
1:15; Isa 40:26; Jer 15:9 Amos
4:7; Hag 1:1; Mark 1:8; Luke
2:14; John 3:8; Acts 27:25;
Rom 5:14; Colossians; 1 Tim
4:13; 1 Pet 2:10; 3 John 1:10;
Rev 21:9-27
Weapons Jer 8:22
Wedding Gen 17:17; Prov 31:28;
SofS 1:2; John 4:18; Eph 5:22;
Heb 13:4; 1 Pet 3:6; 1 John
4:18
Wicked Heb 3:11; 2 Pet 3:9-10
Wife/Wives Gen 2:21; 4:17; 11:9; 1
Kgs 11:3; Prov 12:4; Eccl 9:9;
Acts 4:19; Eph 5:22,23,33; 1
Tim 3:2; 5:2; 1 Pet 3:1,7
Wills Deut 18:11

Wisdom/Wise Num 11:29; 1 Kgs
3:9, 16-27; 11:3; Ps 119:99;
Prov 5:7; 9:10; Matt 2:1,10;
14:6-10; 2 Cor 6:3; 1 Tim
4:12,13

Woman/Women Gen
2:3,18,21,22,23; 8:24; Est 8:3;
Prov 21:9; 27:15; 31:16; Isa
3:16; Eph 5:22; Rev 8:1

Wood Gen 6:14

Words (also see Speech) Isa 8:12;
Ezek 43:14; Dan 4:30; John
14:26-27

Work Gen 1:5; 7:8-9; Deut 5:12-
14; Neh 6:15; Prov 6:9-10;
10:4, 5; 12:11; 20:13; 21:9;
31:28; Matt 6:26; Acts; 1 Cor
3:12-13; Gal 6:9; Eph 4:28; Col
3:22; 1 Thess 4:11-12,14; 5:14;
2 Thess 3:6,10; 1 Tim 5:14;
Titus 2:5; Heb 3:13; James
5:16; 1 Pet 2:18; Rev 20:3

World Isa 11:12

Worry Gen 1:26; 2:15; Deut 1:21; 2
Sam 12:23; Job 2:13; Ps 23:1;
37:8; Eccl; Matt 6:34; Phil 4:6;
2 Tim 4:2

Worship 1 Chr 25:1; Ps 23:2

Writing Corinthians

Youth Prov 3:1-5; 1 Tim 4:12; 5:1;
1 Pet 3:3

Zeal James 1:22

Zoo Isa 65:25; 1 Pet 3:6

Printed in Great Britain
by Amazon

48310253R00278